Functional Curriculum

for

Elementary, Middle, and Secondary Age Students with Special Needs

Functional Curriculum

for

Elementary, Middle, and Secondary Age Students with Special Needs

Edited by

Paul Wehman
John Kregel

pro·ed
An International Publisher
8700 Shoal Creek Boulevard
Austin, Texas 78757-6897
800/897-3202 Fax 800/397-7633
Order online at http://www.proedinc.com

An International Publisher

© 1997 by PRO-ED, Inc.
8700 Shoal Creek Boulevard
Austin, Texas 78757-6897
800/897-3202   Fax 800/397-7633
Order online at http://www.proedinc.com

Library of Congress Cataloging-in-Publication Data

Functional curriculum for elementary, middle, and secondary age
    students with special needs / [edited by] Paul Wehman, John Kregel.
       p.   cm.
    Includes bibliographical references and index.
    ISBN 0-89079-721-8 (alk. paper)
    1. Special education—United States—Curricula.   2. Handicapped
students—Education—United States—Curricula.   3. Curriculum
planning—United States.   I. Wehman, Paul.   II. Kregel, John, Ed.
D.
LC3981.F85   1997
371.9'0973—dc21   96-53194
                                         CIP

This book is designed in 11 point Palatino.

Production Manager: Alan Grimes
Production Coordinator: Karen Swain
Managing Editor: Tracy Sergo
Art Director: Thomas Barkley
Reprints Buyer: Alicia Woods
Editor: Charlotte Saikia, Publications Development Company of Texas
Editorial Assistant: Claudette Landry
Editorial Assistant: Suzi Hunn

Printed in the United States of America

   3 4 5 6 7 8 9 10   00

Contents

10 LIVING AT HOME   227

Daniel E. Steere and Teri L. Burcroff

11 TEACHING PERSONAL CARE AND HYGIENE SKILLS   251

Fred Spooner and Wendy M. Wood

12 HEALTH AND SAFETY   283

Martin Agran

Preface

In this book we have developed a framework for a functional and longitudinal curriculum for children and adolescents with disabilities and other special needs. There is a stronger demand than ever to provide functional curriculum for students; that is, curriculum with everyday usefulness and value in making the student more competent and independent. In addition to the focus on functional curriculum, there is a strong emphasis on showing how to tie curriculum from the elementary to the middle school and on up into the secondary school as well as adulthood. We believe that not enough attention has been paid to connecting the different curriculum levels so that there is a continuity of educational service for students and their families.

In this book, we have assembled contributions from some of this nation's leading authorities in curriculum design; they have provided dozens of highly relevant tables, charts, and instructional programs for direct service providers. At the same time, each chapter is based on the most recent research and the most contemporary thinking to help teachers and other instructional personnel be current in their planning. The chapters in this book deal with areas of expertise that most students will need. For example, self-determination skills, functional academics, transportation, home and community living, and activities of daily living, as well as work preparation and socialization, are all critical to success in adulthood. The chapters have a heavy curriculum format that is designed to be as user friendly as possible to teachers, instructional personnel, counselors, and occupational therapists, as well as other people in the special education, psychology, and rehabilitation fields with interest in this area.

We are extremely grateful to the contributors in this book. People such as Paul Sale, James Martin, Pam Wolfe, Wendy Harriott, Kathryn Banks, Shirley Chandler, Sara Pankaskie, Marty Agran, Cheryl Hanley-Maxwell, Michael West, Kathe Wittig, Vicki Dowdy, Lana Collet-Klingenberg, Daniel Steere, Stacy Dymond, Fred Spooner, Wendy Wood, and Teri Burcroff all willingly gave their time to make this an outstanding curriculum book for either preservice or in-service use. We are most grateful to them as well as our many colleagues who provided insights about the best way to develop this book. It is our hope that it will have tremendous utility to students in training as well as professionals in the field.

PAUL WEHMAN
JOHN KREGEL

1

Curriculum Design

PAUL WEHMAN

Margaret is an 8-year-old with profound mental retardation and multiple sensory physical handicaps. She is cortically blind but responds to sounds with gazes and turns her head toward sounds on occasion. She smiles and coos when stimulated by touch, and she seems to enjoy music. A team of professionals, using modern technology, has rigged switch devices that allow Margaret to activate toys and musical devices by eyebrow and tongue movements. She is also physically prompted to use switches to control devices in her environment such as the toaster. This technology allows her to participate partially in daily activities. Staff members also communicate with her by telling her what is happening and by using tactile prompts during all activities. Different staff members wear different colognes to facilitate her identity of them. Opportunities for choice are constantly presented to Margaret. For example, two flavors of toothpaste are offered as well as two scents of soap during daily activities. Many instructional activities take place in community settings such as the mall or fast-food restaurant. The family and professionals plan together to be sure that everyone exposes Margaret to multiple sensory experiences.

Randy attends a middle school and has been learning to participate in grocery shopping at a neighborhood supermarket. Because he uses a walker for support, he has been paired with a peer for the shopping activity. Typically, Randy identifies the correct item while the peer pushes the cart. For the past year, the school occupational therapist has become increasingly discouraged with the use of an isolated therapy model. She works with Randy in the occupational therapy room twice a week and is concerned that he may or may not use newly learned skills in natural settings. When she expressed these feelings to Randy's teacher, they decided to incorporate the occupational therapy objective of transferring to and from the walker with the grocery shopping activity. The therapist developed a program to teach Randy to leave his walker at the front of the store, transfer to the grocery cart, and use the cart as support while he shops. At first, this task was difficult for Randy because the cart would roll as he attempted to transfer. Also, Randy could not let go of the cart with both hands when retrieving an item or he would lose his balance. Thus, they taught him to move through an aisle of the store selecting items only on the right-hand side. At the end of the aisle, he makes a U-turn so that he can pass down the aisle again to select items on the left side. Although he still shops occasionally with a peer, Randy is especially proud that he can go through the store alone while his teacher waits at the front of the store or his mother completes her own shopping.

Samuel is a young man with severe mental retardation who is involved in a high school vocational training program. His mother expressed her concern to the instructional team during the Individual Education Plan (IEP) conference that her son is not involved in household routines. In fact, he is very dependent on family members for most activities of daily living such as selecting clothing, grooming, preparing meals, and maintaining his bedroom. Samuel can count to five, but has not mastered many academic skills such as color identification, reading, and typical readiness skills.

Samuel recently began training at a new work site that requires employees to wear uniforms. The instructional staff noticed immediately that Samuel was highly motivated to wear the uniform. In fact, his mother had problems with Samuel wanting to wear his uniform every day rather than only on Tuesdays and Thursdays when he reports to the training site. The instructional team worked with the family to incorporate this newfound motivation in critical home routines. The teacher adapted a calendar by placing large green dots on Tuesdays and Thursdays and attaching a red marker on a string. Now when Samuel gets up in the morning, he goes to the refrigerator with his mother to look at the calendar. He locates the current day to determine whether or not it is a uniform day. After making this decision, he takes the marker and places an X on the day so that he will know where to look for the next day. Now he is ready to assist in the selection of clothing. The instructional team also decided to teach Samuel to participate in washing the uniform. This has now become a Saturday chore in the home. At this time, Samuel is not able to perform all the steps, but he does load and unload the machine as well as operate the controls, which are adapted with colored tape. Even though Samuel is still not independent in the performance of household tasks, he is certainly more involved than he was before. Not only are his parents pleased with his progress, but his younger siblings have begun to comment about their older brother going to work.

These three case studies all represent individual students with disabilities who could be found in any school system throughout the country. These are students who have significant learning and behavioral challenges and who require extensive training in independent living skills before they become adults. This book has been developed because in today's complex society there is a greater need than ever before for students with disabilities to receive a comprehensive independent living skills curriculum. In the past 20 years, thousands of such children have entered the public school system for the first time; furthermore, state institutions and other segregated programs are on the wane. As a result, the need for competence in a broad array of independent living skills has become paramount for students with all disabilities and throughout the school system.

The primary purpose of this book is to provide a solid foundation of longitudinal curriculum for teachers and other direct service providers as they design and implement independent living skills training programs. Longitudinal curriculum involves continuity of planning, instruction, and communication across the age levels by teachers and parents. The enormous amount of research literature published over the past 10 years needs to be utilized by teachers in their classrooms and other training environments toward this goal of a longitudinal curriculum. One of the major goals of this book is to use this research information as a basis for sound educational planning that will lead to positive community outcomes for students as they leave school.

A second major focus of this book is to present curriculum across the major age levels within schools at the elementary, middle, and secondary levels. Although a number of curriculum books have been published, many of them focus exclusively on those with mild versus severe disabilities or on elementary versus the secondary age levels. In this book, we will cover the major independent living areas in which students need to demonstrate competence and adapt them across the different age levels.

MAJOR PRINCIPLES OF CURRICULUM DESIGN

There are numerous approaches to designing curriculum, from commercially available "canned" programs to those that are more "homemade." Many schools also provide a standardized curriculum that all teachers must follow for students. In some cases, state departments of education have mandated the use of certain types of curricula for students, which presumably leads to the passing of competency or literacy tests. These differing approaches to curriculum design are some of the reasons that many students leave school without the necessary independent living skills building blocks that are essential for competence in today's society. To truly achieve continuity across the age groups in school for the purpose of having a genuine longitudinal curriculum, four key design tenets need to be followed. The curriculum must be:

1. Individualized and person centered.
2. Functional or practical.
3. Adaptive.
4. Ecologically oriented.

INDIVIDUALIZED AND PERSON CENTERED

Each child is an individual and requires a specialized set of instructional objectives that are particularly suited for his or her needs. In all too many American classrooms, the students' Individual Education Plans are virtually identical in content and scope. This type of blanket programming does a grave injustice to a child's particular needs. We should not assume, for example, that all 16-year-olds with a label of educational mental retardation should learn the capitals of all 50 states. It may be that this is an inappropriate instructional objective for all these students; on the other hand, there may be a justification for one or two to be learning something like this in the academic area because they hope to go on to a community college.

The concept of person-centered planning has become increasingly popular (Mount & Zwernik, 1990). Person-centered planning provides an in-depth look at a given student and his or her world, particularly home and community, with a special focus on the student's vision for the future. The concept of person-centered planning is especially important for children who need a road map of what the future can hold for them. It is the primary theme of this book that longitudinal curriculum is the best way to provide educational programming to children with special needs. A person-centered planning approach is highly consistent with this type of long-term curriculum planning.

A person-centered planning approach in the context of longitudinal curriculum means that teachers must communicate across the different age spans and there must be *continuity* between the curriculum objectives from year to year.

The absence of this form of individualized person-centered planning has been the hallmark of many special education programs, thereby depriving students with disabilities the opportunity to reach their fullest potential.

FUNCTIONAL OR PRACTICAL

The second design requirement of curriculum objectives for all students, regardless of their disability or level of disability, is to be functional or practical in nature (Clark, 1996). A functional curriculum has been written about extensively, but many schools continue to provide nonfunctional instructional objectives to the long-term disadvantage of the students. There is nothing especially complicated about designing and implementing functional objectives. What is involved is a careful analysis of each student's individual needs, which are then weighed in the context of what the student needs the most. This often means determining what the student will be able to utilize most effectively to develop competence and make life less challenging.

The functional aspects of each child's curriculum cannot be emphasized enough. No matter how good the quality of instruction or how sophisticated the equipment or how new the school facilities, if the student is being offered inappropriate subject matter, then he or she loses the opportunity to benefit from a more useful education. For example, assume a teenager named Mike has severe mental retardation and some slight physical disability and cerebral palsy. Mike has had an IEP objective to tie his shoelaces into a knot. Assume further that Mike has attempted to learn this over the past 5 years, pretty much unsuccessfully: Why would any teacher continue to teach this skill when alternative styles of shoes and fasteners are available? Good common sense would suggest that Mike needs to be learning some other skills that will allow him to be competent at home and in the community rather than spending day after day—with at best marginal success—on a skill that does not build on his strengths or respond to his most pressing needs.

Hundreds of persons like Mike can be identified for any type or level of disability. The key question that the teacher must ask the student and the family is, "What activities does your son [daughter] need the most to be effective and competent as a human being in the weeks and months ahead?" When families have unrealistic expectations, then the teacher must work carefully with them in an educative fashion to suggest alternative goals. Figure 1.1 shows a strategy for identifying functional activities.

ADAPTIVE

In addition to being person centered and functional, the curriculum design must also be adaptive to the specific goals and capabilities of a given child. On one hand, it

FIGURE 1.1   Identifying Functional Activities for Instruction Across All Curriculum Domains

1. Select a broad curriculum domain (recreation, community, vocational, domestic) to be analyzed.
2. Identify a list of environments within home, school, and community settings where students may perform activities related to the identified domain.
3. Identify additional environments by surveying other professionals, the parents, and the students.
4. Observe these identified environments and list those skills that are essential for competence in each environment.
5. Verify the list of skills with other professionals and with parents.
6. Repeat this process for all domains.
7. Review and revise as needed (with a minimum of one review annually).

should be obvious that to provide an individualized and functional curriculum adaptations will be necessary; on the other hand, this principle also suggests that a curriculum objective identified by the IEP committee at the beginning of the school year may have to be altered two or three months later. If all are in agreement that a modified objective makes sense, then nothing whatsoever is wrong with changing the goal. It is much more problematical to continue providing instruction to students who are not learning because the objective is inappropriate. The teacher must remember, however, that it may take some time to reach a definitive decision about adapting an objective. It may very well be that the general area of curriculum is appropriate (e.g., functioning independently in the community), but that riding a bus is not the right target objective at this point; instead, crossing the street might be more appropriate. This type of adaptation is critical for students with some sophistication in cognitive problem solving and academics. The resource teacher who is working with a student to improve reading skills must be flexible enough to change the targeted goals if the student is becoming increasingly frustrated due to failure. This is also true in learning computer skills, calculation, arithmetic skills, or improving handwriting. The need to modify goals frequently is a problem for some teachers because they are too rigid or do not wish to take the time to go through the often lengthy process of identifying new objectives to work on with the student.

Adaptive curriculum instruction has been shown to be an effective way of providing instruction for students with significant disabilities. In this book, we will focus on using an adaptation approach to help students learn the curriculum objectives and reach their fullest potential. Each curriculum objective identified in this book is subject to adaptation and redesign based on students' needs. The teacher must think in terms of the need to adapt when the student is continuing to have problems in acquiring the skills that were originally targeted.

ECOLOGICALLY ORIENTED

Approximately 20 years ago, Brown and his colleagues (1976) wrote eloquently about the importance of examining the student's environments when making decisions about what curriculum objectives to teach the child. Two decades later, these ideas are more viable than ever, especially when complemented with person-centered planning, functional instruction, and adaptation. The underlying notion of an ecologically oriented program requires the student, teacher, and family to sit down and discuss the student's high-priority activities and each of the major living environments. For example, what are the student's main activities at home and in his or her immediate neighborhood? What are the major activities that the student performs or wishes to perform in the community (e.g., going to church, shopping for groceries, visiting the mall)? What are the student's major recreational activities or are activities the student would like to become involved with? Many potential environments, or what Brown terms *subenvironments*, can be analyzed for different activities. These activities then provide the foundation for the curriculum objectives. Therefore, if a student goes with his father to church every Saturday morning to participate in a men's brunch, the student might need to place high priority on learning how to perform clean-up activities. The student could then be helpful to the father and participate with other adults in a meaningful activity.

There are no end to objectives that can be identified using an ecological approach. This design feature has usually been seen as being most useful for those with severe intellectual disabilities, but this is not really the case. Any student with a disability is going to have some skill deficits within environments outside the school, and it is up to the teacher and student, along with the family to prioritize the skills to focus on in the coming school year.

These four principles of curriculum design—individualized and person-centered planning, functional or practical curriculum, adaptive instruction, and ecologically oriented curriculum—are the glue that hold the longitudinal curriculum design together. To provide continuity of instruction across the different age levels, all participants in the educational process must follow and understand these tenets. Because teachers do not always "buy in" to these ideas, parents will sometimes have to take a larger proportion of the responsibility, but over the long term, the school system must have a longitudinal curriculum philosophy that teachers and administrators ultimately adhere to and put into practice.

Many types of curriculum and curriculum objectives are discussed in this book, but running through all the forthcoming chapters will be these four major principles that are critical for students' effective learning and behavioral competence. Figure 1.2 provides a series of activities for prioritizing instructional targets for students.

CRITICAL AREAS OF INDEPENDENT LIVING

CAREER EDUCATION AND WORK

When teachers think of independent living, they do not usually think about career education or work as a curriculum area. However, the ability to get a job, hold a job, and identify some type of career path is an extremely important aspect of successful independent living. Most people cannot expect to have a happy and enjoyable life without some form of productive work activity.

Students need to develop an understanding of the relationships among work responsibility, pay, and getting along with others. They need to understand how their involvement in the community workforce is important to the way they are perceived.

FIGURE 1.2   Prioritizing Activities for Instruction

1. Identify with the student and his or her family the student's performance in each of the domain categories. Then identify desired relevant future environments in which it is projected the student will be functioning.
2. Identify activities and skills relevant to the student's current environment; identify skills necessary to function in projected future environments.
3. Review all relevant current and future activities and indicate those activities that occur in two or more domains and that are age-appropriate.
4. List these activities from most to least-frequent in occurrence.
5. From this list, identify those activities that are crucial for the student's safety. Next identify those activities that are critical for functioning independently in the identified future environments.
6. Select for immediate instruction:
   (a) Those activities essential to the student's safety within current environments.
   (b) Those activities that the student must perform frequently to function independently within current and identified future environments.
7. Select remaining objectives from the list of activities (Step 4).

Students at all levels of disability need to develop a work ethic. For example, students who work at the local grocery store not only must be able to bag groceries and carry them out to the car, but also need to know how to speak politely and communicate in a positive way to all customers, even though some customers are unfriendly or rude. All too often, schools have been slow to provide ongoing career education and vocational education instruction for students, yet the multiple stages of career development are very important. Figure 1.3 shows how this progress unfolds as the child grows older. This shows up repeatedly in students' ability to gain employment once they leave school. While still in school, most students should have some form of job or employment so they can truly learn what a work ethic is all about. Many kinds of vocational training can be considered in the curriculum; these goals will be covered in a later chapter. In general, the selection of training tasks can be best accomplished by checking with the student and family about the student's

FIGURE 1.3   Stages of Career Education

	Career Awareness	Career Exploration	Career Preparation	Job Placement
Elementary	██	██		
Junior high		██	██	
Senior high			██	
At graduation				██

vocational interest and by considering his or her aptitudes. The needs of the community labor market also are a determining factor. It is imperative for vocational education teachers and school administrators to communicate with employers operating businesses in or near the school district. It is these employers who will judge the success or failure of the school's efforts in the area of vocational education. In taking on this responsibility, the schools need to establish realistic employment goals for students. The following list suggests five employment goals for entry-level positions for students or recent graduates:

1. Mary will work part-time in a beauty salon with the help of a job counselor.
2. Marcie will become employed full-time as a baker's assistant.
3. Joseph will work as a stocker in Lowe's building store.
4. Elroy will be employed in a toy factory doing quality control with supported employment.
5. Michael will work part-time as a library page.

COMMUNITY LIVING

Community living skills are frequently grouped into broad clusters related to such areas as domestic skills, mobility skills, activities of daily living, personal social interactions, and communication. Actual independence, however, depends on the competence the individual shows in community living, as well as the availability and quality of support services in the community. The adequacy of support is a critical factor that will determine whether a student will do well. For example, a student with cerebral palsy and mild intellectual disability may live in a community with several different transportation options that are easily accessible, very strong adherence to the Americans with Disabilities Act (ADA) by community facilities, and a telecommunication system that serves public places and is user friendly for people with disabilities. This person will do much better accessing the community and living in the community than an individual with comparable physical abilities who lives in an environment where there has been indifference or apathy to making facilities more accessible.

What this means to the teacher is that despite even herculean efforts at instruction, it may still be difficult for a student to get around the community successfully if that community has resisted implementing ADA guidelines. Nevertheless, it is extremely important to give students every opportunity to develop their fullest skill capacity in community living. Listing community living skills is almost impossible because there are so many. However, the principles of curriculum design described earlier (e.g., person-centered planning, functionality) will be helpful in narrowing down the key target skills for instruction to a manageable number.

Community living skills allow persons with disabilities to establish a better identity and become assimilated into the community. It is one thing for children and youth to go to school and to live at home, but once they "age-out" a school, they will face the major transition to a postschool world. As students become adults, they will have to develop some form of a career, find their own place to live, and learn how to get about in the complex challenging community. A later chapter in this book identifies the skills needed to meet the challenges of the community. It also is necessary to recognize the roadblocks to making this successful transition as well as the supports that will bolster an individual's competence in the community. These are key points in generating a community living goal. The following five examples of home living and independent living goals range from cooking and finances to taking care of personal needs:

1. Sam will develop a repertoire of cooking skills for dinner and lunch.
2. Jean will set financial goals.
3. Nick will independently perform all basic self-care tasks.
4. Tina will independently take care of personal needs including meal preparation and household chores.
5. Marcie will live with her family until age 22.

SAFETY

Increased efforts to assimilate students with disabilities into their neighborhood schools and communities as well as work environments obviously will create a greater risk of injury. It is imperative that students with disabilities learn appropriate responses to potential threats to their health and safety. Students with significant disabilities may be at much greater risk for accidents and emergency situations than other children, despite the typical at-risk behavior of many middle school and high school students. Health and safety are not new areas of instruction; for almost 30 years, students with mild disabilities have received basic training in crossing streets, listening to railroad signals, and so on. This text, however, presents a more sophisticated approach to safety skill instruction in the way that Agran, Marchand-Martella, and Martella (1995) have suggested. With dangers such as AIDS, playground injuries, and drugs in schools, it is easy to see where students with disabilities could be at risk. In creating an educational plan for each student, it is essential to include issues related to safety and health such as the following goals:

1. Garland will maintain control over seizures.
2. Scott will be aware of health precautions when handling and grooming animals.
3. Elvis will eat at least one nutritious meal per day.
4. David will receive wheelchair maintenance and adjustment as needed.
5. Michael will reduce incidents of self-injury through stress management or other self-management techniques.

SELF-ADVOCACY

Many community programs are beginning to teach self-advocacy skills to people with disabilities (Wehmeyer, 1995). These programs help individuals with disabilities learn more about the choices that are available to them in the community, as well as their rights. Self-advocacy can be introduced into all areas of the school curriculum, but this will require some thought. As educators, we must go beyond simply teaching basic items of knowledge, and instead help students with disabilities more actively protect themselves. The idea that students will acquire self-determination and self-advocacy on a long-term scale is extremely important if they are to become truly independent and reasonably self-sufficient adults. Here are five examples of self-advocacy goals:

1. Margaret will, with her family, set up a 5-, 10-, and 15-year future life plan.
2. Krystal will actively participate in discussions around graduation, college, work, independence, and money during the Individualized Transition Plan (ITP) meeting.
3. Brody will benefit from the advocacy of a nonprofit organization providing such services.
4. Cara will develop coping skills for his illness.
5. Dorothy will benefit from alternative guardianship.

Transportation

Getting to and from places in the community is a major aspect of transitioning from childhood/dependence to adulthood/independence. This goal is all too often passed over by educators and left to family members or others. Although most secondary school students can enroll in driver education programs, schools seldom consider the transportation needs of those youngsters who cannot drive because of their disability.

The transportation goal needs to reflect a continuum of mobility options ranging from selection of an appropriate wheelchair to use of a specially equipped vehicle. Transportation goals may also include using public transportation, gaining a driver's license, finding one's way around the community, reading a map, or learning how to ask for help.

With the passage of the Americans with Disabilities Act, physical accessibility of public facilities in the community is now mandatory and seen by the U.S. Congress as a civil right. This law provides statutory support to facilitate travel for people with disabilities. However, if funds are not available to purchase necessary equipment or if individuals do not receive appropriate training and support in certain travel skills, the impact of this law cannot be realized.

As with a number of these ITP goals, the student and family, along with the educational team, must prioritize their transportation goals. Remember, many goals in other areas will be extremely difficult to implement unless the student has adequate transportation skills. Going to college, holding a steady job, or participating on the YMCA jogging team requires the ability to get from one point to the other. The more travel skills the student develops, the more other avenues will open up.

The integral relationship between community mobility and community functioning requires educators to focus on preparing individuals with disabilities to travel more independently. How much self-empowerment and control over life are realizable for a person with serious travel restriction? Program initiatives in this area must focus on increasing the opportunity for community travel and teaching specific mobility skills. Although the ADA addresses only accessibility, instruction and support are also needed to improve the mobility of persons with disabilities in the community. Here are five examples of transportation goals:

1. Joseph will travel independently to designated locations within a 2-mile radius of his residence.
2. Darla will become independent at finding her way around the shopping mall.
3. Susan will initiate her own transportation needs through STAR.
4. Nick will use public transportation to get to work and other places he frequents.
5. Tom will travel safely in his wheelchair in the community.

HOME LIVING SKILLS

Home living skills include many different activities. While many of these skills such as toileting or washing one's hands are used in other environments, home living skills are defined as those skills that are not directly related to a specific vocational skill or community task. The importance of home living skills is most evident with individuals who have significant disabilities and continually need help. Even in the 1990s, a person with a significant disability who is unable to perform key activities of daily living in the home may very well be sent to a nursing home because no one in the natural home is able to provide adequate care. It is imperative for teachers to assess the home living competence of students because these skills are critical building blocks for a long-term community adjustment. An individual who cannot perform the necessary home living skills will be at great risk for long-term institutionalization and will be less likely to engage in other more exciting activities such as employment or integrated community living. Independence or semi-independence in a home setting is often a requirement for a community vocational placement as well.

The wide range of skills required for community domestic living means that educators must systematically priortize these skills for training. Involvement of the family and student to decide which of these skills is optimal is absolutely essential. Special attention should be directed toward developing methods for self-instruction and self-management of a home setting. The ultimate goal of instruction is to teach students skills that will increase their independence in daily adult life. The earlier this type of instruction can occur, the greater likelihood of success as a student becomes older. Skills that include activities of daily living must be in the curriculum, particularly for those students who come to school with significant deficits in their abilities to perform them.

POSTSECONDARY EDUCATION/FUNCTIONAL ACADEMICS

Historically, special education programs for students with disabilities, as well as nondisabled children, have emphasized academic skills training. Students who were not ready for instruction and academics were taught prerequisites such as sorting colors and shapes. Many students with disabilities, especially significant disabilities, do not learn at the rate of nondisabled children and often do not progress beyond learning these prerequisites. Protracted instruction on such basic academic skills not only becomes boring, but is a tragic waste of resources for students who have limited time before losing their school entitlement. Sorting colors and shapes is pretty low in functionality when compared with being able to order a meal at a fast-food restaurant or purchase a ticket to a local movie theater.

The solution to this problem is a move toward a functional academic curriculum that involves life skills, independent living skills, daily living skills, vocational and career education, and career development concepts. The key consideration in determining whether to teach an academic skill is, Will the student be able to use this information currently or in the future? The most definitive way to determine whether this is likely or not is to study the environments that the student is in right now and will probably be in the future and then identify those academic or academiclike skills that are necessary. The functionality of an academic skill will be defined by the student and his or her family based on their home and community environments.

The involvement of students in functional academics in an increasing level may determine whether or not some movement into postsecondary education is viable. At a certain level of functioning, concentrating on postsecondary education does not make much sense; getting a job is more important and particularly identifying a job that requires very little in the way of academics. On the other hand, many students with traumatic brain injury, learning disabilities, sensory impairments, and severe physical disabilities, are all beginning to increase their applications for some form of higher education. If possible, the student's educational team and family need to aim as high as possible in terms of goals and expectations. A goal of postsecondary education will be appropriate for thousands of students who decide to focus less on vocational training and more on higher education while working part-time. For some young adults, the dual track of some employment and a limited educational load in a two-year or four-year college or trade school makes a great deal of sense. Educational goals for these students are associated with establishing interviews with admissions counselors, visiting classes, spending several days on campus, and talking to other students with disabilities who are currently enrolled at the college. The student and family must keep in mind, however, the importance of developing the necessary building blocks for a career, as opposed to an isolated job. Increasing academics at a selective level, along with providing meaningful employment experiences—as in the following five examples—can make all the difference in the world for students as they grow into adulthood:

1. Sam will complete a 4-year Bachelor of Social Work degree.
2. Mona will take 2 courses at the community college in computer education.
3. Mary will attend/complete a 2-year community college associate program in culinary arts, with support services.
4. Robert will increase skills in computer science.
5. Lori will continue to add to his English vocabulary.

FINANCIAL PLANNING AND MANAGEMENT

Economic self-sufficiency is a major goal for most citizens, and individuals with disabilities are no different. Amazingly, we in education do not help students focus adequately on financial planning, investment strategies, and comparative shopping.

Not surprisingly, individuals with disabilities are among the most vulnerable to being taken advantage of by scams and unfair marketing practices.

If employment and postsecondary education are worthwhile transition goals, then certainly the financial/income needs area cannot be far behind in importance. Considering that social security payments and medical assistance account for the overwhelming number of dollars spent on disability in the United States, individuals with disabilities need to be educated in their rights and entitlements as related to these payments. Because Social Security regulations are complex and sometimes difficult to understand, students need to learn how to get help in resolving special questions.

Educational goals may involve many different areas ranging from simple money management to more complex topics such as estate planning, using credit, and long-term financial planning. Even selecting coins for a drink machine may have to be taught. This ITP goal may require a parent or other family member to take a major role and responsibility.

Money management has always been part of the special education curriculum, but most schools have not advanced to a more contemporary and functional approach for many areas of financial planning and economic self-sufficiency. Many school programs do not even teach money skills in community settings. There is an assumption that students will automatically know how to perform in the community a skill learned in the classroom. The world is much more complicated for today's youth than it was for previous generations. Personal competence is heavily dependent on the ability to manage financial affairs, know what questions to ask, know how to obtain help, and know what pitfalls to avoid. The ITP team needs to help students attend to needs such as these:

1. Tiffany will seek employment while taking courses at the community college.
2. Sid will be financially independent of his sister/guardian.
3. Chris will receive financial aid for college.
4. Susan will open a checking account and learn how to make three department store purchases.
5. Tashell currently receives Supplemental Security Income (SSI) and Social Security Disability Income (SSDI). She will earn an income and develop an individual support plan for her 1st year of employment.

SOCIALIZATION, RECREATION, AND LEISURE

Leisure is supposed to be fun, not work; furthermore, it should be reinforcing, not unpleasant. At the same time, socialization is very important for students to learn. This individualized goal should be emphasized unless a student is already very active with many friends.

Many wonderful materials and curricula have been developed for age-appropriate social and leisure activities (Kelley & Frieden, 1989; Schleien & Ray, 1988; Wehman & Schleien, 1981). Selecting appropriate ITP recreation goals hinges on these criteria:

- What recreational interests does the student demonstrate and are these interests consistent with his or her intellectual and physical capabilities?

- What opportunities are available in the student's community and home to enjoy this leisure activity?

There are so many leisure activities that this goal can be overwhelming. As a rule of thumb, it will be most advantageous to select a goal that has a high probability of being enjoyed over and over again. The best approach is to ask parents, siblings, and the student not only what they like, but what is available. Wanting to be on the swimming team may be great, but if the pool is 40 miles away and there is no transportation, this might be a futile plan. Common sense must enter into goal planning, as in these examples:

1. Terri will develop a daily exercise/therapy routine to strengthen healthy muscles with YWCA and physical therapist.
2. Robert will use a TV remote control and operate a VCR independently by 1/98.
3. Wendy will join the community volleyball team.
4. Charles will get involved with a recreational activity of his choosing.
5. Karen will participate in a bowling league with older adolescents and young women.

WHAT DO PARENTS NEED TO KNOW ABOUT TRANSITION PLANNING FOR THEIR CHILDREN?

When considering these different curriculum areas, it is also important to look at school from the eyes of a parent. Parents and teachers often have very different perspectives about what is best for a student; the parents' attitude may depend partially on the severity of the child's impairment without their support and involvement. The following sections provide three scenarios of how parents might plan a teenager's transition depending on the level of disability experienced. Table 1.1 summarizes the main points.

Scenario 1. Significant Impairment

If my child has been labeled "multiply disabled," "severely retarded," "severely emotionally disturbed," or "autistic," then I need to work closely with my teachers, counselors, and school administrators to see that several key points are covered in my child's individual education plan and transition plan.

While every child has different needs, as a parent, I know that because my child has significant impairments the more planning, help, supports, and training I can provide, the more capable my child will be once school is over. This will make my life easier, too. Therefore, the two features that I want to try very hard to get into my program are:

1. *Real-life training experiences in community settings, home-living settings, and work settings.* I want to communicate directly with the teachers about the skills

TABLE 1.1   As a Parent, What Should I Be Looking for in Planning Transition for My Child?

Mild Impairment Individual needs some extra help to get to an even level with others in most areas.	• Significant planning time with school guidance counselor, teacher on postsecondary school options. • Planned, *extended* community college or 4-year college experience. • Part-time employment before leaving school. • School/community volunteer experience.
Moderate Impairment Individual needs substantial help in one or more academic or behavioral areas.	• Focused efforts on specific career/trade/skill training for a given occupation. • Work experience at job sites. • Part-time employment before leaving school. • On site *short* experiences in local community colleges with arranged help/supports by public school.
Significant Impairment Individual needs help/support most of time to complete major aspects of life skills.	• High proportions of time receiving training/instruction in community sites. • Work experience in community. • Part-time employment before leaving school.

that I think my son or daughter needs to know the most and negotiate an educational/transition plan that reflects areas such as good behavior during shopping at the grocery store, shopping skills, improved travel and/or mobility skills, improvement or competence in activities of daily living, and use of leisure time in a constructive fashion, either with siblings or with other community members. I know that the best way to train these skills will be to *teach them on a daily basis in the places where they occur the most,* which usually is not in the classroom.

2. *Work experience and, if at all possible, some form of part-time employment that increases as my child gets older.* The idea of work for students with severe behavioral or intellectual impairments may seem unlikely to some, but through job coaching and behavioral training support, many students with significant impairments can acquire necessary competitive employment skills for selected jobs. Job coaching is part of a program called supported employment.

While there are other key areas to focus on, real-life community training and work preparation, work experience, and part-time employment are extremely high priorities. Competence in these areas will increase the likelihood of getting better post-21 services in the community from vocational rehabilitation and the community service board.

SCENARIO 2. MODERATE IMPAIRMENT

If I am the parent of a child labeled as having "mental retardation," "severe learning disability," "cerebral palsy," or any other impairment which tends to significantly impact the student's normal *academic progression,* then I will work closely with the teachers, counselors, and administrators to see that my child gets a program reflecting the following points:

1. *Vocational training.* As these students become teenagers, they must increasingly focus on a possible skill, trade, or occupation. Although it is unrealistic to identify a lifelong occupation for a teenager, receiving training as a cosmetologist, licensed practical nurse, plumber, or plumber's helper, gives the child an important leg up on others who have no specific skill. A major reason for unemployment of young people with disabilities is that they have no training or experience in specific occupations.

2. *Work experience and part-time employment while in school.* The greatest tragedy for many of these students is that they leave school with a certificate of completion, but have no specific vocational trade, aptitude, or skill; and perhaps more importantly, they have not learned appropriate work habits or had work experiences that would allow them to get a job and keep a job.

3. *Academic skills.* Students need to have an opportunity to develop academic skills to the fullest level possible and utilize those skills in a functional manner. For example, the student who has some competence in math, can use these skills to improve quality of life.

Scenario 3. Mild Impairment

If I am the parent of a child who has been labeled as having a "mild disability," "mild ADHD," "learning disability," "educable mental retardation," then transition planning for my child should include significant amounts of time with the school guidance counselor and teachers to arrange the best array of classes that mesh with what the student wants to do after leaving school. I will want my child's program to fulfill the following requirements:

1. *Involvement of community colleges, course offerings, and certificate programs into the high school planning process.* Teenagers with a mild impairment should have a coordinated on-site program in local community or four-year colleges so that they have a sense of what the college experience is like. College can be an overwhelming experience for students without disabilities, and those with impairments will need extra help to level the playing field. Some colleges, however, are more "friendly" to those with disabilities than others. Parents and school personnel need to work closely to identify suitable colleges and, at the same time, develop close working relationships with senior higher education personnel at these schools. Many students with mild impairments never move ahead because they have received no postsecondary education. This trap can be avoided through coordinated on-site and extended experiences for students during summer and even during the regular school year at community colleges.

2. *Employment.* Students need to enter the world of work and demonstrate good competitive employment skills. This should be a key prerequisite for students before leaving their school program.

3. *Development of self-esteem.* Many of these students have been unfairly taken advantage of or teased by other classmates or people in the community; one way to overcome this lack of self-esteem is to encourage them to serve as a volunteer or participant in school/community extracurricular activities. These students will not succeed without having a better feeling about themselves, and schools can help answer this need. School and community work experiences, employment, and targeted postsecondary internships as part of an IEP for 15- to 19-year-olds can be an excellent prescription for success after they leave school.

CONCLUSION

The purpose of this chapter has been to describe the importance of longitudinal curriculum in the education of students with disabilities. There is a strong need for a functional and individualized curriculum. What we teach children will influence their adult lives and provide them with the competence needed for problem solving in the community and workplace. It is the responsibility of the schools to present curriculum content that has integrity, value, and relevance. In this book, the chapters are specifically targeted at fulfilling this mandate.

REFERENCES

Agran, M., Marchand-Martella, N., & Martella, R. (1995). *Safety for persons with developmental disabilities.* Baltimore: Paul H. Brookes.

Brown, L., Nietupski, J., & Hamre-Nietupski, S. (1976). Criterion of ultimate functioning. In M. Thomas (Ed.) *Hey don't forget about me!* (pp. 212–242). Reston, VA: Council of Exceptional Children.

Clark, G. (1996). Transition planning for secondary level students with learning disabilities. *Journal of learning disabilities, 29*(1), 79–92.

Kelley, J., & Frieden, L. (1989). *Go for it: A book on sports and recreation for persons with disabilities.* Chicago, IL: Harcourt Brace Jovanich.

Mount, B., & Zwernik K. (1990). *Making futures happen: A manual for facilitators of personal futures planning.* St. Paul, MN: Metropolitan Council of the Twin Cities Area.

Schleien, S., & Ray, M. (1988). *Community recreation and persons with disabilities: Strategies for integration.* Baltimore: Paul H. Brookes.

Wehman, P., & Schleien, S. (1982). *Leisure programs for handicapped persons.* Austin, TX: Pro-Ed.

Wehmeyer, M. L. (1995). *Whose future is it anyway? A student-directed transition planning process.* Arlington, TX: Arc National Headquarters.

2

Designing Instructional Programs

JOHN KREGEL

Instructional technology is always changing. Teaching strategies now viewed as state of the art will someday be questioned and rejected. Research and technological advances have led to a series of current "best practices" in instructional approaches for students with disabilities. First, instructional goals should be determined by analyzing the employment, educational, residential, community, and recreational environments the student will encounter both in and out of school. Second, whenever possible, tasks should be grouped and taught as integrated activities, as opposed to merely teaching isolated skills. Third, instruction should not prepare students just to perform skills in one setting; it should enable them instead to generalize their new abilities to new, previously unexperienced environments in their own communities. Finally, instruction, to the extent possible, should occur in community-based settings where students will actually use these skills.

This chapter is not designed to provide a comprehensive discussion of all aspects of instructional technology and program development. Many fine resource texts do this quite well and should be consulted (e.g., Orelove & Sobsey, 1987; Snell, 1993). Rather, the chapter is intended to familiarize the reader with the terminology used in the remaining chapters, provide an outline of the key decisions a practitioner should make when using the programs and curriculum suggestions in this text, and provide general guidelines for instructional programming for students with significant disabilities.

DECIDING WHETHER TO TEACH A SPECIFIC SKILL

Chapter 1 described the process of using information from a variety of sources to assess an individual's strengths and weaknesses; involving the student, his or her family, and community members in the assessment; and developing individualized goals and objectives that address the individual's primary educational needs. The first decision to be made after an interdisciplinary assessment reveals a skill deficit is whether or not the skill deficit is significant enough to initiate instruction. While there are many reasons for teaching or not teaching a specific skill to an individual student, at least three criteria should be applied to the decision-making process—functionality, feasibility, and student preferences.

FUNCTIONALITY

The first decision to be made is whether the skill or behavior being considered for instruction is functional for the student. Will this skill enable the student to be more independent? If the student can use learned skills in his or her home, community, or on the job, the likelihood is far greater that the skills will be retained over time. This implies that functionality is different, depending on environments that are most relevant to each student. A skill that is functional for one individual may be irrelevant for another. The principle of functionality implies that no "universal" curriculum exists that is equally applicable for all students.

It is also important to consider how well the student's environment will support a skill once it is acquired. Will the student be able to practice what he or she has been taught? If the student performs it successfully, will he or she receive the naturally occurring consequences that will reinforce the behavior? For example, will a student who is taught to make purchases in retail stores or order food in restaurants be able to use these skills outside the instructional setting? The actual test of whether a skill has been acquired is whether it is performed in the environment where the student will need it to be an independent citizen, homemaker, or worker. If these opportunities don't exist, it may be appropriate to delay instruction on a particular skill.

Another consideration is whether the student will be able to use the skill in both current and future environments. For example, learning to fill out a job application may be useful for some students at some point in time, but teaching this skill may be questionable if the student is several years or more away from actually applying for a job. Ideally, skills should be taught that have both immediate relevance and the opportunity for long-term use.

FEASIBILITY

A second important decision is whether instruction on a skill is feasible at this time. While there are literally thousands of potentially functional skills that might be taught to a given student, it may be that other skills have higher educational priority at this time. From one perspective, it may be argued that we can teach almost any skill to a learner if we use the proper techniques and devote a sufficient amount of instructional time. However, the anticipated length of time to teach a particular skill may be so great that only a portion of a skill should be taught at one time, or an alternative approach to performing a skill should be identified to reduce the required time.

The feasibility criterion is routinely applied in educational decision making. For children at the elementary level, the decision of focusing on verbal speech as opposed to alternative communication modalities is often decided in part based on the feasibility of instruction. The skills of driving (vs. using public transportation), making change, and writing checks are often considered in terms of feasibility when identifying the most relevant options for a particular adolescent.

STUDENT PREFERENCES

The criteria of functionality and feasibility in no way outweigh the importance of student and family preferences in the identification of potential skills for instruction. Of crucial importance is whether the student is interested in the skill and has had a role in selecting the instructional objectives. A student who has been involved in selecting instructional objectives likely will be more motivated to learn the skill. Self-selected skills will be far more likely to be used outside the school setting. Also, acquiring a skill that one feels is important can often add to an individual's positive self-concept and sense of accomplishment.

In some areas, the importance of student preferences is readily apparent. Few would discount the significance of student preference in areas such identifying a job or selecting potential recreational activities. However, student likes and preferences should be considered in all areas of instruction. For example, how an individual styles his or her hair, the menu items selected for cooking instruction, and the community settings frequented by the individual should all be based on the preferences and desires of a student and his or her family.

DEVELOPING INSTRUCTIONAL PROGRAMS

Developing an instructional program to teach a specific skill requires the teacher to make important choices. How should the individual complete the task? How should it be broken down for instruction? When the student makes an error during instruction, what feedback should be provided? When making these decisions, the teacher should focus on the unique needs of a specific student with specific learning deficits. The particular disabilities of a student will determine the most effective method of performing a task, organizing task content, and providing instruction. It is far more effective to design a program for an individual with a distinguishing set of skills and deficits than to develop instructional programs that are supposed to be usable with all individuals with disabilities. For example, the student's ability to speak, have full use of all extremities, or profit from various types of feedback will dramatically affect the strategies used to deliver instruction. Some of the major decisions involved in developing instructional programs are identified in Figure 2.1.

The effort to individualize instructional programming should be reflected in all aspects of the program format. For example, some programs may be designed to use specific sensory modalities in the learning process and would therefore be appropriate for a deaf, blind, or deaf-blind individual. Consideration can also be given to how the task is to be performed. Many of the instructional programs described in

FIGURE 2.1   Steps in the Design of Instructional Programs
_____

1. Developing the instructional objectives.
2. Identifying the method of performing the task.
3. Completing the task analysis.
4. Determining program format.
5. Collecting baseline information.
6. Developing instructional prompts:
   A. System of least prompts.
   B. Time delay.
7. Scheduling the training session:
   A. Massed versus distributed training trials.
   B. Community-based instruction.
8. Developing reinforcement strategies.
9. Planning for generalization.
_____

other chapters reflect alternate methods for performing conventional skills in ways that capitalize on an individual's strengths and abilities. For example, a teacher may be working with three students on purchasing items in a grocery store, training each student to use a different method to perform the task. As a result of this need for individualization, almost all instructional programs are specific in nature and frequently need to be significantly modified for use with other students.

DEVELOPING INSTRUCTIONAL OBJECTIVES

After the teacher has decided to teach a particular skill to a specific student, a behavioral objective should be written. Numerous resources are available that do an excellent job of teaching the process of writing instructional objectives (e.g., Rusch, Rose, & Greenwood, 1988). Behavioral objectives are statements that describe what is to be taught (the *behavior*), where and when the behavior is to occur *(conditions)*, and a standard of performance *(criterion)*, which is used to determine successful acquisition of the objective.

The behavior statement within an instructional objective specifies the target response that we want the student to perform. What will the student be able to do after instruction has been completed? Behavioral objectives are important components of the individualized planning process. However, they also serve a practical function in the development of instructional programs. The behavioral objective defines the *scope* of the task to be taught. If the task is washing clothes, an appropriate objective might be, "The student will sort, load, wash using bleach and fabric softener, dry on line, fold, and put away three loads of clothes." Another acceptable objective might be, "The student will load, wash, dry in automatic dryer, and fold one load of laundry." These are two distinct tasks that will be analyzed differently, taught differently, and evaluated differently.

The behavior component of the objective may focus on teaching the student the entirety of a specific task or provide instruction on only a portion of the skill to allow the partial participation of individuals unable to acquire the whole skill. The principle of partial participation (Baumgart et al., 1982) holds that even if a student is unable to perform all aspects of a task due to the severity of a disability, he or she should learn how to perform those parts of a skill that can be acquired. In other words, the inability to perform all aspects of a task in the way most people perform it should not prohibit instruction on any part of the task. Teachers have the responsibility to work toward student participation on components of tasks identified by the student or his or her family as meaningful and relevant.

The principle of partial participation is highly related to the notion of entry behaviors or prerequisite skills. A prerequisite skill is one that a student must have to benefit from instruction on a program as it is written. It does not necessarily mean that the student should not be taught the task involved, simply because he or she cannot perform a prerequisite skill. There are two reasons for this. First, the student may learn the prerequisite skill within the context of the program. If the student is learning to operate a pay telephone, functional use of a pincer grasp would seem to be a prerequisite skill enabling the student to pick up the dime and place it in the slot. If the student being taught does not have a functional pincer grasp, it might be possible to develop the grasp by teaching it during this highly motivating task.

A second reason for not excluding a student from instruction on a skill because he or she lacks a prerequisite skill is that a prerequisite skill is one necessary to complete a program *as it is written*. If a student cannot perform a specific prerequisite skill, the instructor can devise a method for performing the task that doesn't require the particular skill. In working with students who possess multiple disabilities, a critical programming component is the teacher's ability to devise alternative methods of performing a given task.

The conditions in a behavioral objective stipulate where the behavior should occur, when it should occur, and the environmental stimuli and factors that should be present. For example, a behavioral objective might be designed to teach the individual to cross a four-lane street. When and where the student should perform this task would dramatically impact the instructional strategies used and the criterion for successful mastery. Potential conditions for the objective of street crossing are described in Figure 2.2.

FIGURE 2.2   Conditions Under Which a Street
Crossing Objective Might Occur

When:
    Rush-hour traffic.
    Non-rush-hour traffic.
Where:
    Familiar street.
    Unfamiliar street.
    Near school.
    Near home.
Environmental Factors:
    Traffic light.
    Two-way or four-way stop sign.
    Crosswalk or no crosswalk.
    Presence of parent or adult.
    Presence of street crossing guard.
    Sidewalk or no sidewalk.

The criterion component of the behavior objective delineates the anticipated standard of success. Criteria are usually stated in quantifiable terms, such as frequency, rate, duration, or percentage correct. The criteria specified for a particular objective reflect the unique characteristics of both the individual and the skill under instruction. For example, in the street-crossing example, the criterion to be established would necessarily be quite rigid (e.g., 20 consecutive performances with no errors), due to the dangers inherent in just one situation where the individual fails to perform the skills successfully. A recreational task, such as shooting a basketball through a hoop, could have a much less demanding criterion (e.g., 30% accuracy across 10 trials on two consecutive days), since 100% accuracy on this skill is neither necessary nor anticipated. Similarly, the criterion level established for a student whose performance is stable on a day-to-day basis may be significantly different from that developed for a student whose disability causes wide variation in performance on a daily basis. A student with significant memory deficits resulting from a traumatic brain injury would require an extremely stringent criterion on tasks that rely heavily on memory skills (e.g., distinguishing between poisonous and nonpoisonous materials in a work setting).

Any criterion level identified for a particular student is little more than an arbitrary designation of a level of proficiency at which the student can be said to have learned the task. There is nothing magical about the criteria delineated in an IEP or for an instructional objective. Just because the student performs a skill with 80% accuracy for three consecutive days, does this mean that the skill has been learned to a point at which it can be used at all times in all places? To answer this question is a complex task involving a number of variables. Does the student perform the skill well enough and fast enough? Will the student be able to perform the skill after a vacation or illness? How well will the skill generalize to other environments? It may be useful for teachers to distinguish achievement of an artificial criterion for education measurement purposes and the actual performance of the skill in the environment in which it was intended to be used.

ACQUISITION, FLUENCY, MAINTENANCE, AND GENERALIZATION

To ensure the instruction results in functional skills that can assist the individual in varied settings, the instructor must develop a systematic plan for moving the individual from initial acquisition to complete mastery of the skill. Mastery may be viewed as having four components: Acquisition, fluency, generalization, and maintenance.

The *acquisition* phase refers to the student's ability to learn the skill under the conditions and criteria established in the original objective. However, the student's ability to initially perform a task such as enter data into a computer, make a bed, or prepare a meal may not reflect the ultimate standards that would be expected of an experienced performer. *Fluency* refers to the increased accuracy and speed of performance reflecting an individual's improved competence with further practice. *Generalization* reflects a further expansion of the individual's abilities. Generalization is usually defined as exhibiting a behavior or performing a skill under different conditions (stimuli, settings, time of the day, etc.) than were present in the initial acquisition phase. Specific procedures for promoting generalization are described in this chapter. Finally, *maintenance* refers to the individual retaining the ability to perform a skill over time. For skills such as counting money to be truly

TABLE 2.1   Mastering the Use of a Pay Telephone

Acquisition	Michael will deposit the appropriate amount of money and dial the correct telephone number 70% of the time across 10 consecutive opportunities.
Fluency	Michael will deposit the correct amount of money and accurately dial an appropriate telephone number 90% of the time across 20 consecutive opportunities.
Generalization	Michael will use various coin combinations to dial different telephone numbers, using a number of different pay telephones, 90% of the time across 20 consecutive opportunities.
Maintenance	Michael will use various coin combinations to dial different telephone numbers, using a number of different pay telephones, at random monthly intervals over a period of two years.

functional, the individual must be able to perform those skills months or years after they were initially learned.

Table 2.1 provides an example of the acquisition, fluency, generalization, and maintenance stages for the skill of using a pay telephone for a student named Michael. Initially, Michael learns to use a single pay phone with 70% accuracy. However, to stop instruction at this point would leave Michael in a situation where he might be considered a "marginal" telephone user, prone to frustration and more than occasionally dialing a wrong number. During the fluency stage, efforts are undertaken to improve his accuracy. In the generalization phase, Michael expands his abilities so that his ability to use the phone isn't limited by the change in his pocket, the number he is dialing, or the type of telephone that might be available. Finally, it is important that after spending a considerable amount of effort learning this skill, Michael is able to perform it for the foreseeable future. Maintenance procedures are used to ensure that, once acquired, students can use skills for an indefinite period.

METHOD OF PERFORMING THE TASK

The method is the manner in which the task is performed, or the process or strategy that the student will use to complete a complex activity such as cleaning a bedroom, playing a video game, or self-administering medication. This area of instructional program development requires a great deal of innovation and creativity from the teacher. The method selected for instruction will determine (1) whether the student will acquire the task, (2) the amount of time required for instruction, and (3) the potential for the acquired skill to generalize across a large number of settings.

Several factors influence the method that will work best with a given student. When possible, the student should be taught to perform a task in the same manner that most other individuals complete it. A student who dresses very differently from his or her peers, orders meals differently in a restaurant, or uses a different procedure to swim the length of a swimming pool may unnecessarily feel that his or her accomplishments are somehow inferior to those of others. For this reason, it is important to determine the typical way that various skills are performed and teach students the method used by most people in our society. This can be identified by observing people if an independent living skill is involved, interviewing individuals in employment settings, or by consulting developmental literature or curriculum guides in areas such as motor or communication skills.

When the most common method cannot be used, two factors should be considered and balanced in developing alternative methods. The first factor is the speed and convenience of the method for the learner. If the task can be performed more quickly and with less effort, the alternative method may be advisable. Examples of alternative methods that will improve the speed and efficiency of an individual's performance include having the student thread a belt through belt loops while holding the pants on his or her lap rather than while wearing them, using a language board method for ordering in a fast-food restaurant, or using Velcro® fasteners instead of zippers or snaps.

Another factor in identifying an alternative method of performing a task is whether the method will enable the student to perform the task in a variety of environments. For example, an alternative method may enable a person who cannot count money to operate a vending machine but may limit the number of different vending machines the student can operate. In this case, the alternative method identified may make the task easier for the student to perform, but limit the environments in which the student can use the skill. Consider the following methods for teaching a student with limited money-counting skills (unable to combine coins into various amounts of money) to use drink or snack food vending machines that cost between $0.25 and $1.50:

Method 1.   The student is provided a small number of one-dollar bills. The student uses the bills to purchase items from vending machines. When approaching the machine, the student locates the dollar bill slot, inserts the bill, and selects the desired item. If the item is not dispensed, the student inserts a second bill (in case the item costs more than $1.00). The student never inserts more than two bills.

This method is effective when used with vending machines that accept currency in addition to coins. It does not require any counting skills. However, if the vending machine approached by the student does accept currency, the student will be frustrated in attempts to obtain an item. In addition, if the machine is malfunctioning (bills are inserted but not returned and nothing is dispensed), the individual will lose $2.00.

Method 2.   The student is provided several quarters. The student approaches the vending machine, locates the slot where coins are inserted and inserts a single quarter. The student then pushes the button (pulls the selection lever, etc.) that dispenses the desired item. If the item is not dispensed, the student repeats the process of inserting another quarter and again pushing the button. The process is continued until the item is dispensed.

Method 2 has the advantage of working on a wider range of vending machines than Method 1, including machines that do not accept currency. However, it fails to keep the student from losing money if a machine is malfunctioning (inserting coins and pressing selection buttons before putting in the correct amount of change may increase the likelihood of malfunction).

Method 3.   The student is provided a large number of dimes and one or more nickels. The student approaches the machine and locates the writing on the machine that identifies the amount a specific item costs. The student points to the number in amount that is on the right (either 0 or 5). If the number is a "5," the student inserts the nickel. The student then covers that number with his or her finger and looks at the remaining number(s). The student then inserts that many dimes into the machine and presses the button to select the desired item.

Method 3 has several advantages. It will work on all vending machines with items costing up to $1.50. It enables the student to enter all the needed coins before selecting the item, thereby reducing the chance of causing a malfunction. It ensures that the student will not insert up to $2.00 in coins or currencies into machines that are not working. This approach, however, is significantly more complicated than the other identified strategies. It requires the student to (1) discriminate dimes from nickels, (2) discriminate left from right in a series of numerals, and (3) count accurately up to 15.

Each of the three methods may be appropriate for an individual student. Many other effective methods have been devised to teach generalized use of vending machines to students with significant disabilities. The precise method that will be best for a specific student depends on the skill under consideration, the student's ability to perform various components of the tasks, and the range of settings in which the skills must be used after instruction. What is important is that the instructor not use the lack of prerequisite skills to limit the student's ability to learn functional and meaningful skills.

TASK ANALYSIS

After the method has been selected, the next step is the development of a formal task analysis. Task analysis is the process of breaking down a skill or set of skills into its component parts to help a student learn the skill. The number and specificity of the steps identified in the task analysis should be related to the student's ability level. For example, one student may benefit from instruction on the task of washing dishes in a sink when the task is broken down into a series of 10 distinct steps. For another student, 10 steps in the task analysis may not be sufficient, and a 30-step or 40-step task analysis should be developed.

Numerous strategies can be used to generate task analyses. Published resources can be consulted; they may provide a basic guide that teachers can modify or adapt for their students. In employment settings, businesses may have developed detailed procedures for training all employees, and these can form the basis of individualized task analyses for a specific student. Task analyses should be individually developed and put to use. In most instances, therefore, a teacher will have to construct a task analysis without any additional resources.

The teacher who must develop a task analysis without help from a published resource can use several approaches. The teacher may analytically perform the task by him- or herself. Alternatively, the teacher can simply list the steps based on a logical analysis of the steps to be performed. Another approach would be to observe an individual performing the task. Finally, if the teacher is analyzing complex vocational or recreational skills, he or she may interview an experienced individual to learn his or her skill techniques.

The following guidelines are useful for listing the various steps in a task analysis:

1. Each step of the task analysis should be stated in a way that allows the instructor (or other individual) to accurately and objectively determine whether the individual has completed the step.

2. Each step of the task analysis should be written so that it can also be used as a verbal prompt to the student during instruction. For example, a step could state, "put the quarter in the machine" as opposed to "use a pincer grasp to grasp a quarter and insert into appropriate slot."

3. If important to the completion of the task, specify the hand the individual will use to perform a specific action.

4. If a step has the word "and" in it, carefully review the step to determine whether to break it into multiple steps. For example, in the step "put ketchup and mustard on the hot dog," the student may successfully complete part of the step but have difficulty completing the entire step. Separating this step into two steps will allow the identification of the specific component of the task on which the student is experiencing difficulty.

5. After developing the task analysis, the teacher should "pilot-test" the task analysis with the student and make modifications based on the results of the test before initiating instruction.

An example of a task analysis for washing a number of dirty dishes in a sink is contained in Figure 2.3. While the 15-step task analysis may be overly detailed for some individuals, the task analysis is based on a large number of assumptions. First, the task is designed for a kitchen that has a double sink (one for washing and one for rinsing) and a single faucet (where hot and cold water are mixed). If this is not the case in the student's home, the task analysis would need to be modified.

FIGURE 2.3   Task Analysis of Washing Dishes

Steps
1. Place the drain cover over the drain.
2. Turn on the water.
3. Adjust the water temperature.
4. Squeeze the dishwashing liquid into the sink under the water flow.
5. Determine when the sink is full.
6. Move the faucet to the other side of the sink.
7. Adjust the water temperature to cold.
8. Place dirty dishes in sink.
9. Pick up dishwashing sponge.
10. Wash front of dish with sponge.
11. Wash back of dish with sponge.
12. Rinse front of dish under cold running water.
13. Rinse back of dish under cold running water.
14. Check dish for cleanliness.
15. Place dish in rack.

Second, in the task design, cold water runs constantly throughout the washing process. This may be viewed by the teacher, the student, or his or her family as an unacceptable waste of resources. Third, the task assumes that the individual is able to use one hand to manipulate the dish under the rinse water. Some individuals might require the intermediate step of setting down the wash sponge while using both hands to rinse. Finally, the task analysis only applies to dishes. Significant modifications would need to be made for silverware, glasses, pots and pans, or other items.

The remaining chapters include several types of task analyses. Most task analyses are sequential listings of the steps to be performed in completing complex behavioral chains. Other task analyses are distance based—the steps listed are used to teach the student to perform the skills across increasing distances. These types of analysis are particularly useful in teaching vocational skills or recreational skills in situations that require the student to orient throughout a large area. With other skills, the student performs the same action through the course of the task; what is analyzed may be the complexity of the conditions under which the skill will be performed, the amount of assistance given to the student while performing the skill, or the duration or rate at which the skill is performed.

INSTRUCTIONAL PROCEDURES

Thus far, all the steps discussed in developing instructional programs deal with designing the task for presentation to the student. The remaining components will deal with designing teaching strategies and methods for evaluating learner performance on the task. The following components will be discussed: program format, description of a training session, teaching strategies and correction procedures, reinforcement, criteria for mastery, and generalization.

PROGRAM FORMAT

Program format relates to how much and what part of the task will be presented to the student for instruction during one training trial. The three most common program formats include forward chaining, backward chaining, and total task presentation. The primary difference between the chaining procedures and the total task procedure is that in the chaining procedures the student receives instruction on just one step of the program on any given trial. In the total task presentation format, the student receives instruction on all steps of the task analysis during each instructional period.

In forward chaining, the student learns the first step of the task first. Instruction is provided on the first "unlearned" step of the analysis. The teacher allows the student to attempt to perform the designated step. If successful, reinforcement is delivered. If unsuccessful, assistance is provided. After the student has mastered that step, instruction proceeds to the next step. In general, few skills are taught using forward chaining, since this approach prevents the individual from successfully completing the last step of the task and experiencing the natural consequences of successful performance until all steps in the task analysis have been completely learned. Forward chaining may have its greatest application on tasks such as tying shoes, in which the last steps of the task analysis are generally the most difficult to acquire. The student can benefit from the assistance received on the latter steps of the analysis while practicing and learning the initial steps.

In backward chaining, the last step of the task is taught first. This approach has the advantage of linking the naturally occurring reinforcement, which inherently results from the completion of the task, with the performance of the activity. Backward chaining may be beneficial for tasks on which the individual is able to complete a large number of the steps at the end of the task analysis. In the dishwashing example contained in Figure 2.3, the student would first be taught to place the dish in the dish rack. The student would then be taught to complete the last two steps of the task, inspect for cleanliness and place in the rack, and so on.

In the total task format, the student will receive training on every step of the task analysis. In the dishwashing example, the student will be allowed to attempt to perform Step 1, placing the drain cover on the drain. If he or she is successful, reinforcement may be provided; if unsuccessful, assistance will be delivered. In either situation, instruction will move on to the next step and the student will independently attempt Step 2, and again receive either reinforcement or assistance. Using the same routine, the student will move through all the remaining steps.

Total task presentation has several advantages. Some research is available to indicate that total task presentation is more effective than chaining strategies for some students with disabilities (Kayser, Billingsley, & Neel, 1986). Total task presentation is generally viewed as more "natural" because instruction is generally provided in the context of daily routines. Also, strategies sometimes can be used in combination. For example, a particularly difficult step of a task could be further broken down and isolated for instruction using a chaining strategy, while the main task is taught through a total task format.

To further illustrate the differences between the three formats, assume the task we wish to teach is hand washing. If a forward chaining procedure is used, the student will first learn Step 1 of the task: "Turn on the cold water." During the training session, several trials may be provided on the same step. After the child learns that step, another step is added and the student attempts to perform the first and second steps of the task: "Turn on the cold water, turn on the hot water." Additional steps are added to the chain until the student performs the whole task. In a backward chaining program, the student first learns the last step, then the last two steps, and so on. In all chaining programs, a criterion is set (called a phase-change criterion), which is used to determine when to add an additional step. For example, when the student performs the first step correctly for three consecutive times, the second step will be added, and so on.

In a total task presentation, the student attempts to independently perform each step of the task on each trial. In the hand-washing example, the student first attempts to independently perform the first step: "Turn on the cold water." If the student performs the step correctly, reinforcement is given. If the student does not perform the step correctly, a correction procedure is initiated and the student is given assistance until he or she is able to perform the step. Then, on the same trial, the student continues the task, attempting to perform the second step; this process continues, with the student attempting to perform each step of the task independently, and then receiving reinforcement or assistance, until the task has been completed. The total task presentation is generally used when the teacher feels that the student can benefit from instruction on more than one step of a training program within a single training session.

COLLECTING BASELINE INFORMATION

After the instructor has identified a method of task performance and developed a task analysis, instruction may be initiated. The first step in the actual instructional process is the collection of baseline, or assessment, information. The purposes of the baseline assessment are to (1) determine whether instruction on the task is required, (2) verify that the task analysis developed for the skill is appropriate for the student, and (3) identify any particular steps of an analysis that may cause particular problems for the student.

The actual format of the baseline assessment may vary depending on the task. If the task being assessed contains a lengthy list of complex steps, it may be appropriate to observe the student's performance across all steps of the task. On shorter tasks, assessment may stop at the first mistake made by the student. Some skills, such as the introduction of a new vocational skill that the student has never seen or attempted before, may only need to be assessed once or twice. Other skills, such as time-telling or money counting, may require lengthier baseline periods since the student's first response may not indicate his or her overall level of mastery. Whatever assessment strategy is used, it is important to ensure that assessment occurs under the same conditions that the task is ultimately intended to be performed. Community-based skills must be assessed *in the community*, at the time of day on which they typically occur.

INSTRUCTIONAL PROMPTS

The preceding teaching procedures assume that the student learns the skill with no difficulty whatsoever. If a teacher's only task was to reinforce the student for tasks performed correctly, it would be an easy job. In reality, students may make numerous errors and require significant assistance on many steps of a program until they acquire the desired skill. When the student performs a step incorrectly, or fails to perform a step after a specified period of time, assistance, in the form of a *prompt*, should be delivered to allow the student to successfully perform the task.

Many types of prompts can be used to help students with disabilities acquire complex skills. The most effective prompt in a specific situation depends on the characteristics of the learner, the type of task being taught, and the specific step within the task on which the student is experiencing difficulty. Figure 2.4 lists a number of prompts that have proven effective in many instructional settings. The following paragraphs describe these prompts.

Ambiguous Verbal Prompts.   In some situations, an individual needs only minimal assistance to complete the next step of a task analysis. He or she may be uncertain, or lack confidence about performing the step correctly. In these situations, an ambiguous verbal statement such as "What's next?" can prompt the student to initiate the next step of the task analysis. Ambiguous verbal cues have their greatest applicability when the teacher feels that the student knows the next step, or has completed the step properly in the past, but is reluctant for whatever reason to initiate the procedure.

FIGURE 2.4   Instructional Prompts

Ambiguous verbal/manual prompt. Comments such as, "Keep going," or "What's next?" prompt a student to go on without specifying what needs to be done.

Specific verbal/manual prompt. Specific information tells the student what to do next (e.g., "Pick up the plate").

Demonstration (modeling). Trainer performs the correct action and then allows the student to attempt to perform the step.

Gestures. These cues refer to nonverbal communication without words, such as pointing to the place where an object belongs, or gesturing to the student to turn an object over.

Priming. The student is given just enough physical assistance to initiate completion of the step. When the student begins to move independently, the trainer's assistance is removed.

Physical assistance. The student is given hand-over-hand assistance to enable completion of the task. When this assistance is faded from the hand, to wrist, to forearm, to elbow, to shoulder, the process is called graduated guidance.

Specific Verbal Cues.   Direct verbal instruction is an effective way to guide the individual into performing the correct action. Verbal prompts must be presented in a form that the student understands. A consistent verbal prompt should be developed for each step of a task analysis, which is why the steps in a task analysis should be written in a manner that allows them to be directly stated as specific verbal cues. These cues are most applicable in the initial stages of teaching a task with students who can benefit from verbal instructions. In addition, verbal cues are most applicable for steps of the task analysis involving discrimination among actions, objects, or other stimuli. Verbal cues will be less effective with behaviors that require complex motor movements.

Modeling.   As an instructional prompt, modeling refers to demonstrations of the appropriate action completed by an instructor, who then allows the student to copy (model) his or her action. Modeling is an effective strategy in situations where the individual is able to benefit from demonstrations performed by the instructor and the step of the task analysis to be completed does not lend itself to verbal cues.

The use of models assumes that the student will attend to the model and copy the actions to complete the task. Since the student turns his or her attention away from the instructional task to attend to the teacher's demonstration, modeling should only be used when other strategies are ineffective. In addition, when models are used, they should be combined with verbal cues so that over time the verbal prompt becomes an effective prompt.

In most instances, modeling refers to actions performed by the individual. However, modeling may also be done by a classmate or other individual in the actual setting where instruction is taking place. In employment settings, a coworker may model an action for an individual. In recreational settings such as a fitness center, other participants may be used to model actions.

Gestures.   Gestures are simply motions or actions by the instructor that serve a communicative function and indicate to the student the next action that should be performed. Gestures are most appropriate for situations in which the student does not understand a specific verbal prompt provided by the instructor or the action required at a specific step of a task analysis is difficult to state. For example, if the student does not know what a Phillips-head screwdriver is, it is difficult for him or her to respond to a specific verbal prompt such as, "Pick up the Phillips-head screwdriver." In this case, pointing to a Phillips-head screwdriver (gesture) may be an effective prompt. As with modeling, gestures should be paired with a specific verbal prompt, so that over time the verbal direction becomes an effective prompt. Gestures are also effective prompts when the step of the task analysis requires the individual to place an object in a specific location or orientation. Prompts such as "Turn it over" or "Rotate it 90 degrees" may be very difficult to understand for many students if not accompanied by a gesture.

Priming.   Priming is a physical prompt in which the teacher provides gentle physical contact that directs the student to initiate action on a step of the task analysis. Priming is sometimes referred to as partial physical assistance. Priming is often effective in situations where the step involved requires physical manipulation and the individual seems to know what to do next, yet is hesitant about initiating the step. A gentle touch on the elbow or shoulder may help the student complete the next step of the task analysis, such as clicking the left mouse button, inserting a token into a machine, or pressing a doorbell.

Physical Prompts.   Physical prompts involve hand-over-hand assistance to complete a specific step of the task. Physical prompts are the most intrusive of all prompts and should be used only when absolutely necessary. The prompts should be delivered in a gentle manner that provides the minimal required assistance. Physical prompts are most effective on steps that require complex physical manipulations. In these situations, the instructor can assist the student to develop the appropriate motor movements, as well as control the pace of the action, as in a swimming stroke, turning a key in a lock, or shifting a manual transmission of an automobile.

System of Least Prompts

Prompts are most frequently used in combination. In most instances, they are ordered into a hierarchy that can be delivered in a "most to least" or "least to most" sequence. A prompt hierarchy is basically a two-part delineation of what the teacher will do when the student makes a mistake. First, the teacher should stop the student's ongoing behavior. Second, the teacher should provide the minimal assistance that will enable the student to complete the step.

When the individual begins to make an error on a step of a task analysis, the teacher should move quickly to stop the behavior. There is abundant evidence that "errorless" learning is the most effective approach to instruction. In other words, learning occurs most efficiently when the student makes few errors. When an individual starts to perform a step incorrectly, (e.g., turning on the cold water when the hot water should be turned on), he or she is in effect "practicing" making mistakes. Stopping an error at its inception and then immediately providing enough assistance to enable the individual to perform the step independently will allow the person to learn the task in the shortest amount of time.

As previously described, there are a variety of ways to give assistance to a student. These can be arranged in a hierarchy from a minimal amount to a maximum amount of assistance. Generally, a prompt hierarchy contains three levels of assistance. If a student starts to make an error, the teacher should stop the ongoing behavior and deliver the assistance identified on the first level of the prompt hierarchy. If the student still does not complete the step, the second level of the prompt hierarchy should be implemented, and then the third.

Different prompt hierarchies can be employed depending on whether the student makes a *discrimination error* or a *manipulation error*. A discrimination error occurs when an individual's behavior is not under the control of the appropriate discrimination stimulus (S^D). The most frequently occurring discrimination errors involve selecting an inappropriate object, placing an object in an inappropriate place, or orienting an object incorrectly. A specific feedback hierarchy can be delineated for each of the types of error. As a general rule, ambiguous verbal prompts, specific verbal prompts, and gestures are considered the most effective prompts for discrimination errors.

The other major category of errors concerns manipulation error. A manipulation error occurs when an individual is unable to perform the physical manipulation necessary to complete a step. For example, an eight-year-old student named Emily is attempting to learn to insert a compact disk into a CD player, but is unable to easily grasp the outside edges of the CD and insert it into the narrow slot on the player. In this situation, the following prompt hierarchy could be used to correct Emily's manipulation errors. Initially, Emily will be allowed to attempt the physical manipulation (inserting the compact disk) for a period of 15 seconds. If she has not completed the step in that time period, the trainer will:

1. Provide a physical prompt in the form of hand-over-hand physical manipulation, beginning with the fingers and hand.
2. This manipulation will be faded from the fingers to the back of the hand to the wrist as the individual becomes more proficient at the task.

It is important to emphasize that the types of prompt used to correct discrimination and manipulation errors do not, and perhaps should not, be the same. For example, if Emily is attempting to insert the compact disk into the player upside down, a specific verbal cue or gesture indicating that she should turn it over might be effective. However, if she is having difficulty grasping and inserting the disk into the slot, verbal or gestural prompts may have limited value. Discrimination errors and manipulation errors frequently require different prompt hierarchies.

If the individual is making the same error on the same step over successive trials, it might prove effective to provide assistance to the learner *prior* to the performance of the step. This assistance will preclude the possibility of the individual independently performing the step correctly, but it has several advantages. First, it enables the student to practice performing the appropriate action, and that action only, in the presence of the particular S^D for that step. Second, it maintains the continuity and rhythm of the task. Third, it prevents incorrect responses from being practiced, which lessens the risk that the student will develop ineffective habits. The type of prior assistance given will again be determined by the type of error made.

If an individual makes an error on a specific step for three consecutive trials, the trainer should provide prior assistance. The trainer should intervene and provide assistance at the level that was effective during feedback on previous trials. As the individual progresses through training, the amount of assistance should decrease until none is being provided. If at any time during the fading process, an individual makes an error even after having been given prior assistance, more assistance will be given until the learner is performing the step accurately.

TIME DELAY

Time delay is a prompting procedure that is especially useful in promoting errorless learning. In time delay, prompts are initially provided immediately after the instructional cue, thereby greatly reducing the number of errors that will be made by the student. As the student begins to master the task, the time period between the cue and the prompt is gradually and systematically faded. In the *progressive delay approach*, the length of time between cue and prompts increases by small increments. In a *constant delay approach*, the length of time between cue and prompt varies from immediate to a constant (e.g., 5-second) level.

Time delay has been used effectively to teach skills such as using a vending machine (Browder, Snell, & Wildonger, 1988) and reading sight words (Ault, Gast, & Wolery, 1988). While in some instances, time delay has been used to teach lengthy behavioral chains, such as bed making (Snell, 1982), the procedure is most suited for teaching skills such as communication and functional academics.

For example, Mr. Young uses time delay to teach Lance, a 12-year-old boy with significant memory deficits how to state his home telephone number. Mr. Young first gives the cue, "Lance, what is your telephone number?" and immediately prompts (0-second time delay) Lance by verbally stating the first digit of his telephone number, and then the second digit and so on until the number is complete. After a series of practice trials, Mr. Young initiates a 1-second delay between the cue and each of the prompts. As practice sessions are completed, Lance begins to occasionally say a digit of his phone number in the interval between the cue and Mr. Young's verbal prompt. Over time, as Lance's performance improves, Mr. Young fades the period of time from 1 second to 3 seconds and then 5 seconds as Lance gains mastery of the skill. Lance is then ready to generalize the use of this skill to a wide range of community-based settings.

SCHEDULING THE TRAINING SESSION

Scheduling where and when instruction will occur is often one of the most challenging aspects of instructional planning. Current trends emphasize instruction of entire tasks and activity sequencing (in areas such as grooming, home maintenance, etc.), as opposed to instruction on isolated skills. Activity sequencing requires lengthy instructional periods that may not easily fit into the structure of the school day. In addition, instruction should be provided in the natural environments where the skill is to be performed, such as the local grocery store or post office. This emphasis often runs counter to trends such as inclusion, which stresses the importance of students spending a maximum amount of time with their same-aged peers, and minimum competency testing which emphasizes instruction on academic skills necessary for basic adult literacy. Within this environment, finding the time and resources necessary to teach the type of skills identified in the remaining chapters often becomes difficult.

Massed Versus Distributed Trials.   Twenty years ago, best practices in the instruction of individuals with significant disabilities suggested that instruction for students should be "massed" in certain periods of the day. For example, if a student was learning to turn on a radio, he or she would practice turning it on, the teacher or student would turn it off, the student would practice the task again, and this sequence would be repeated three, five, or ten times until an instructional session was completed.

In the 1980s, a number of professionals began to question this concept of massed trials (Guess & Helmstetter, 1986; Mulligan, Guess, Hoelvet, & Brown, 1980). The procedure was rejected as an artificial, overly rigid technique that reduced the likelihood that skills taught in the training setting would transfer to natural community settings. As an alternative, the concept of "distributed trials" was developed. Training should occur in community-based, in vivo, settings and should focus on *activities* as opposed to isolated skills. Considerable evidence suggests that distributed trials result in improved performance and more positive student responses than mass trials (Dunlap & Keogel, 1980; Mulligan, Macy, & Guess, 1982). While the intensive practice afforded by the mass trial approach may be beneficial in a limited number of situations, the advantages of community-based training have proven significant.

Community-Based Instruction.   Community-based instruction offers the student the opportunity of learning new skills in the environment in which the skills will be applied. The student is able to experience the environmental factors that form the context for the skills the student is to acquire. For example, the presence of coworkers, the relationship to an employment supervisor, the duration of the workday are all factors that influence an individual's ability to learn new job skills. Similarly, adjusting to the pace and noise of downtown sidewalks is crucial to learning bus-riding skills. Distributed trial approaches are more likely to take place at various times and across settings, thereby promoting generalization.

While scheduling may be affected by the student, the task being taught, and the structure of the school, a number of guidelines can be offered. First, whenever possible, instruction should focus on activities rather than isolated skills. Meal preparation could focus on preparing the meal, eating, and performing kitchen cleanup chores. Students in work experience situations could learn to perform a series of photocopying activities in a local retail setting. Second, instruction should take place at the time of day at which the task is usually performed. Third, when possible, the student should spend the maximum amount of time possible with his or her same-aged peers. The concept of community-based instruction is not inconsistent with the concept of inclusion. Students without disabilities, family members, employers, and community members can all be involved in instructional settings. Fourth, the length of time between instructional sessions should be determined by the needs of an individual student and the nature of the task being taught. For some students, instruction one time per week may enable them to acquire community skills. Other students may benefit from more frequent community-based instruction. Some activities, such as doing one's laundry, may occur once or twice per week. Other activities, such as banking, may occur less than one time per week.

REINFORCEMENT

Little has been said about the role of reinforcement in the design of instructional programs. Although it is often overemphasized in simplistic explanations of the learning process, few would deny that a motivated learner will be more likely to quickly learn a task than one who is not motivated. Reinforcement is a form of feedback that cues the learner whether his or her behavior was correct and motivates the person to try to be correct again in the future.

In many instances, no specialized reinforcement program is needed because completing the task will lead to inherently reinforcing results (e.g., cooking a meal, making a purchase). Some students, however, will require additional reinforcement in the form of activities or verbal praise. A few students may need more tangible reinforcement. Some individuals may feel that the use of tangible reinforcement is not a natural approach and that it bribes students to perform skills they should want to learn on their own. However, giving a tangible reinforcement during the initial stages of instruction on the task does not mean the student will always require that reinforcement to perform the task. Reinforcement can be faded, just as physical assistance can be faded. If a student is not learning a skill, and appears to be unmotivated and having a difficult time paying attention to the task, tangible reinforcement techniques may be highly appropriate.

GENERALIZATION

The final component of instructional program design that will be discussed is generalization. Generalization refers to situations in which the student (1) demonstrates a skill learned in one setting in related, but not previously experienced, environments, (2) continues to display a behavior after the training conditions have been removed (also known as maintenance), or (3) develops new, untrained responses as a result of initial training. Despite its importance, generalization is an area of educational programming that is often neglected. After all, students need to be able to cross all streets of a specific type, not only the single street or streets on which instruction occurred, or to be able to purchase foods in all types of grocery stores, not just a single location.

Generalization can be said to have occurred if the change endures over time, occurs in a variety of settings, or occurs across a set of related behaviors. Generalization can take place along a number of different dimensions. These are usually identified as stimulus generalization, maintenance, and response generalization. Examples of each of the three generalization dimensions are provided in Figure 2.5.

A wide variety of strategies can be used to promote the generalization of newly learned skills across employment, residential, community living, and recreational situations.

Rely on Natural Reinforcers. In some instances, providing reinforcement through verbal praise or activity reinforcers is an effective way of motivating students with disabilities to learn new skills. However, an overemphasis on artificial

FIGURE 2.5   Dimensions of Generalization

Stimulus generalization. The student should be able to perform a skill in a variety of community settings, or with a variety of materials. For example, a student who has learned to purchase a meal in a fast-food restaurant should be able to use a variety of fast food settings. A student who has learned to use a screwdriver should be able to use screwdrivers of various shapes and sizes.

Maintenance. The student should be able to independently perform a skill learned several weeks or months earlier without any of the prompting or reinforcement provided in the initial training stages. For example, a student who has learned to prepare a specific meal should be able to prepare the meal in the absence of any instruction 6 to 12 weeks after receiving the initial training.

Response generalization. A student who learned to perform a skill in the presence of a specific stimulus will perform related skills in the presence of the same stimulus. For example, a student who has learned to use a written checklist to assist in completing a part of their job (e.g., watering plants in a greenhouse) begins to develop and use written checklists to assist with housecleaning or car maintenance activities.

reinforcement during the initial training period may actually reduce the likelihood that skills taught in one setting may generalize to an array of settings throughout the community. Whenever possible, instructional programs should be designed so that the student experiences the natural consequences of completing an activity. For example, the natural consequence of completing an employment task may be praise from a supervisor or a paycheck. The consequence of successfully operating a CD player may be to listen to music. Exposing students to the consequences of task completion, as opposed to adding artificial reinforcements that must ultimately be faded, is an effective strategy of encouraging stimulus generalization.

Train Sufficient Examples.   If the intent of instruction is to enable an individual to perform a skill in a variety of settings and situations, then special care should be taken to ensure that training sites reflect the range of settings the individual will experience after learning the skill. One process for generalizing skill usage across various community settings is *general case instruction.* General case instruction emphasizes the careful selection of teaching examples to enable students to learn to perform skills across a variety of settings (e.g., Horner & McDonald, 1982; Sprague & Horner, 1984). This approach has proved effective with skills ranging from using telephones and vending machines, to vocational skills, to appropriate social behaviors.

When using general case instruction, the teacher should first identify the universe of possible settings in which a skill might be used. The teacher then carefully selects a set of "teaching examples" and "testing examples" that reflect the natural variation across all the settings that make up the universe. For example, if the task being taught is purchasing food in a fast-food restaurant, teaching examples should reflect fast-food restaurants that have salad bars and those that do not, restaurants with condiments in various locations, restaurants where the customer is responsible for serving his or her own drink from a drink machine, and so on. Instruction then begins on several (2–4) teaching example sites. After the student is able to order food at these teaching example sites, testing occurs at a similar number of testing sites to see if the student can generalize his or her newly learned skill to untrained settings. If generalization has not yet occurred, instruction continues in additional teaching sites until the individual can easily perform the task in a variety of untrained settings.

Train Loosely.   For many years, best practices in the instruction of individuals with significant disabilities emphasized standardized instructional strategies and rigid adherence to proven learning principles. Baer (1981) has argued that if instruction is too rigid (repeated the same way each time without variation), it may actually inhibit generalization. To promote generalization, Baer suggested randomly varying the number of instructors, the settings in which instruction occurred, and the time of day at which instruction would take place. The teacher is encouraged to vary his or her tone of voice, position in relation to the student, and the words used during instruction. The instructional setting can also vary in terms of lighting, sound, decorations, or presence of other individuals. Baer (1981) then urges teachers, "Do all this as often and unpredictably as possible" (p. 25).

Program Common Stimuli.   Another effective strategy for promoting both stimulus and response generalization is to identify stimuli (e.g., items or objects) that can be present in both the initial training and generalization environments. The extent to which common stimuli are available in all settings to prompt the student's appropriate behavior will greatly determine the amount of generalization the individual will display. Pocket calculators, written checklists of daily activities at school, work, or home, or even portable computers can be stimuli that assist the student to perform a newly learned behavior across a variety of settings.

For example, promoting the use of pocket calculators in many settings may promote stimulus generalization in students learning basic financial management skills. Using a calculator to make purchases in a grocery store may generalize to restaurants, banks, and other retail settings. The common stimulus (the pocket calculator), enhances the student's confidence in each of these settings. Similarly, response generalization can be enhanced when a common stimulus, such as a written checklist, is used to manage a student's morning routine at home, manage time effectively at work, and organize errands that must be run during the weekend.

Self-Management Strategies.   Using self-management strategies to promote generalization refers to involving students directly in their own instruction. While this might sound odd at first, all children and adults use numerous self-management strategies on a daily basis. We make lists to prompt us about what to buy at the grocery store. We reinforce ourselves with a short break and a cool drink after completing a tiring activity such as mowing grass or playing basketball. We record data about ourselves when we keep track of how much we weigh or the number of laps we swim. When used as an instructional technique for students with disabilities, self-management may refer to activities such as self-instruction, self-monitoring and evaluation, and self-reinforcement.

Self-instruction occurs when the student prompts himself or herself to perform one of the steps involved in the task analysis for a particular skill. Recipe cards, picture booklets (Wacker & Berg, 1984), pocket-size calendars, and tape-recorded instructions (Alberto, Sharpton, Briggs, & Stright, 1986) have all been used to help students acquire and maintain new skills. Self-instruction strategies have been particularly effective in assisting individuals to learn and perform job-related duties in employment situations.

Kreutzer and Wehman (1991) describe an array of compensatory strategies and other self-instructional strategies that have been used by individuals to overcome memory and other learning problems and successfully maintain employment.

Self-monitoring and evaluation refers to situations where individuals observe and record their own behavior. A child who checks off the various tasks involved in cleaning her own room (making bed, emptying trash, dusting, etc.) as the tasks are completed, an adolescent who keeps track of his high score on a video game, and an adult who checks off job duties as they are completed are all using self-monitoring strategies. Self-monitoring is effective for several reasons. Some evidence suggests that the very act of recording one's own behavior may change it for the better. Self-monitoring can also involve the subjective evaluation of the quality of one's own efforts, such as when an individual samples a dish that he or she has prepared, or evaluates the cleanliness of a kitchen after cleaning it.

Self-reinforcement occurs when the individual selects a reinforcer that will be administered when a behavior has occurred, or actually makes the decision to implement the reinforcement contingency. Employee determination of when to take breaks and what is done during break time has effectively enhanced employee performance in a variety of work settings. Rewarding oneself by watching a favorite television program after completing a series of housekeeping activities such as doing laundry and ironing can enhance the maintenance of these skills over a long period.

The need to plan and program for generalization places a difficult burden on the instructional staff. Programming for generalization is a complex problem. But what is certain is that generalization will occur if systematically planned for, whereas it may not spontaneously occur without specific interventions designed to promote it. The teacher should work both during and after initial training to encourage generalization.

CONCLUSION

Effective instruction for students with disabilities involves many decisions and an ability to adapt basic strategies to the unique characteristics and needs of individual students. This chapter described some of the important decisions and steps involved in developing instructional programs in the curricular areas described in the remainder of the book. Determining whether to teach a particular skill, developing a behavioral objective, developing a creative method for performing the task, and completing a task analysis require commitment and cooperation by a number of individuals, including the student, his or her family, and members of the community. Developing prompting procedures, providing reinforcement, and promoting generalization emphasize building on an individual's current skills to enable the achievement of self-selected instructional goals.

A growing body of literature identifies effective guidelines for the design and delivery of instruction for individuals with disabilities. Best practices include task-analytic instruction, training in actual community settings, use of coordinated prompting procedures and planning instruction so as to maximize generalization. Through careful planning and the cooperation of everyone involved, effective instructional strategies can promote the independence and inclusion of individuals with disabilities in employment, educational, and recreational settings in their communities.

REFERENCES

Alberto, P., Sharpton, W., Briggs, A., & Stright, M. (1986). Facilitating task acquisition through the use of a self-operated auditory prompting system. *Journal of the Association of Persons with Severe Handicaps, 11*, 85–91.

Ault, M., Gast, D., & Wolery, M. (1988). Comparison of progressive and constant time-delay procedures in teaching community sign-word reading. *American Journal on Mental Retardation, 93*, 44–56.

Baer, D. (1981). *How to plan for generalization.* Austin, TX: Pro-Ed.

Baumgart, D., Brown, L., Pumpian, I., Nisbet, J., Ford, A., Sweet, M., Messina, R., & Schroeder, J. (1982). Principle of partial participation and individualized adaptations in educational programs for severely handicapped students. *Journal of the Association of Persons with Severe Handicaps, 7*, 17–27.

Browder, D., Snell, M., & Wildonger, B. (1988). Simulation and community-based instruction of vending machines with time delay. *Education and Training in Mental Retardation, 23*, 175–185.

Dunlap, G., & Koegel, R. (1980). Motivating autistic children through stimulus variation. *Journal of Applied Behavior Analysis, 13*, 619–627.

Guess, D., & Helmstetter, E. (1986). Skill cluster instruction and the individualized curriculum sequencing model. In R. Horner, L. Meyer, & H. D. Fredericks (Eds.), *Education of learners with severe handicaps* (pp. 221–248). Baltimore: Paul H. Brookes.

Horner, R., & McDonald, R. (1982). A comparison of single instance and general case instruction in teaching a generalized vocational skill. *Journal of the Association for the Severely Handicapped, 7*, 7–20.

Kayser, J., Billingsley, F., & Neel, R. (1986). A comparison of in-context and traditional instructional approaches: Total task, single trial versus backward chaining, multiple trials. *Journal of the Association for Persons with Severe Handicaps, 11*, 28–38.

Kreutzer, J., & Wehman, P. (Eds.). (1991). *Cognitive rehabilitation for persons with traumatic brain injury.* Baltimore: Paul H. Brookes.

Mulligan, M., Guess, D., Hoelvet, J., & Brown, F. (1980). The individualized sequencing model: 1. Implications from research on massed, distributed, or spaced trial training. *Journal of the Association for the Severely Handicapped, 5*, 229–323.

Mulligan, M., Macy, L., & Guess, D. (1982). Effects of massed, distributed, and spaced trial training on severely handicapped students' performance. *Journal of the Association for the Severely Handicapped, 7*, 48–61.

Orelove, F., & Sobsey, R. (1987). *Educating children with multiple disabilities: A transdisciplinary approach.* Baltimore: Paul H. Brookes.

Rusch, F., Rose, T., & Greenwood, C. (1988). *Introduction to behavior analysis in special education.* Englewood Cliffs, NJ: Prentice-Hall.

Snell, M. (1982). Analysis of time delay procedures in teaching daily living skills to retarded adults. *Analysis and Intervention in Developmental Disabilities, 2*, 139–156.

Snell, M. (Ed.). (1993). *Instruction of students with severe disabilities* (4th ed.). New York: Macmillan.

Sprague, J., & Horner, R. (1984). The effects of single instance, multiple instance, and general case training on generalized vending machine use by moderately and severely handicapped students. *Journal of Applied Behavior Analysis, 17*, 273–278.

Wacker, D., & Berg, W. (1984). Use of peer instruction to train a complex photocopying task to severely retarded adolescents. *Analysis and Intervention in Developmental Disabilities, 4*, 219–234.

3

Self-Determination

PAUL SALE

JAMES E. MARTIN

Zeke is a 15-year-old young man living with his aging adoptive parents in a midsize suburban western city. Zeke has received special education support services since the third grade. At that time, he had significant problems reading and experienced many poor social interactions with peers and educators. During grade school and the first few years of middle school, the education system placed Zeke into a self-contained program where he spent all day with other children who had social interaction and academic problems. Toward the end of his middle school years, the district changed philosophies and began placing most students from self-contained classrooms into general education programs. Zeke now receives special education services through an inclusion facilitator who works with general education teachers to provide needed supports, accommodations, and strategies within his high school classes.

Zeke's academic performance plateaued the last two years of middle school and hasn't increased. Even though he received instruction in basic academic skills during elementary and middle school, his performance improved only marginally. He now reads at the 4.1 grade level. His math skills are at a 5.5 grade level, and his written language performance is about that of a typical fourth grader. The more teachers insisted that he spend time learning to read, write, and calculate better, the more he acted out. This avoidance response resulted in him being suspended three times last year. His recent arrest and conviction for burglary and possession of a controlled substance are closely tied to his desire to join a street gang. He told his counselor and probation officer that he may drop out of school. The vice principal and some of the faculty secretly wish Zeke would leave. His parents are frustrated and don't know what to do.

Throughout Zeke's school years, educators and parents have told Zeke what to do, when to do it, and how he did. Zeke is not engaged in the education process. The more his academic and social performance decline, the more direction the adults in his life provide. In short, Zeke does not know what to do, where to go, or how to get there. Peers and situations seem to direct Zeke's life.

A school-based self-determination curriculum may help Zeke learn to decide for himself what to do, where to go, and how to get there. This next section will overview what self-determination is and review sample self-determination assessment and curricula.

DESCRIPTION OF CURRICULUM

Every day I have before me many choices
It is not easy to choose . . .
I know what the past was.
I know what the present is.
But the choice that propels me into the future.
I'm not sure I'll make the right choices . . .
Every day I have before me many choices.
                    —*Wegscheider-Cruse*

Over the past few years, increasing efforts have focused on teaching students with special needs the generalizable skills they need to be successful both during the school years and beyond. Educators have realized that simply teaching the three R's and social skills does not adequately prepare students for life after school. Many policy makers and educators are starting to suggest that self-determination may be one of the keys to success during the school years and afterward. But why focus on self-determination? What is it? Why is self-determination instruction important? The purpose of this section is to look at the foundation of self-determination-based curriculum and to give a general overview of self-determination curriculum and specific examples.

Curriculum Foundation

Self-determination curricula attempt to teach a set of skills that successful people use. The roots of these materials come from the self-determination psychological literature, research in business and sport psychology, from self-efficacy writings, and from the self-management literature, to mention a few. Self-determination materials bring together in one package the best of these different approaches. An understanding of self-determination can be found in an analysis of what successful people do.

What Does It Take to Be Successful?   Successful people know what they want and persistently go after it (Hill, 1960; Hill & Stone, 1987). They decide on major goals, set a timeline, develop specific plans to attain their goals, determine the benefits that reaching the goals will bring, close off discouraging influences and thought, and will build coalitions with others who share similar goals and who will encourage each other in reaching them—something Zeke has never done. Zeke is not different from most of his peers who receive special education services. Most students with special needs are never taught how to be successful.

Garfield (1986) interviewed over 1,500 successful people from business, science, sports, and the arts. He found that successful people excel at making decisions, self-managing their behavior, and adapting to changing situations. When successful people make decisions, they (a) choose a goal, (b) envision and communicate that goal, and (c) develop an action plan consisting of specific objectives and means to evaluate performance. Successful people:

- Learn as they go, using educated risks and building confidence in their skills along the way. "It is not fear of failure that drives them along, but a strong desire for achievement" (Garfield, 1986, p. 138).

- See themselves "as the originator of actions in one's life . . . [viewing] events in life as opportunities for taking action and [seeing] themselves as the agents who must precipitate action" (Garfield, 1986, p. 141).

- Adapt by making course corrections and managing change through lifelong learning, expecting to succeed, mapping alternative futures, and updating their mission.

Garfield reached two conclusions in his study of successful people: First, regardless of age, education, or profession, the most successful people share the same basic set of skills. Second, individuals can *learn* these skills (Garfield, 1986). In education, these are called self-determination skills.

SELF-DETERMINATION

Self-determined individuals know how to choose—they know what they want and how to get it. From an awareness of personal needs, self-determined individuals choose goals, then doggedly pursue them. This involves asserting their presence, making their needs known, evaluating progress toward meeting their goals, adjusting their performance, and creating unique approaches to solve problems (Field & Hoffman, 1994; Martin, Huber Marshall, & Maxson, 1993; Mithaug, 1991, 1993; Schloss, Alper, & Jayne, 1993; Ward, 1988; Wehmeyer, 1992a, 1992b). People who are self-determined choose and enact their choices in persistent pursuit of their best interests (Mithaug, 1994). Self-determined people are their own best advocate (Martin et al., 1993).

Individuals with Disabilities and Success.   Do these same success and self-determination behaviors apply to people with disabilities? Yes, they do. In a unique study, Gerber, Ginsberg, and Reiff (1992) interviewed a group of adults with learning disabilities to determine why some succeeded and others failed. They found that successful individuals with learning disabilities had:

- A desire to succeed.
- Well thought-out goals.
- Persistence.
- Adapted to their environment.
- Built a social support network that facilitated their success.

Gerber et al. (1992) realized that successful individuals decided, long before they became successful, that they would be successful. The authors concluded that successful adults with severe learning disabilities wanted to succeed, set achievable goals, and confronted their learning disability so that they could take appropriate measures to increase the likelihood of success. One highly successful young man explained it like this: "Successful people have a plan. You have to have a plan, goals, strategy, otherwise you are flying through the clouds and then you hit the mountain" (Gerber et al., 1992, p. 480).

Summary

The special education process does little to empower youth with learning and behavior problems. As a result, these youth do not learn the skills needed to manage their lives. They remain dependent on other people to make decisions, provide support, and make needed changes (Mithaug, Martin, & Agran, 1987). Little effort is expended to teach students how to gain control of their lives and to adapt to changes in their environments (Martin & Huber Marshall, 1995).

Self-Determination Curricula Exemplars

Over the past several years, the U.S. Department of Education, Office of Special Education Programs, has funded numerous self-determination curriculum development projects across the country. In addition, several other curricula have been developed through other efforts. The curricula use a variety of approaches and strategies to facilitate the development of self-determination skills for students with special needs.

During 1995 and 1996, a team of University of Colorado faculty and public school educators reviewed self-determination curricula from across the country. Team members independently reviewed materials, compiled results, and produced a detailed review (Martin, Huber Marshall, Miller, Kregar, & Hughes, 1996). This section will overview several of these curricula packages.

Become Your Own Expert (Carpenter, 1995). This is a well-written curriculum that may be used to teach high school students with learning disabilities self-advocacy skills during a one-semester course. The self-advocacy skills that are directly taught in this curriculum include identifying individual academic strengths and weaknesses, learning styles, and setting goals for completing high school and continuing postsecondary education and training. In addition, students learn about classroom and workplace accommodations that help them be successful, and about federal and transition laws that support them in their efforts. The skill development activities utilize a variety of instructional techniques and strategies such as structured group problem solving, videotaped self-evaluations, site visits to post secondary programs, and activities involving postsecondary students and adults with learning disabilities. A corresponding parent program accompanies this curriculum, and many parents may learn how to support students while they acquire new skills. Available from Winnelle D. Carpenter, MA, Minnesota Educational Services, Capitol View Center, 70 West Colorado Road, B2, Little Canada, MN 55117-1402 (1-800-848-4912, ext. 2401).

Connections: A Transition Curriculum for Grades 3 Through 6 (Aspinall, Roberts, & Robinson, 1992).   This curriculum provides an equal balance between several concepts, including career awareness, attitudes, values, and habits, human relationships, occupational information, and acquisition of job and daily living skills. Its purpose is to impact work personalities early on in the school years through teaching crucial career education and self-determination concepts. Self-determination is not directly addressed, but many self-determination concepts are discussed. Emphasized in three units are career development, career orientation, and career exploration. Unit 1, entitled "Me and My Shadow," introduces the self-determination skills of self-awareness and goal setting through sections on "getting to know me," "positive self-esteem," and "goal-setting." The other two units present typical career development concepts such as the role of the worker and identification of jobs that exist in the student's community. Available from Colorado Department of Education, Special Education Programs, 201 East Colfax, Denver, CO 80203 (303-866-6694).

Learning with PURPOSE: An Instructor's Manual for Teaching Self-Determination Skills to Students Who Are At-Risk for Failure (Serna & Lau-Smith, 1995).   This is a comprehensive self-determination curriculum designed for students with mild and moderate disabilities, and students who are at risk for failure in home, school, and community environments. The program is appropriate for students between the ages of 12 and 25 years. Self-evaluation, self-direction, networking, collaboration, persistence and risk taking, and dealing with stress are the self-determination skills systematically taught in this program. Students define the skill, understand how the skill will be useful to them, rehearse the skill, evaluate their own performance, reach skill mastery, and participate in activities that will help them use their skills in other environments. A corresponding parent program accompanies this curriculum, and many parents may learn how to support students while they acquire new skills. Available from Loretta A. Serna, PhD, University of New Mexico, College of Education 215, Albuquerque, NM 87131 (505-277-5119).

I Want My Dream, New Hat, and Profile Decks—It's My Life-Preference-Based Planning, Facilitator's Guide, and Goal Planner's Workbook (Curtis, 1995).   A facilitator uses numerous "It's My Life" awareness building materials to show how students can take an active role in making decisions, self-advocating, and creating their own lifestyle plans and goals. Preference-based planning supports a process whereby individuals learn how to string together thoughts to get an idea, make a plan, evaluate the progress, and adjust. Materials include the New Hat Card Deck, I Want My Dream Deck, *It's My Life* workbook, and other materials. The contents of the workbook include "Organizing My Planner," "Hopes, Dreams, and Preferences," "Possibilities, Priorities, and Goals," and "My Meeting." Supplemental materials, which are available from the author, are used in different workbook chapters. Available from Emilee Curtis, New Hats Inc., PO Box 57567, Salt Lake City, UT 84157 (801-268-9811).

Steps to Self-Determination (Field & Hoffman, 1995).   This curriculum supports students in developing skills, knowledge, and experiences to help them be more self-determined. The activities engage students in experiences designed to increase their self-awareness and self-esteem, and provides instruction in skills to assist them in reaching their goals. The curriculum follows a five-step model: (1) know yourself, (2) value yourself, (3) plan, (4) act, and (5) learn. Each curriculum activity relates back to one of these steps. The lessons begin with a six-hour workshop session, followed by 16 weekly sessions that take place in a scheduled class or extracurricular activity. The 16 sessions include topics such as "What Is Important to Me?" "Setting Long-Term Goals," "Creative Barrier Breaking," "Assertive Communication," "Negotiation," and "Conflict Resolution." Available from Pro-Ed Publications, 8700 Shoal Creek Boulevard, Austin, TX 78757-6897 (512-451-3246).

Whose Future Is It Anyway? A Student-Directed Transition Planning Process (Wehmeyer, 1995b). This instructional package provides students the opportunity to acquire the knowledge and confidence to take part in the transition process of an equal partner. The package emphasizes disability as a part of the human condition and stresses that students need to be aware of their own learning abilities and needs. Each session teaches students something they can use in their transition or other educational meeting. Students learn how to write and track goals, identify community resources, how informed consent affects them, how to communicate in small groups, and how to participate in a meeting. Students select a coach to help them through the process. The six major parts of the program are (1) getting to know you, (2) making decisions, (3) how to get what you need, (4) goals, objectives, and the future, (5) communication, and (6) thank-you. Students use the materials on their own—they read and complete the 40 lessons in about 5 days. The materials are designed for students to read and complete most of the activities independently. A detailed facilitator's guide is included to help with this process. Available from Michael Wehmeyer, PhD, The Arc National Headquarters, 500 East Border Street, Suite 300, Arlington, TX 76010 (817-261-6003).

ChoiceMaker Self-Determination Transition Curriculum: Self-Directed IEP, Choosing Employment Goals, and Take Action (Martin, Huber Marshall, Maxson, & Jerman, 1996). These three instructional packages teach seven self-determination constructs: self-awareness, self-advocacy, self-efficacy, decision making, independent performance, self-evaluation, and adjustment through leadership and management of the Individual Education Plan (IEP) process. The *Self-Directed IEP* (Martin, Huber Marshall, Maxson, & Jerman, 1996) is designed for use by students receiving special education services, the others are for use by all secondary students. The *Self-Directed IEP* teaches students the leadership skills needed to manage their IEP meeting, disclose their interests, skills, and limits, and build necessary support to reach their goals. *Choosing Employment Goals* (Huber Marshall, Martin, Maxson, & Jerman, 1996) teaches students a process to learn and articulate their employment interests, skills, limits, and goals. *Taking Action* (Huber Marshall, Martin, McGill, Maxson, & Jerman, 1996) teaches students how to break their long-term goals into tasks that can be accomplished in a week, and shows students a process they can use to attain goals. Each package comes with at least one student video, teacher guide, and student materials. Somewhat unique to the ChoiceMaker curriculum is the inclusion of a detailed self-evaluation process where students reflect about their choices and then compare them with reality. For example, in *Choosing Employment Goals,* students identify the job characteristics they like then compare those choices with the characteristics that exist at different job sites. Similarly, in *Choosing Employment Goals*, students self-evaluate their work, social, and personal behaviors; then this rating is compared with that done by a job-site supervisor. In both examples, students decide if their initial evaluation matches that of the site or supervisor.

Additional choosing goal packages for the remaining transition areas (in-school, postsecondary, personal matters, etc.) will be developed in the next two years. Available from Sopris West Publishers, 1140 Boston Avenue, Longmont, CO, 80501 (303-651-2829).

GENERAL APPROACHES TO ASSESSMENT

Assessment of self-determination knowledge and skills possessed by individual students is an essential beginning point prior to instruction, and as a follow-up to instruction. This assessment of self-determination skills and knowledge is complimentary to but distinct from assessment of specific task-related or academic skills. For example, when assessing a student on a particular community-based training site, information such as rate, endurance, and quality of task performance is measured. These narrow data need to be complimented by an assessment of the process that the student uses to self-evaluate, formulate plans, and implement changes in task related, social, and other behaviors.

The measurement of the student's self-determination knowledge and skills is primarily accomplished through the use of third-party assessment checklists or self-report tools. Each self-determination assessment tool is rooted in the authors' unique understanding of what self-determination is and its major constructs. This section will present four examples of different assessment approaches and the associated tools.

The Arc Approach.   Wehmeyer (1995a) describes self-determination as "acting as the primary causal agent in one's life and making choices and decisions regarding one's quality of life free from undue external influence or interference" (p. 1). The *Arc's Self-Determination Scale* uses this definition for individuals with disabilities to assess their own beliefs about themselves and their self-determination. It also provides a means for individuals with disabilities and educators to work together to identify strengths and limitations relative to self-determination goals and objectives (Wehmeyer, 1995a). The scale is designed for use by adolescents with disabilities, particularly students with mild mental retardation and learning disabilities.

The *Arc's Self-Determination Scale* is a student self-report measure of self-determination designed for use by adolescents with cognitive disabilities. In constructing his scale, Wehmeyer (1995a) used the findings from numerous other researchers' work. The scale has 72 items divided into four sections: (1) autonomy, (2) self-regulation, (3) psychological empowerment, and (4) self-realization. Behavioral autonomy consists of four activity categories: (1) self- and family care, (2) self-management, (3) recreational, and (4) social and vocational. Self-regulated behavior includes self-management strategies, goal setting and attainment behaviors, problem-solving behaviors, and observational learning strategies. Psychological empowerment refers to perceived control including its cognitive, personality, and motivational domains. Self-realization is self-knowledge and self-understanding through experience and interpretation of one's environment and is influenced by evaluations of significant others, reinforcements, and opinions of one's own behavior.

The *Arc's Self-Determination Scale* requires a different type of response for each of the four sections. The autonomy section asks the individual to respond to a Likert type scale for 32 questions. The self-regulation component requests respondents to fill-in the middle of the story given the beginning and ending of the story for six situations. The self-regulation section also asks three open-ended questions related to living, working, and transportation plans for the future. The psychological empowerment subscale provides 15 two-item forced choice questions. Last, self-realization provides 15 forced choice (agree/disagree) items. The *Arc's Self-Determination Scale* is scored in a five-step process that converts the raw section scores into percentile scores from a nationwide norming sample of 500 special education students primarily with learning disabilities (44%) and mental retardation (35%).

The *Arc's Self-Determination Scale* is available from Michael Wehmeyer at The Arc, 500 East Border Street, Suite 300, Arlington, TX 76010 (817-261-6003).

The AIR Approach.   Wolman, Campeau, DuBois, Mithaug, and Stolarski (1994) believe that self-determined people know and express their needs, interests, and abilities. They set goals, make plans, and follow through with actions to achieve their goals. Wolman et al. believe that "self-determination depends on students' capacities and opportunities" (p. 5). Capacity is defined as the student's knowledge and skills, while opportunity refers to the student's chances to use their self-determination skills. Capacity, opportunity, and conditions are the foundation of the *AIR Self-Determination Scale.* Thinking, doing, and adjusting are all components of the AIR assessment process. The purpose of the scale is to provide an easy tool to assess and teach self-determination. The tool is designed for all school-age students—with and without disabilities.

Four versions of the scale are available. The parent, educator, and research versions are all third-party report scales relying on already obtained information. The student version can be completed independently by students with sufficient reading skills or with assistance for those who can not read the scale.

The educator version of the scale is the most comprehensive. It has three capacity sections (knowledge, ability, and perception) and two opportunity sections (school and home). Knowledge is the understanding a student has about self-determination. Ability includes those skills needed to identify one's interests and needs, and to satisfy those needs. Perception includes motivation, confidence, self-esteem, and the "sense of freedom to meet interests and needs" (Wolman et al., 1994, p. 15). Opportunities at school and at home are those supporting environmental events that can enable the student to become more self-determined. Each section has 6 items for a total of 30 items. "The student and parent forms are shorter and the headings on them are slightly different. For example, the ability section is called 'What Do I Do' in the student form and 'Things My Child Does' in the parent form. The student and parent forms include six items each for ability, opportunity at school, and opportunity at home. The student form also includes six items for perception" (Wolman et al., 1994, p. 22).

The educator's version of the *AIR Self-Determination Scale* uses previous observations of the student to complete a 5-point Likert scale for each of the 30 items. The raw scores for each of the five sections are tabulated, graphed, and compared with the total points available to find the percentage level of self-determination. This tool is a criterion-referenced assessment used in a nonnormative manner. The tool was validated on 450 students with and without disabilities in San Jose, CA, and New York City.

The *AIR Self-Determination Scale* is available from Dennis Mithaug, Special Education Program, Teachers College, Columbia University, New York, NY 10027 (212-678-3859).

The University of Colorado Approach.   Martin et al. (1993) believe that self-determined people know how to choose—they know what they want and how to get it. From an awareness of personal needs, self-determined individuals will choose goals and then persistently pursue them. This involves asserting their presence, making their needs known, evaluating progress toward meeting goals, adjusting performance, and creating a plan to solve problems. The *ChoiceMaker Self-Determination Transition Assessment* (Martin & Huber Marshall, 1996) is based on the ChoiceMaker Curriculum (see Table 3.1). The tool is unique in that it can be tied directly to the ChoiceMaker curriculum and thus can be used as a curriculum-based assessment (CBA). The scale is designed for middle and high school students who have mild to moderate learning and behavior problems.

The *ChoiceMaker Self-Determination Transition Assessment* is a third-person scale used by educators to assess their students' skills, and opportunities provided by the school environment. The assessment tool consists of 62 items to evaluate student self-determination skills; it also evaluates the opportunities at school to exercise these skills. Each domain is divided into three major sections: Choosing Goals, Expressing Goals, and Taking Action. The Choosing Goals section assesses skills and opportunities related to students' understanding of their rights and goal-setting roles, expression of transition interest across school, employment, post high school education and other areas, expressing of skills and limits of the foregoing transition areas, and options and goals for those transition areas. The Expressing Goals section assesses student leadership and expression of interest, skills, limits, and goals at their IEP and transition meetings. The Taking Action section measures planning, action taking, self-evaluation, and adjustment.

The *ChoiceMaker Self-Determination Transition Assessment* requires completion of a 5-point Likert scale response for each of the 62 items across the student skills and opportunities at school domains. The raw scores for each of the three sections are tabulated, graphed, and compared with the total points available to find the percentage level of self-determination in each domain. This tool is a criterion-referenced assessment used in a nonnormative manner. The assessment has been validated using over 300 students with learning disabilities, mental retardation, and behavior problems from four states.

The *ChoiceMaker Self-Determination Transition Assessment* is available from Sopris West, Inc., 1140 Boston Avenue, Longmont, CO 80501 (303-651-2829).

CURRICULUM DESIGN

We have discussed the general parameters of self-determination, reviewed several curricula, and described several assessment tools. The essential components of a

TABLE 3.1   ChoiceMaker Self-Determination Transition Curriculum Matrix

Sections	Teaching Goals	Teaching Objectives						
1: Choosing Goals	A. *Student Interests*	A1. Express *school* interests	A2. Express *employment* interests	A3. Express *post-high school education* interests	A4. Express *personal* interests	A5. Express *housing & daily living* interests	A6. Express *community participation* interests	
(through school & community experience)	B. *Student skills & limits*	B1. Express *school* skills & limits	B2. Express *employment* skills & limits	B3. Express *post-high school education* skills & limits	B4. Express *personal* skills & limits	B5. Express *housing & daily living* skills & limits	B6. Express *community participation* skills & limits	
	C. *Student Goals*	C1. Indicate options & choose *school* goals	C2. Indicate options and choose *employment* goals	C3. Indicate options & choose *post-high school education* goals	C4. Indicate options & choose *personal* goals	C5. Indicate options & choose *housing & daily living* goals	C6. Indicate options & choose *community participation* goals	
2: Expressing Goals	D. *Student Leading Meeting*	D1. Begin meeting by stating purpose	D2. Introduce participants	D3. Review past goals & performance	D4. Ask for feedback	D5. Ask questions if don't understand	D6. Deal with differences in opinion	D7. State needed support	D8. Close meeting by summarizing decisions
	E. *Student Reporting*	E1. Express interests (from A1-6)	E2. Express skills & limits (from B1-6)	E3. Express options & goals (from C1-6)				
3: Taking Action	F. *Student Plan*	F1. Break general goals into specific goals that can be completed now	F2. Establish *standard* for specific goals	F3. Determine how to get *feedback* from environment	F4. Determine *motivation* to complete specific goals	F5. Determine *strategies* for completing specific goals	F6. Determine *support* needed to complete specific goals	F7. Prioritize & *schedule* to complete specific goals	F8. Express *belief* that goals can be obtained
	G. *Student Action*	G1. Record or report performance	G2. Perform specific goals to *standard*	G3. Obtain *feedback* on performance	G4. *Motivate* self to complete specific goals	G5. Use *strategies* to perform specific goals	G6. Obtain *support* needed	G7. Follow *schedule*	
	H. *Student Evaluation*	H1. Determine if goals are achieved	H2. Compare performance to *standards*	H3. Evaluate *feedback*	H4. Evaluate *motivation*	H5. Evaluate effectiveness of *strategies*	H6. Evaluate *support* used	H7. Evaluate *schedule*	H8. Evaluate *belief*
	I. *Student Adjustment*	I1. Adjust goals if necessary	I2. Adjust or repeat goal *standards*	I3. Adjust or repeat method for *feedback*	I4. Adjust or repeat *motivation*	I5. Adjust or repeat *strategies*	I6. Adjust or repeat *support*	I7. Adjust or repeat *schedule*	I8. Adjust or repeat *belief* that goals can be obtained

From: *ChoiceMaker Self-Determination Assessment*, by James Martin and Laura Huber Marshall, 1996, Colorado Springs, CO: University of Colorado at Colorado Springs. Reprinted with permission.

self-determination curriculum are goal-setting, choice, self-evaluation, and adjustment components. These self-determination components must be infused into the daily instructional cycle, as they cannot be taught in a vacuum. Learning self-determination is a function of opportunity to practice and opportunity to learn. It is important to remember that real choice must be available, too, once students and their IEP team have chosen goals across curriculum domains and decided which environments they wish to meet those goals in. Students, in conjunction with other IEP team members, need also to choose the strategies they want to use, the supports they will need, and the criteria they want to be evaluated by. This requires teachers, schools, and districts to provide flexible, individualized, student-driven curricula, as opposed to only set, group-oriented, and teacher-directed activities.

To fully implement a self-determination philosophy, goal-setting, choice, and self-evaluation must occur across common curricular domains, such as reading, math, science, and social studies. Or, in the case of some students, goal-setting, choice, and self-evaluation will occur within the common domains of functional academics, including domestic, recreational, community, and vocational activities. Students must also engage in choice and goal-setting related to where needs can best be met. Rather than educators or parents always deciding where students should go, students need to have a strong voice in this decision, too.

How can self-determination instruction be implemented on an individual, schoolwide, and district level? This section will provide examples of how this can be done at the elementary, middle school, and high school levels.

ELEMENTARY SCHOOL CURRICULUM CONSIDERATIONS

The self-determination activities during the early elementary years focus on teaching students helpful strategies for setting goals, planning how to achieve their goals, and self-evaluating their performance. During the elementary years, students have repeated opportunities to practice goal-setting, planning, and self-evaluation. This may occur in many different ways.

Student Assessment.   Currently, one of the few elementary self-determination assessment tools available is the *AIR Self-Determination Scale* (Wolman et al., 1994). As mentioned earlier, the *AIR Self-Determination Scale* measures opportunity and capacity (student skills) at school. Assessing self-determination capacity and opportunities is critical for students in elementary schools.

Zeke, the student described at the beginning of this chapter, will be used as an elementary assessment example. Figure 3.1 is a hypothetical profile of Zeke's level of self-determination as measured with the educator's version of the *AIR Self-Determination Scale* when he was in the fourth grade. The profile shows Zeke at an overall self-determination level of 61 of the possible 150 points, for a score of 40%. His capacity and opportunity scores were similar at 28 and 33, respectively. Interestingly, he had many more opportunities at home to practice self-determination than were available at school. Please note that the *AIR Self-Determination Scale* provides no normative data from which to compare Zeke's score with that of other students his age. Zeke's overall scores are used to compare his current profile with that scored later in life. These data can't be used to compare Zeke with other students in the fourth grade.

FIGURE 3.1 The AIR Self-Determination Profile Educator Form

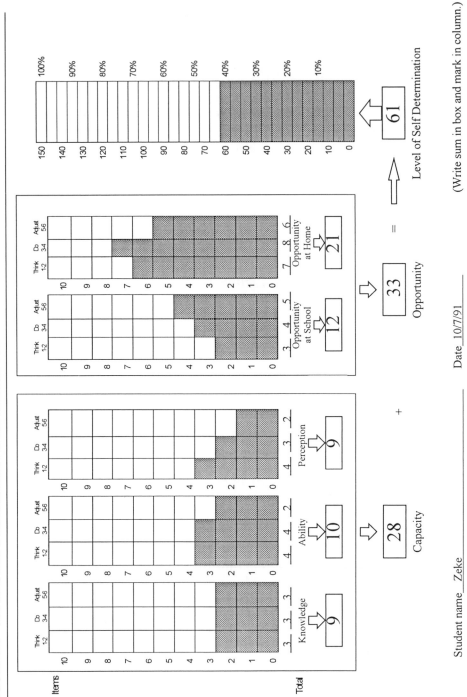

Level of Self Determination

61

(Write sum in box and mark in column.)

Student name Zeke   Date 10/7/91

Note. From *AIR Self-Determination Scale© and User Guide,* by Jean M. Wolman, Peggie L. Campeau, Phyllis A. DuBois, Dennis E. Mithaug, and Virginia S. Stolarski, 1994, New York: American Institutes for Research. Reprinted with permission.

Zeke had not received any self-determination instruction at this point in his life. The first step to use the assessment results is to determine an instructional beginning point for Zeke. The IEP team looked at the responses to each assessment item. Figure 3.2 shows how Zeke's teacher scored his knowledge of self-determination behaviors. The results of these items and the others provide insight into Zeke's relative self-determination behavioral strengths and deficits. For example, Zeke almost never identifies his personal strengths and talents, and therefore never sets expectations and goals to satisfy his own interests and needs. Likewise, the school almost never provides opportunities for that behavior and never asks Zeke to identify his goals and expectations. Remember, these examples do not represent the complete assessment—they are illustrative only.

Sample IEP Goals.   The IEP team, with Zeke's input and agreement, next sets goals based upon these findings. Likewise, Zeke's educational team decides to provide increased opportunity for Zeke to practice these skills. The team used the *Air Self-Determination User Guide* (Wolman et al., 1994) to arrive at the following two annual goals.

Annual Goals

1. To increase Zeke's knowledge of own interests, abilities, and limitations.

   Sample Activities:
   a. Racing against the clock five students (including Zeke) in a cooperative group list 15 school and out-of-school interests in five minutes.
   b. The five students will discuss with the teacher their skills and limitations associated with each interest.
2. To increase Zeke's knowledge of how to set goals that satisfy interests.

   Sample Activities:
   a. Students will interview three adults to determine the adults' goals.
   b. Students will examine the commonalties of the goals identified during their interviews (e.g., long-range nature of goals, type of goals).
   c. Students will write two goals for their academic work to be achieved in the next week (e.g., 90% correct on spelling test, 24 math facts completed in a minute).

Elementary Self-Determination Curricula.   Little elementary level self-determination curricula exist. Much of what teachers will need to do is to take the basic assessed skills and develop activities. The preceding activities are illustrative of how this can be done. One of the few available elementary packages that we know about is *Connections: A Transition Curriculum for Grades 3 Through 6* (Aspinall et al., 1992). This curriculum provides an equal balance between several concepts, including career awareness; attitudes, values, and habits; human relationships; occupational information; and acquisition of job and daily living skills. Its purpose is to impact work personalities in the early school years through teaching crucial career education and self-determination concepts. Self-determination is not directly addressed, but many self-determination concepts are discussed. Emphasized in three

FIGURE 3.2   Zeke's Knowledge of Self-Determination Behaviors

PERCEPTION of Knowledge and Ability to Perform Self-Determination Behaviors	1 Never	2 Almost Never	3 Sometimes	4 Almost Always	5 Always
1. Student feels free to express own needs, interests, and abilities, even when facing opposition from others—*Example:* Fran defends her needs and interests to anyone who questions them.	1	2	③	4	5
2. Student feels free to set own goals and expectations, even if they are different from the expectations others have for the student—*Example:* Trevor does not feel constrained by others' opinions in setting goals and expectations for himself.	①	2	3	4	5
			Perception Total: Items 1–2		[4]
3. Student feels free to make own choices, decisions, and plans, to meet own goals and expectations—*Example:* Corine often considers her parents suggestions when making choices and plans, but the final plans taken to meet her goals are her own.	①	2	3	4	5
4. Student feels confident about being able to successfully complete own plans—*Example:* When Nicholas schedules his own activities, he is confident he can complete them accurately and on time.	1	②	3	4	5
			Perception Total: Items 3–4		[3]

FIGURE 3.2 *(Continued)*

PERCEPTION of Knowledge and Ability to Perform Self-Determination Behaviors	1 Never	2 Almost Never	3 Sometimes	4 Almost Always	5 Always
5. Student is confident about using feedback to evaluate results of own work—*Example:* Amanda is confident that she will be able to benefit from the feedback she receives from her parents, teachers, and peers.	①	2	3	4	5
6. Student changes plans again and again to meet a goal without getting discouraged—*Example:* Levar is motivated to work on a project as long as it takes, using whatever approaches are necessary to get it right.	①	2	3	4	5
				Perception Total: Items 5–6	[2]

Note. From *AIR Self-Determination Scale© and User Guide,* by Jean M. Wolman, Peggy L. Campeau, Phyllis A. DuBois, Dennis E. Mithaug, and Virginia S. Stolarski, 1994, New York: American Institutes for Research. Reprinted with permission.

units are career development, career orientation, and career exploration. Unit 1, entitled "Me and My Shadow" introduces the self-determination skills of self-awareness and goal-setting through sections on "getting to know me," "positive self-esteem," and "goal-setting."

MIDDLE SCHOOL CURRICULUM CONSIDERATIONS

The self-determination activities during the middle school years focus on refining students' strategies for setting goals, planning how to achieve their goals, and self-evaluating their performance. It is during the middle school years that students begin to focus in increasing amounts on goals and plans beyond middle and high school. Career exploration (Brolin, 1989) is a common focus during these years, with students assessing career interests and abilities and setting some trial plans for meeting those goals.

Student Assessment. The Arc's Self-Determination Scale is a good assessment for use with middle school students because it examines autonomy, self-regulation, psychological empowerment, and self-realization. Figure 3.3 is a hypothetical profile of Zeke's level of self-determination as measured with *The Arc's Self-Determination Scale* when he was in the seventh grade. Unlike the *AIR Self-Determination Scale,* Arc's scale provides normative data from which to compare Zeke's score with other adolescents.

FIGURE 3.3   Zeke's Level of Self-Determination

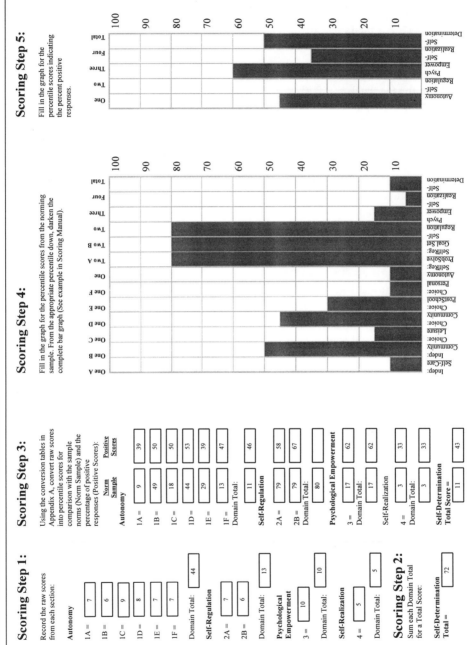

Note. From *The Arc's Self Determination Scale—Adolescent Version*, by Michael Wehmeyer and Kathy Kelchner, 1995, Arlington, TX: The Arc National Headquarters. Reprinted with permission.

Zeke's self-determination level overall is better than only 11 out of 100 students (as noted in the graph under Step 4 and based on the normative sample of 500 adolescent students). Compared with the normative sample, Zeke's skills related to self-regulation are relatively strong. Autonomy and self-realization are Zeke's two weakest assessed areas at the 11th and 3rd percentile, respectively.

The IEP team looked at the responses to each assessment item. Figure 3.4 shows how Zeke's teacher scored the Independence: Personal Care section. For example, Zeke never cares for his own clothes but he always keeps together his own personal items. He will sometimes make his meals, do home chores, do simple first aid, and groom himself. Figure 3.5 depicts the results of Zeke's psychological empowerment subscale. Of the 16 possible items Zeke felt empowered on 10 responses. Although this gave Zeke a high positive score (see Figure 3.3), when compared with the norm group, Zeke's results were low. For example, Zeke said "Trying hard at school doesn't do me much good," "I need good luck to get what I want," and "My choices will not be honored." These responses provide an excellent beginning point for the IEP team to start determining Zeke's goals for the next school year.

Sample IEP Goals.   Like the elementary IEP team, Zeke's middle school IEP team, with Zeke's input and agreement, sets goals based on the assessment results. In this instance, the first goal is for Zeke to use the assessment tool himself to develop a plan of action prior to his IEP meeting.

Annual Goals

1. To increase Zeke's knowledge of his own self-determined behaviors and attitudes.

   Sample Activities:
   a. Quarterly, Zeke completes the *Arc's Self-Determination Scale* (e.g., the current assessment demonstrates that Zeke needs to improve his performance in the areas of personal autonomy and psychological empowerment).
   b. Discuss the assessment results with peers, parents, and school personnel.
   c. Develop a plan of action to improve at least one subdomain per quarter and discuss weekly with peers, parents, and educators his progress. For example, Zeke has asked his dad for instruction in how to do his laundry. Zeke has asked his peers and school staff to point out to him how each lesson relates to his adult life.
   d. Zeke will present his assessment, his plan of action, and results at his next IEP meeting.
2. To increase Zeke's participation in school activities.

   Sample Activities:
   a. Zeke will identify with a counselor all extracurricular activities options available at his school.
   b. Zeke will select three extracurricular activities to explore.
   c. Zeke will regularly participate in at least one extracurricular activity throughout the school year.

FIGURE 3.4 **Zeke's Scores on the Independence Section of the Arc**

SECTION ONE AUTONOMY		**Directions:** Check the answer on each question that BEST tells how you act in that situation. There are no right or wrong answers. Check only one answer for each question. (If your disability limits you from actually performing the activity, but you have control over the activity (such as a personal care attendant), answer like you performed the activity).							
1A. Independence: Routine personal care and family oriented functions								**1A. Subtotal** 7	
1.	I make my own meals or snacks.	[ ]	I do not even if i have the chance	[X]	I do sometimes when I have the chance	[ ]	I do most of the time I have the chance	[ ]	I do every time I have the change
2.	I care for my own clothes.	[X]	I do not even if I have the chance	[ ]	I do sometimes when I have the chance	[ ]	I do most of the time I have the chance	[ ]	I do every time I have the chance
3.	I do chores in my home.	[ ]	I do not even if I have the chance	[X]	I do sometimes when I have the chance	[ ]	I do most of the time I have the chance	[ ]	I do every time I have the chance
4.	I keep my own personal items together.	[ ]	I do not even if I have the chance	[ ]	I do sometimes when I have the chance	[ ]	I do most of the time I have the chance	[X]	I do every time I have the chance
5.	I do simple first aid or medical care for myself.	[ ]	I do not even if I have the chance	[X]	I do sometimes when I have the chance	[ ]	I do most of the time I have the chance	[ ]	I do every time I have the chance
6.	I keep good personal care and grooming.	[ ]	I do not even if I have the chance	[X]	I do sometimes when I have the chance	[ ]	I do most of the time I have the chance	[ ]	I do every time I have the chance

Note. From *The Arc's Self Determination Scale—Adolescent Version*, by Michael Wehmeyer and Kathy Kelchner, 1995, Arlington, TX: The Arc National Headquarters. Reprinted with permission.

FIGURE 3.5   Zeke's Psychological Empowerment Subscale

SECTION THREE
Psychological Empowerment

Directions:

- Check the answer that BEST describes you.
- Choose only one answer for each question.
- There are no right or wrong answers.

42. [X] I usually do what my friends want...or
    [ ] I tell my friends if they are doing something I don't want to do.

43. [X] I tell others when I have new or different ideas or opinions...or
    [ ] I usually agree with other peoples' opinions or ideas.

44. [X] I usually agree with people when they tell me I can't do something...or
    [ ] I tell people when I think I can do something that they tell me I can't.

45. [ ] I tell people when they have hurt my feelings...or
    [X] I am afraid to tell people when they have hurt my feelings.

46. [X] I can make my own decisions...or
    [ ] Other people make decisions for me.

47. [X] Trying hard at school doesn't do me much good... or
    [ ] Trying hard at school will help me get a good job.

48. [ ] I can get what I want by working hard...or
    [X] I need good luck to get what I want.

49. [ ] It is no use to keep trying because that won't change things...or
    [X] I keep trying even after I get something wrong.

50. [X] I have the ability to do the job I want...or
    [ ] I cannot do what it takes to do the job I want.

51. [ ] I don't know how to make friends...or
    [X] I know how to make friends.

52. [X] I am able to work with others...or
    [ ] I cannot work well with others.

53. [ ] I do not make good choices...or
    [X] I can make good choices

54. [X] If I have the ability, I will be able to get the job I want...or
    [ ] I probably will not get the job I want even if I have the ability.

55. [ ] I will have a hard time making new friends...or
    [X] I will be able to make friends in new situations.

56. [X] I will be able to work with others if I need to...or
    [ ] I will not be able to work with others if I need to.

57. [X] My choices will not be honored...or
    [ ] I will be able to make choices that are important to me.

Section 3 Subtotal   10

Note. From *The Arc's Self Determination Scale—Adolescent Version,* by Michael Wehmeyer and Kathy Kelchner, 1995, Arlington, TX: The Arc National Headquarters. Reprinted with permission.

HIGH SCHOOL CURRICULUM CONSIDERATIONS

The activities during the high school years focus on teaching self-determination through student leadership of the IEP process. While in the elementary and middle school grades, Zeke actively participated in his IEP meetings and collaborated with his educators to develop goals, interventions, and self-evaluation strategies. Now, Zeke needs to develop these skills further to learn the self-determination skills he will need after leaving school. The IEP process provides the perfect opportunity to learn these crucial skills.

Student Assessment. The *ChoiceMaker Self-Determination Transition Assessment* evaluates the self-determination skills students will need to be successful in their adult life and the opportunities available to engage in these skills. This scale is designed for use by middle and high school students with learning and behavior problems. The ChoiceMaker Assessment measures students self-determination skills and opportunities across three areas: Choosing Goals, Expressing Goals, and Taking Action. Figure 3.6 is a hypothetical profile of Zeke's level of self-determination and the opportunities his school provides as measured with *ChoiceMaker Self-Determination Transition Assessment* from his freshman year. Unlike the other assessments, the ChoiceMaker tool is a curriculum-based assessment keyed directly to the Choice-Maker Self-Determination Transition Curriculum, which teaches self-determination skills through active participation and leadership of the IEP process. This criterion-referenced scale profiles Zeke's skills in relation to the ChoiceMaker curriculum. Zeke performs only about 44% of the Choosing Goals skills, 15% of the Expressing Goals skills, and 25% of the Taking Action skills. It should be noted, however, Zeke's skill performance is only slightly below the opportunities available at his school. In addition to Zeke's skill development, systematic reform must occur at Zeke's school to provide greater opportunities for self-determined behaviors.

Zeke's IEP team looked at the assessment results section by section to develop goals and activities. Figure 3.7 shows how Zeke's teacher scored the Student Interests section of Choosing Goals. Zeke's teachers have never seen him express any employment, post-high school education, or housing and daily interests. Not surprisingly, Zeke's school program provided little to no opportunity for him to express interests in these areas, except for asking him about his school interests, which carried over from his middle school educational plan. Expressing Goals results are depicted in Figure 3.8. Zeke attended his IEP meetings, but did little once there. He talked briefly about his past goals and his performance and responded to questions when asked about his school interests and goals.

Sample IEP Goals. Once Zeke's IEP team reviewed the Opportunity at School section they realized they needed to improve their curriculum to allow for more self-determined behaviors to occur at school. Concurrently, Zeke and his IEP team set goals and discussed activities to achieve those goals based on the *ChoiceMaker* assessment results. The IEP team used the goals and objectives from the ChoiceMaker Transition Curriculum Guide to assist them in this process.

Annual Goals

1. Zeke will express his employment and post-high school education interests, skills, limits, and goals at his next IEP meeting.

FIGURE 3.6 Part II: ChoiceMaker Self-Determination Transition Assessment Profile

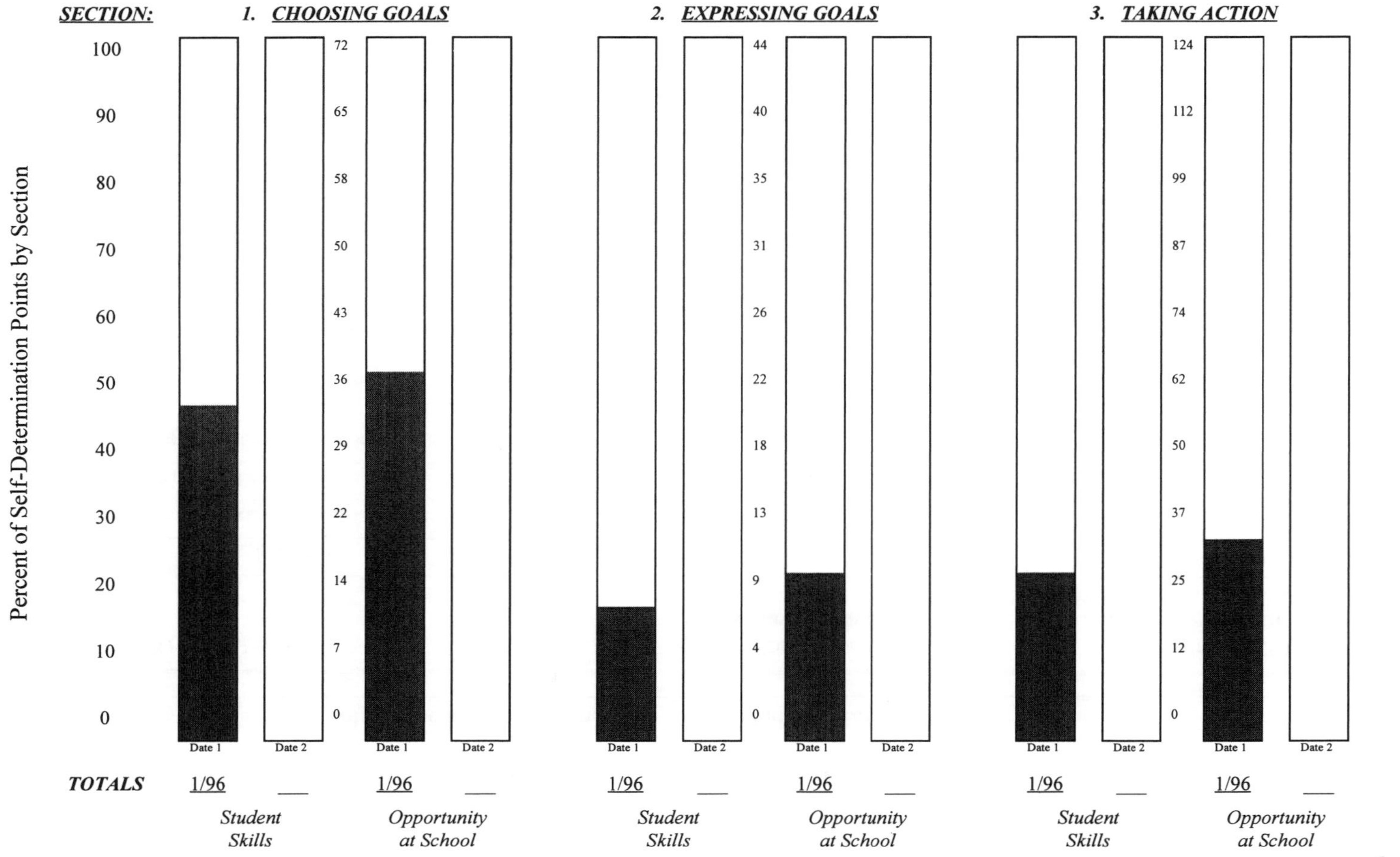

Note. From *ChoiceMaker Self-Determination Assessment,* by James Martin and Laura Huber Marshall, 1996, Colorado Springs, CO: University of Colorado at Colorado Springs. Reprinted with permission.

FIGURE 3.7   Part I: ChoiceMaker Self-Determination Transition Assessment, Section 1

SECTION 1: CHOOSING GOALS	Student Skills (Does the student do this?)					Opportunity at School (Does school provide structured time?)				
A. Student Interests – Does the student:	(not at all)				100%	(not at all)				100%
A1. Express school interests (e.g. classes, sports, clubs)?	0	1	2	3	4	0	1	2	3	4
A2. Express employment interests (e.g., jobs, careers)?	0	1	2	3	4	0	1	2	3	4
A3. Express post-high school education interests (e.g. colleges, trade school)?	0	1	2	3	4	0	1	2	3	4
A4. Express personal interests (e.g., relationships, leisure, health, legal?	0	1	2	3	4	0	1	2	3	4
A5. Express housing & daily living interests?	0	1	2	3	4	0	1	2	3	4
A6. Express community participation interests (e.g. transportation, adult services)?	0	1	2	3	4	0	1	2	3	4
	Subtotal 6					**Subtotal 10**				

Note. From *ChoiceMaker Self-Determination Assessment*, by James Martin and Laura Huber Marshall, 1996, Colorado Springs, CO: University of Colorado at Colorado Springs. Reprinted with permission.

FIGURE 3.8 Part I: ChoiceMaker Self-Determination Transition Assessment, Section 2

SECTION 2: EXPRESSING GOALS	Student Skills (Does the student do this?)						Opportunity at School (Does school provide structured time?)					
	(not at all)					100%	(not at all)					100%
D. Student Leading Meeting- Does the student:												
D1. Begin meeting by stating purpose?	0	1	2	3	4		0	1	2	3	4	
D2. Introduce participants?	0	1	2	3	4		0	1	2	3	4	
D3. Review past goals and performance?	0	1	2	3	4		0	1	2	3	4	
D4. Ask for feedback from group members?	0	1	2	3	4		0	1	2	3	4	
D5. Ask questions if student doesn't understand something?	0	1	2	3	4		0	1	2	3	4	
D6. Deal with differences in opinion?	0	1	2	3	4		0	1	2	3	4	
D7. State needed support?	0	1	2	3	4		0	1	2	3	4	
D8. Close meeting by summarizing decisions?	0	1	2	3	4		0	1	2	3	4	
			Subtotal	2					Subtotal	3		
E. Student Reporting-Does the student:												
E1. Express interests (from SECTION 1: CHOOSING GOALS?)	0	1	2	3	4		0	1	2	3	4	
E2. Express skills & limits (from SECTION 1: CHOOSING GOALS)	0	1	2	3	4		0	1	2	3	4	
E3. Express options and goals (from SECTION 1: CHOOSING GOALS)	0	1	2	3	4		0	1	2	3	4	
			TOTAL (E+F)	7					TOTAL (E+F)	11		

Note. From *ChoiceMaker Self-Determination Assessment*, by James Martin and Laura Huber Marshall, 1996, Colorado Springs, CO: University of Colorado at Colorado Springs. Reprinted with permission.

Sample Activities:
   a. In his transition class and community work experiences, Zeke completes the Choosing Employment Goals lessons. These lessons provide Zeke the opportunity to learn the job characteristics he likes and whether they match different community job sites.
   b. In his learning strategies class, Zeke will complete the Choosing Education Goals lessons. Among other skills, Zeke will learn to identify the classroom characteristics he likes best (e.g., lecture or hands-on, small group activities) and compare them with available next semester classes.
2. To increase Zeke's leadership of his IEP process.

Sample Activities:
   a. Zeke will complete the Self-Directed IEP lessons. For example, Zeke will learn the 11 steps needed for him to lead his own IEP meeting.
   b. Prior to his IEP meeting, Zeke will videotape a role play using the 11 steps needed to lead his own IEP meeting. Students and his teacher will each assume varying roles. After the role play, Zeke will review his performance with assistance from his peers and teacher.

CONCLUSION

Self-determination skill development should be an integral part of every student's educational program. Various self-determination assessment and curricula are now becoming available to facilitate the teaching of self-determination skills within the overall curriculum. Opportunities must be created across elementary, middle school, and high school programs for students to exercise self-determination. Self-determination-oriented goals need to become a part of each student's IEP. Successful adults use self-determination skills. Doesn't it make sense to teach students the skills needed to be successful while they are still in school?

REFERENCES

Aspinall, R. S., Roberts, L., & Robinson, R. (1992). *Connections. A transition curriculum for grades 3 through 6.* Denver, CO: Colorado Department of Education.

Brolin, D. E. (1989). *Life centered career education: A competency based approach* (3rd ed.). Reston, VA: Council for Exceptional Children.

Carpenter, W. D. (1995). *Become your own expert! Self-advocacy curriculum for individuals with learning disabilities.* Minneapolis, MN: Minnesota Educational Services.

Curtis, E. (1995). *It's my life: Preference-based planning, facilitator's guide and goal planner's workbook.* Salt Lake City, UT: New Hats.

Field, S., & Hoffman, A. (1994). Development of a model for self-determination. *Career Development for Exceptional Individuals, 17*(2), 159–169.

Field, S., & Hoffman, A. (1995). *Steps to self-determination.* Austin, TX: Pro-Ed.

Garfield, G. (1986). *Peak performers: The new heroes of American business.* New York: Avon.

Gerber, P. J., Ginsberg, R., & Reiff, H. B. (1992). Identifying alterable patterns in employment success for highly successful adults with learning disabilities. *Journal of Learning Disabilities, 25,* 475–487.

Hill, N. H. (1960). *Think and grow rich.* New York: Ballantine Books.

Hill, N. H., & Stone, W. C. (1987). *Success through a positive mental attitude.* New York: Prentice-Hall.

Huber Marshall, L., Martin, J. E., Maxson, L. L., & Jerman, P. (1996). *Choosing employment goals.* Longmont, CO: Sopris West.

Huber Marshall, L., Martin, J. E., McGill, T., Maxson, L. L., & Jerman, P. (1996). *Taking action.* Longmont, CO: Sopris West.

Martin, J. E., & Huber Marshall, L. H. (1995). ChoiceMaker: A comprehensive self-determination transition program. *Intervention in School and Clinic, 30*(3), 147–156.

Martin, J. E., & Huber Marshall, L. H. (1996). *ChoiceMaker self-determination transition assessment.* Longmont, CO: Sopris West.

Martin, J. E., Huber Marshall, L., & Maxson, L. L. (1993). *Career Development for Exceptional Individuals, 16*(1), 53–61.

Martin, J. E., Huber Marshall, L., Maxson, L. L., & Jerman, P. (1996). *Self-directed IEP.* Longmont, CO: Sopris West.

Martin, J. E., Huber Marshall, L., Miller, T. L., Kregar, G., & Hughes, W. (1996). Self-determination curricula: A detailed review. In S. Field, J. E. Martin, R. J. Miller, M. Ward, & M. L. Wehmeyer (Eds.), *Student self-determination guide.* Reston, VA: Council for Exceptional Children, Division of Career Development and Transition.

Mithaug, D. E. (1991). *Self-determined kids: Raising satisfied and successful children.* Lexington, MA: D. C. Heath.

Mithaug, D. E. (1993). *Self-regulation theory: How optimal adjustment maximizes gain.* Westport, CN: Praeger.

Mithaug, D. E. (1994). *Self-determination.* Manuscript in preparation.

Mithaug, D. E., Martin, J. E., & Agran, M. (1987). Adaptability instruction: The goal of transitional programs. *Exceptional Children, 53*, 500–505.

Schloss, P. J., Alper, S., & Jayne, D. (1993). Self-determination for people with disabilities: Choice, risk, and dignity. *Exceptional Children, 60*(3), 215–225.

Serna, L. A., & Lau-Smith, J. (1995). *Learning with PURPOSE: An instructor's manual for teaching self-determination skills to students who are at-risk for failure.* Albuquerque: University of New Mexico.

Ward, M. J. (1988). The many facets of self-determination. *National Information Center for Children and Youth with Handicaps: Transition Summary, 5*, 2–3.

Wehmeyer, M. L. (1992a). Promoting self-determination using the Life-Centered Career Education Curriculum. In D. E. Brolin (Ed.), *Life-Centered Career Education Curriculum.* Reston, VA: Council for Exceptional Children.

Wehmeyer, M. L. (1992b). Self-determination: Critical skills for outcome-oriented transition services. *Journal for Vocational Special Needs Education, 15*, 3–9.

Wehmeyer, M. L. (1995a). *The Arc's self-determination scale.* Arlington, TX: Arc National Headquarters.

Wehmeyer, M. L. (1995b). *Whose future is it anyway? A student-directed transition planning process.* Arlington, TX: Arc National Headquarters.

Wolman, J. M., Campeau, P. L., DuBois, P. A., Mithaug, D. E., & Stolarski, V. S. (1994). *AIR self-determination scale and user guide.* Palo Alto, CA: American Institutes for Research.

4

Functional Academics

PAMELA S. WOLFE

WENDY A. HARRIOTT

In this chapter, you will be introduced to two students with disabilities: Michael, who has a mild learning disability, and Jennifer, who has more severe disabilities. Within the chapter, we will examine specific learning objectives for both Michael and Jennifer as well as functional academic activities to achieve those goals. Completed Individualized Education Plans (IEPs) for Michael and Jennifer are included in Appendix 4.A.

Case Study: Michael

Michael is a male of average intelligence who has a specific learning disability. He was referred for special education services by the multidisciplinary team when he was in the second grade. His regular classroom teachers wanted to retain him in first grade, but his mother wouldn't agree to this placement. He was promoted into second grade but continued to receive failing grades and began to act out due to his increasing frustration. Michael was then placed into a Learning Support classroom for part-time instruction.

Michael lives at home in a suburban neighborhood within a single-parent household. His mother works full-time at the local grocery store as a cashier to support the family. His father has visitation rights and spends time with Michael on the weekends. Michael is the middle child of three children. Both his older brother and his younger sister are in regular education classrooms.

Among Michael's strengths are his sense of humor, a generally cheerful attitude, his desire to be involved in school activities with his peers, and his strong verbal expressive

The authors would like to acknowledge the assistance of Terri Lindner and Bella Bregar of State College, PA, and Katie Beldon and Janie Mattern of Centre Hall, PA, for their help in the preparation of this chapter. Their excellent teaching materials helped create many of the practical applications used in the chapter.

skills. According to Michael's special and regular education teachers, Michael needs to improve his skills in interacting appropriately both with his peers and adults. He does initiate interactions, but he tends to use inappropriate language and doesn't utilize common courtesies (e.g., shaking an adult's hand, saying "please" and "thank-you"). Michael also has difficulty with his receptive language skills and consequently, inaccurately interprets social situations. He also tends to display a low self-esteem. Individuals interacting with Michael report that he is easily distracted from tasks and often does not complete his assigned work. Michael's reading and writing skills are several grade levels lower than his chronological-age peers. In the area of mathematics, Michael is able to perform calculations, however his ability to problem-solve is significantly below that of his peers.

Case Study: Jennifer

Jennifer has severe mental retardation and cerebral palsy. She was identified as in need of special services at birth and began receiving early intervention services when she was 3 years old. When Jennifer was of age to attend school, she received most of her instruction within a Life Skills Support classroom. She was also integrated into regular education classes for many of her nonacademic activities.

Jennifer lives at home with her mother and father both who are employed full-time. Her mother works in the school district as a secretary and her father is an accountant. Both of her parents are actively involved in her educational planning and placement decisions, and are also active in a number of advocacy groups. Jennifer is an only child; however, she is rarely alone since many of her friends from the community often visit her at home after school.

Due to severe cognitive disabilities, Jennifer has low receptive and expressive language skills. Even though she has no functional speech, she does communicate using a Dyna Vox® (an assistive device to augment communication). Jennifer points to a picture board menu with icons that represent words. The Dyna Vox permits Jennifer to "say" words to her nondisabled peers. Jennifer does not usually initiate interactions with peers and adults; however, she does respond to their communications.

A paraprofessional assists Jennifer with her hygiene, toileting, eating, and mobility needs. She uses a manual wheelchair to travel throughout her environment. She is also able to use a computer in her classroom using a single switch.

Perhaps one of most difficult yet fundamental questions facing teachers is "What is the goal of education?" Educators have long struggled with issues such as what should be taught in the school versus the home, and who is best suited to impart this information. Terms such as "most appropriate education" and "outcome-based education" highlight basic issues that continue to pervade the educational community. What should teachers be doing with the valuable but limited time they have to educate students, particularly in special education settings where students need more time and practice to master skills? Traditional models of education have suggested that students be taught academic and enrichment/content skills with the expectation that students will acquire other skills needed for living and working incidentally and on their own (Brolin, 1995). When this model was applied to students in special education, many students were found to lack some of the necessary "survival" skills to function beyond the classroom. Additionally, when students with disabilities were taught traditional content in a "bottom-up" approach that requires students to go through stages of development before they can master skills, frequently students were being taught skills that were nonfunctional, artificial, and inappropriate for their chronological age (Brown et al., 1979).

The need for more meaningful curriculum is perhaps highlighted most starkly in data illustrating graduation rates and postschool outcomes for special education students. The Fifteenth Annual Report to Congress (U.S. Department of Education, Office of Special Education Programs, 1993) reported that 39% of students with disabilities drop out of school before graduation. Student outcome data reveal that students with disabilities are less frequently employed, earn less than those without disabilities, and generally are rated as less able to adequately perform functional mental skills such as counting change, telling time, and reading common signs (Wagner et al., 1991). Given such data and mandates, educators are realizing that students like Michael and Jennifer need to be exposed to a functional curriculum that will enable them to succeed beyond the school's doors.

FUNCTIONAL ACADEMIC CURRICULUM

The ideology behind providing students with meaningful skills has been evident for much of educational history; as early as 1937, Dewey spoke of the need to learn by doing (Weaver, Landers, & Adams, 1991). Special educators have long sought to provide functional curriculum to students. Terms associated with functional curriculum within special education have included criterion of ultimate functioning, life skills, independent living skills, daily living skills, work experience, vocational education, career education, and career development (Brolin, 1995; Brown, Nietupski, & Hamre-Nietupski, 1976). The construct of functionality can be conceptualized as a thinking process used by teachers to answer questions such as, "How, when, and where will my students use this knowledge in their lives now and in the future?" (Weaver et al., 1991). Functional skills are those skills that can be used in natural environments and focus on concepts and skills needed in areas such as employment/education, home and family, leisure pursuits, community involvement, physical/emotional health, and personal responsibility/relationships (Clark, 1994; Cronin & Patton, 1993). In contrast, nonfunctional skills have a low probability of being required in daily activities (Brown et al., 1979). The functionality of skills is contextually defined by each student and his or her own family. What is functional for one student may not necessarily be functional for another student in the same class. To determine whether a skill is functional for a student, teachers can ask themselves several questions (Clark, 1994):

- Is the instructional content of the student's current educational placement appropriate for meeting the student's personal and social, daily living, and occupational adjustment needs?
- Does the content focus on necessary knowledge and skills to function as independently as possible in the home, school, or community?
- Does the content provide a scope and sequence for meeting future needs?
- Do the student's parents think the content is important for both current and future needs?

- Does the student think the content is important for both current and future needs?
- Is the content appropriate for the student's chronological age and current intellectual, academic, or behavioral performance level?
- What are the consequences of not learning the content or skills inherent in the current educational placement?

Functional curricula traditionally have been associated with students having severe disabilities. It was assumed that traditional academic content would not be useful for persons with severe disabilities but that training in adaptive skills would be necessary. Adaptive skills, sometimes called independent living skills, describe the skills that are needed by students to be integrated into the community and gain as much independence as possible (Langone, 1986). Adaptive skill areas were often viewed as dichotomous with the traditional academic content covered in many schools. Greater numbers of educators, however, are now arguing that functional curricula should be a priority for all students (Algozzine & Audette, 1992; Brolin, 1995). That is, any skill taught in school should be examined to determine how it will be useful to the student and when it will be used in everyday life. Further, educators are now beginning to realize that functional academic content encompasses far more than a worksheet detailing information about math facts and can include such activities as creating a weekly budget, using a calculator, or purchasing a drink from a vending machine with an assortment of coins. Table 4.1 lists traditional academic content areas and examples of functional activities that may be used to convey academic subject matter. Students who are not able to master all the academic skills needed for participation in an activity, can be taught to use adaptations (Browder & Snell, 1993). For example, if a student is unable to read a daily schedule of events in text form, the teacher could teach the student to use an adaptation such as a picture schedule of the day's events. Similarly, if the student cannot identify coins to purchase an item, the teacher could teach the student to use a money envelope containing a predetermined amount of money. In both cases, the student is using functional academic skill adaptations to participate in activities.

Because functional academics can encompass a variety of life skills, it is important to identify activities that students may undertake when they leave the school system. Several authors have identified major activities or life demands that most adults must be able to perform (e.g., Cronin & Patton, 1993; Dever, 1988). These curricula provide teachers with an idea of what skills may be needed and enable them to identify objectives, goals, and daily instructional activities. For example, within the domain of leisure pursuits, an academic competency may be filling out a magazine order form. A teacher could use this information to devise an instructional objective and then plan activities so that his student can practice filling out forms in a number of settings where the student would be required to perform the needed skill. Table 4.2 presents matrices for elementary and secondary students developed by Cronin and Patton (1993) that illustrate the relationship between scholastic/social skills and adult domains. The matrix illustrates how functional academic skills can be taught across a variety of curricular domains. Table 4.3 lists a number of existing functional curricula and guides that are available to educators.

TABLE 4.1   Functional Academic Activities

Reading

    Read a newspaper article.
    Read a recipe.
    Read the signs on rest-room doors indicating "Men" and "Women."
    Read instructions for video game.

Math

    Add sales tax to purchase order.
    Use calculator to add grocery item totals.
    Compare prices at local video store.
    Calculate income tax return.

Science

    Calculate boiling point for candy recipe.
    Chart medication use.
    Plant and harvest vegetable garden.
    Identify weather to select appropriate clothing.

Social Studies

    Register to vote.
    Identify cultural holidays and customs.
    Identify headlines in newspapers.
    Determine bus route in the community.

Health

    Brush teeth/oral hygiene.
    Plan balanced meals.
    Identify and purchase items for class first-aid kit.
    Identify health services in the community.

Educators are still examining ways to incorporate traditional academic subjects with more functional knowledge; however, all educators should use meaningful adjustment beyond school as a measure of success. Later in the chapter, strategies are presented for integrating functional curriculum content into academic subject matter in regular education classrooms.

ASSESSMENT OF FUNCTIONAL ACADEMIC SKILLS

Assessment is an essential feature of meaningful educational programming; teachers assess students to gain information for the purposes of screening, placement, curriculum development, and student evaluation (Salvia & Ysseldyke, 1995). Traditional assessment measures have consisted mainly of standardized tests that compare a student's performance with that of other students on academic, behavioral, interest, and attitudes. However, given the trend toward more functional curricula, educators have found the need for assessment that will yield practical and meaningful information about how well an individual will perform in natural settings and environments (Brolin, 1995). Although some functional academic skills can be

TABLE 4.2   Matrices for Relationships—Elementary and Secondary School Students

	Employment/ Education	Home and Family	Leisure Pursuits	Community Involvement	Emotional/ Physical Health	Personal Responsibility/ Relationships
Reading	Read library books on various occupations	Read directions to prepare brownies from mix	Look for ads in the newspaper for toys	Read road signs and understand what they mean	Locate poison control numbers in the phone book	Read a story to a younger child
Writing	Write to the school board about a pothole in the school driveway	Make a list of items needed from the grocery store	Fill out a magazine order form completely	Complete an application to play Little League	Keep a daily diary of food you eat in each food group	Write a thank-you note to a relative for a gift
Listening	Listen to a lecture by a bank official on savings accounts	Listen to a lecture on babysitting tips	Listen to radio/TV to see if a ball game is rained out	Listen to a lecture on how children can recycle	Listen to the school nurse explain the annual eye exam for your class	Listen to a friend describe their family vacation
Speaking	Discuss reasons we work	Ask parents for permission to stay at a friend's house	Invite friends over to play Monopoly	Discuss park and playground improvements with the mayor	Ask the school nurse how to care for mosquito bites	Discuss honesty, trust, and promise. Define them.
Math Applications	Calculate how much you would make babysitting at $1.25 an hour for 3 hours	Compute the cost of a box of cereal using a coupon	Compute the cost of going to the movies	Compute tax on a video game	Calculate and compare the cost of different types of Band-Aids. Include tax.	Ask a friend to share a candy bar. Calculate your part of the cost.
Problem-Solving	Decide which environment you work best in: out or in; quiet or noisy; active or at a desk, etc.	Decide how to share TV time with a sibling	Given $15 for the afternoon which would you do: go to the movies, go bowling, or play videos?	Role-play the times you would use the 911 emergency number	Decide how many hours of sleep you need per night	Decide if you have enough coins to purchase a vending machine soda for you and your friend
Survival Skills	Keep homework assignments in a special notebook	Develop a checklist of what to do before and after school	Use a map to find the best way to the mall	Draw a map of the way you go to/from school	Mark the calendar for your next dental appointment	Identify important table manners
Personal/ Social	Ask a classmate to assist you with a job	Settle a dispute with a sibling	Call a video store to see if they have a specific movie	Role-play asking a police officer for help if you're lost	Ask a friend to go bicycling with you	Role-play appropriate behavior for various places (movies, church, restaurant, ballpark)

Elementary Matrix: Relationship of Scholastic/Social Skills to Adult Domains.

assessed using standardized tests, a number of functional assessment strategies are gaining popularity with educators such as rating scales and inventories, performance-based assessments, and ecological inventories.

RATING SCALES AND INVENTORIES

Rating scales and inventories can be developed commercially or by teachers to assess functional academic skills. Information for assessment is collected through a number of different ways including review of the student's file, staffing notes, interview results, observations, test and work sample administrations, situational assessments, and curriculum-based assessments (Brolin, 1995). Scales and inventories typically list a number of functional competencies that teachers, parents, and other persons involved in the student's life can use as a benchmark to assess whether or not the student has the needed competency. Functional competencies can include skills in areas such as physical, cognitive, personal, and social domains (Brolin, 1995). Table 4.4 lists

	Employment/ Education	Home and Family	Leisure Pursuits	Community Involvement	Emotional/ Physical Health	Personal Responsibility/ Relationships
Reading	Reading classified ads for jobs	Interpreting bills	Locating and understanding movie information in a newspaper	Following directions on tax forms	Comprehending directions on medication	Reading letters from friends
Writing	Writing a letter of application for a job	Writing checks	Writing for information on a city to visit	Filling in a voter registration form	Filling in your medical history on forms	Sending thank-you notes
Listening	Understanding oral directions of a procedure change	Comprehending oral directions about making dinner	Listening for forecast to plan outdoor activity	Understanding campaign ads	Attending lectures on stress	Taking turns in a conversation
Speaking	Asking your boss for a raise	Discussing morning routines with family	Inquiring about tickets for a concert	Stating your opinion at the school board meeting	Describing symptoms to a doctor	Giving feedback to a friend about the purchase of a compact disc
Math Applications	Understanding difference between net and gross pay	Computing the cost of doing laundry in a laundromat versus at home	Calculating the cost of a dinner out versus eating at home	Obtaining information for a building permit	Using a thermometer	Planning the costs of a date
Problem-Solving	Settling a dispute with a co-worker	Deciding how much budget for rent	Role-playing appropriate behaviors for various places	Knowing what to do if you are the victim of fraud	Selecting a doctor	Deciding how to ask someone for a date
Survival Skills	Using a prepared career planning packet	Listing emergency phone numbers	Using a shopping center directory	Marking a calendar for important dates (e.g., recycling, garbage collection)	Using a system to remember to take vitamins	Developing a system to remember birthdays
Personal/ Social	Applying appropriate interview skills	Helping a child with homework	Knowing the rules of a neighborhood pool	Locating self-improvement classes	Getting a yearly physical exam	Discussing how to negotiate a price at a flea market

Secondary Matrix: Relationship of Scholastic/Social Skills to Adult Domains.

Matrix Illustrating the Relationship of Scholastic/Social Skills to Adult Life Domains

Note. From *Life Skills Instruction for All Students with Special Needs* (pp. 32–33), by M. E. Cronin and J. R. Patton, 1993, Austin, TX: PRO-ED, Inc. Reprinted with permission.

a selection of commercially available functional assessment scales and inventories as well as a brief description of each instrument.

PERFORMANCE ASSESSMENT

Performance assessment is concerned with what the student is able to do with knowledge rather than simply acquiring knowledge or facts. The central difference between traditional and performance assessment is the type of response required by the student. Standardized tests require that a student select and mark the correct response; performance assessment requires the student to produce or perform a response (Poteet, Choate, & Stewart, 1993). Closely related to performance assessment is authentic assessment. Performance assessment becomes authentic when it requires the tasks to be performed in natural contexts and under natural conditions and demands (Meyer, 1992). Authentic performance assessments frequently have been used in vocational

TABLE 4.3   Commercially Available Functional Curricula

Curriculum - Publisher	Description
Life Centered Career Education: The Complete Curriculum and Assessment Package (Council for Exceptional Children)	Contains lesson plans for the areas of Daily Living Skills, and Occupational Skills. Also included are Knowledge and Performance Batteries, Administration Manuals, and a Technical Report.
Lifeschool (Pacemaker Learning Materials)	10 modules focusing on money, housing, groceries, and clothing. Reading level 3.5–4.5.
Adaptive Living Skills Curriculum (The Riverside Publishing Company)	Contains 24 skill modules from 4 domain areas: personal living skills, home living skills, community living skills, and employment skills.
Independent Living Skills Curriculum (University of Oregon)	Includes paying bills, menu planning, grocery shopping, cooking, and personal hygiene.
The Syracuse Community Referenced Curriculum Guide (Paul H. Brookes)	Manual for teaching community living, academic, social, communication, and motor skills.
Survival Skills System and Resource Guide for Transition Materials from School to Work (The Conover Company)	Includes assessment and training for vocational exploration, career planning, gaining employment, and social skills.

Note. Adapted from Brolin, D. E. (1995).

domains through the use of situational assessments, work samples, and simulations (Poteet et al., 1993) and are easily applied to assessment of functional academic skills. An example of an authentic performance assessment for Michael was when his teacher videotaped his job interviews in the community and then provided him with constructive feedback. Types of authentic performance assessment include portfolio and curriculum-based assessment, and ecological inventories.

Portfolio Assessment.   Portfolio assessment is also gaining favor among educators as a means to collect observable evidence or products of performance assessment (Poteet et al., 1993). Portfolio assessment is the use of records of a student's work over time that illustrates the depth, breadth, and development of the student's academic abilities. It should be a purposeful and systematic collection of the student's work (Pierce & O'Malley, 1992). The purpose of the portfolio will determine its content; however, two types are widely used: working portfolios, which represent the student's academic work in progress, and permanent portfolios, which represent the best and most comprehensive assessment of the student's work (Grady, 1992). For example, Michael's elementary Language Arts teacher maintained a working portfolio of Michael's functional writing activities. Figure 4.1 illustrates the kinds of materials that can be used in an assessment portfolio in a variety of functional academic domains.

Curriculum-Based Assessment.   Curriculum-based assessment (CBA) is another type of performance assessment. It is appealing to educators because assessment is

TABLE 4.4   Commercially Available Adaptive Behavior Scales and Inventories

Scale/Inventory Name	Description
Inventory of Essential Skills (1987)	Covers academic areas of reading/language arts, math, and study skills.
Brigance Life Skills Inventory (1994)	Assesses listening, speaking, reading, writing, comprehending, and computing skills in 9 life-skills sections: speaking and listening skills, functional writing skills, words on common signs and warning labels, telephone skills, money and finance, food, clothing, health, and travel and transportation.
Vineland Adaptive Behavior Scales (1984)	Contains the Interview Edition, Interview Edition Expanded Form, and Classroom Edition. Contains 11 subdomains organized into 4 domains of communication, daily living, socialization, and motor skills.
The Adaptive Behavior: The Street Survival Skills Questionnaire (1983)	Contains 9 subtests: basic concepts, functional signs, tools, domestics, health and safety, public services, time, monetary, and measurements.
Functional Assessment Inventory (1984)	Includes 2 rating forms with 30 functional items. Items include memory, use of hands, interest in working, personality, motivation.
The Prevocational Assessment and Curriculum Guide (1978)	Assesses 46 school and workshop skills: attendance/endurance, independence, production, learning, behavior/communication skills, social skills, grooming/eating skills, toileting skills.

Note. Adapted from Brolin, D. E. (1995).

conducted in the curriculum of the local school and is tied to the actual classroom material that is being taught, which enables teachers to directly determine the extent that students are learning (Fuchs & Deno, 1994). Although a number of curriculum-based assessment methods are available, all the methods share three features: (1) student proficiency is sampled from materials found in the school's curriculum; (2) assessments must recur over time; and (3) information from the assessment is used to formulate instructional decisions (Tucker, 1987). Figure 4.2 presents an example of a curriculum-based assessment conducted for Michael in the functional academic area of reading. A graph of Michael's sight words learned and recalled is displayed. Fuchs and Deno (1994) have identified several critical features of CBA that are necessary to ensure that the assessment is useful for instruction: (1) repeated testing on materials of comparable difficult over time; (2) use of valid tests; and (3) use of quantitative and qualitative data.

Ecological Inventory.   Ecological inventories, another way to conduct a functional assessment, are typically associated with students having more severe disabilities. The ecological inventory is based on the top-down approach to skill development

FIGURE 4.1   Assessment Portfolios

Reading Portfolio
Audiotape of oral reading of selected passages.
Original story grammar map.
Transcript of story retelling.
Log of books read with personal reactions, summaries, vocabulary.
Representative assignments: responses to pre/post reading questions.
Favorite performance.
Journal entries including self-evaluation.

Science Portfolio
Representative work samples.
Student-selected best performance.
Report from hands-on investigation.
Notes on Science Fair project.
Journal entries including self-evaluation.
Learning progress record.
Report cards.
Personal journal.

Writing Portfolio
Scrapbook of representative writing samples.
Selected prewriting activities.
Illustrations/diagrams for one piece.
Log/journal of writing ideas, vocabulary, semantic maps, compositions, evaluations.
Conference notes, observation narratives.
Student-selected best performance.
Self-evaluation checklists and teacher checklists.

Social Studies Portfolio
Representative work samples.
Student-selected best performance.
Design of travel brochure, packet, or itinerary of trip.
Notes on History Fair project.
Journal entries including self-evaluation.

Generic Portfolio
Tests.
Significant daily assignments.
Anecdotal observations.

Mathematics Portfolio
Reports of mathematical investigations.
Representative assignments.
Teacher conference notes.
Descriptions and diagrams of problem-solving processes.
Video, audio, or computer-generated examples of work.
Best performance.
Journal entries including self-evaluation.

Arts Portfolio
Best performance.
Favorite performance.
First, middle, and final renderings of projects.
Tape of performance.
Journal entries including self-evaluation.
Photographs.
Awards.
Personal goals.

Note. From "Performance Assessment and Special Education: Practices and Prospects," by J. A. Poteet, J. S. Choate, and S. C. Steward, 1993, *Focus on Exceptional Children, 26,* p. 9. Reprinted with permission.

FIGURE 4.2   Curriculum-Based Assessment (CBA) for Michael

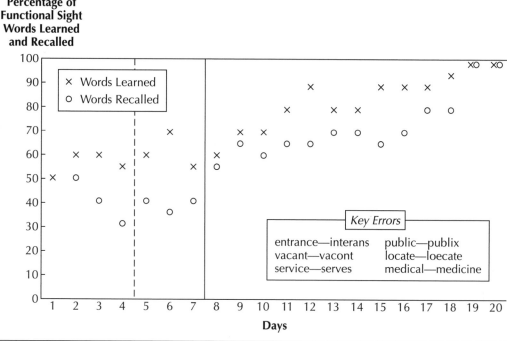

that focuses on the skills needed in the natural environment as the source of curriculum content (Brown et al., 1979). Ecological inventories assess a student's strengths and weaknesses within natural environments; information from the inventories can help determine how well a student performs activities within frequently accessed environments. Environments that are selected to be inventoried typically are identified through parent interviews and represent activities that are of present and future importance to the student (Browder, 1987). Results of ecological inventories are of particular use in functional assessment because instructional objectives can be directly identified from functional performance of the skill. The results of the inventory can be used to help decide whether to teach an adaptive skill or adapt the situation to facilitate student performance (Downing & Perino, 1992). Steps in conducting an ecological inventory include:

- Identifying the appropriate curriculum domain.
- Identifying the environment.
- Identifying subenvironments within the environment.
- Identifying activities that occur in the subenvironment.
- Determining whether the student has the skills to perform the activities required in the subenvironment.
- For students who do not have the skills, deciding how to teach the skill, teach an adaptation, or modify the environment (Falvey, 1989).

Table 4.5 presents an ecological inventory that has been conducted for Jennifer. Notice that the inventory revealed a number of functional academic skills that Jennifer's teacher could use as instructional objectives for her IEP. Table 4.5A lists discrepancies between the student's skill level and skills needed to perform the tasks as well as "what-to-do" options to teach the skill.

FUNCTIONAL ACADEMIC CURRICULUM DESIGN

Because the functionality of curriculum is contextually bound, each individual student will need different skills to function in future environments. Common to all published curricula and those developed by teachers are several concepts that serve to make the materials used and the skills taught functional including: a top-down model for curriculum development; social validation of methods, materials, and outcomes; programming for generalization; appropriate use of assistive technology; transition planning; and development of appropriate Individual Education Plans (IEPs).

TABLE 4.5   Ecological Inventory for Jennifer

Domain: Domestic

Environment: Elementary Classroom

Subenvironment: Kitchen

Activity: Lunch preparation

Activity 1: Planning lunch menu
    Skill 1: Determine meal (sandwich, milk, dessert).
    Skill 2: Determine if ingredients are available in cupboards and refrigerator.
    Skill 3: If item is unavailable, place on shopping list.
    Skill 4: Determine amount of food necessary to make meal.

Activity 2: Food preparation—sandwich
    Skill 1: Read recipe.
    Skill 2: Locate ingredients and utensils.
    Skill 3: Take bread out of wrapper.
    Skill 4: Using butter knife, spread peanut butter on one slice of bread.
    Skill 5: Spread jelly on the other slice of bread.
    Skill 6: Assemble sandwich.
    Skill 7: Cut sandwich in half.

Activity 3: Food preparation—beverage
    Skill 1: Take milk out of refrigerator.
    Skill 2: Get glass out of cupboard.
    Skill 3: Pour milk into glass.

Activity 4: Food preparation—dessert
    Skill 1: Choose fruit from cupboard or refrigerator.
    Skill 2: Open can of fruit.
    Skill 3: Obtain bowl from cupboard.
    Skill 4: Pour fruit into bowl.

TABLE 4.5A Skill Discrepancies for Jennifer

Student: Jennifer Godshall	Domain: Domestic	Subenvironment: Kitchen
Date: November 1, 1995	Environment: Elementary Classroom	Teacher: Wendy Harriott

Nonhandicapped Person Inventory	Student Inventory	Discrepancy Analysis	What-to-Do Options
Activity: Planning lunch menu			
Skills: Determine meal (sandwich, milk, dessert)	+		
Determine if ingredients are available in cupboards and refrigerator	–	No strategy to determine	Add picture cues to cupboards and refrigerator
Place on shopping list if unavailable	–	Unable to write	Develop a menu of pictures to use to construct shopping list
Determine amount of food needed to make meal	+		
Activity: Food preparation—sandwich			
Skills: Read Recipe	–	Not able to read	Develop picture recipes and teach
Locate ingredients and utensils	–	Unable to find	Add picture cues for ingredients and utensils and teach
Take bread out of wrapper	–	Lacking pincer grasp	Use bread without twist ties and improve pincer grasp skills
Spread peanut butter on one slice of bread	–	Bread tears	Use toast or slightly stale bread

(Continued)

TABLE 4.5A (*Continued*)

	Nonhandicapped Person Inventory	Student Inventory	Discrepancy Analysis	What-to-Do Options
	Spread jelly on the other slice of bread	–	Bread tears	Use toast or slightly stale bread
	Assemble sandwich	+		
	Cut sandwich in half	+		
Activity:	Food preparation—beverage			
Skills:	Take milk out of refrigerator	–	Not enough muscle strength to open refrigerator	Teach her to use two hands or provide hand-over-hand assistance
	Get glass out of cupboard	–	Drop glass	Use unbreakable cup
	Pour milk into glass	–	Often tips glass over	Use holder to steady glass
Activity:	Food preparation—dessert			
Skills:	Choose fruit from cupboard or refrigerator	–	Unable to find	Provide picture cues on cupboard and refrigerator
	Open can of fruit	–	Lack of muscle strength and pincer grasp	Teach to use electric can opener
	Obtain bowl from cupboard	+		
	Pour fruit into bowl	+		

Note. Adapted from *Community-based Curriculum*, Second Edition, by M. Falvey, 1989, Baltimore, MD: Paul H. Brookes.

Top-Down Model for Curriculum Development.   The top-down curriculum approach suggests that the skills needed for functioning as an adult are identified and then instructional content is based on this information (Helmke, Havekost, Patton, & Pollaway, 1994). This approach contrasts with the more traditional bottom-up approach to curriculum development in which skills are taught in developmental stages. The top-down model is more suited to a student's current and future needs and reinforces the concept of transition planning outlined in current legislation such as the Individuals with Disabilities Education Act (IDEA) (Helmke et al., 1994). Cronin and Patton (1993) have identified a four-stage model of functional curriculum development outlined in Figure 4.3. The model suggests that functional curriculum can be developed by:

- Identifying the major adult domains and subdomains that students need to function in as adults such as employment/education, home and family, leisure pursuits, community involvement, physical/emotional health, and personal responsibility and relationships.
- Identifying major life demands or situations that most adults will encounter.

FIGURE 4.3   Top-Down Approach to Curriculum Development

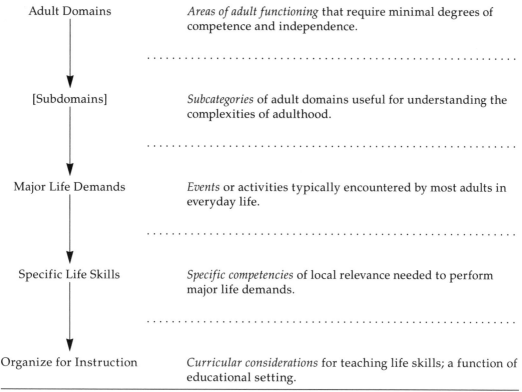

Adult Domains — *Areas of adult functioning* that require minimal degrees of competence and independence.

[Subdomains] — *Subcategories* of adult domains useful for understanding the complexities of adulthood.

Major Life Demands — *Events* or activities typically encountered by most adults in everyday life.

Specific Life Skills — *Specific competencies* of local relevance needed to perform major life demands.

Organize for Instruction — *Curricular considerations* for teaching life skills; a function of educational setting.

Note. Adapted from *Life Skills Instruction for All Students with Special Needs*, by M. E. Cronin and J. R. Patton, 1993, Austin, TX: PRO-ED, Inc. Copyright 1993 by PRO-ED, Inc. Adapted with permission.

- Identifying specific life skills needed to meet each of the life demands that will be used as the basis for instructional objectives on the student's IEP or Individualized Transition Plan (ITP).
- Organizing instruction to teach the functional skills by deciding what content to cover and how to accomplish it.

SOCIAL VALIDATION OF METHODS, MATERIALS, AND OUTCOMES

The concept of social validity, used to evaluate the acceptability or viability of interventions, is a critical component in the development of functional curriculum. That is, for a curriculum to be deemed functional, it must be judged to be socially valid. Social validity can be determined by asking whether the goals, procedures, and effects of an intervention or instructional goal are acceptable as judged by the person with a disability, educators, and the community at large (Bernstein, 1989). Closely related to the concept of social validity is the concept of age-appropriateness. Functional curriculum focuses on the development of skills that are representative of an individual's chronological age rather than developmental age. For example, even though Jennifer may be functioning on a lower cognitive level, as her IEP indicates, when she turned 17 she was working on skills and competencies similar to other 17-year-old students. Attention to the social validity of goals, instructional procedures, and outcomes cannot be stressed enough; research has shown that individuals with disabilities who are depicted engaging in nonfunctional and age-inappropriate activities are perceived by others in the community less favorably (e.g., having lower IQs, reading levels, future earning capacities, needing more restrictive residential and educational placement options; Bates, Morrow, Panscofar, & Sedlak, 1984; Calhoun & Calhoun, 1993). Educators must ensure that their students are learning functional, age-appropriate skills that are taught in a socially valid manner.

PROGRAMMING FOR GENERALIZATION

A common difficulty for many students with disabilities is the transfer of skills from one setting to a different setting. To ensure that students are able to perform skills under a variety of conditions and circumstances, teachers must actively plan to facilitate generalization (Horner, McDonnell, & Bellamy, 1986). One method of planning for generalization is general case programming. General case programming centers on the selection of examples of learning that sample the range of ways in which a functional activity is conducted in the community (Steere, Wood, Panscofar, & Butterworth, 1993). When conducting general case programming, a teacher must analyze the environment to determine variations in how activities are conducted so that students are taught to respond in any given situation. Steps when conducting general case programming include (1) defining the instructional universe; (2) selecting what conditions will be taught; (3) conducting training and collecting data; (4) modifying instruction based on an analysis of error patterns; (5) training under exceptional conditions; and (6) determining when to stop training based on student performance in untrained conditions (Horner, Sprague, & Wilcox, 1982). Teachers using a functional curriculum can employ general case programming to ensure that students are able to function and use their skills in a variety of settings.

APPROPRIATE USE OF ASSISTIVE TECHNOLOGY

Assistive technology can be defined as any item, device, or piece of equipment that is used to increase a person's ability to participate in the tasks of daily living and function as independently as possible (Parette, Hourcade, & VanBiervliet, 1993; Reed & Bowser, 1991). Technology can be used in a number of ways to facilitate the acquisition of functional academic content. Teachers can use assistive technology to design functional curricula through use of interactive videodiscs that provide community-based simulations for practice with functional skills (Wissick, Lloyd, & Kinzie, 1992). Further, computer-assisted instruction can be used to impart information as well as serve as a means to practice and reinforce skills (Kinzer, Sherwood, & Bransford, 1986). Computers have been found to increase a student's engagement time on learning tasks (Cosden, Gerber, Semmel, Goldman, & Semmel, 1987). Finally, assistive technology can be used to implement functional academic curricula through adaptive devices that permit students with disabilities to participate in activities. Computer-based video games can be used by students with severe disabilities as a leisure activity performed with a nondisabled peer (Powers & Ball, 1983; Sedlack, Doyle, & Schloss, 1982). Video games are age-appropriate and also require sequencing, directionality, and strategy skills. Computers have also been used to enhance self-esteem and confidence, or to motivate students with special needs (Male, 1988). Jennifer's educational program was greatly enhanced when she learned to use her communication device, the Dyna Vox; she is now able to communicate with her peers. Adaptive devices can include toys, mobility and seating devices (wheelchairs, carts), augmentative communication aids (manual and electronic communication devices), personal computers and modifications (switches, alternate keyboards, computer outputs), environmental controls (devices used to activate lights, TV, games), and vocational adaptations (workstation modifications, use of telecommunication devices) (Reed & Bowser, 1991).

TRANSITION PLANNING

Transition implies movement from one educational setting to another. IDEA mandates that an Individual Transition Plan (ITP) be developed for each student with a disability by the age of 16 to better assure a smooth transition from the school to the community. The ITP provides a plan for services rather than a plan for skill or knowledge acquisition. The ITP generally has no set format and is often included as part of the IEP. Typically, the ITP is organized around areas similar to those included in functional curricula such as employment/education, home and family, leisure activities, community involvement, emotional-physical health, personal responsibility, and relationships (Polloway & Patton, 1993). Transition planning is an integral part of teaching functional academics because once placement options and services are identified, a teacher can identify skills needed in future environments and can help students acquire the skills they will need once they leave school.

Although IDEA only mandates transition for students with disabilities who are preparing to leave the school system, longitudinal transition planning throughout the student's educational career is necessary to ensure that necessary functional skills are being taught and reinforced in each setting (Steere, Wood, Panscofar, & Rucker, 1993). Provision of longitudinal and ongoing planning ensures that students with disabilities are receiving instruction in the skills they need to function in future environments within the school and the community. Examples of how to program for transition throughout a student's school career are given throughout the following section including sample objectives and activities for Michael and Jennifer.

IMPLEMENTING FUNCTIONAL CURRICULA

ORGANIZATION OF ACADEMIC CONTENT

It has been argued by some educators that functional curriculum cannot be taught in regular education classrooms given the typical academic content that is covered in such a setting. However, functional skills can be taught to students with special needs in any educational setting or environment (Cronin & Patton, 1993). Figure 4.4 depicts a model developed by Cronin and Patton (1993) for integrating functional curricula into a student's educational program as well as a practical example of each integration strategy. As depicted, the bottom of the continuum represents a situation in which the majority of the curriculum is life skills oriented; the top of the continuum represents a situation in which academic subject matter is emphasized. The model illustrates how functional content can be infused throughout the curriculum and the day. Figure 4.4 also includes examples from Michael's program to illustrate the components of the model.

If a comprehensive grouping of life skills courses is chosen for a student with disabilities, strategies can be used to ensure that the curriculum can be carried out

---

FIGURE 4.4   Functional Integration Curricula Strategies and Examples for Michael

1. Infusion of life skills topics into established content of existing courses.

   In the elementary school, Michael was included in regular education classes. When the regular education teacher taught handwriting and spelling skills in isolation, Michael's special education teacher infused life skills by teaching the class how to write letters, address envelopes, and fill out real forms.

2. Portion of existing course dedicated to life skills topics.

   In Michael's elementary science class, the teacher prepared a unit on health and safety. Life skills topics were added to the unit such as reading warning labels on containers, saying "no" to strangers, and opening your door only after identifying the visitor.

3. Single generic life skills course.

   When Michael was of high school age, his special education teacher developed an elective course for both special and regular education students entitled "Coping 101." It covered many topics including peer pressure, dating and relationships, after-school activities, dealing with parents and other authority figures, and employment-seeking skills.

4. Select topical life skills course.

   Michael's high school program included a required course in health. This course was cotaught by a regular education teacher and a special education teacher. Topics included CPR training, first aid, sexuality, disease and illness, and drug and alcohol awareness.

5. Comprehensive grouping of specific life skills courses.

   This option was not available at the high school Michael attended; however, the staff was working toward developing a series of integrated life skills courses. These would cover all subject areas.

Note. Adapted from *Life Skills Instruction For All Students with Special Needs* (p. 9), by M. S. Cronin and J. R. Patton, 1993, Austin, TX: PRO-ED, Inc. Copyright 1993 by PRO-ED, Inc. Adapted with permission.

in an integrated setting such as the regular education classroom. Figure 4.5 lists the strategies as well as a practical example of how such strategies could be implemented for Jennifer. Strategies for providing functional academic instruction in integrated settings include:

- Providing partial assistance through a peer or classmate within the context of regular classroom activities.
- Identifying downtimes during the school day when functional skills can be taught without disrupting normal classroom routine.
- Providing parallel instruction (provide functional skills training for students with disabilities while nondisabled students participate in academic work).

FIGURE 4.5   Functional Academic Instruction in Integrated Settings and Examples for Jennifer

Strategy

1. Provide partial assistance via peers within the context of regular classroom activities.

Practical Example

1. Ordering lunch in elementary school. Student peer assists Jennifer. Jennifer chooses meal from picture menu and chooses milk from empty cartons. Peer makes sure that Jennifer's lunch is included in class lunch count. Jennifer also asks (using Dyna Vox) peer to get her wallet out of her locker in order to buy her lunch ticket. Peer assists Jennifer in purchasing her lunch ticket in the cafeteria.

Strategy

2. Identify downtimes when functional skills can be taught without disrupting normal classroom routine.

Practical Example

2. During breaks between classes in middle school, Jennifer can practice reading functional signs within building (e.g., "Women" and "Men") with her peer tutor.

Strategy

3. Provide parallel instruction within regular classroom.

Practical Example

3. While middle school math class is learning how to add and subtract positive and negative integers; Jennifer can practice identifying coins and choosing the appropriate coins to pay for lunch.

Strategy

4. Briefly remove student for specialized instruction when regular activities are beyond her skill level.

Practical Example

4. At the high school level, Jennifer was removed from regular class when the content was too difficult. When her peers were learning Economics in math class: Jennifer went to her community-based Apartment program to work on shopping for personal items and learning how to use the ATM.

Note. Adapted from Hamre-Nietupski, McDonald, & Nietupski (1992).

- Briefly removing the student with disabilities for specialized instruction but only when all activities are clearly beyond their skill level (Hamre-Nietupski, McDonald, & Nietupski, 1992).

COMMUNITY-BASED INSTRUCTION

With the shift toward the development of more functional curricula, the emphasis of instruction has moved from simulated classroom settings to the community itself (Wehman, Moon, Everson, Wood, & Barcus, 1988). Community-based instruction (CBI), discussed in greater detail in Chapter 2, underlies most functional academic curriculum because the demands of the natural environment can be readily identified and taught under the natural conditions. In addition, students with disabilities are afforded greater opportunities to interact with persons without disabilities (Stainback, Stainback, & Forest, 1989). Community-based instruction has been found to increase the acquisition of adaptive behaviors (McDonnell, Hardman, Hightower, Keifer-O'Donnell, & Drew, 1993) and has been used to teach a wide variety of functional academic skills and activities to students with disabilities including community service work (Everington & Stevenson, 1994), shopping in supermarkets (Ford, 1983), eating in fast-food restaurants (van den Pol et al., 1981), and playing pinball (Hill, Wehman, & Horst, 1982).

DEVELOPMENT OF FUNCTIONAL INDIVIDUAL EDUCATION PLANS

Individual Education Plans, which typically consist of annual goals and short-term objectives, are used by many teachers as a basis for daily instructional programming and curricular development (Sands, Adams, & Stout, 1995). The skills and objectives selected for inclusion on the IEP should reflect skills that will be needed by the student in current and future environments that have been identified through functional assessments such as rating scales and inventories, and performance assessments as noted previously in the chapter. Because the IEP represents an important legal and working document, it should be developed carefully with attention given to the appropriateness of the objectives to future environments. Sailor et al. (1989) have developed a checklist that can be used to determine whether IEPs reflect best practice indicators. When developing IEPs, Sailor et al. suggest that educators ask whether (1) the materials and tasks outlined are age-appropriate; (2) the activities and skills are basic, represent a critical activity and provide an opportunity for interaction with peers without disabilities; and (3) the skill can be generalized to a variety of environments and in natural settings (Sailor et al., 1989).

Examples of Functional Academic IEP Objectives. The following IEP objectives have been selected for Michael and Jennifer who were presented in the case studies at the beginning of the chapter. Objectives are presented for each student in elementary, middle, and secondary school. Complete IEPs are provided in Appendix 4.A. These IEPs illustrate that, although the goals and objectives for the students may differ due to age and disability, their academic goals and objectives were taught in a functional and meaningful manner. Michael has a specific learning disability and was placed into special education in second grade. Michael's teachers reported that Michael needed to improve in many areas including interacting appropriately with peers and adults, reading and writing skills, and mathematics problem-solving skills. Specific learning objectives will be provided along with corresponding activities designed to meet those objectives for the elementary, middle, and secondary school settings.

Elementary School—Michael

Michael was included in regular education classrooms for the majority of his day throughout elementary school. His regular classroom teachers worked collaboratively with his special education teacher to provide a functional academic program for him. Following are two examples of specific learning objectives and classroom activities for Michael from his fifth-grade regular education Language Arts and Science classrooms:

Objective for Language Arts Skills
• When asked to provide personal identification information, Michael will orally or in written form, provide the following information: name, complete home address, phone number, parent's name, school's name, and teacher's name with 100% accuracy in 8 out of 10 trials.

Functional Activities
1. Write letters to class pen pals using appropriate format including return address and heading.
2. Address envelopes using home address and/or school address.
3. Type letters to class international pen-pals using computers and the Internet.
4. Make personal identification card.
5. Fill out real forms with personal information (for example: catalog order form, library card application, sports application).
6. Practice calling 911 and providing pertinent emergency information.
7. Prepare for transition into middle school by writing a letter to teachers he will have in the middle school, and making new ID card containing middle school information.

Objective for Science Skills
• Identify a product as safe or unsafe by reading warning labels on various household containers with 100% accuracy.

Functional Activities
1. Read labels from items in various settings (nurse's office, art class, main office).
2. Identify bottles as safe or unsafe (empty containers of typical household and school items).
3. Place poison stickers on unsafe containers in school and home (with parent assistance).
4. Prepare for transition into middle school by: surveying classrooms and offices in the middle school and practice reading warning labels for his future environment.

Elementary School—Jennifer

Jennifer was enrolled in a Life Skills Support classroom in elementary school. Within this classroom, she often worked with peer tutors. She also ate lunch in the cafeteria, went to recess, and attended classes in art, music, and physical education in integrated settings. Jennifer's regular education teacher, her special education teacher, and her physical therapist worked together to provide a functional program to meet her individual needs. Following are examples of behavioral objectives and classroom activities for Jennifer in fifth grade in the skill areas of Language Arts/Communication and Health/Physical Education:

Objective for Language Arts/Communication
- While completing required daily living activities, Jennifer will initiate use of her communication device on a daily basis to make her wants and needs known in this area.

Functional Activities
1. Cafeteria lunch activities:

   Chooses pictures of menu items.

   Chooses type of milk (white, chocolate, or strawberry) desired from empty cartons.

   Uses money from wallet to buy lunch ticket.

   Within cafeteria, uses picture board to ask for items needed.

   Communicates with peers during lunch.

   As a transitional activity, begin teaching Jennifer prices and menu choices from the middle school cafeteria.

2. Making lunch activity:

   Chooses simple meals from menu picture cards (e.g., soup, sandwich, spaghetti, ravioli, macaroni and cheese, dessert).

   Checks cupboards and refrigerator to determine if all ingredients are available.

   If item is not available, must place on picture shopping list and go shopping to buy the needed items.

   Uses picture recipe to make lunch.

   Identify and invite peer tutor to eat lunch.

   Make simple meals at home with parents' assistance (with different menu items) using communication device.

   To assist in transition, make simple meals in Home Economics room in middle school.

3. Conducting lunch count for school (this activity is completed daily with a peer tutor):

   Uses colored marker to mark top of lunch count page.

   Places papers in appropriate colored folders.

   Distributes colored folders outside teachers' doors (peer reads teacher's names on folders and assists with wheelchair as needed).

Objective for Health/Physical Education Skills
- While in daily school routine, will initiate interactions with nonhandicapped peers and become more actively involved in group activities.

Functional Activities
1. Personal grooming:

   Uses communication device to request needed items from personal basket (cup, comb, brush, toothbrush, toothpaste, hand cream).

Uses requested items appropriately.

Places items back into basket.

Uses grooming materials and picture board at home.

To prepare for transition into middle school, gradually add typical grooming items her peers use in middle school (e.g., barrette, perfume).

2. Gross motor activities (with regular education peers):

Obstacle course relay race.

Dodge ball, Red Rover, soccer, tag.

Parachute games.

Modified exercises.

Softball tournament (partial participation).

3. Use of picture schedule to greet, say good-bye, and cheer for peers during activities. Use peer confederates as needed (trained peers to initiate interactions with Jennifer).

4. To prepare for middle school transition, introduce Jennifer to middle school teachers using communication device.

Middle School—Michael

In the middle school, Michael required more time for instruction in his special education class. He received the majority of his instruction for academic subject areas within his Learning Support classroom. Following are sample IEP objectives for Michael in his eighth-grade mathematics and social studies classes. Notice that the subject areas are not clearly distinct and overlap (e.g., math skills are included within the social studies activities).

Objective for Math Skills
• Given a specified budget, Mike will prepare a shopping list, use newspaper circulars to compare prices, and identify items to purchase within budget guidelines.

Functional Activities
1. Grocery purchasing activity:

Construct a shopping list of grocery items to make a simple meal.

Using circulars from local grocery stores, make price comparisons to determine the better buy.

Choose and cut out appropriate coupons for items on grocery list.

Compute total for purchases including special prices and coupons.

Shop for items for Home Economics class at the local grocery store.

To assist in transition: Shop for items at grocery store located close to Michael's home.

2. Catalog purchasing activity:

Using catalogs and local circulars, choose items to purchase within a set budget.

Fill out order form for those items and calculate price including sales tax and shipping costs.

Calculate the total for the same order using a credit card (including finance charges).

To assist in transition into high school: Prepare a personal weekly expense budget utilizing prices from the high school.

Objectives for Social Studies
- Identify and participate in discussions on local, national, and world current events topics from newspapers, television, and current periodicals.
- Use a map to plan a trip, calculating number of miles for the trip, identifying restaurants and hotels, and estimating the total cost for the trip.

Functional Activities
1. Current events activities:

   Using newspapers, identify current events topics.

   Discuss current events issues with regular education peers.

   Watch news and discuss events with parents, peers, and teacher.

   Read and recall current events articles from periodicals (e.g., *Newsweek*).

   Participate in current events games.

   To prepare for transition: Interview and orally report on high school sports figures.
2. Planning a trip activity:

   Choose a rental car from a local dealership. Call or visit dealerships, compare prices, miles per gallon, safety features, available options.

   Determine items needed for trip based on location, planned activities, season of the year. Write a detailed packing list.

   Plan route using map: Include miles, cities, routes to follow, time required for trip, and when to stop for gas.

   Call travel agencies (e.g., AAA) for literature on hotels, restaurants, leisure activities, and local tourist attractions.

   Read literature using symbols and abbreviations.

   Estimate cost of trip.

   State simple rules for driving a car (using driver's manual).

Middle School—Jennifer

In the middle school setting, Jennifer continued to receive most of her instruction within the Life Skills Support classroom. Her teachers continued to work collaboratively and gradually increased her exposure to integrated environments. Much of her academic instruction also was located in the community. Following are examples of Jennifer's objectives and functional activities in the seventh grade for the areas of mathematics and reading skills.

Objectives for Mathematics Skills
- Identify and select appropriate type and number of coins to purchase lunch.
- Demonstrate knowledge of concept of one-to-one correspondence through work activities.
- Select appropriate picture from picture schedule for daily scheduled activities.

Functional Activities

1. Identify coins and the amounts they represent (using real coins).
2. Choose appropriate coins and dollars to pay for lunch daily.
3. Match coins with lunch items (e.g., one quarter will buy a carton of milk).
4. Using a carton with individual compartments, place one item in each compartment.
5. Set table placing one plate, napkin, fork, knife, spoon, cup, and saucer at each place setting in Home Economics class.
6. Select appropriate picture menu for various activities in daily schedule.
7. To prepare for transition into the high school setting, count coins needed to pay for high school lunch.
8. Use appropriate coins in vending machines in high school.

Objectives for Reading Skills

- Will recognize her name by pointing to it in a variety of locations.
- Will read functional signs and demonstrate the meaning of each sign.

Functional Activities

1. Find school locker, gym locker, personal basket, and work materials by using her printed name as a cue (picture cues provided as needed).
2. Use functional signs to distinguish between women's and men's restrooms in school and in the community.
3. Will recognize basic safety signs and follow them (e.g., stop, green light, railroad).
4. Read picture thermometer and select clothing appropriate for the weather.
5. To prepare for transition into the high school setting, locate and use women's restrooms in the high school by reading the functional signs.

High School—Michael

When Michael reached high school age, his program focused more on skills to prepare him for his life after graduation. He was involved in a transition program that included job experience placements and part-time employment in addition to his functional academic program within the school setting. The following sample IEP objectives for Michael from his Language Arts and Social Studies classes show that his subject matter was integrated a great deal at this level.

Objectives for Language Arts

- Read and write using functional materials such as street signs, recipes, community signs, and job applications.
- Participate in job interviews using appropriate language and social interactions.
- Display appropriate behavior, language, and social skills in school and at job sites.
- Write sentences describing job experiences and explain orally.

Functional Activities

1. Functional materials activities:

    Read street and community signs and describe the meaning of each (e.g., "No Loitering," "Laundromat," "Yield to Pedestrians," or instructions on how to pump gas at self-service stations).

Read recipes and prepare meals in Home Economics class and at home for family.

Read want-ads from newspaper and apply for desired positions.

To prepare for transition into adult life: complete various job applications for job experience sites and local communities.

2. Job and job interview activities:

View and discuss examples and nonexamples of job interviews and job behaviors on videodisc.

Participate in videotaped role plays of job interviews.

To prepare for transition into adult life: Participate in real job interviews in the local community.

Describe orally and write sentences about the specific requirements of various jobs.

Display appropriate language and behavior in role plays of realistic job situations.

Display appropriate behavior at various job sites.

Objectives for Social Studies Skills
- Identify community resources and community leaders. List community services and demonstrate how to access those resources (using directories, phone, or written communication). Use appropriate community resources as needed.
- Michael will list at least 10 local laws and describe the meaning of each law with 90% accuracy.

Functional Activities
1. Use phone book (yellow pages) and newspapers to identify available community resources.
2. Contact needed resources and obtain necessary information.
3. Arrange interviews with community leaders to obtain more information.
4. To assist in transition after high school graduation: Develop list of references for job applications.
5. Access local ordinances from government officials.
6. Discuss the meanings of local laws and consequences for breaking the law.

High School—Jennifer

Jennifer's program in high school was not only functional within her Life Skills classroom, but a major portion of her instruction was located within an apartment setting in her local community where she could practice daily living, leisure, and recreational skills. Her activities were completed with a peer, a teacher, a parent, or the transition coach. The following objectives and activities for Jennifer are from her twelfth-grade program for Health/Physical Education and Mathematics. At this time in her program, subject areas were highly integrated and taught in actual community settings.

Objectives for Health/Physical Education
- Participate in appropriate community leisure activities.
- Differentiate between public and private settings for sexual behavior.

Functional Activities
1. Shoot pool with peers in community and at apartment site.
2. Initiate conversation with peers using communication device.

3. Listen to favorite music with peers.
4. Swim in community and apartment pool.
5. Participate in role-play situations regarding sexual behavior in public and private settings.
6. Use communication board to say "no" to unwanted physical touch.

Objectives for Mathematics
- Measure liquid and powdered substances using measuring cups.
- Use appropriate amount of money to pay for items in community settings.

Functional Activities
1. Measure to prepare simple meals.
2. Measure detergent to wash laundry.
3. Sort colors to wash laundry.
4. Use vending machines to buy items (e.g., soda, candy, gum, laundry detergent).
5. Use public telephones.
6. Use public transportation.
7. Shop and buy needed personal hygiene materials.
8. Use automated teller machine (ATM) as needed.

APPENDIX 4.A

Sample Individualized Education Plans for Michael and Jennifer

MICHAEL'S PLAN

Smithtown Area School District
Special Education Office
222 North Second Street, Smithtown, PA 10000

INDIVIDUAL EDUCATION PLAN

Student Name: Michael Fleetman   **ID:** 100–00-0000

Meeting Date: 9/01/95

Parent/Guardian: Henry and Marion Fleetman

Student Address: 108 Park Avenue Smithtown PA 10000

Phone: 358–8546   **Birthdate:** 8/18/85   **Age:** 10

School Year: 1995–1996   **School District:** Smithtown Area

Present Educational Levels

Evaluations used:
Burns/Roe Individual Reading Inventory
Brigance Inventory of Basic Skills
Curriculum-Based Assessment
Classroom Observation
Student and Parent Interview

Language Arts

On the Burns/Roe IRI, Michael was able to read words with 100% accuracy at the second grade level. At the third-grade level, he was able to identify words with 75% accuracy. In the reading comprehension section of the test, he was able to read and comprehend short passages on the third-grade level. He was able to identify the main idea, and answer vocabulary questions. His interpretations of cause and effect and sequencing skills were weak. Michael was very distractible during this session. The test was administered in a quiet room with only Michael and myself present.

In the area of written expression, Michael's skills are similar to a second grader's skills. He has a great deal of difficulty with spelling, use of proper grammar, and expressing his ideas on paper or orally.

Mathematics

Michael is able to perform the four basic operations on whole numbers at a level slightly below his grade-level peers. He can add and subtract numbers with simple regrouping. He is able to perform multiplication problems using a multiplication chart. Long division is difficult for him. In the area of problem solving, his limited reading skills hinder his progress. When the problem is read to him, he is able to complete simple word problems on the 2.5 level.

Functional Skills

Michael has made many friends both within his special education classes and regular education classes. He likes to joke with his peers, often at inappropriate times. He tends to display inappropriate social skills around adults.

Michael has a difficult time getting started and completing assigned tasks. He often gets distracted and does not finish his work. He also often strays from the topic of class discussions.

He likes to work in group situations; however, he rarely completes his work.

Michael does complete chores around his house such as taking out the trash and cleaning his room.

Strengths

Self-confident.
Strong verbal expressive skills.
Volunteers to help with classroom duties.
Sense of humor.
Generally friendly, cheerful attitude.
Desire to be involved in group activities.
Math calculation skills.

Needs

Improve reading and written communication skills.
Improve math skills.
Needs to curb inappropriate social behaviors with peers and adults.
Improve use of social courtesies.
Improve self-esteem.
Completion of assigned tasks.

Annual Goals

To improve Language Arts skills.
To improve Mathematics skills.
To improve basic Science skills.
To improve understanding of current events though Social Studies program.
To improve social communication skills.
To foster self-confidence in social and academic situations.
To increase awareness of job awareness and job behavior skills.
To increase appropriate behaviors both in and out of the classroom.
To increase physical health through physical education.

Short-Term Instructional Objectives

Michael will increase skills in the following with at least 75% accuracy. Evaluation will be based on teacher observation, curriculum-based assessment, parent input, student self-evaluation, and construction of a learning portfolio:

1. Identify a product as safe or unsafe by reading warning labels on various household containers.
2. When asked to provide personal identification information, will orally or in written form, provide the following information: name, complete home address, phone number, parents' names, school's name, and teacher's name.
3. Improve basic math computational skills in applications problems.
4. Improve skills in the areas of money and measurement.
5. Increase vocabulary skills (e.g.. circle, draw, write, poison).
6. Increase comprehension through more fluent reading.
7. Improve written expression through use of word processing.
8. Improve understanding of current events.
9. Identify and correct communication failures.
10. Use clarification skills when he does not understand another speaker's meaning.
11. Interpret and use functional/appropriate nonverbal communication skills (gestures, voice quality and volume, posture, etc.) in a variety of communication tasks.
12. Improve understanding of current events through daily newspaper activities.
13. Identify and describe various occupations.
14. Improve physical health by participating in sports and games in physical education class and in after-school activities.
15. Improve self-esteem and independence by participating in mainstreamed activities.
16. Improve ability to select appropriate comments to participate in group discussions.

Special Designed Instruction

Continual, immediate feedback and reinforcement.
Repeated practice.
Continued support and communication with family.
Extended time on test if necessary.
Take test in learning support classroom if necessary.

Small group instruction.
Use of manipulatives and concrete materials when possible.
Support for mainstream classes.
Adaptation of regular class curriculum and activities if necessary.
Consultation among special education teacher and regular education teachers.
Individualized instruction or curriculum when necessary.

Related Services: Speech and Language Support. Small group instruction with coaching, feedback, and monitoring for one class period per week.

Instructional Group (Assignment): Learning support.

Level of Intervention: Part-time.

Location of Intervention: Smithtown Elementary School.

Inclusion in Regular Education: Participates in regular education classes for Science, Social Studies, and nonacademics (music, art, physical education, library).

Date When Services and Programs Will Begin: September 1, 1995.

Anticipated Duration of Services and Programs: September 1, 1996.

Exit Criteria: When the student no longer requires specially designed instruction in academic areas as well as socially appropriate behavior as listed on his IEP.

IEP TEAM HAS ALSO CONSIDERED: N/A

TEAM MEMBERS:

NAME (typed or printed)	**POSITION** (typed or printed)	**SIGNATURE**
	Parent/Guardian	
	Building Principal/LEA	
	Special Education Teacher	
	Regular Education Teacher	
	Speech/ Language Specialist	
	Other (Specify)	
	Other (Specify)	

JENNIFER'S PLAN

Smithtown Area School District
Special Education Office
222 North Second Street, Smithtown, PA 10000

INDIVIDUAL EDUCATION PLAN

Student Name: Jennifer Godshall   **ID:** 200–00-0000

Meeting Date: 11/01/95

Parent/Guardian: Robert and Marjorie Godshall

Student Address: 330 Hamilton Avenue Smithtown PA 10000

Phone: 358–1992   **Birthdate:** 10/27/78   **Age:** 17

School Year: 1995–1996   **School District:** Smithtown Area

Present Educational Levels

Evaluations used:
Brigance Inventory of Basic Skills
Curriculum-Based Assessment
Classroom Observation
Parent Interview
Receptive One-Word Picture Vocabulary Test

Communication

Jennifer is a nonverbal student who communicates using gestures, and an assistive communication device, the Dyna Vox. She continues to need reminders to use her picture board. Results of the Receptive One-Word Picture Vocabulary Test indicate that Jennifer has a receptive language age of 3 years 2 months. This is a very low estimate of her receptive language skills: Some of the items she missed on the test she has used correctly on her communication board. Within the classroom and the Apartment program, Jennifer usually responds to her peers, but she does not initiate conversations with them.

Mathematics

Jennifer is able to identify a quarter as the coin required to buy a soda. She needs to improve her skills in identifying and using other coins.

Functional Skills

Jennifer requires assistance with her hygiene, toileting, eating, and mobility needs. She occasionally self-propels her wheelchair, but she needs to become more independent in this area. She does not feed herself.

Jennifer experiences difficulty adjusting to changes in her routine and her environment.

Strengths

Generally friendly attitude, is well-liked by peers.
Desire to be involved with group activities.
Improving skills in using Dyna Vox.
Can identify a quarter.
Responds well to peers.

Needs

Initiate interactions with peers and adults.
Improve independence skills.
Develop recreation/leisure interests.
Improve awareness of own sexuality.
Use appropriate coins to purchase items.

Annual Goals

Improve functioning within community.
Improve communication skills.
Improve overall functional movement.
Improve domestic skills to become more independent.

Short-Term Instructional Objectives

Jennifer will increase skills in the following to a functional level. Evaluation will be based on performance monitoring, teacher, job coach, and transition coordinator observations, parent interview, ecological inventory, and videotapes of her activities within the community:

1. Will activate the computer.
2. Will initiate communication with peers and adults.
3. Will prepare simple meals.
4. Will interact appropriately with peers and adults.
5. Will increase her ability to communicate through the use of augmentative communication.
6. Will make requests.
7. Use wheelchair for mobility.
8. Will participate in leisure activities at home and within the Apartment Program.
9. Will load a washing machine with clothes of similar colors, add appropriate amount of laundry detergent, and start the machine.
10. Will use microwave oven to prepare meals and snacks.
11. Will purchase personal items at store paying with proper amount of money.
12. Will participate in daily functional activities at the Apartment Program.

Specially Designed Instruction

Use of a touch window for computer.
Obtain student's attention prior to giving directions.
Present directions in small steps.
Use of on-task prompting.
Use of positive reinforcement.
Use of augmentative communication device: electronic device (Dyna Vox) gestures.
Small group and individualized instruction.
The Apartment Life Program.
Provide repeated opportunities for practice in classroom and in the community.
Use of computer-assisted instruction to reinforce vocabulary and basic concepts.
Use of positioning exercises recommended by physical therapist.
Use of range of motion exercises recommended by physical therapist.
Task-analysis for multistep activities.
Individualized curriculum.
Consultation among all teachers, job coach, transition coordinator, Apartment Life staff.
Job Coaching services.

Related Services: Speech/Language Therapy, Transportation for school, Apartment Program, and Community-Based Instruction, Physical and Occupational Therapy Consultation.

Instructional Group (Assignment): Life Skills Support, Speech/Language Support, Physical Therapy Support, Occupational Therapy Support.

Level of Intervention: Part-Time Life Skills, Supplemental Speech (2 times a week), OT/PT Consultative.

Location of Intervention: Smithtown Area High School and Apartment Life Program.

Inclusion in Regular Education: Homeroom, Adapted Physical Education, Lunch, Vo-Tech food service (1 period).

Date When Services and Programs Will Begin: November 1, 1995.

Anticipated Duration of Services and Programs: Graduation or November 1, 1996.

Exit Criteria: When the student no longer requires assistive devices or specially designed instruction as specified within IEP.

IEP TEAM HAS ALSO CONSIDERED:

{X} Adaptive Physical Education   {X} Assistive Devices

{X} Extended School Year   {X} Graduation Planning

{ } Student Health Concerns   { } Enrichment

{ } Information for Instructional Support Team   { } Behavior Management

{X} Transition Services   {X} Vocational Assessment

                                       { } Other (specify)

TEAM MEMBERS:

NAME (typed or printed)   **POSITION** (typed or printed)   **SIGNATURE**
Parent/Guardian
Building Principal/LEA
Special Education Teacher
Regular Education Teacher
Speech/Language Specialist
Physical Therapist
Transition Coordinator
Job Coach
Other (Specify)

REFERENCES

Algozzine, B., & Audette, B. (1992). Free and appropriate education for all students. Total quality and the transformation of American public education. *Remedial and Special Education, 13*(6), 8–18.

Bates, P., Morrow, S. A., Panscofar, E., & Sedlak, R. (1984). The effect of functional vs. nonfunctional activities on attitudes/expectations of nonhandicapped college students: What they see is what we get. *Journal of the Association for Persons with Severe Handicaps, 9*(2), 73–78.

Bernstein, G. S. (1989). In response: Social validity and the report of the ABA task force on right to effective treatment. *Behavior Analyst, 12*(1), 97.

Brolin, D. E. (1995). *Career education: A functional life skills approach* (3rd ed.). Englewood Cliffs, NJ: Prentice-Hall.

Browder, D. (1987). *Assessment of individuals with severe handicaps: An applied behavior approach to life skills assessment.* Baltimore: Paul H. Brookes.

Browder, D., & Snell, M. E. (1993). Functional academics. In M. S. Snell (Ed.), *Instruction of students with severe disabilities* (pp. 442–479). New York: Merrill.

Brown, L., Branston, M. B., Hamre-Nietupski, S., Pumpian, I., Certo, N., & Gruenewald, L. (1979). A strategy for developing chronological-age-appropriate and functional curricular content for severely handicapped adolescents and young adults. *Journal of Special Education, 13*(1), 81–90.

Brown, L., Nietupski, J., & Hamre-Nietupski, S. (1976). Criterion of ultimate functioning. In M. A. Thomas (Ed.), *Hey, don't forget about me!* (pp. 2–13). Reston, VA: Council for Exceptional Children.

Calhoun, M. L., & Calhoun, L. G. (1993). Age-appropriate activities: Effects on the social perception of adults with mental retardation. *Education and Training in Mental Retardation, 28,* 143–148.

Clark, G. M. (1994). Is a functional curriculum approach compatible with an inclusive education model? *Teaching Exceptional Children, 26*(2), 36–39.

Cosden, M. A., Gerber, M. M., Semmel, D. S., Goldman, S. R., & Semmel, M. I. (1987). Microcomputer use within micro-educational environments. *Exceptional Children, 53,* 399–409.

Cronin, M. E., & Patton, J. R. (1993). *Life skills instruction for all students with special needs.* Austin, TX: Pro-Ed.

Dever, R. B. (1988). Community living skills: A taxonomy. In D. E. Brolin (Ed.), *Career education: A functional life skills approach* (3rd Ed., p. 47). Englewood Cliffs, NJ: Prentice-Hall.

Dewey, J. (1937). *Democracy and education: An introduction to the philosophy of education.* New York: Macmillan.

Downing, J., & Perino, D. M. (1992). Functional versus standardized assessment procedures: Implications for educational programming. *Mental Retardation, 30*(5), 289–295.

Everington, C., & Stevenson, T. (1994). A giving experience: Using community service to promote community living skills and integration for individuals with severe disabilities. *Teaching Exceptional Children, 26*(3), 56–59.

Falvey, M. (1989). *Community-based curriculum: Instructional strategies for students with severe handicaps* (2nd ed.). Baltimore: Paul H. Brookes.

Ford, A. (1983). *The performance of moderately and severely handicapped students in community environments as a function of the cues available and the antecedent versus consequential teaching procedures used.* Unpublished doctoral dissertation, University of Wisconsin, Department of Behavioral Disabilities, Madison.

Fuchs, L. S., & Deno, S. L. (1994). Must instructionally useful performance assessment be based in the curriculum? *Exceptional Children, 61*(1), 15–24.

Grady, E. (1992). *The portfolio approach to assessment* (Fastback 341). Bloomington, IN: Phi Beta Kappa Educational Foundation.

Hamre-Nietupski, S., McDonald, J., & Nietupski, J. (1992). Integrating elementary students with multiple disabilities into supported regular classes: Challenges and solutions. *Teaching Exceptional Children, 24*(3), 6–9.

Helmke, L. M., Havekost, D. M., Patton, J. R., & Pollaway, E. A. (1994). Life skills programming: Development of a high school science course. *Teaching Exceptional Children, 26*(2), 49–53.

Hill, J., Wehman, P., & Horst, G. (1982). Toward generalization of appropriate leisure and social behavior in severely handicapped youth: Pinball machine use. *Journal of the Association for the Severely Handicapped, 6*(4), 38–44.

Horner, R., McDonnell, J. J., & Bellamy, G. (1986). Teaching generalized skills: General case instruction in simulation and community settings. In R. H. Horner, L. H. Meyer, & H. D. Fredericks (Eds.), *Education of learners with severe handicaps: Exemplary service strategies* (pp. 289–294). Baltimore: Paul H. Brookes.

Horner, R., Sprague, J., & Wilcox, B. (1982). General case programming for community activities. In B. Wilcox & G. Bellamy (Eds.), *Design of high school programs for severely handicapped persons* (pp. 61–98). Baltimore: Paul H. Brookes.

Kinzer, C., Sherwood, R., & Bransford, J. (1986). Computer strategies for education: Foundations and content-area applications. Columbus, OH: Merrill.

Langone, J. (1986). *Teaching retarded learners: Curriculum and methods for improving instruction.* Boston: Allyn & Bacon.

Male, M. (1988). *Special magic: Computers, classroom strategies, and exceptional students.* Mountain View, CA: Mayfield.

McDonnell, J., Hardman, M. L., Hightower, J., Keifer-O'Donnell, R., & Drew, C. (1993). Impact of community-based instruction on the development of adaptive behavior of secondary-level students with mental retardation. *American Journal on Mental Retardation, 97,* 575–584.

Meyer, C. A. (1992). What's the difference between authentic and performance assessment? *Educational Leadership 49*(8), 39–40.

Parette, H. P., Hourcade, J. J., & VanBiervliet, A. (1993). Selection of appropriate technology for children with disabilities. *Teaching Exceptional Children, 25*(3), 18–22.

Pierce, L. V., & O'Malley, J. M. (1992). *Performance and portfolio assessment for language minority students.* Washington, DC: National Clearinghouse for Bilingual Education.

Polloway, E. A., & Patton, J. R. (1993). *Strategies for teaching learners with special needs* (5th ed.). New York: Merrill.

Poteet, J. A., Choate, J. S., & Stewart, S. C. (1993). Performance assessment and special education: Practices and prospects. *Focus on Exceptional Children, 26,* 1–20.

Powers, J., & Ball, T. S. (1983). Video games to augment leisure programming in a state hospital residence for developmentally disabled clients. *Journal of Special Education Technology, 6*(1), 48–57.

Reed, P., & Bowser, G. (1991). *The role of the occupational and physical therapist in assistive technology.* Washington, DC: U.S. Department of Education, Center for Special Education Technology.

Sailor, W., Anderson, J., Halvorsen, A. T., Doering, K., Filler, J., & Goetz, L. (1989). *The comprehensive local school: Regular education for all students with disabilities.* Baltimore: Paul H. Brookes.

Salvia, J., & Ysseldyke, J. E. (1995). *Assessment* (6th ed.). Boston: Houghton Mifflin.

Sands, D. J., Adams, L., & Stout, D. M. (1995). A statewide exploration of the nature and use of curriculum in special education. *Exceptional Children, 62,* 68–83.

Sedlak, R. A., Doyle, M., & Schloss, P. (1982). Video games: A training and generalization demonstration for severely retarded adolescents. *Education and Training of the Mentally Retarded, 17*(5) 332–336.

Stainback, S., Stainback, W., & Forest, M. (1989). *Integration of students with severe handicaps into public schools.* Baltimore: Paul H. Brookes.

Steere, D. E., Wood, R., Panscofar, E. L., & Rucker, R. E. (1993). Vocational training for secondary-level students with severe disabilities. *Teaching Exceptional Children, 25*(4), 7–11.

Tucker, J. (1987). Curriculum-based assessment is no fad. *Collaborative Educator, 1*(4), 4, 10.

U.S. Department of Education, Office of Special Education Programs. (1993). *Fifteenth annual report to Congress on the implementation of the Individuals with Disabilities Act.* Washington, DC: Author.

van den Pol, R., Iwata, B., Ivanic, I., Page, T., Neef, N., & Whitley, F. (1981). Teaching the handicapped to eat in public places. *Journal of Applied Behavior Analysis, 14,* 61–69.

Wagner, M., Newman, L., D'Amico, R., Joy, E. D., Butler-Nalin, P., Marde, C., & Cox, R. (Eds.). (1991). Youth with disabilities: How are they doing? The first comprehensive report from the National Longitudinal Transition Study of Special Education Students. In D. E. Brolin (Ed.), *Career education: A functional life skills approach* (p. 9). Englewood Cliffs, NJ: Prentice-Hall.

Weaver, R., Landers, M. F., & Adams, S. (1991). Making curriculum functional: Special education and beyond. *Intervention in School and Clinic, 25,* 284–287.

Wehman, P., Moon, M. S., Everson, J., Wood, W., & Barcus, M. (1988). *Transition from school to work.* Baltimore: Paul H. Brookes.

Wissick, C. A., Lloyd, J. W., & Kinzie, M. B. (1992). The effects of community training using a videodisc-based simulation. *Journal of Special Education Technology, 11,* 207–222.

5

Financial Planning and Money Management

KATHRYN CLELAND BANKS

The goal of a longitudinal curriculum to develop financial planning and money management skills is financial independence as an expected educational outcome for the mild to moderate cognitively impaired learner upon transition from school to adult life.

Case Study: Thomas

Thomas is 21 years old. He completed high school in 1995 with a special education diploma. He is mildly intellectually disabled with a measured full-scale IQ of 58. He participated in the work evaluation and work adjustment program at Goodwill Industries through funding provided by the local rehabilitation office. After six months of training, he had a productivity rate of 85% to 90% of the industry standard required to hold a competitive job.

Over a three-year period, Thomas held three jobs. His first placement was as a janitor for a local restaurant. Thomas learned to travel independently, the duties of the job, and the social skills necessary to maintain employment. Tom's money management and financial planning skills, however, were not identified as deficient. He developed the habit of cashing his checks and stopping by the mall to make unnecessary purchases. He would return home without the money he needed for bus fare or lunch the following week. Tom's teachers talked to him about being more responsible with his money, but they did not intervene with his behavior. They felt that money management and financial planning were issues that were up to Thomas and his mother to address.

Tom's family experienced a loss of income directly related to his earnings. As a result of this development as well as his inability to manage money and plan for expenses, his mother encouraged him to quit work. His mother insisted that he return to school. She complained to his teachers that Thomas did not understand how to manage his money. She asked his teachers to help him build money management skills.

The total dollar amount spent by the local rehabilitation office and the Joint Training Partnership Program on work evaluation, work adjustment, job coach assistance, and subsidized employment training came to approximately $10,000. This figure does not include the cost of Tom's special education program at school.

For the next year, Thomas remained in school where his teachers attempted to help him develop money management and financial planning skills. They were able to increase his counting skills from sums of up to $5.00 to sums of up to $20.00. He demonstrated an understanding of job-related expenses using class work and drill activities.

Tom's next job placement lasted only three weeks. He was unable to gain the speed necessary to maintain employment in the area of his expressed interest as a pants presser for a local dry cleaners. He was then placed at a neighborhood grocery store as a courtesy clerk earning minimum wage plus tips. A job coach was provided to assist Thomas with locating merchandise in the store. He was able to transfer the mobility skills he developed from the placement at the restaurant. He is currently maintaining employment at the grocery store; however, his mother reports that he continues to cash his checks and return home with little or no money. He makes inappropriate purchases, and she fears that he is cheated out of some of the money. He often needs her assistance with transportation and lunch money to return to work.

DESCRIPTION OF CURRICULUM

Financial independence is an appropriate and necessary educational outcome for individuals with disabilities. Adequate money management and financial planning skills are necessary for any individual to function independently in society. Financial independence as an outcome of the educational experience for youth with disabilities requires mastery of the same money management and financial planning skills that are required of all learners. However, the curriculum and methods of instruction for these students will differ significantly from the instructional requirements of their nondisabled peers (Langone, 1992).

SPECIAL NEEDS

Individuals with mild cognitive deficits fall significantly behind general education students academically. By the time they reach high school, the functional grade level scores attained will be six or more years behind the grade levels of their nondisabled peers (Dreshler & Schumaker, 1986). The ability to generalize or transfer skills from one setting to another is poor for those with mild retardation and increases in difficulty as the level of cognitive impairment increases (Langone, 1992). These factors make it difficult for instructors to teach money management and financial planning skills in the context of a traditional classroom setting. Yet, individuals with mild to moderate mental retardation are most often served in traditional classroom settings that afford limited opportunity for community-based instruction (Roessler, 1991). The curriculum accepted by most classroom teachers of mild to moderate cognitively impaired students will focus primarily on money management and financial planning skills taught in isolation using methods focused on the repetition of facts and lists (Langone, 1992).

It is well documented that this population retains and transfers, to the greatest degree, those skills learned in the situation where the skills are to be used. Although individuals with mild disability express the same need and desire for financial independence as their nondisabled peers, their slower ability to learn, retain, and transfer skills requires a more concrete approach to instruction. Instructional approaches that use functional materials in the most realistic setting available will promote the retention and transfer of money management and financial planning skills better than any other curriculum design (Brolin, 1993).

Curriculum for this population needs to be longitudinal in design where money management and financial planning skills are systematically presented beginning in the elementary grades. The curriculum should build continuously on a network of prerequisite skills and should be presented throughout the secondary grades until the special needs learner transitions into adult life as a financially independent individual. Materials used in instruction must mimic those most often used in adult environments. For example, money used to teach counting skills should always be copies of real currency. All materials used to facilitate the mastery of money management and financial planning skills from elementary to high school, should be as close as possible to the same items used by financially independent adults.

SEQUENCE OF INSTRUCTION

A longitudinal curriculum for money management and financial planning also reflects, as closely as possible, the sequence of events that will take place when the skill is to be used. For example, where shopping takes place once a week, the concept that food purchases are planned ahead using lists and coupons involves financial planning skills. To develop these skills, teachers can plan lessons using a classroom shopping center and activities that build skills for the shopping process. Community-based shopping trips can reinforce the skills introduced and practiced in the classroom center. An example plan would be to develop activities that reinforce shopping skills by practicing the skills first in a classroom shopping center. In Table 5.1, the sequence of activities for students to practice grocery store skills in a real-life environment is described.

Teachers should use variations of these activities to encourage mastery and promote the transfer of money management and financial planning skills. Community-based sites can vary as much as possible to further encourage the transfer of skills. Skill maintenance activities should continue after student mastery has been documented. More complex shopping trips that involve major purchases such as appliances, electronics, furniture, or real estate can be added as the student's skill levels increase.

The sequence of activities described in Table 5.1 is at an advanced level and is appropriate for the upper grades. Students on advanced levels can also develop the skills to compare layaway purchases with credit card and rent-to-own purchases. Too often, mild to moderately retarded adults are tempted by high-priced items at the rent-to-own store over the delayed gratification of a layaway plan. The difference in cost is extreme and difficult for these individuals to distinguish without training.

TABLE 5.1   Learning Grocery Purchasing Skills

Sequence	Activity
Monday	Students will plan individual weekly menus to include food items needed for breakfast, lunch, supper, and snacks.
Tuesday	Students will compile an individual list of items and food amounts needed to complete the menu. Menus are based on student preference.
Wednesday	Students will check weekly advertisements and coupons against items needed. Substitutions may be made for specials and coupon items that save money.
Thursday	Students will compute the approximate cost of the menu using pricing information obtained from store advertisements and coupons. Students will compare the cost of the items with their personal weekly budget. Weekly budgets are based on realistic income potential.
Friday	Students will visit the supermarket and practice selecting the items on the list. Students will calculate the difference between estimated and actual cost. Calculators with tapes can be used to total items for purchase as these items are selected. Students will record the information in a weekly budget ledger.

Using credit, checking interest rates, and understanding billing procedures are important skills that need to be addressed at the secondary level (Brolin, 1993).

Prerequisite skills are needed to accomplish the plan outlined in Table 5.1. Elementary and middle school teachers can develop students' mastery of these skills by using lessons similar in scope and sequence, but with less skill content required for mastery.

Table 5.2 shows how an elementary or middle school teacher would plan a group lesson around a shopping trip. Group activities for elementary and middle school students will develop prerequisite skills such as measurement, vocabulary, and creative writing in a context that students will use as adults. Teachers could promote a contest where classes compete for prizes for the best cookie or the best advertisement. The income produced by the sale provides a tangible and realistic avenue for teaching prerequisite skills such as counting and projecting food costs. Students with well-developed skills could serve as peer tutors for those students needing more extensive remediation and drill. Activities such as these promote inclusion in the regular education classroom (Jones & Carlier, 1995).

Lessons using a similar "plan of action" format are useful in teaching money management and financial planning skills because they focus on the development of skills in the context of their use. They are also much more interesting than the paper-and-pencil rote learning activities taught in many special needs classrooms today. The prerequisite skills that are developed in the learning process will be needed for the individual to begin to develop the higher order skills required for learning to budget money and prepare for both expected and unexpected expenses as an adult. If these concepts are started in the early grades, students will become accustomed to planning for expenses, comparing prices, calculating food amounts, estimating costs, and adjusting menus to save money. Students involved in this instructional format will learn how to write number words using a check. They will learn how to

TABLE 5.2   Planning and Shopping Trip

Sequence	Activity
Monday	As a group, students will discuss and make plans for a cookie sale. They decide on the cookie of choice. Students will plan the sale and begin to advertise the sale to peers, adults, and family.
Tuesday	Students will make a list of the required ingredients needed to make the cookie of choice. Amounts needed for each ingredient are calculated. Students will continue to advertise the sale to peers, adults, and family.
Wednesday	Students will compute the estimated cost of ingredients needed. They will look at advertisements and coupons available to reduce costs. Students will estimate the cost of the ingredients and determine the price of the cookie. Students will add the price per cookie to the advertised sale. Orders will be taken and money will be collected.
Thursday	Students will go to the supermarket to select and purchase ingredients. They will compare estimated costs to actual costs. Students will return to school and make a schedule for baking and distributing the cookies the next day. They will continue to collect money.
Friday	Students will bake, package, and deliver cookies to customers. Students will compute the cost and profit of the sale. The students will evaluate their sale, discuss possible changes, and decide how to continue the program.

sign their name using the method that they will most often employ as adults. They will be exposed to and master the prerequisite skills that are necessary for true financial independence.

SELF-DETERMINATION

Individuals with mild to moderate cognitive impairments need training that will empower them to take control of their finances. Assuming that they cannot achieve financial independence, especially at an early age, will delay the instruction and support that fosters independence. The delay may also serve to perpetrate the assumption in the general public that these individuals are unable to attain this goal. Taking control of the cognitively impaired individual's personal finances may seem like appropriate assistance, but in reality, this kind of help fosters dependence. When adults with disabilities depend on others to perform money management and financial planning tasks, they are unlikely to feel empowered by their income. This perception will diminish their ability to function in the community independently in their own mind as well in the minds of others (Wehmeyer & Kelchner, 1995). Individuals with disabilities have a right to expect that their planned educational program will focus on the acquisition of skills that will foster their financial independence as adults. Professionals have the responsibility for providing instruction and support that will promote the educational outcome of financial independence for mild to moderate cognitively impaired individuals. This responsibility begins with school entry and does not end until transition to adult life.

COMMUNITY-BASED INSTRUCTION

Community-based instruction is an essential tool in a longitudinal curriculum for money management and financial planning for the mild to moderate cognitively impaired learner. Teachers need to develop relationships with local bankers and retail managers that allow frequent access to community sites for instructional purposes. Relationships with community sites should begin in the elementary grades and continue throughout the secondary level as a regular component to any curriculum designed to teach financial planning and money management skills. Educators will find support from the community because programs that develop money management and financial planning skills in potential customers are useful to local businesses. Well-trained consumers make good customers. Usually banks and retail stores have slow periods that will facilitate student visitation. Many have customer service representatives eager to assist teachers with training. Some communities have established school-business partnerships in an organized effort to link the school and community. These business partners often provide time and resources that encourage employee involvement in school-related activities.

CLASSROOM LEARNING CENTERS

Teachers who videotape community-based trips will find these tapes useful in the development of authentic classroom learning centers. Written permission to videotape both students and locations should be secured prior to taping (Salend, 1995). Learning centers are important links to community sites in the classroom setting and can be used to reinforce a variety of skills. These centers could be developed at every grade level to replicate the essential functions of the community sites. For example, a banking center that is equipped with necessary forms using an appropriate format can be developed by a team of teachers and shared between classroom locations. A banking center allows students in the classroom to concentrate on the repetition of banking skills using a realistic banking environment. Local banks should be helpful in providing the forms needed to build money management and financial planning skills. Teachers can adapt the forms based on the instructional level of the learner. The center should be constructed as close as possible to the physical structure of a local bank.

Other centers, such as a supermarket or drugstore center can be developed using the same format. Teachers who work together to create realistic centers will improve the quality of instruction for the essential functions of community sites as well as increase the availability of a variety of centers for use in their classrooms. Realistic banking and marketing centers will enhance students' ability to generalize financial planning and money management skills in different locations. The classroom that resembles the community is more functional than one that is traditional in appearance.

PARENTAL SUPPORT AND PARTICIPATION

Perhaps the single most often overlooked factor in the process of developing skills related to financial independence for mild to moderate cognitively impaired individuals is that of parental participation and support. Too often, teachers will have limited contact with parents. This contact usually centers around annual review meetings or behavioral problems that occur in the school setting. Parental participation and support for the development of skills that lead to financial independence for this population is critical. Without support, teachers will find that their most creative and coordinated instructional plans are taught in a vacuum that precludes student success.

There are several barriers to parental participation and support. Parents may feel out of place or intimidated by the educational setting. They may be uncomfortable with the professionals involved with their child. Educational jargon may be difficult for parents to translate into the action steps they must take to be true participants in the skill-building process. They may be reluctant to accept their child's disability and not able to provide assistance at that particular time.

The amount of time needed for the parent to participate may be difficult to arrange around the care of small children or elderly family members. The parent's level of competence in the skills related to financial independence may be deficient or below those levels necessary to assist in the skill-building process.

There may be a cultural or a language barrier. Parents may have a different financial agenda for their child than one that leads to financial independence. They may place academic skills such as reading or general math skills at a higher priority than money management or financial planning skills. This barrier may be especially true in the elementary grades. The parents may be physically or emotionally disabled themselves.

Teachers may feel it is easier to plan and carry out objectives for their students without the interference of parents. Teachers may make little effort beyond what is required by law to involve parents because it is time consuming and difficult to maintain. The problem with this approach is that very little personally appropriate or realistic financial skills training can occur in a vacuum. Individuals with mild retardation often need the help and support of everyone involved in their educational program to successfully develop the skills they need to become financially independent adults.

Each family has a unique method for managing household finances. Issues surrounding personal finances are extremely private in this culture and are often considered off limits to everyone but the individuals immediately involved. The subject is, at best, tricky to discuss in the school setting. Despite the barriers involved, teachers who recognize parental support and participation as critical components to a student's success in developing financial skills will be ahead of those professionals who resist. The teacher who shows true concern for the student's need and desire for a financially independent future can overcome many of the barriers involved in promoting parental participation. A teacher who is tactful and nonjudgmental in approaching parents, will more easily gain true support for the development of money management and financial planning skills in mild to moderate cognitively impaired students.

When questions are focused on the student's access to money, parents will be more willing to share personal information. In addition, the parents' responses will give the teacher an idea of how money is managed in the home. Teachers can determine the parents attitude concerning their child's ability to become financially independent using this type of dialogue. It goes without saying that parents must feel that personal information will be kept strictly confidential. Privacy is of particular importance when dealing with personal issues related to money management and financial planning.

When the teacher has built a bridge of support, the following question should be asked of the parent: What goals do you have for your child related to money management and financial planning in the coming year? This question can never be asked too early. When a parent responds, wise teachers will work diligently to develop the particular skill that is requested. They will pay close attention to the parent's wishes, and contact the parent often to report progress and solicit help in reaching the goal. Even if the parent wants a teacher to teach skills not related to money management and financial planning, it is important for the teacher to stick to the skill that is requested first. Many parents of special needs students complain that teachers do not give homework. This approach provides the perfect opportunity to give homework because teachers can count on parental support.

As the desired skill is developed, the teacher can ask the parent for additional assistance in skill building. Teachers should share this information in the minutes of the next IEP review so that the new teacher will be able to continue to build the bridge of support. If possible, teachers should contact each other to share information such as "Tom's mother is really sensitive about his inability to count money. She will welcome any home assignments you send to reinforce this skill." Teachers will save time if they do not have to uncover this type of information. This knowledge will assist the new teacher in making a positive initial contact with the parent. This process will also build esteem in parents as they will feel that they are important to their child's educational progress. Parents who feel like they are an active participant will be more available to support the teacher (Roessler, 1991). These parents may also help to build support from other parents as well.

As parents begin to see increases in the skills related to financial independence, it will become easier for them to relinquish some of the control that fosters dependence in the mild to moderately retarded population. A true partnership between the school and home can help build the confidence and the self-determination skills that these individuals need to become financially independent as they reach adulthood. When the process begins in the early grades and is fostered throughout high school, and into adult life, financial independence as an educational outcome for mild to moderate cognitively impaired individuals will be closer to reality than it is at the present time.

GENERAL APPROACHES TO ASSESSMENT

The purpose of assessment is to determine the present level of performance of the individual skill or group of skills related to money management and financial planning for the mild to moderate special needs learner. An accurate assessment of present levels of performance will enable the IEP team to develop goals and objectives that will target skills that need to be developed or increased. An ongoing evaluation of performance levels will assist teachers with the task of moving as rapidly as possible from one skill level to the next. The assessment process is a key component to the success of a longitudinal curriculum for money management and financial planning. By targeting the specific skill areas that need work, teachers can make the best use of instructional time.

The main components of an accurate assessment involve observation, task analysis, situational assessment, and a measurement of general knowledge. The evaluator would combine the results of these components to reflect an accurate picture of the learner's present levels of performance related to money management and financial planning skills. Consistently accurate data collected over a designated period is a key factor to the results of any assessment. Simply measuring a student once or twice per year to obtain a general grade level score will do little to document the present level of student performance for money management and financial planning skills. The data collection process is painstaking and time consuming. It is not usually the favorite teaching activity of most professionals. Yet, this aspect of the assessment process is extremely important to an accurate evaluation of the present levels of skill performance. Teachers who are disciplined in the collection of data will find that the process will enable them to make the best use of limited instructional time.

GENERAL KNOWLEDGE ASSESSMENT

There are many excellent instruments available to determine the general performance level of money management and financial planning skills for mild-to-moderate cognitively impaired individuals. The Brigance Diagnostic Inventory of Essential Skills is often used to determine functional skill levels for the mildly disabled student. The section of the test related to money and finance skills is an accurate general measure of these functional skill levels in the individual learner (Brigance, 1981). The recently introduced Brigance Diagnostic Life Skills Inventory also has a comprehensive assessment for money and finance skills. The test ranges in difficulty from second- to eighth-grade levels. There is also a "quick screen" battery that contains a small sample of items to provide teachers with a short diagnostic placement level. Teachers may also use the screen to verify results obtained from other assessments and to identify those skills that need more extensive evaluation. The Money and Finance sections of the Brigance Diagnostic Life Skills Inventory provide thorough coverage of the skills necessary for financial independence (Brigance, 1995). A number of these skills are listed in Figure 5.1. Both inventories are comprehensive criterion-referenced assessments that identify the precise skills mastered by the learner to determine the next step in the instruction of the curriculum.

The Woodcock-Johnson Scales of Independent Behavior also include a section on money and value that can be used with students who function below second-grade level. This battery would be useful for individuals who have not yet reached the skill level assessed by the Brigance Diagnostic Life Skills Inventory. Both instruments include norms to obtain standard scores when this information is needed.

These examples of assessment batteries are useful tools for evaluating a student's present level of performance in general knowledge related to money and finance skills.

SITUATIONAL ASSESSMENT

Situational assessment involves the process of observing a student when performing a skill or group of skills and recording the level of independence demonstrated by the individual performing the task. The situation where the skill is observed and

FIGURE 5.1   Brigance Life Skills Inventory: Money and Finance Sections

Introduction

Assessment for Basic Skills
   Equivalent Values of Coins and the Dollar Bills
   Totals Values of Groups of Coins
   Convert Coins
   Price Signs
   Make Changes
   Computes Totals for Purchases
   Comprehends and Computes Savings on Purchases
   Uses Charts and Tables to Compute Expenses
   Completes Application for Credit Card
   Completes Deposit Slips, Writes Checks, and Computes Balance

Supplemental and Related Lists/Skill Sequences
   Equivalent Values of Collections of Bill
   Totals Values of Groups of Bills
   Convert Bills
   Price Signs
   Price Signs
   Makes Change
   Makes Change
   Computes Totals, Including Tax, for Purchases
   Determines How Many Items of a Given Price Can Be Purchased with a Given Amount of Money
   Addition of Whole Numbers
   Totals for Purchases
   Comprehends and Computes Savings on Purchases
   Subtraction of Whole Numbers
   Spends Money Wisely (Thrifty Buying)
   Uses Locally Available Charts and Tables to Compute Savings/Differences
   Interprets Information from Graphs
   Credit Skills and Knowledge
   Computes Interest on Loans
   Bank Statement and Checkbook
   Checking Account Skills and Knowledge
   Savings Account Skills and Knowledge
   Miscellaneous Money Management and Consumer Skills

Note. From *Brigance Life Skills Inventory*, by A. H. Brigance, 1995, N. Billercia, MA: Curriculum Associates.

recorded can be a classroom setting or a community site. The location will depend on the skill being assessed and the instructional level of the student (Clees, 1992).

Situational assessments are extremely valuable to a total assessment battery to determine the present level of performance because teachers are able to observe and rate the skill as it is being performed by the student. The student's general knowledge of the skill in isolation will not indicate the extent that the skill will transfer to a real-life situation.

For example, a situational assessment for check-writing skills would involve teacher observation of the student writing a real check. The assessment would be even more accurate if the student was using his or her own checkbook to write a check for a purchase such as a class ring. The closer the situation is to the real-life event, the more accurately a teacher can determine true performance levels.

An elementary teacher performing a similar situational assessment of check-writing skills would observe a student writing a check using an enlarged check format. If, over a designated period, the student has correctly written the vocabulary and placed the appropriate information on the correct lines and in the correct boxes, then the teacher can assume that the student has mastered the prerequisite skills for writing a personal check. The teacher can then move on to more complicated skills while providing activities for the maintenance of check-writing skills.

If teachers use a vocabulary, spelling, and cursive writing test to evaluate the skills in isolation of the real format for writing a check, they will probably find that the student has not yet mastered the ability to transfer these skills to a realistic check-writing situation. Teachers may then find they will need to devote additional instructional time to the development of check-writing skills related to real-life situations.

Data sheets such as the one depicted in Figure 5.2 document skill acquisition and help the teacher reflect which skills are to be assessed. Wise teachers will combine grading responsibilities with data collection duties to document student progress. The data sheets enable parents and students to understand exactly how a grade is calculated. Students who see their progress and know the next step can recognize that they are moving steadily toward a shared goal and are less likely to appear bored and lazy in class.

CURRICULUM DESIGN

The design for a longitudinal curriculum for money management and financial planning consists of a systematic series of goals and objectives formulated to build skills from elementary, to middle, to high school levels until the mild to moderate cognitively impaired learner has developed the highest level of personal financial independence possible. The design begins with the identification of the prerequisite skills needed to develop money management and financial planning skills at the elementary level. Once the prerequisite skills have been identified, they should be taught in the context that best allows the student to transfer the skill to the next level.

An example of a longitudinal curriculum design for writing a personal check is described in Table 5.3. The format used is related to the Life Centered Career Education Curriculum developed by Brolin (1978). Elementary teachers begin to develop check-writing skills as soon as a student has mastered the basic prerequisite skills of manuscript and cursive writing. Basic vocabulary and arithmetic skills needed for financial planning and money management are introduced using an enlarged check format to practice writing the words and symbols appropriately.

Students build check-writing vocabulary and cursive writing skills throughout elementary grades until they demonstrate a level of independence that allows them to move to a standard size check format. Teachers increase check-writing skills by creating more complicated scenarios for students to write personal checks. To reinforce skills, students work in groups where advanced-level students tutor peers who need additional reinforcement for skill mastery.

Middle school teachers continue the skill-building process. They will introduce more complex situations that involve check writing and use variations of the different personal check formats available at local banks. Middle school banking centers should include a variety of the materials currently used by adults to write personal

FIGURE 5.2   Data Sheet for Documenting Skill Acquisition

Student Name: _____   Date: _____

Day	Things to Do	Entry	Intermediate	Advanced	Exit
Monday	Breakfast Menu				
	Lunch Menu				
	Supper Menu				
	Snack Menu				
	Generic Menu				
Tuesday	Breakfast List				
	Lunch List				
	Supper List				
	Snack List				
	Generic List				
Wednesday	Breakfast-Coupons/Specials				
	Lunch-Coupons/Specials				
	Supper-Coupons/Specials				
	Snack-Coupons/Specials				
	Generic-Coupons/Specials				
Thursday	Breakfast-Cost Estimate				
	Lunch-Cost Estimate				
	Supper-Cost Estimate				
	Snack-Cost Estimate				
	Generic-Cost Estimate				
Friday	CBI Items Found				
	Items Totaled				
	Items Compared with Budget				
	Items Recorded in Ledger				

Key: Entry: Needs Total Assistance.
Intermediate: Needs Prompts.
Advanced: Needs Minimal Assistance.
Exit: Independent Skill.
Generic: Butter/Sugar/Salt etc.

checks. Parents can include their child in check-writing duties in the home (Brolin, 1993). The use of a variety of formats will enable students to transfer skills. They will also be better able to make an informed choice regarding the particular format they will use when they open a personal checking account.

High school teachers will reinforce check-writing skills using banking centers, personal budget lessons, and community-based field trips to local banks. If high school teachers do not have to spend instructional time teaching students how to

TABLE 5.3   Curriculum Design for Money Management

DOMAIN:	*Daily Living Skills Elementary Level*
COMPETENCY:	*Managing Personal Finances*
SUBCOMPETENCY:	*Prerequisite Skills for Writing a Personal Check*

Objective	Activities/Strategies	Adult/Peer Roles
Master prerequisite skills for writing a personal check.	• Students will demonstrate mastery of basic manuscript and cursive alphabet and number symbols. • Students will use an enlarged check format to develop the following skills: Write number words on appropriate lines. Write corresponding number symbols in appropriate boxes. Write proper nouns related to purchase. Sign name on appropriate line. • Students will demonstrate an understanding of the basic vocabulary involved in writing a check. • Students will practice skills in a classroom banking center. • Students will visit local banks to obtain information related to check writing.	• Parents will assist student with homework related to writing a check using an enlarged check format. • Parent will allow student to observe the parent writing personal checks for household expenses. • Bank personnel will discuss the types of checks and account services offered by the bank in basic terms. • Student will work in groups where students with advanced skills can tutor those needing additional instruction.

Note. Adapted from *Life Centered Career Education: A Competency Based Approach* (4th edition), by D. E. Brolin, 1993, p. 27, Reston, VA: The Council for Exceptional Children. Copyright 1993 by the Council for Exceptional Children.

write a personal check, they can devote more instructional time to visiting local banks. They will be able to determine which bank has the best services related to the individual needs of the student. Students will have a distinct frame of reference in which to choose a bank and the appropriate check format for their individual needs. High school teachers will be able to assist working students with opening and maintaining a personal checking account. Parents who have been actively involved in the skill-building process will be better able to assist their mild to moderately retarded child to enter adulthood with the skills necessary to open and maintain a personal checking account.

An enormous variety of resources are available for teachers to use in developing a longitudinal curriculum for money management and financial planning. The

Life Centered Career Education (LCCE) competency-based curriculum developed by Brolin (1978) is one comprehensive resource that is excellent for this purpose. Modifications to the LCCE curriculum for the moderately retarded population are currently being developed by Loyd and Brolin (1995). Elementary teachers can use these materials to scale down the objectives of the LCCE curriculum into the prerequisite skills required for the mastery of money management and financial planning skills. The breakdown for the prerequisite skills needed to write a personal check is described in Table 5.3. Additional goals and objectives for teaching money management and financial planning skills could be developed using the LCCE format such as described in Table 5.4. Elementary teachers can focus on instruction for identified prerequisite skills at the earliest available time using materials that are as much like those used in real life as possible.

   Life Skills Instruction for All Students with Special Needs: A Practical Guide for Integrating Real Life Content into the Curriculum, by Cronin and Patton (1993), is also an outstanding resource for the development of a longitudinal money management and financial planning curriculum. Information related to age level, reading level, and instructional format is given for commercially available resources in an extensive

TABLE 5.4   Additional Goals for Teaching Money Management

DOMAIN:	*Daily Living Skills Secondary Level*
COMPETENCY:	*Managing Personal Finances*
SUBCOMPETENCY:	*Use Banking Services*

Objective	Activities/Strategies	Adult/Peer Roles
Write checks, make deposits, and record checking transactions.	• Students take a field trip to a bank to discuss procedures to follow when writing checks, making deposits, and recording checking account transactions. • Students list on a poster the process of writing checks, making deposits, and recording transactions. • Class practices with mock checks, deposit slips, check registers, and monthly bank statements. • Class discusses the importance of accurate checking account record keeping. • Class devises mock checking system and students use checks to purchase classroom items.	• Parents inform the student of the procedures for writing checks, making deposits, and recording transactions. • Parents discuss with the student the family's checking account transactions and recording. • Bank personnel discusses the procedures for writing checks, making deposits, and recording transactions. • Parents assist student in making an actual transaction and in record keeping. • Parents involve the student in balancing the family's checking account.

Note. From *Life Centered Career Education: A Competency Based Approach* (4th edition, p. 27), by D. E. Brolin, 1993, Reston, VA: The Council for Exceptional Children. Copyright 1993 by The Council for Exceptional Children. Reprinted with permission.

appendix. Detailed advice from community resource professionals in the field is also given. Although not as detailed as LCCE, the book is well written and easy to use by professionals in the process of curriculum development.

SAMPLE INDIVIDUAL EDUCATION PLAN

Thomas: One Dollar at a Time

Tom's mother feels that he should let her cash his checks and handle his money. She feels he should contribute to household expenses. Thomas refuses to comply and asserts his resentment that his mother wants to control his life as well as his money. He acknowledges his responsibility for family expenses, but expresses the desire to move into his own place. He feels he can be independent if he can learn money management and financial planning skills.

Instead of assuming responsibility for Tom's finances, his mother can assist him with the task of developing the skills he needs to manage his money. The assistance of an advocate may be useful to help set the plan in motion and encourage its completion. For a six-month period, Thomas and his mother will agree and commit to the following plan. They will acknowledge to each other that a positive change in Tom's behavior regarding financial independence is important to both of them.

Each payday, Thomas will go to the bank with the advocate and cash his check in the form of one-dollar bills. Thomas will count his money with the teller. With permission from Thomas, the advocate could pre-arrange this process with the bank. Tom's mother may or may not go to the bank. This is a personal choice that will be made by Thomas. The advocate will decrease the bank visits as soon as Thomas is independent in the skills necessary to complete the task on his own.

Thomas earns about $60.00 per week. He works 5 to 6 days on a part-time basis. His weekly transportation expense is $12.00, and his weekly snack and lunch expense is $18.00. He needs a new supply of soap, shaving cream, razors, toothpaste, and deodorant. These items will cost approximately $12.00. He will soon need two new work shirts, one pair of work pants and a pair of walking shoes. If he puts aside $5.00 per week for three months, he will have saved $60.00 toward those purchases. The items listed will cost approximately $120.00.

At home, Thomas and his mother list each expense on a single sheet of paper and arrange them in order of their importance. Thomas will keep a ledger of income, expenses, and savings. He will need assistance at first but will be able to develop the skills to do this task independently. Thomas will count out the amount of each expense from the stack of one-dollar bills. He will, with his mother's assistance, decide where to keep the money safe for the next week's expenses. When finished, he will have $13.00 left as discretionary income. Thirteen dollars sounds like a lot of spending money for someone who makes $60.00 per week; but Thomas has grown accustomed to having his entire paycheck as discretionary income.

It will be difficult for Thomas and his mother to follow through with this plan of action. They will both need encouragement, support, and a high level of commitment to make it successful. If Thomas returns to his former habits, his mother will have to make the decision to continue to allow his dependence, or to let him walk to work and miss lunch until he receives the next paycheck.

Tables 5.5 and 5.6 show a sample individual education plan for the development of money management and financial planning skills for Thomas. If Thomas were still a student, the special education teacher would assume the responsibilities of the advocate.

TABLE 5.5 Individual Educational Program Semiannual Goal and Short-Term Instructional Objectives Mild Intellectual Disabilities/Advocate—Family Support Program Service

Student: *Thomas*   Person to Provide Service: *Advocate/Parent*   DOB: *1/1/74*   Date: 9/1/95–3/1/96

Semiannual Goal: *To increase skills related to cashing a payroll check, making a budget, and keeping a journal of expenses over a six-month period.*

Short-Term Instructional Objectives Thomas will:	Criteria for Mastery	Method of Evaluation	Projected Date of Review	Mastery (Dates) Yes	No
1. Practice cashing a copy of his payroll check using photocopies of one-dollar bills.	Build mastery levels until he can maintain 100% or 10 of 10 attempts.	Observation Data Sheets	11/1/95		
2. Count the one-dollar bills to equal the amount of his check. Begin with photocopies and convert to real currency.	Build mastery levels until he can maintain 100% or 10 of 10 attempts.	Observation Data Sheets	11/1/95 3/1/96		
3. Count the one-dollar bills related to his travel and lunch expenses. Begin with photocopies and convert to real currency.	Build mastery levels until he can maintain 100% or 10 of 10 attempts.	Observation Data Sheets	11/1/95 3/1/96		
4. List expected expenses and estimate the cost of the items.	8 of 10 attempts to list and estimate actual cost of future expenses.	Lists/Discussion Observation/Data Sheets	1/1/96 3/1/96		
5. Make a list of items he wants, but does not need to purchase and estimate the cost of the items.	8 of 10 attempts to list and estimate actual cost of desired items.	Lists/Discussion Observation/Data Sheets	1/1/96 3/1/96		
6. Make a weekly budget of expenses related to personal needs and desires.	8 of 10 attempts to make a realistic budget of needs and desires.	Budget Forms Discussion Observation/Data Sheets	3/1/96		
7. Record amounts of each expense in a journal. Document weekly and monthly amounts accurately. Review each prior week's expenses.	Build a mastery of recording skills until he can maintain 100% accuracy or 10 of 10 attempts.	Journal Sheets Discussion Observation/Data Sheets	3/1/96		

TABLE 5.6   Individual Educational Program Semiannual Goal and Short-Term Instructional Objectives
Mild Intellectual Disabilities/Advocate—Family Support Program/Service

Student: *Thomas* Person to Provide Service: *Advocate/Parent*   DOB: *1/1/74*   Date: *9/1/95–3/1/96*
Semiannual Goal: *To increase banking skills related to cashing a payroll check using a local banking facility over a six-month period.*

Short-Term Instructional Objectives Thomas will:	Criteria for Mastery	Method of Evaluation	Projected Dates of Review	Mastery (Dates) Yes	No
1. Obtain a picture ID using his original birth certificate and Social Security card.	100% of one attempt.	Copy of ID card	9/15/95		
2. Travel to a local bank of choice and cash his payroll check with the assistance of the advocate.	100% of one attempt per week for 8 weeks.	Self-Report by Thomas/observation/data sheets/cash from check	11/1/95		
3. Without assistance, request that the teller cash the check with one-dollar bills.	100% of one attempt per week for 8 weeks.	Observation/Data Sheets/Self-Report by Thomas/correct amount of cash	11/1/95 3/1/96		
4. Count the cash prior to leaving the bank with the assistance of the advocate and/or teller for the first 8 weeks and independently for the next 4 weeks.	100% of one attempt per week for 8 weeks.	Observation/Data Sheet/count cash with advocate/count cash with teller/Self-Report by Thomas	11/1/95 3/1/96		
5. Secure the money on his person in a safe place and return home immediately with all cash with assistance.	100% of one attempt per week for 8 weeks with assistance. 100% of one attempt per week for 4 weeks independently.	Safe return home with appropriate amount of cash/Observation/Data Sheet/Self-Report by Thomas	12/1/95 3/1/96		
6. Correctly complete Steps 1–5 independently.	100% of one attempt per week for 4 weeks.	Observation/Data Sheet/Self-Report by Thomas/Observation by Mother/Safe return home with all cash	3/1/96		

Initially, Thomas will use photocopies of one-dollar bills to practice the plan prior to cashing his checks. The guided practice will move to real money as soon as Thomas feels he can complete the task. The advocate will assist Thomas' mother in gradually taking a secondary role while sticking to the decision not to encourage his dependence on her for additional money. As Thomas develops skills in financial planning and money management, he and his mother will determine together how he will meet his financial obligations to his family. As Thomas begins to see the reality of financial planning and money management related to his income, expenses, and personal desires, he will become more responsible in his spending decisions.

CONCLUSION

The purpose of this chapter has been to highlight the necessity of money management and financial independence for individuals with disabilities. A number of figures and tables have been presented to provide examples of the types of different money management skills that might be taught. These skills need to be presented across the school-age curriculum, from elementary through secondary.

REFERENCES

Brigance, A. H. (1981). *Brigance Diagnostic Inventory of Essential Skills*. N. Billercia, MA: Curriculum Associates.

Brigance, A. H. (1995). *Brigance Life Skills Inventory*. N. Billercia, MA: Curriculum Associates.

Brolin, D. E. (1978). *Life centered career education: A competency based approach*. Reston, VA: Council for Exceptional Children.

Brolin, D. E. (1993). *Life centered career education: A competency based approach* (4th ed.). Reston, VA: Council for Exceptional Children.

Clees, T. (1992). Community living. In P. J. McLaughlin & P. Wehman (Eds.), *Developmental disabilities: A handbook of best practices* (pp. 228–267). Boston: Andover/Butterworth/Heinemann.

Cronin, M., & Patton, J. (1993). *Life skills instruction for all students with special needs: A practical guide for integrating real-life content into the curriculum*. Austin, TX: Pro-Ed.

Dreshler, D., & Schumaker, J. B. (1986). Leaving strategies: An instructional alternative for low achieving students. *Exceptional Child, 52*, 583–590.

Jones, M. M., & Carlier, L. L. (1995). Creating inclusionary opportunities for learners with multiple disabilities: A team teaching approach. *Teaching Exceptional Children, 27*(3), 23–27.

Langone, J. (1992). *Developmental disabilities: A handbook of best practices* (pp. 1–15) Boston: Andover/Butterworth/Heinemann.

Loyd, R., & Brolin, D. E. (1995). *Life centered career education: Modified curriculum for individuals with moderate disabilities*. Reston, VA: Council for Exceptional Children.

Roessler, R. (1991). A problem solving approach to implementing career education. *Career Development for Exceptional Individuals, 14*(1), 59–66.

Salend, S. J. (1995). Using video cassette recorder technology in special education classrooms. *Teaching Exceptional Children, 27*(3), 4–9.

Wehmeyer, M. L., & Kelchner, K. (1995). Measuring the autonomy of adolescents and adults with mental retardation: A self report from Autonomous Functional Checklist. *Career Development for Exceptional Individuals, 18*(1), 3–21.

6

Socialization, Peer Relationships, and Self-Esteem

Shirley K. Chandler

Sara C. Pankaskie

Accurately or not, much of society today views students with disabilities as socially incompetent because of their behaviors. These behaviors may include disrupting the classroom environment, fighting, name calling or withdrawal, isolation, and avoidance of peers. They may have trouble making or sustaining relationships, interacting with others, and may also have problems with diminished self-esteem. The following case study is typical of many of the students receiving special education services today.

Case Study

Michael is a 15-year-old middle school student. He is the older of two children, with a brother, age 10. Michael, his brother, and his mother reside in an apartment complex near the school he attends. Michael's father and mother are divorced, and he sees his father on an irregular basis. His mother works full-time as a secretary/bookkeeper for an auto dealer.

Starting in the first grade, Michael has had a great deal of difficulty in school. His major difficulties began with the development of reading skills. He was unable to stay on task and had difficulty grasping basic reading concepts. By the third grade, Michael was exhibiting poor social skills, was fighting with his classmates, and had low impulse control. He was held back in the third grade, but exhibited no significant gains by the end of that school year.

Prior to his entry into fourth grade, Michael was referred to the school psychologist for an evaluation. The results of this evaluation showed that Michael had a severe learning disability in the area of reading comprehension. He also exhibited Attention Deficit Disorder (ADD) tendencies that, according to the psychologist, might be the result of frustration over his inability to understand his schoolwork and the repeated failures he was experiencing in the classroom. This evaluation resulted in his placement in a Resource Room for help with his reading skills.

By the time Michael reached middle school, he had been placed in a self-contained special education classroom. He currently has a primary diagnosis of severe learning disability and a secondary diagnosis of an emotional disability. His only mainstreamed classes are art, music, and gym.

On his last triennial psychological, Michael's full-scale IQ was 103. However, scores on the academic tests showed him to be three to four years behind his peers on academic subjects. Achievement testing showed abilities and strengths in understanding mechanical principles; visualizing in three dimension; and working rapidly and accurately with his hands. Michael also exhibited strengths in utilizing basic math computational skills. These strength areas are consistent with Michael's desire to work as an auto mechanic. Testing observations by the psychologist note that Michael has trouble concentrating and staying on task. Michael's teachers also note that he acts out in class, picks fights with his classmates, is a discipline problem, and has been placed on in-school suspension on several occasions. He does not complete assignments or bring required materials from home when directed to. Michael copes with discipline by lashing out when directly confronted. He will swear and/or start a fight with his classmates or brother.

During Michael's latest IEP conference, his mother stated that Michael has been staying out late at night, and has been experimenting with alcohol. She states that he does not appear to have any friends and she is afraid that he will drop out of school rather than face more failure at the high school level. She also states that he fights constantly with his younger brother, who is a high achiever and is in the gifted class at the same middle school.

When interviewed by the school psychologist, Michael stated that he hated school and felt it was a waste of time. He was unwilling to accept any blame for his behavior and placed the blame on his classmates for his discipline problems. He states that his classmates are "retards" and that he does not belong in that class. He also stated that his mother and father like his brother better because he is smarter. Michael blames his mother for the parents' divorce and the father's failure to visit on a regular basis. When asked about his use of alcohol, Michael denied it and denied the use of any drugs.

Michael stated that he would like to work on cars or maybe join the Army but was unable to articulate the requirements for either of these two jobs. He also stated that he will quit school if he has to stay in that "retard" class when he goes to high school. When asked what he would do if he quit school, Michael said he wasn't sure and that maybe he would get a job at Pizza II.

Based on his observations and his interview with Michael, the school psychologist has recommended that Michael become involved in individual counseling for self-esteem and impulse control. He also recommended participation in group counseling for peer relationship and social skill development. Additionally, he has recommended to the mother that Michael and his family become involved in some form of family counseling.

DESCRIPTION OF CURRICULUM

For most of us, success in everyday life is tied to our ability to get along with others. We think of socialization as something that takes place naturally, while we are growing up (Gaynor, Breland, Harlacher, Tondorf, & Zivkovich, 1992). Research and classroom records have shown us that this process does not work for many students with disabilities. Failures in the area of socialization occur on a daily basis in our classrooms. While Dodge (1989) and Gaynor et al. (1992) have noted that the "socially rejected" child is identified as being liked by few or no peers, Kendrick (1991) and Bergen (1993) point out that the development of positive self-esteem does not occur without "at least one truly caring, accepting friend."

Becoming competent in social skills "is no more inevitable than becoming competent in academics. Both require the opportunity to learn" (Gaynor et al., 1992). The teaching of social skills is often left to chance. However, many students with disabilities may not learn these skills unless they are taught.

For students with learning disabilities or poor academic achievement, the classroom becomes a "breeding ground for feelings of inadequacy and worthlessness" (Curwin, 1993). Students who are continually confronted with failure have little opportunity to develop a positive self-esteem.

The parents of students with disabilities have begun to call for a restructure of the special education system. Prompted by their dissatisfaction with a dual system of education (Stainback & Stainback, 1984), parents are calling for not only a restructuring of special education (Reynolds, Wang, & Walberg, 1987), but a revamping of the entire delivery system for individuals with disabilities (Gartner & Lipsky, 1987). This dissatisfaction arises not only from the poor academic performance of students who have been removed from regular education classes, but also from the effects segregated classes have had on the social development of their children (Gaynor et al., 1992). Not only does segregation limit the opportunities that students with disabilities have to develop appropriate relationships with their peers without disabilities, it also limits their opportunities to learn important social skills and lowers self-esteem.

SOCIALIZATION

Socialization in the current context refers to how an individual interacts with others and participates in society. Along with the skills needed for positive peer relationships and good self-esteem, as described in this chapter, socialization addresses those skills, behaviors, and attitudes necessary for an individual to survive as a member of a group. The things we are learn in this area help us become better family members, workers, and citizens, regardless of our culture or social status. Each culture (and subculture) establishes its own set of minimum expectations. Individuals who ignore or violate these group expectations (or never acquire the skills and behaviors necessary to meet them) may be isolated, ostracized, or, at worst, punished.

The importance of socialization cannot be overstated. The necessity of teaching basic social skills, behaviors, and attitudes is obvious. Teachers who are responsible for teaching students with disabilities have a special need to become familiar with assessments and curricula that address these skills.

There are many curricula that address the general area of socialization. Some of them are listed in Table 6.1. This list represents only a sample of the curricula available commercially. It is intended to represent a cross-section of approaches to teaching social skills, presentation modes, and target ages and groups. Some "classics" (e.g., Skillstreaming) as well as some relatively new and innovative approaches (e.g., The Nine Steps) are included. For further discussion on assessing and teaching social skills, see those sections in this chapter.

SELF-ESTEEM

Individuals who feel good about themselves find it easier to feel good about things around them, including school. These positive feelings often lead to increased effort, resulting in praise that, in turn, results in even better self-feelings. A very positive cycle. But what of people who do not have a history of success? They may have diminished feelings of self-worth and negative feelings about the world around them. They may, in fact, even blame the world for their failures. They do not approach school with much enthusiasm and therefore often are low achievers. Low achievement is met with criticism that results in even lower self-esteem.

Many students with disabilities have low self-esteem. Whether a result of repeated failure and criticism or a cause of it, if not reversed or ameliorated, it often leads to school failure or dropping out. If students are to make progress in school, they need to feel at least confident enough to make a reasonable effort. Teachers can be a positive force in this respect. They can be a positive role model and can set reasonably high standards and project a positive mind-set that students can attain them.

Certain principles of self-esteem help in the understanding of the way it affects behavior:

- Children will act in ways that increase their sense of self-worth and satisfaction.
- Children will act in ways that confirm their self-concept.
- Children will act in ways that maintain a consistent self-image, regardless of changing circumstances.

What these mean in a practical sense is that (1) it may be difficult to change a child's self-image once it has been ingrained, and (2) a teacher should not be discouraged if first attempts at raising low self-esteem are met with a continuation of behaviors that lead to failure. The child may simply be trying to "correct" the misconception that he or she is a worthwhile individual. In time, this can change if the teacher provides enough opportunities for success and teaches coping skills. One of the most basic things a teacher can do to help students feel better about themselves is to give assignments or tasks early in the lesson that they know students can accomplish successfully. Other things a teacher can do throughout the day is to praise good effort, reinforce successive approximations, and provide feedback in such a way as not to criticize the child, but to point out how the response falls short of the desired outcome—something they are both working on together.

TABLE 6.1   Sample Curricula

Curriculum Name	Type			Comments
	SE	PR	SO*	
ACCEPTS. Walker, McConnell, Holmes, Todis, Walker, & Golden. (1983). Pro-Ed.			X	Elementary school students with mild to moderate disabilities. Manual, activities manual, and videos.
ACCESS. (1987). Walker, Todis, Holmes, & Horton. Pro-Ed.	X	X	X	Secondary school students with mild to moderate disabilities. Manual, activities manual, and videos.
ASSET: A Social Skills Program for Adolescents. (1981). Hazel, Schumaker, Sherman, & Sheldon-Widgen. Research Press.		X	X	Ages 13–18. Group activities. Leader's guide, home notes, questionnaires, skill sheets, videos, and audiotapes.
Developing Understanding of Self and Others, (Rev. ed.). (1982). Dinkmeyer & Dinkmeyer, Jr. American Guidance Service.			X	Levels for grades K–2 and 3–4. Problem-solve with role play and discussion. Audiotapes, pictures, puppets, activity cards and guide. *Drug Free,* an extension program created by Joyce L. McKay and the DUSO authors, available separately.
Esteem Builders: A K–8 Self-Esteem Curriculum for Improving Student Achievement, Behavior and School Climate. (1989). Borba. Jalmar Press.	X			Grades K–8. Leader's manual with activities outlined.
Getting Along with Others: Teaching Social Effectiveness to Children. (1983). Jackson, Jackson, & Monroe. Research Press.			X	Elementary students with suggested modifications for other levels. List of suggested assessment tools, activity notebook, and program guide with teacher scripts. Secondary level also available.
Learning to Live Drug Free: A Curriculum Model for Prevention. (1990). U.S. Dept. of Educ. Washington, DC.	X	X	X	Grades K–12. Teachers manual, teaching tips and activities, with supplemental list of resources.
Mind Your Manners. (1987). Leighton & Stanfield. James Stanfield.			X	Teens and young adults with developmental disabilities. Teacher-training video, guide, and 6-part video.
PEERS: A Program for Remediating Social Withdrawal in School. (1978). Hops, Guild, Fleischman, Paine, Street, Walker, & Greenwood. CORBEH.			X	Socially withdrawn students in primary grades. Teacher and consultant guides, packet, and program materials.
Personal Power: Peer Interaction Skills. (1983). Wells. Pro-Ed.		X		Exceptional and at-risk students in Grades 4–12. Instructor's guide, handouts, pretests, and lesson plan manual.

(continued)

TABLE 6.1   *(Continued)*

Curriculum Name	SE	PR	SO*	Comments
Skillstreaming in Early Childhood. McGinnis & Goldstein. Research Press.		X	X	Preschool and kindergarten. Program booklet and reproducible.
Skillstreaming the Adolescent. (1980). Goldstein, Sprafkin, Geershaw, & Klein. Research Press.		X	X	Adolescents.
Skillstreaming the Elementary School Child. (1984). McGinnis & Goldstein. Research Press.		X	X	Mainstreamed students with LD, MH and BD. Teacher guide, reproducible and self-monitoring forms. Audio and video tapes available.
Social Skills for Daily Living. (1988). Schumaker, Hazel, & Pederson. American Guidance Service.			X	Students with mild disabilities, ages 12–21. For individual or small group instruction. Manual, student workbook, materials, management forms and progress wall chart.
Social Skills in the School and Community. (1991). Sargent, (Ed.). CEC Publications.			X	Mainstreamed primary, intermediate, junior high and high school levels.
Social Skills Strategies, Books A & B. (1989). Gajewski & Mayo. Thinking Publications.			X	Adolescents with BD, LD, MR, SLI; or anyone with skill, performance or self-control deficits. Two-year program with daily activities.
Social Decision-making Skills: Curriculum Guide for the Elementary Grades. (1989). Elias & Clabby. Aspen Publishers, Inc.			X	Students in regular and special education, Grades K–6. Guide with scripted lessons and student worksheets.
Taking Part: Introducing Social Skills to Young Children. (1991). Cartledge & Kleefeld. American Guidance Service.			X	Preschool to Grade 3, regular and exceptional students. Manual, puppets, stickers, posters and activity sheets.
Teaching Social Skills: A Practical Instructional Approach. (1992). Rutherford, Chipman, DiGangi, & Anderson. CEC Publications.			X	
The Nine Steps of Self-Esteem: The Ta Da Video Series. (1990). Nimco, Inc. Piney Mountain Press, Inc.	X			Teens. Ten 30-minute video lessons.
The Integrated Preschool Curriculum Procedures for Socially Integrating Young Handicapped. (1988). Odom & Associates. University of Washington Press.		X	X	Preschool.

TABLE 6.1   *(Continued)*

Curriculum Name	Type			Comments
	SE	PR	SO*	
Thinking It Through. Foxx & Bittle. Research Press.			X	Separate guides for teachers of adolescents with developmental disabilities, chronic mental illness, brain injuries, and emotional problems.
Thinking, Feeling, Behaving. (1989). Vernon. Research Press.	X	X	X	Levels for Grades 1–6 and 7–12. Small groups or individuals in regular and special education settings. Uses art, stories, games, and discussion.

Key: SE = Self-esteem; PR = Peer relationships; SO = Socialization.

Helping others has been found to help certain students feel better about themselves (Curwin, 1993). Students experiencing problems at school or at home may be assigned to assist less able children (those with profound retardation or physical disabilities). Students reported better attitudes toward school when they felt needed and appreciated. Being in a helping mode rather than a needing mode appears to increase self-esteem and feelings of control over the school environment.

Cooperative learning methods have been found to increase self-esteem as well as academic skills (Slavin, 1991). Cooperative learning involves having learners of different ability levels work in small groups or teams to help one another. It may be used as a supplement to direct teacher instruction in all kinds of settings (e.g., academic and vocational).

Self-esteem is linked to achievement, but it is also closely related to peer acceptance. Students who lack the skills necessary to make and keep friends will suffer greatly, especially during the middle school years. Students in included settings often exhibit gains in general adaptability, normalization, and socialization, but there are some possible disadvantages for students in the area of self-esteem. Students with disabilities in the mainstream may exhibit lower self-esteem than their nondisabled peers (Kauffman, Gerber, & Semmel, 1988). Another issue surrounding self-esteem and inclusion is the lack of opportunity to associate with other people with disabilities (Stainback, Stainback, East, & Sapon-Shevin, 1994). This problem may be addressed by inviting role models to career days, by showing films about people with disabilities who have succeeded in life, or by giving students opportunities to attend support meetings or social events for people with like disabilities. This not only benefits students with disabilities but also helps to change attitudes among students without disabilities.

The conditions that improve self-concept include feeling connected, feeling unique, and feeling empowered. Anything teachers can do to see that these conditions exist in the classroom and throughout the school, the more likely it is that students will have good feelings about themselves.

Several of the curricula in Table 6.1 address self-esteem along with other topics in socialization. Two address it specifically: *Esteem Builders,* and *The Nine Steps of Self-Esteem.*

PEER RELATIONSHIPS

Peer relationships are defined as the interactions an individual has with others of the same general age and life situation. Human beings are by nature gregarious. Since the beginning of recorded history, the ability to get along with family, clan, and tribe members has often meant the difference between survival and extinction. The area of peer relationships is related to the general area of socialization but differs from it in that the focus is on the relationship with one's age and situational cohorts rather than all the people and things in one's environment.

The exact relationship between good peer relationships and social skills is unclear. Many general social attributes (such as friendliness) as well as specific behaviors (such as sharing) appear to be correlated to peer acceptance, but it is still a mystery why some children are "popular" and some are neglected or overtly rejected by peers.

Peer relationships are important at all ages: We learn from peers as small children, we share with them as young people, we benefit from their support and friendship as adults, and we depend on them as we get older. In terms of development, however, they are probably most important during early adolescence. This is the time when being like one's peers takes on a special significance as young people struggle with separating their identity from that of their parents.

In general, a teacher who wants to help an individual student be better accepted by his or her peers should (1) observe what the popular students do (and do not do) in particular situations; (2) compare this with what the target student does in similar situations; (3) identify the discrepancies, if any; and (4) teach the missing skills. (A note of caution: Sometimes popular students can engage in what might be considered inappropriate or unfriendly behaviors and the "halo" effect will cover them. The same behaviors on the part of an unpopular child would probably not be condoned by the peer group.) An example of teaching to the template (the model presented by the popular child) follows:

> The teacher observes that popular students join activities in progress by praising one of the group members ("Nice throw, Jack! Can I toss one?"), whereas the unpopular student may push into the group and grab the ball away ("Watch me, I can throw way better than that"). The teacher would attempt to teach the target student how to use praise to enter a group.

Most of the social skills curricula in Table 6.1 include peer relationships, and one, *Personal Power,* targets peer relationships for exceptional and at-risk students.

No description of curriculum development would be complete without examining two of the major areas of difficulty that students with disabilities, and all students for that matter, face as they grow, mature, and attempt to develop peer relationships and a self-identify. Pressure to use/abuse alcohol and drugs and to have early and/or unprotected sex is a common occurrence for today's student. A child who is seeking to be accepted by his or her peers may succumb to this pressure.

Substance Abuse.   Drug and alcohol abuse are not just the scourge of some elements of our society. People from all classes and races have been affected in one way or another. Relevant to this discussion is the prevention of drug and alcohol abuse among persons with disabilities. It is difficult to find data on the prevalence of substance abuse specifically among school-age students with disabilities. There may be several reasons for this. First, most data of this type, while reported for age, sex, and race, is seldom reported by disability. Also, there is a feeling in some disability communities (e.g., the deaf community) that this is a shameful weakness and should not be discussed outside the family. Families and friends of people with disabilities sometimes view substance abuse as an entitlement. That is, people with disabilities have a rough life and so should be excused if they take refuge in drugs (Cavaliere, 1995). Data can be found, however, for drug use among young people in general. Cavaliere cited a recent survey by a national parents organization that shows that substance abuse among schoolchildren is up again for the fourth year in a row. The survey findings include the following: One out of five high school seniors smokes marijuana at least monthly in high schools, the use of cocaine and hallucinogens has reached its highest level since 1988. Cigarette use was reported by 44% of high school students. Only 34% said that their parents talked to them frequently about the dangers of drug use, 33% indicated that parents do not set strict rules, and half (50%) said they are not disciplined consistently for breaking rules (Levy, 1995). Though there is no information specifically related to students with disabilities, if the preceding information about drug and alcohol use is indicative, the seriousness of the problem and the need for interventions are clear. There are several approaches to substance prevention and reduction for children and young adults. In a general sense, they are similar to approaches used to teach other social skills (e.g., cognitive, affective, social learning). The difference in programs that specifically target substance prevention and reduction is in the focus. In the curricula listing (Table 6.1), three programs with this focus are included: one for the early years (*Developing an Understanding of Self and Others*) and one that spans the K–3, 4–6, 7–8, and 9–12 grades (*Learning to Live Drug Free*).

Self-Protection.   Children and young adults with disabilities are not immune to social problems other than drug and alcohol abuse. They also must protect themselves from physical, psychological, and sexual abuse. The question of whether children with disabilities are more likely to be victims of abuse is still unanswered because of a lack of longitudinal, community-based studies (Martin, 1995). But teachers are aware that some special education students are either at risk for exploitation or misuse their sexuality in a misguided attempt to attain popularity (Walker-Hirsch & Champagne, 1991). Many social skills curricula devote a portion of their training to teaching young people to resist peer pressure, but few specifically address the area of protection from inappropriate behavior by nonpeers. One such program, *Circles,* helps students with limited cognitive and communication skills distinguish different kinds of touching from people who are at different levels of intimacy in their lives (e.g., family, intimate friends, acquaintances). It also teaches students that it is okay to say "no" to inappropriate kinds of touch. Other curricula that address these areas are included in the social skills curriculum matrix in Table 6.1.

GENERAL APPROACHES TO ASSESSMENT

Assessment of an individual's social skills, self-esteem, or the ability to develop relationships with one's peers may be done for a variety of reasons. These reasons may include determining eligibility for services, identifying specific areas of need for training, or tracking student progress during an intervention program. Assessment may also be needed for educational decision making, and it is often requested because someone (teacher, parent, administrator) feels the child has a problem such as excessive undesirable behaviors or deficient prosocial behaviors. The type and method of assessment will depend on the purpose of the assessment. Table 6.2 displays some of the more commonly used assessment instruments in the three areas related to social skills: self-esteem, peer relationships, and socialization.

The type and method of assessment used will depend primarily on the purpose of the assessment. Although there are many commercially available instruments, teachers often find that direct observation is the shortest distance between a problem and its solution. Carter and Sugai (1989) point out that "although it may be difficult, direct observation of student performance should be used as much as possible." Assessment may be accomplished in many ways: rating scales, interviews; formal testing; previous anecdotal reports; but for classroom interventions, direct observation is best because it provides direct information about the frequency, duration, intensity, and context of the behavior.

Additional considerations in making an assessment and ultimately choosing an intervention are whether the student's problem is due to a skills deficit or a performance deficit and whether the student has an emotional or conduct disorder. One way of making this determination is through the use of the *Behavior Problem Checklist* listed in Table 6.2. This model helps teachers decide, after observing the student and reviewing pertinent records, whether the student has certain prosocial behaviors in his or her repertoire, and if so, what may be interfering with their consistent performance. Once this determination has been made, an appropriate intervention may be developed.

FUNCTIONAL ASSESSMENT OF CHALLENGING BEHAVIORS

For persons with the most severe disabilities, the assessment of social skills presents a different set of issues. Students who display such challenging behaviors as hitting self or others, running away, destruction of property, and other disruptive behaviors present serious problems for teachers. To intervene with students who display such behaviors, it is extremely important to know the *why* of these acts. The most effective way to do this is to conduct a functional assessment (Foster-Johnson & Dunlap, 1993). The results of the assessment may then be used to write a meaningful program to replace the disruptive behavior with other, more productive and prosocial behaviors.

The first step in functional assessment (after identifying and defining the target behavior) is to gather information about when, where, and under what conditions the student exhibits the behavior. Answer the questions: (1) What happens right after? (2) What were the conditions in the classroom before, during, and after the behavior (which staff were present, what tasks were being presented, what were the other students doing, what was I doing)? It puts the focus on the environment instead of entirely on the student. This is because one of the basic assumptions of this approach is the *challenging behaviors are related to the concept in which they occur.*

TABLE 6.2   Selected Assessments

Assessment Name	Assessment Method	SE	PR	SO*	Comments
AAMR Adaptive Behavior Scale—School Edition: 2 Lambert, Leland, & Nihira (1993). Riverside Publishing, Inc.	Interview			X	Primarily for use with children with mr ages 3–16. Assesses social and daily living skills and behaviors.
Assessment of Interpersonal Relations Bracken (1993). Riverside Publishing, Inc.	Observer-rater		X	X	Designed for use with adolescents. Co-normed with the MDSCS.
Behavior Problem Checklist—R Quay & Peterson (1987). Quay Publishers	Observer-rater checklist		X	X	For grades K–8. More useful for classifying than for specifying behavior deficits.
Behavior Rating Profile—2 Brown & Hammill (1990). Pro-Ed	Interview and self-report		X	X	For Grades 1–12. School, home, and peer ratings. Extensive validity measures.
Burks' Behavior Rating Scales. Burks (1977). Western Psychological Services	Observer-rater			X	For grades 1–9. Assesses 18 categories with 10 min. administration.
Child Behavior Checklist R Achenback & Edelbrock (1991). Achenback Press	Interview and self-report		X	X	For ages 4–16. Multiple informants/environments. Useful for placement and programming.
Coopersmith Self-Esteem Inventories Coopersmith (1981). Publishers Test Service	Self-report	X			Measures attitudes in social, academic, and personal contexts.
Culture-Free Self-Esteem Inventories—2nd Battle (1981). Psychological and Educational Publications, Inc.	Self-report	X			For children and adults. Assesses five areas. Standardized on special populations.
Devereaux Behavior Rating Scales Smith (1966). Devereaux Foundation Press	Observer		X	X	Three scales covering K–age 18. Covers wide range of behaviors.
Matson Evaluation of Social Skills Matson et al. (1983). *Behavior and Research Therapy, 21,* 335–340.	Observer-rater or self-report			X	For ages 4–18. Assesses observable social behaviors.
Multi-Dimensional Self-Concept Scale (MDSCS) Bracken (1992). Riverside Publishing, Inc.	Self-report	X			For ages 9–19. Assesses social affect, competence, academic, family and physical functioning.

(continued)

TABLE 6.2   *(Continued)*

Assessment Name	Assessment Method	SE	PR	SO*	Comments
Perceived Competence Scale Hartner (1982). *Child Development, 53,* 87–97.	Interview (parent report)			X	For preschool-adolescence. Screens for developmental as well as emotional problems.
Personality Inventory for Children Wirt, Lachar, Klienedinst, Seat, & Broen (1977). Western Psychological Press	Self-report	X			For elementary and jr. high students. Assesses general self-worth and three subareas.
Piers-Harris Self-Concept Scale Piers & Harris (1969). Western Psychological Services	Self-report	X			For Grades 3–12. Assesses physical appearance, popularity, and happiness.
Scales of Independent Behavior Bruininks, Woodcock, Weatherman, & Hill (1984). Riverside Publishing, Inc.	Interview			X	For infant–adult. Assesses three major areas plus a problem behavior scale. Statistically linked to the Woodcock-Johnson Psych Ed Battery.
Self-Esteem Index Brown & Alexander (1991). Psychological and Educational Publications, Inc.	Self-report	X			For ages 7–19. For group or individual. Results in self-esteem quotient.
Social-Emotional Dimension Scale Hutton & Roberts (1986). Pro-Ed	Observer-rater		X	X	For ages 5–6 to 18–6. Covers six areas including avoidance of peer and teacher interaction.
Social Skills Rating System Gresham & Elliott (1990). AGS	Observer-rater and self-report		X	X	For preschool–high school. Age, gender, and disability normed. Multiple informants rate both frequency and importance.
Test of Pragmatic Language Phelps-Terasaki & Phelps-Gunn (1992). Riverside Publishing, Inc.	Interview (test prompt)			X	For K–jr. high. Assesses how students use language socially to achieve goals.
Vineland Adaptive Behavior Checklists Sparrow, Balla, & Cicchetti (1984). AGS	Interview or direct observation			X	Three versions cover birth–adult (including classroom version for ages 3–13).
Weller-Strawser Scales of Adaptive Behavior Weller & Strawser (1981). Academic Therapy Publications	Observer-rater		X	X	Elementary and secondary versions. Results in profile with recommendations.

* *Key:* SE = Self-esteem; PR = Peer relationships; SO = Socialization.

The next step is to determine the purpose served by the behavior based on the information gathered. This step addresses another basic assumption: *challenging behaviors serve a purpose for the student.* What are some of these possible purposes? Teachers often assume that the purpose is to gain attention, and undoubtedly, these behaviors do get attention. Consider, however, some other possibilities such as (1) escape from an undesirable or difficult task; (2) avoidance of nonreinforcing activities or events; (3) need for more sensory stimulation; or (4) the desire for something for which the student has no words or way to communicate. Students with a limited repertoire of behaviors may use the same behavior to signal different things, and a certain behavior exhibited by one student may have an entirely different function when exhibited by another student.

The final step is to develop an intervention based on the most likely reason for the behavior. This intervention may be as simple as attending to behaviors incompatible with the challenging behavior, and as complex as developing a communication system that provides the student with an alternative way of asking for what he or she wants instead of acting out to obtain it.

FUNCTIONAL ASSESSMENT FOR STUDENTS WITH MILD DISABILITIES

Students with mild disabilities who have problem behaviors are often not viewed in the same way as their peers with more severe disabilities. This is probably because students with mild disabilities have the ability to use language to communicate. For some students, however, including those with normal and above intelligence, part of their disability is the inability to express ideas and feelings in a socially appropriate way. People act with purpose. Even when a child exhibits what appears to us to be aberrant behaviors, there is a goal. This desired goal has been called "behavioral intent" (Neel & Cessna, 1993). Behavioral intent is the purpose sought by the student and it can only be inferred by analyzing the student's behaviors in a variety of settings.

The assessment of problem behaviors usually focuses on what needs to be reduced or eliminated, rather than on what skills need to be taught. The present level of performance and the goals and objectives on the Individualized Education Plan (IEP) of a student with problem behaviors would be greatly altered if there were a different mind-set from the beginning of the assessment process. For example, if a student's problem behaviors are thought to be serving the need for attention, then other ways may be found to give attention in an academic (or social or physical) activity. If a student's intent is power (control), then ways may be found to give the student more control over his or her own learning environment, tasks, and responses mode. This diagnostic approach, as with the functional assessment of challenging behaviors, can only be evaluated by whether or not the behaviors decrease and the desired prosocial and academic behaviors increase.

CURRICULUM DESIGN

Curriculum has been defined as how teachers and students spend their time in school (Wilcox & Bellamy, 1987). This seems especially true in an area such as social skills which pervades every aspect not only of school life, but of life at home, in the community, and at work. Because of this, the teaching of social skills does not lend itself to strict scheduling (Tuesdays and Thursdays from 9 A.M. to 10 A.M.), but is more effective when infused and embedded whenever and wherever students are in the school day. Unlike academic areas, the scope and sequence of social skills are loosely defined and more open to values interpretation.

This does not mean, however, that social skills should not be assessed and taught in a systematic manner. Almost everyone can agree that children and young adults should be able to get along with authority figures and peers and have feelings of self-worth that allow them to make and pursue positive life goals. There are generally accepted methods for social skills instruction and excellent models of each are available commercially. Teachers want to know what social skills to teach, when to teach them, and how to go about it. Some also want to know why.

The "why" of social skills instruction represents a sad commentary on our society. Educators are often asked to teach skills, behaviors, and values that were previously taught at home or in the churches and synagogues. The breakdown of family structure and the increasing amount of violence in society (as too often reflected on television) have made it increasingly important to teach prosocial skills to students in school. It has also been noted that the procedures and techniques used by schools in the past—programs that focused on extinguishing or reducing inappropriate behaviors—have not been very successful in the long run.

A partial answer to the "what" question may be found in the section on social skills assessment. There are many considerations when deciding what social skills to teach and when. Certain skills and behaviors are more appropriate for certain ages (developmental and chronological) than others (see "Considerations for Teaching Social Skills"). Young school-age children need to be taught the basics of social interaction, sharing, care of animals and the environment (the things we learned in kindergarten). Middle school is a time of intense pressure to be like the group. Knowledge about how and when to be like the group and how and when to resist peer pressure are critical skills at this age. In high school, students are preparing to enter the real world of work and/or college. They will need self-advocacy skills, knowledge of appropriate workplace social skills, and, above all, the ability to solve complex social problems and make social decisions (see Figure 6.1 for a more complete list of social skills).

Students with mild disabilities will be better able to learn context-free skills and generalize them to many settings and situations. They should be taught social problem-solving strategies and social decision-making skills. Students with moderate to severe cognitive disabilities will probably need to be taught skills that will be useful to them in the settings/contexts in which they are most likely to be living, working, and playing.

The answer to the "how" of teaching of social skills is both simple and complex. It is simple in that the methods used by most of the widely accepted social skills programs have many common elements. It is complex in that hardly anyone seems to agree on how much of which element goes into acquisition, mastery, maintenance, and generalization.

General Social Instruction.   There are some generally accepted practices for teaching almost any skill that apply equally well to teaching social skills. Among these are direct instruction, prompting, coaching, positive reinforcement, shaping,

FIGURE 6.1   Social Skills List

Social Skills Training Project (Volusia, 1992)

I. Basic Interpersonal Skills

Body Language
1. Using good posture
2. Facing the person
3. Keeping a comfortable distance
4. Making eye contact

Contact Initiation
5. Using a pleasant voice
6. Greeting
7. Introducing yourself

II. Conversation Skills

Beginning and Ending
8. Beginning a conversation
9. Ending a conversation

Maintaining
10. Listening attentively
11. Making sense
12. Taking turns talking
13. Asking and answering questions
14. Sharing personal conversation

III. Participation Skills

Group Interaction
15. Joining an activity in progress
16. Inviting others
17. Performing introductions
18. Taking "no" for an answer

Cooperation and Competition
19. Asking for help
20. Offering help
21. Following rules
22. Showing sportsmanship
23. Dealing with losing

IV. Friendship Skills

Respect
24. Using polite words
25. Touching the right way
26. Giving a compliment
27. Receiving a compliment

Mutuality
28. Sharing
29. Asking a favor
30. Expressing affection
31. Apologizing

V. Conflict Skills

Assertiveness
32. Giving criticism
33. Resisting peer pressure
34. Standing up for a friend
35. Responding to teasing

Coping
36. Receiving criticism
37. Coping with your own anger
38. Dealing with anger of others
39. Negotiating

Skills of Handicapped Children (Walker, Holmes, Todis, Walker, & Golden, 1983)

Area I: Classroom Skills

Listening to the teacher
Doing what the teacher asks
Doing your best work (work quietly and write neatly)
Following classroom rules

Area II: Basic Interaction Skills

Eye contact
Using the right voice
Starting a conversation
Listening
Answering
Making sense
Taking turns talking
Asking questions
Keeping the conversation going

Area III: Getting Along Skills

Using polite words
Sharing
Following rules
Assisting others
Touching the right way

Area IV: Making Friends

Good grooming
Smiling
Complimenting
Friendship making

Area V: Coping Skills

When someone says "no"
When you express anger
When someone teases
When someone tries to hurt you
When someone asks you to do something you can't do
When things don't go right

(continued)

FIGURE 6.1   *(Continued)*

Social Skills in the Classroom (Stephens, 1992)	**Environmental Behaviors**
Self-Related Behavior	Dealing with emergencies
Accepting consequences	Lunchroom behaviors
Ethical behavior	Movement around the environment
Expressing feelings	Care for the environment
Positive attitude toward self	**Interpersonal Behaviors**
Task-Related Behavior	Accepting authority
Asking and answering questions	Coping with conflict
Classroom discussion	Gaining attention
Completing tasks	Greeting others
Following directions	Helping others
Group activities	Making conversation
Independent work	Organized play
On-task behavior	Positive attitude toward others
Performing before others	Playing informally
Quality of work	Property: own and others

fading, and positive practice. There are also some techniques that are more appropriate for students with mild disabilities than for students with moderate to severe cognitive disabilities.

Social Skills Instruction for Students with Mild Disabilities.   The steps for teaching a social skill are:

1. *Present the skill.* Name it, define it, give a rationale for it, and model it.
2. *Practice the skill.* Provide guided practice, talk through the skill, generalize the skill, assign its use to other settings, and reinforce its use in many settings.

A much more detailed explanation of the sequence of instruction may be found in the Skillstreaming® materials by Goldstein, Sprafkin, Geershaw, and Klein (1986) and McGinnis and Goldstein (1984).

There are further considerations in teaching the skills for social problem solving. For example, to teach a student to react appropriately in social situations, the teacher must first determine whether the student recognizes the feelings and affect of others. If not, the student will have to be taught to recognize and put names to certain feelings and affects. There are programs that assist students in putting names to different feelings (e.g., anger, sadness, boredom) so they may learn to respond to them (Cartledge & Kleefeld, 1991).

Cognitive behavior modification (the cognitive method) has been found particularly effective in teaching social problem solving. This approach, based on the work of Donald Meichenbaum (1977) and others suggest solving social problems with the same approach used for solving other types of problems: (1) Identify the problem,

(2) generate solutions, (3) determine the pros and cons of each solution, (4) pick a solution, (5) evaluate the efficacy, and (6) reinforce self if successful.

With cognitive behavior modification, the major difference is how the student is taught the "self" component. The teacher, after having provided a rationale for the strategy, talks aloud through the steps of the general problem-solving strategy (or the same steps using a specific situation). Then the student talks aloud through it until it is fairly certain that he or she knows it. The student then talks it through speaking softly, then subvocally, then silently. An example follows:

Step 1

"This very large Assistant Principal has just told me to get to class, but if I don't go to my locker first to get my homework, I am toast in Ms. Gritz's class."

Step 2

"I could just make a dash for it and yell out an explanation as I run past him; or

I could tell him to get off my case, that I can tell time; or

I could walk calmly up to him with my explanation and hope he lets me pass."

Step 3

"The first one might work or it might tic him off.

The second one would be stupid because he already thinks I'm a wise guy.

The third one has a chance and is less likely to surprise him—and Mr. Holt (alias, The Hulk) does not like surprises!"

Step 4

"I'd better take the third one."

Step 5

"Well, that worked pretty well. He let me through and now maybe he gives me credit for being at least a semiserious student."

Step 6

"Yessss!"

There are other, less instructionally intense methods for assisting students with social skills deficits. Strategic placement is one of these. Simply put, strategic placement refers to the practice of putting a student needing social skills training in situations with other students who are positive role models. This works particularly well for those students who learn incidentally, but may be lost on some students unless the "good" students' behavior is praised specifically in the target student's presence.

Social Skills Instruction for Students with Moderate to Severe Disabilities. The earliest social skills—those we hope to develop in early childhood—are understood to be linked inextricably to cognitive and communication skills. The baby who smiles and coos in response to interaction with a parent or who cries to get picked up is exhibiting early reciprocal social skills. Later, in play with parents (e.g., peekaboo) or in social play with peers, the same skills (social, cognitive, communication) are linked.

There is, perhaps, a tendency to forget these linkages as children grow older and the three areas diverge and become more complex. Cognitive and communication skills continue to play an important part in social skill development.

What, then, of people who lack the cognitive and/or communication abilities to automatically learn or spontaneously perform the requisite social behaviors? Children and youth with moderate to severe disabilities are often lacking in these very skills. This is when the elements of functional curricula should be revisited with an eye to social skills. The general rules for functional curricula are that it should be:

- Useful to the student immediately and/or in the foreseeable future.
- Enhance his or her social value.
- Age appropriate.

Teachers can use these same criteria as guidelines for determining which social skills to teach. Parental input is very important. If the skills taught are those valued by parents, they are more likely to be prompted and reinforced at home. Skills for functioning in inclusive settings are important considerations (see "Special Cases" later in this chapter).

Instruction of social skills for students with moderate to severe disabilities will generally be carried out using the same instructional techniques used for other areas of instruction—a basic behavioral approach. Teachers are always encouraged, however, not to focus on extinction of inappropriate skills, but on teaching prosocial skills. The rule of thumb is *think replacement*. Don't take away a behavior from a person who may have few skills. Replace those that are not working for the student (and you) with those that do. Focus on purposeful, active learning that involves students in doing things that are incompatible with the interfering behaviors. For example, instead of spending a lot of time trying to get a student to stop a noisy repetitive movement, engage him in an activity that is so interesting he chooses to be still. Or engage him in an activity that involves movement and noise in a positive way (clapping to music) but does not reinforce stereotypic behaviors. Always keep in mind that however nonfunctional and irritating the behavior is to you, it is serving some function for that student. Figure that out and you are well on the way to finding a replacement behavior that is more useful for the student (and less annoying to you).

Special Cases.   While all students need social skills training, some students show warning signs of needing immediate and intensive interventions. Among these indicators are many discipline referrals; temper tantrums; fighting with peers; destroying/damaging property; few positive interactions with peers (giving or receiving); uncooperative behavior in the classroom; and/or withdrawn behavior.

The following list outlines a plan to provide intervention for a troubled student who has had to be taken out of the mainstream due to one or several of the listed indicators:

1. Choose the behaviors to be targeted by surveying the regular classroom and determining which behaviors are essential and useful, and acceptable levels of performance of each; then identify behaviors that will be reinforced by peers and teachers (e.g., offering to share) and behaviors that can be used in many settings (e.g., smiling).

2. Teach behaviors in a special class up to or above criterion. Use direct instruction, prompting, modeling, rehearsal, and reinforcement for initial acquisition; social script and role play to attain fluency.

3. Evaluate nondesirable behaviors. Determine which less-than-desirable behaviors occur normally in a regular education setting (e.g., swearing, teasing) and reduce to acceptable limit. Behaviors that are totally socially unacceptable (display of private parts) must be eliminated.

4. Prepare for generalization into the regular classroom using trained peers or a group-oriented process (the entire class gets reinforced when target student displays appropriate behaviors); prepare a checklist for the regular (mainstream) teacher and/or the student.

When all else fails, think of the Golden Rule: "Treat others the way you want to be treated." If every behavior, every act, were measured against this, perhaps there would be less hitting, stealing, and cruel teasing among children and fewer murders and rapes among adults. In one way or another, most people do follow this rule. The problem centers on those children and adults who hold themselves and their own value as human beings in contempt and then apply that same standard to others.

Teachers have the unusual opportunity to impact all areas of students' development, including social development. Remember that you as a teacher must value yourself and model appropriate social behavior for your students. Socialization is more than the sum of the social skills a person has acquired. It is also how that person feels about him- or herself, and his or her peers, family, community, and environment.

Considerations for Teaching Social Skills

Teachers should consider the age and developmental characteristics of a child when trying to decide which social skills to teach. Each developmental stage has characteristics that will be helpful to keep in mind. What may be considered a behavior problem at one age may be appropriate behavior for another age or stage of development. Some social skills and behaviors are complex; attempting to train a student in skills for which the or she is not developmentally ready dooms both the teacher and the child to failure.

Many educators and social psychologists have addressed stages of development. Three among them—Jean Piaget, Erik Erikson, and Lawrence Kohlberg—provide very different but useful views of the stages of cognitive, emotional/social, and moral development. The following paragraphs provide a brief description of three broad stages of development, as well as a statement from the three educators/psychologists about this stage. Common themes and their implications for training of social skills are then summarized.

1. *Early Childhood (1–7 years).* The child has about 3,000 words in speech. He or she is learning to think and reason, not just respond to sensory input.

In the Piagetian scheme, these ages cover the Sensory-motor and the Preoperational stages of development. During this period, the child is organizing and constructing a sense of how the world works primarily through imitation and play and also learning about object permanence and the consequences of actions. The child's view of the world is very much centered on self.

Erikson speaks of these ages as important in resolving three issues: trust versus mistrust, autonomy versus doubting/shame, and initiative versus guilt. Under this construct, we must have trust, autonomy, and initiative in order to develop into socially competent adults.

For Kohlberg, these ages cover the three levels of moral development in which rules are set down by others and goodness or badness (right or wrong) of actions are determined by their physical consequences. The emphasis during this period is on the child's own needs, although the beginnings of fairness and reciprocity are emerging.

Common Themes: The main theme during this period is the importance of the child's concrete and observable interactions with the external environment. Therefore, social skills programs should be simple, have concrete goals, and offer immediate consequences and material rewards. Teachers should avoid subtleties, long, moral arguments, and long delays between behavior and consequences.

2. *Middle Childhood (7–12 years).* There is development in the social arena, especially with playmates. There is also an increasing awareness and mastery of the physical environment.

Piaget refers to these years as the Concrete Operations stage. The child is able to handle complex operations but they are restricted to concrete objects (real or imagined).

For Erikson, this is the time the child is resolving the issue of industry versus inferiority. In school, this means mastering academics. If there is failure here, a sense of frustration, incompetence, and inadequacy may develop, and the stage is set for a difficult adolescence.

In Kohlberg's model, moral development continues to be strongly influenced by the consequences of actions. Rewards and punishments are still shaping the child's "morality" and there is a need to maintain order and stability. As the child approaches adolescence, he or she begins to develop internal standards (rules) but these are based primarily on approval or disapproval of others (teachers, family, etc.).

Common Themes: Although cognitive abilities are developing, there is still a great deal of dependence on external forces. Therefore, more complex social skills procedures may be taught. This is the best time for reaching potential problem children because they are able to understand but are still somewhat malleable. Adolescence may be too late.

3. *Adolescence (13–young adulthood).* This is the storm-and-stress period of life with great physical and emotional changes.

Piaget's stage of formal operations comes into play. The young person is capable of abstract, logical thought and hypothesis testing.

Erikson proposes that the young person is dealing with identity versus role confusion. It is a time of integration of the person's many roles (e.g., son, student, friend) and may be characterized by indecisiveness.

Kohlberg's model points to the parallel of moral development with cognitive development. The young person may go from conventional (influenced by others) to postconventional thinking (internal sense of standards—conscience) where ethical principles mean more than rules. Some young people fail to develop a set of internal rules for ethical and moral development or develop one that is so far outside the mainstream as to create immediate and obvious consequences. Techniques used in earlier years may still need to be maintained while trying to work with troubled young adults to develop socially acceptable internal guidelines.

Common Themes: There is confusion and a seeking for an identity separate from parents and teachers. Students with intact cognitive systems may begin testing both conventional rules and some of their own hypotheses. It is useful for teachers to be able to spot when a student is functioning at a stage younger than expected for his or her age, but this is not a reason to fail to address social skills with that youngster. It may mean using a different approach more appropriate to the student's developmental level.

For all of the developmental stages, several things need to be considered. Children are not miniature adults, they grow and develop at different rates. Not all movement through these stages just happens. Some children may need some help. However, labeling behavioral attributes as a "stage" doesn't explain or change them (e.g., don't just chalk things up to the "terrible twos").

INDIVIDUALIZED EDUCATION PLAN (IEP) DEVELOPMENT

For an IEP to truly meet the needs of the intended student, a number of quality indicators must be present regardless of the content area. Foremost, these indicators need to utilize a family-centered process that focuses upon person-centered planning and choice, and the development process must provide for coordination of services and interventions, with input from all relevant sources. Depending on the individual student, the activities and services should be either community based, integrated within the general school program, or both. Specific resources and time commitments for services should be listed along with any modifications or accommodations that might be needed.

In this chapter, we will be examining the components of the IEP that focus on skill development in the areas of socialization, peer relationships, and self-esteem. Figure 6.2 contains a list of possible IEP goals and short-term objectives. This list is intended to assist teachers in writing annual goals and short-term objectives (STOs) for students' Individualized Education Plans. These examples for elementary and secondary students are not intended to be complete or exhaustive, but to be examples of goals and objectives that teachers might write after formal or informal assessment of the student. Although there are certain skills that all children need early and throughout their lives, it is never too late to begin teaching even the most basic skills. It is also important for teachers to model these skills and to reinforce them whenever they are practiced.

There are also some general questions that teachers, family members and the student should answer as they develop this section of the IEP. These questions might include:

1. How does the student respond to different social situations?
2. What are the student's work habits?

FIGURE 6.2   Individualized Education Plan Goals and Objectives

Elementary

Classroom Survival Skills

   Goal: The student will complete assignments in class.

   Objective: Arrange assignments in a reasonable sequence.

   Objective: Prioritize assignments.

Friendship Making

   Goal: The student will introduce himself appropriately.

   Objective: State the occasions when it is appropriate to introduce oneself.

   Objective: Say "Hello, my name is Henry" and extend his hand for a handshake to three new people at school or in the community.

Dealing with Feelings

   Goal: The student will be able to express her feelings without becoming upset.

   Objective: Identify (name) feelings.

   Objective: Describe her feelings to the teacher without crying, raising her voice, or throwing anything.

Alternatives to Aggression

   Goal: The student will respond to teasing in a socially appropriate way.

   Objective: Identify when other students are teasing in a playful way.

   Objective: Develop and use three ways to divert teasers and respond without crying, hitting, or becoming verbally abusive.

Dealing with Stress

   Goal: The student will deal with accusation by an authority figure in a socially appropriate way.

   Objective: Identify when he is being accused of some misdeed (not just being corrected in class).

   Objective: Use a problem-solving approach to respond to the accusation.

Self-Esteem

   Goal: The student's self esteem will improve.

   Objective: Make positive self-statements related to school, home, or personal appearance.

   Objective: Identify three ways in which she will improve herself academically or personally.

Secondary

Problem Solving

   Goal: The student will be able to determine a reasonable course of action in social situations using the ASSET problem-solving process.

   Objective: Name the steps in the problem-solving process.

   Objective: Demonstrate three in-class and one out-of-class use of the problem-solving process.

Resisting Peer Pressure

   Goal: The student will resist peer pressure to skip school.

   Objective: Generate a list of reasons she should not skip school and keep them in her purse.

   Objective: Use some or all of these reasons when responding to peer pressure to skip school.

Coping

   Goal: The student will be able to protect herself if anyone tries to hurt her.

   Objective: Identify the names and phone number of people to call for assistance in the event of potentially abusive situations.

   Objective: Repeat three possible ways to remove herself from a potentially abusive situation.

FIGURE 6.2   *(Continued)*

Interpersonal Relationships

   Goal: The student will be able to send an "I'm interested" message appropriately to another person.

   Objective: Differentiate between appropriate and inappropriate ways of showing interest in another person.

   Objective: Develop and use at least three ways of demonstrating interest (e.g., complimenting, sending a gift, extending an invitation).

Asking for Directions/Assistance

   Goal: The student will ask for assistance with vocational assignments appropriately.

   Objective: Identify the appropriate person to ask for assistance with a work task (e.g., when one task is finished, when the next task is not clear).

   Objective: Request assistance in homeroom.

Self-Esteem

   Goal: The student will participate actively and positively in his own Transition IEP meeting.

   Objective: Identify own strengths and weaknesses in academic areas.

   Objective: Identify interests and aptitudes for one or more vocational areas.

3. How does the student respond to environmental stresses such as emergencies, deadlines, and, pressure?

4. How does the student work as part of a group and alone, show leadership skills, give supervision, receive supervision, perform special tasks and duties, perform routine tasks and duties, and perform high-speed tasks and duties?

SAMPLE INDIVIDUAL EDUCATION PLAN FOR MICHAEL

Keeping these questions in mind, as well as all the things, Michael, his family, and the school personnel have told us, let us begin to develop an IEP for him. First, we will assess his current level of performance.

Michael reads with comprehension at a 3.7 grade level. He is at the 5.2 level in math. Michael's areas of strength are in manipulating objects and understanding their mechanical functioning. He always volunteers to fix broken items in the classroom. Michael has expressed an interest in working on cars or joining the army when he graduates from high school.

Michael currently demonstrates poor impulse control and has difficulty interacting with authority figures and peers. He appears to be experimenting with alcohol.

Figure 6.3 gives a list of possible long-term goals for Michael with specific objectives that will enable Michael to accomplish his goals. Figure 6.3 also gives an example of a form to use in developing IEP goals with Michael; it also lists who will be involved, what supports are needed, and when that part of the IEP will be addressed.

FIGURE 6.3   IEP Goals and Objectives

Socialization, Peer Relationships, and Self-Esteem

I. Goal: Michael will demonstrate interpersonal skills necessary for cooperative participation in group activities.

I. Short-Term Objectives
1. Michael will demonstrate appropriate behavior when participating on a group task.
2. Michael will demonstrate various methods of effective communication with other people.
3. Michael will verbalize his responsibilities when accepting and completing tasks in a learning group.
4. Michael will verbalize the importance of getting along with others.
5. Michael will demonstrate appropriate social skills in a role-play situation.

II. Goal: Michael will understand the individual differences that contribute to acceptance by his peers.

II. Short-Term Objectives
1. Michael will be able to verbalize positive things about himself.
2. Michael will recognize individual differences and be able to verbalize positive things about his classmates.
3. Michael will demonstrate attitudes and skills that contribute to elimination of stereotyping of his classmates with disabilities.

III. Goal: Michael will recognize and identify personal needs and set goals to support successful transition to high school.

III. Short-Term Objectives
1. Michael will discuss and identify strategies for problem solving in personal relationships in the home, school, and community.
2. Michael will define attitude and explain how it affects behavior in personal relationships in the home, school, and community.
3. Michael will define stress and identify things in his life that cause stress.
4. Michael will describe the qualities he looks for in a friend and the basis for a good friendship.
5. Michael will identify persons and agencies who can be a part of his support network both in and out of school.
6. Michael will verbalize his personal needs, goals, and dreams in the social and interpersonal realm and will discuss strategies for achieving his goals.

IV. Goal: Michael will demonstrate increased self-esteem.

IV. Short-Term Objectives
1. Michael will express positive things about himself.
2. Michael will accept praise appropriately.
3. Michael will accept criticism appropriately.
4. Michael will be able to describe his learning and behavior problems.

V. Goal: Michael will demonstrate socially responsible behavior in the classroom and at home.

V. Short-Term Objectives
1. Michael will follow the instruction of teachers and parents.
2. Michael will demonstrate appropriate behavior in school and the community.
3. Michael will be able to verbalize how his behavior affects others.

FIGURE 6.3   *(Continued)*

VI. Goal: Michael will demonstrate and maintain good interpersonal skills.	*VI. Short-Term Objectives* 1. Michael will establish and maintain close relationships. 2. Michael will make and maintain friends.

Note. Adapted from: *FDLRS/Gateway Transition IEP Handbook* (1995); *The Power of Empowerment* (1994); and *Volusia County Schools Teacher Handbook on Social Skills* (Gaynor, Breland, Harlacher, Tondorf, & Zirkovich, 1992).

CONCLUSION

A thorough examination of the literature and discussions with students, teachers, and parents has shown that many students with disabilities require social skills instruction if they are to succeed in interpersonal relationships, develop positive self-esteem, and be able to participate fully at school, at home, and in their community. The IEP goals should reflect each student's individual needs in these areas and direct, systematic instructional methods should be used to enable the student to acquire the skill he or she needs to be successful.

The earlier these skills are taught, the sooner the student will be able to participate in meaningful interactions with their peers, teachers, and family. With the current emphasis on inclusion and community-based learning and employment, these skills are essential for transition to adult life, and successful performance on the job, in the community and at home.

APPENDIX 6.A

Assessment Materials

AAMR Adaptive Behavior Scale-School Edition (ABS-S:2)
Authors: Lambert, N., Leland, H., & Nihira, K. (1993)
Publisher: Riverside Publishing, Inc. (a Houghton Mifflin Company)
            8420 Bryn Mawr Avenue
            Chicago, IL 60631

Assessment of Interpersonal Relations
Author: Bracken, B. (1993)
Publisher: Riverside Publishing, Inc. (a Houghton Mifflin Company)
            8420 Bryn Mawr Avenue
            Chicago, IL 60631

Behavior Problem Checklist-R
Authors: Quay, H. C., & Peterson, D. R. (1987)
Publisher: Quay Publishers
            Coral Gables, FL

Behavior Rating Profile-R
Authors: Brown, L. L., & Hammill, D. D. (1990)
Publisher: Pro-Ed
            8700 Shoal Creek Boulevard
            Austin, TX 78757-6897

Burks' Behavior Rating Scale
Author: Burks, H. F. (1977)
Publishers: Western Psychological Services
            12031 Wilshire Boulevard
            Los Angeles, CA 90025-1251

Child Behavior Checklist
Authors: Achenback, T. M., & Edelbrock, C. (1991)
Publisher: Achenback Press
            Burlington, VT

Coopersmith Self-Esteem Inventories
Author: Coopersmith, S. (1981)
Publisher: Publishers Test Service
            Monterey, CA

Culture-Free Self-Esteem Inventories for Children and Adults, 2nd Edition
Author: Battle, J. (1981)
Publisher: Psychological and Educational Publications, Inc.
            1477 Rollins Road
            Burlingame, CA 94010-2316

Devereaux Behavior Rating Scales
Author: Smith, M. (1966)
Publisher: Devereaux Foundation Publications
            Devon, PA 19333

Matson Evaluation of Social Skills for Youth
Authors: Matson, J. L., Rotatori, A. F., & Helsel, W. J. (1983)
Publishers: Academic Therapy Publications
            20 Commercial Boulevard
            Novato, CA 94947

Multi-Dimensional Self-Concept Scale
Author: Bracken, B. (1992)
Publishers: Riverside Publishing, Inc. (a Houghton Mifflin Company)
            8420 Bryn Mawr Avenue
            Chicago, IL 60631

Personality Inventory for Children
Authors: Wirt, R. T., Lachar, D., Klienedinst, D., Seat, P. D., & Broen, W. D. (1977)
Publisher: Western Psychological Services
            12031 Wilshire Boulevard
            Los Angeles, CA 90025-1251

Piers-Harris Children's Self-Concept Scale
Authors: Piers, E., & Harris, D. (1969)
Publishers: Western Psychological Services
             12031 Wilshire Boulevard
             Los Angeles, CA 90025-1251

Scales of Independent Behavior
Authors: Bruininks, R. H., Woodcock, R. W., Weatherman, R. E., & Hill, B. K. (1984)
Publishers: Riverside Publishing, Inc. (a Houghton Mifflin Company)
             8420 Bryn Mawr Avenue
             Chicago, IL 60631

Self-Esteem Index
Authors: Brown, L., & Alexander, J. (1991)
Publishers: Psychological and Educational Publications, Inc.
             1477 Rollins Road
             Burlingame, CA 94010-2316

Social-Emotional Dimension Scale
Authors: Hutton, J. B., & Roberts, T. G. (1986)
Publishers: Pro-Ed
             8700 Shoal Creek Boulevard
             Austin, TX 78757-6897

Social Skills Rating System
Authors: Gresham, F. M., & Elliott, S. N. (1990)
Publishers: American Guidance Service (AGS)
             4201 Woodland Road
             P.O. Box 99
             Circle Pines, MN 55014-9989

Test of Pragmatic Language
Authors: Phelps-Terasaki, D., & Phelps-Gunn, T. (1992)
Publishers: Riverside Publishing, Inc. (a Houghton Mifflin Company)
             8420 Bryn Mawr Avenue
             Chicago, IL 60631

Vineland Adaptive Behavior Checklists
Authors: Sparrow, S. S, Balla, D. A., & Cicchetti, D. V. (1984)
Publishers: American Guidance Services (AGS)
             4201 Woodland Road
             P.O. Box 99
             Circle Pines, MN 55014-9989

Weller-Strawser Scales of Adaptive Behavior
Authors: Weller, C., & Strawser, S. (1981)
Publisher: Academic Therapy Publications
             20 Commercial Boulevard
             Novato, CA 94947

Games

Communicate. (1986). Mayo, P., & Waldo, P. Thinking Publications.

Communicate Junior. (1988). Mayo, P., Gajewski, N., Hiren, P., & Kofka, J. Thinking Publications.

Stacking the Deck: A Social Skills Game for Retarded Adults. (1988). Foxx, R. M., & McMorrow, M. J. Research Press.

Curriculum and Training Materials

Perkins, D., Bailey, M., Repetto, J. B., & Schwartz, S. E. (1995). *Dare to dream: A guide to planning your future (A student's guide to transition planning).* Tallahassee: Florida Department of Education.

Perkins, D., Repetto, J. B., & Schwartz, S. E. (1995). *Dare to dream: A guide to planning your future (A student's guide to transition planning—Teacher's guide).* Tallahassee: Florida Department of Education.

Gaynor, J., Breland, J., Harlacher, S., Tondorf, N., & Zivkovich, M. (1992). *Social Skills Training Project: Volusia County Schools teacher handbook.* Tallahassee: Florida Department of Education.

Address: Florida Department of Education
Clearinghouse/Information Center
Florida Education Center
Suite 622
Tallahassee, FL 32399-0400

Bragman, R. S. (1994). *Proving for successful transition into work and community life: How to develop individualized transition plans (ITPs).* Indian Rocks Beach, FL: Phillip Roy.

Bragman, R. S. (1994). *Social and Functional Skill Curriculum kit: For the student interacting in today's society (Teacher's guide).* Indian Rocks Beach, FL: Phillip Roy.

Bragman, R. S. (1994). *Lifestyle 90's: Building a good self-concept.* Indian Rocks Beach, FL: Phillip Roy.

Bragman, R. S. (1994). *Lifestyles Curriculum: Social skills unit.* Indian Rocks Beach, FL: Phillip Roy.

Address: Phillip Roy, Inc.
P.O. Box 130
Indian Rocks Beach, FL 34635

Czerlinsky, T., & Chandler, S. K. (1994). *The Power of Empowerment Training Program: Building partnerships in the rehabilitation process.* Cicero, NY: Program Development Associates.

Address: Program Development Associates
5620 Business Avenue, Suite B
Cicero, NY 13039

FDLRS/Gateway (1995). *Transition individual educational plan handbook.* Live Oak, FL: FDLRS/Gateway.

APPENDIX 6.B

Publishers

Academic Therapy Publications
20 Commercial Boulevard
Novato, CA 94947

Achenback Press
Burlington, VT

American Guidance Services (AGS)
4201 Woodland Road
P.O. Box 99
Circle Pines, MN 55014-1796/55014-9989

Aspen Publishers, Inc.
Rockville, MD

Attainment Company, Inc.
P.O. Box 930160
Verona, WI 53593-0160

CEC Publications, Dept. K4092
1920 Association Drive
Reston, VA 22091-1589

CORBEH
Eugene, OR

Devereaux Foundation Publications
Devon, PA 19333

Educational Achievement Systems
Austin, TX

Hawthorne Educational Services
800 Gray Oak Avenue
Columbia, MO 65201

Jalmar Press
2675 Skypark Drive, Suite 204
Torrance, CA 90505

James Stanfield Company, Inc.
Drawer 28
P.O. Box 41058
Santa Barbara, CA 93140

Piney Mountain Press, Inc.
P.O. Box 333
Cleveland, GA 30528

Pro-Ed
8700 Shoal Creek Boulevard
Austin, TX 78757-6897

Psychological and Educational
Publications, Inc.
1477 Rollins Road
Burlingame, CA 94010-2316

Publishers Test Service
Monterey, CA

Quay Publishers
Coral Gables, FL

Research Press
Dept. 96
P.O. Box 9177
Champaign, IL 61826

Riverside Publishing, Inc. (a Houghton
Mifflin Company)
8420 Bryn Mawr Avenue
Chicago, IL 60631

Thinking Publications
Eau Claire, WI

University of Washington Press
Seattle, WA

Western Psychological Services
12031 Wilshire Boulevard
Los Angeles, CA 90025-1251

REFERENCES

Bergen, D. (1993). Teaching strategies: Facilitating friendship development in inclusion classrooms. *Childhood Education*, 234–235.

Carter, J., & Sugai, G. (1988). Teaching social skills. *Teaching Exceptional Children, 20*(3), 68–71.

Carter, J., & Sugai, G. (1989). Social skills curriculum analysis. *Teaching Exceptional Children, 22*(1), 36–39.

Cartledge, G., & Kleefeld, J. (1991). *Taking part: Introducing social skills to children.* Circle Pines, MN: American Guidance Service.

Cartledge, G., & Milburn, J. F. (1978). The case for teaching social skills in the classroom: A review. *Review of Educational Research, 1,* 133–156.

Cartledge, G., & Milburn, J. F. (1995). *Teaching social skills to children and youth: Innovative approaches.* Boston: Allyn & Bacon.

Cavaliere, F. (1995, October). Substance abuse in the deaf community. *The APA Monitor.*

Curwin, R. L. (1993, November). The healing power of altruism. *Educational Leadership, 50,* 36–39.

Dodge, K. A. (1989). Problems in social relationships. In E. J. Mash & R. A. Barkley (Eds.), *Treatment of childhood disorders* (pp. 223–241). New York: Guilford Press.

Dowrick, P. W. (1986). *Social survival for children.* New York: Brunner/Mazel.

Elliott, S. N., & Gresham, F. M. (1991). *Social skills intervention.* Circle Pines, MN: American Guidance Service.

Erikson, E. (1963). *Childhood and society* (2nd ed.). New York: W.W. Norton.

Foster-Johnson, L., & Dunlap, G. (1993). Using functional assessment to develop effective individualized interventions for challenging behaviors. *Teaching Exceptional Children, 25*(3), 44–57.

Gartner, A., & Lipsky, D. K. (1987). Beyond special education: Toward a quality system for all students. *Harvard Educational Review, 57,* 367–395.

Gaynor, J., Breland, J., Harlacher, S., Tondorf, N., & Zivkovich, M. (1992). *Social Skills Training Project: Teacher handbook.* Daytona Beach, FL: Volusia County School District.

Goldstein, A. P., Sprafkin, R. P., Geershaw, N. J., & Klein, P. (1986). The adolescent: Social skills training through structured learning. In G. Cartledge & J. Milburn (Eds.), *Teaching social skills to children: Innovative approaches* (2nd ed., pp. 303–336). New York: Pergamon Press.

Guralnick, M. J. (1993). Developmentally appropriate practice in the assessment and intervention of children's peer relations. *Topics in Early Childhood Special Education, 13*(3), 334–371.

Kauffman, J. M., Gerber, M. M., & Semmel, M. I. (1988). Arguable assumptions underlying the Regular Education Initiative. *Journal of Learning Disabilities, 21*(1), 6–11.

Knaus, W. J. (1974). *Rational emotive education.* New York: Institute for Rational Living.

Kendrick, D. (1991, March 8). Special children need friends most. Alive and well. *The Cincinnati Enquirer,* p. E7.

Knoff, H. (1988). Effective social interventions. In J. Graden, J. Zinn, & M. Curtis (Eds.), *Enhancing social competencies* (pp. 431–453). Washington: National Association of Secondary School Principals.

Kohlberg, L. (1969). Stage and sequence: The cognitive-developmental approach to socialization. In D. A. Goslin (Ed.), *Handbook of socialization theory and research* (pp. 347–480). Chicago, IL: Rand McNally.

Levy, D. (1995, November 3). Drug use is up, students say. *USA Today,* p. 7D.

Martin, S. (1995, October). Are children with disabilities more likely to be abused? *APA Monitor.*

McGinnis, E., & Goldstein, A. P. (1984). *Skillstreaming the elementary school child.* Champaign, IL: Research Press.

Meichenbaum, D. (1977). *Cognitive-behavior modification: An integrative approach.* New York: Plenum Press.

Morgan, D. P., & Jenson, W. R. (1988). *Teaching behaviorally disordered students: Preferred practices.* Columbus, OH: Merrill.

Neel, R. S., & Cessna, K. K. (1993). Behavioral intent: Instructional content for students with behavior disorders. In *Instructionally differentiated programming.* Denver: Colorado Department of Education.

Nelson, C. M. (1988, Summer). Social skills training for handicapped students. *Teaching Exceptional Children, 20,* 19–23.

Piaget, J. (1950). *The psychology of intelligence.* New York: International Universities Press.

Reynolds, M. C., Wang, M. C., & Walberg, H. J. (1987). The necessary restructuring of special and regular education. *Exceptional Children, 53,* 391–398.

Rizzo, J., & Zabel, R. (1988). *Educating children and adolescents with behavioral disorders.* Needham Heights, MA: Allyn & Bacon.

Slavin, R. E. (1991). Synthesis of research on cooperative learning. *Educational Leadership, 48,* 71–82.

Stainback, S., Stainback, W., East, K., & Sapon-Shevin, M. (1994). A commentary on inclusion and the development of a positive self-identity by persons with disabilities. *Exceptional Children, 60*(6), 486–490.

Stainback, W., & Stainback, S. (1984). A rationale for the merger of special and regular education. *Exceptional Children, 51,* 102–111.

Stephens, T. M. (1992). *Social skills in the classroom.* Odessa, FL: Psychological Assessment Resources.

Walker, H. M., Holmes, D., Todis, B., Walker, J., & Golden, N. (1983). *The Walker Social Skills Curriculum.* Austin, TX: Pro-Ed.

Walker-Hirsch, L., & Champagne, M. P. (1991, September). The Circles Concept: Social competence in special education. *Educational Leadership, 48,* 65–67.

Webber, J., & Coleman, M. (1988). Using Rational-Emotive Therapy to prevent classroom problems. *Teaching Exceptional Children, 21*(1), 32–35.

7

Curricular Choices Related to Work

RESTRUCTURING CURRICULA FOR IMPROVED WORK OUTCOMES

CHERYL HANLEY-MAXWELL

LANA COLLET-KLINGENBERG

Donna is 14 years old. She comes from an impoverished family in a rural community. For years, her parents have questioned her teachers about whether she is receiving an appropriate education. Every time they have questioned the content of her program (it has been primarily academic), she has been reevaluated and relabeled. She has been identified as learning disabled, emotionally disturbed, and mildly mentally retarded at various points in her education. Most recently, as her parents have struggled to get functional skills into her Individualized Education Plan (IEP), her reevaluation has resulted in a new label of moderate mental retardation. Frustrated, her parents have appealed to an advocate for help. They contend that, despite her label, she is running out of time to be prepared to live and work as an adult. Her parents feel that if more attention were given to teaching her real-life skills, such as preparing her for the world of work, she would be more interested in school. Thus, she would be more likely to complete school and move successfully into a job. The advocate agrees and is working with the school to prepare an appropriate vocational curriculum and transitional plan for Donna.

Donna's current documented (i.e., in the IEP) skills include functional reading and math. Her parents report that she has good hygiene and personal care skills, and that she follows simple directions well. In addition, they report that she can complete basic domestic skills (e.g., laundry, preparing simple meals, housecleaning chores) without assistance. While she manages to travel independently (by foot or rides from friends) in their small community, Donna's parents report that they are concerned about her safety when they or other adults are not with her. Teachers report that she has trouble with short-term memory, problem solving, task initiation, task completion, self-assessment, self-advocacy, and self-direction. Donna reports that she gets along well with others. However, observations by parents and teachers suggest that because she is often unsure of herself, wants to be liked, lacks social skills, and has difficulty identifying potentially problematic situations, she plays an extremely passive role and is often victimized by her friends, especially her boyfriends. Thus, there are concerns that she may be in danger of becoming pregnant and dropping out of school. She has no career goals, work history (community, school, or home), or readily salable work skills. She does talk about getting her own apartment and possibly getting married and having children someday. When asked about what she might be interested in doing for a job, she does not have any specific jobs in mind. She seems to change her mind weekly about what she would like to do. Some jobs she has listed include child care, retail, banking, waitressing, and doing crafts. Donna also talks about graduating when she is 18 ("like all my friends"), though she is eligible for special education services until she is 21.

CURRICULAR CHOICES RELATED TO WORK

Throughout the history of American education, schools have been the means of educating children to be productive members of society. Transition to work, as it is defined today, has resulted from two previous work-focused trends in education: work/study (Halpern, 1973, 1974, 1992) and career education (Halpern, 1992). In 1986, Madeline Will articulated the school-to-work or transition priority of the Office of Special Education Programs (Will, 1986a, 1986b). Since then the idea of transition has become a national priority for all students (America 2000). While work education has been a priority for students both in regular education and in special education, rarely have programs been directed to both populations simultaneously.

The goal of all curricula for students with disabilities is to prepare them for life after graduation. More specifically, the desired outcome is for students to leave high school prepared to deal with the rights and responsibilities of adult life. Employment is included within these adult rights and responsibilities. The purpose of this chapter is to focus on the vocational preparation of individuals with disabilities as they assume their adult roles in the employment world.

CAREER DEVELOPMENT

One area that teachers need to look to for guidance in the development of individually constructed vocational curricula is career development. Career development is a vital factor in a life-span approach to transition from school to work. Various career development theories attempt to describe the process of career development. One of these theories, work adjustment theory, is based on the constructs of work personality, work competencies, and work goals (Hershenson, 1984). Skills in these three areas develop throughout our lives in combination with each other and in conjunction with environmental influences. There are, however, "primary periods" (Szymanski, 1994) during which each of these foundation pieces tends to develop.

"Work personality develops during the preschool years, work competencies during the school years, and work goals develop during the later school years" (Szymanski, 1994, p. 403). More specifically, play enhances the development of work personality, home/school work responsibilities assist in the development of work personality and work competency, and career fantasy and exposure to work role models provide for the development of work goals, which are further refined by career-related experiences and learning opportunities. Additionally, work adjustment is further influenced by the expectations of family, culture, and community (Szymanski, 1994). In other words, career development theory emphasizes the breadth of transition planning considerations and the longitudinal nature of the transition process. Specific career development theories and their impact on curricular choices are discussed within the context of the design and application of the curricular model proposed in this chapter.

ASSESSMENT

Individualized curriculum that facilitates the development of work-related skills is determined through an ongoing and thorough process involving ecological assessment and functional vocational assessment. Ecological assessment tends to be a broader-based type of assessment that is geared toward a greater understanding of the individual within all of the ecologies or environments of his or her life. Functional vocational assessment is more specific, focusing on the needs, skills, and interests of the individual within the context of future work environments. As this chapter focuses on work-related school curricula, both forms of assessment are presented in order that the reader may differentiate for him- or herself the most useful focus of assessment for the age/needs of the learner being considered.

ECOLOGICAL ASSESSMENT

In ecological assessment, an individual's skills and skill needs are evaluated within the context of current and potential future education, employment, residential, and community setting demands (Browder & King, 1987). According to Brown-Glover (1992), this results in ". . . the ecological curriculum [that] provides a true set of individualized goals" (p. 243). The individual's strengths and limitations in specific tasks are assessed along with existing and potential support systems for that individual (Pancsofar, 1986). In addition, the personal interests and goals of the individual and his or her family are considered. Thus, ecological assessment involves (1) assessment of potential skill needs, (2) assessment of the individual's skill use in real-life settings and of the interests and goals of the individual and his or her significant others, and (3) assessment of support needs and systems. Each of these areas will be discussed.

Potential Skill Analysis. A vital part of a thorough assessment, potential skill analysis includes both task-specific analysis and the analysis of social skills needed for survival in targeted settings. Additionally, the analysis should include process skills or those "integrative" skills needed in various target situations (i.e., known and potential future work and living environments). Observations at the targeted sites, interviews with knowledgeable individuals (e.g., coworkers and supervisors), and reviews of existing curricular materials in the targeted skill area are used to identify potential skill needs. The identified skills then form the basic content of the assessment and instructional components and the basis for consideration of possible adaptation and accommodation needs. Aspects of possible content for assessment may also be adapted from some of the commercially available products designed to measure life skills (e.g., Street Survival Skills Checklist, Linkenhoker & McCarron, 1980; Tests for Everyday Living, Halpern, Irvin, & Landman, 1979; National Independent Living Skills Screening Instrument, Sands, Woolsey, & Dunlap, 1985); and curriculum-based measures that accompany some functional curricula (e.g., Life Centered Career Education Competency Rating Scale, Brolin, 1991).

Individual Assessment.   Not to be confused with readiness testing, tests of eligibility, or the myriad interest inventories available, assessment of the individual is used to determine programmatic needs (Parker, Szymanski, & Hanley-Maxwell, 1989). This determination is accomplished through a systematic examination of the individual's performance of essential skills and the examination of information about the person's learning history, future goals and aspirations, and interests. Assessment of the individual also includes the identification of adaptation needs (e.g., partial participation, materials adaptation, setting adaptation, task resequencing). A related form of assessment, curriculum-based assessment (CBA), is similar in process to the individual needs assessment. However, CBA is typically tied to predetermined curricula. Here skills that are taught within a targeted curriculum form the core of the assessment content. Students are assessed in relation to their performance of various examples of those skills within the targeted curriculum.

Support System Assessment.   This portion of the assessment process identifies potential facilitating and inhibiting relationships that may affect the successful adult outcomes. Support systems examined include friends, family, and potential relationship in future jobs or residences (Hanley-Maxwell & Bordieri, 1989). Self-efficacy of the individual is also considered here, as this will have an impact on the level of support needed in employment settings. Available supports and potential support sources are matched to the current and projected support needs and wishes of the individual.

FUNCTIONAL VOCATIONAL ASSESSMENT

This type of assessment helps to determine what skills and capabilities the individual has and how those skills are used across work and work-related environments (Kellogg, 1995). The type and levels of necessary work-related supports needed and available are also determined through this kind of assessment. While the potential listing of content areas is infinite, a number of areas are universal to most individuals. The following two sections provide a discussion of these areas and how information is best accessed.

Content Areas.   The kinds of information to be accessed using a functional vocational assessment include information on the individual's work and school history, including learning style, work-related skills/concerns, work endurance/stamina, functional use of academic skills, and the ability to follow directions. Information regarding the individual's communication skills, social skills, interaction style, and behavior is regarded as important for job training and placement as well. Additional information should be collected regarding mobility/orientation skills, medical needs/management, fine and gross motor skills, transportation needs, and any other special needs or considerations for employment. Current and future financial information, goals and needs must also be addressed. Finally, and most importantly, the strengths and preferences of the individual must be taken into consideration across all these content areas.

Accessing Information.   According to J. Wheeler (personal communication, October 1995), the process of functional vocational assessment can be likened to a funnel. Information in each of the content areas is sought from a variety of sources. These sources include the individual, his or her significant others, and written documents. Observations and interactions with the individual are first and foremost. The individual conducting the assessment must know or get to know the individual whom she or he is assessing to conduct a fair and accurate assessment (J. Wheeler, personal communication, October 1995). Additional and confirming information may be gathered through interviews and discussions with other people who play significant roles in the life of the individual. Finally, documents such as written reports, case histories, and educational/work records may be accessed to further supplement the information gathered through the other means discussed above. All this information is then compiled (or funneled) into a plan for job development.

SUMMARY

The process of ecological assessment and functional vocational assessment includes identifying current and future environments, the skills necessary for successful functioning in those environments, the abilities of the individual in performing those skills, and the supports available, as well as those needed by the individual to function as independently as possible. Thorough and ongoing assessment (i.e., longitudinal and varied in skills, settings, and materials) helps to identify and revise curricular content that is individualized and focuses on preparing students for adult life. Used together, ecological and functional vocational assessment ensure "goodness of fit" between the realities of an individual's life (in terms of skills, needs, goals) and the instruction that we provide (via the IEP and a well-planned curriculum). It cannot be stressed enough that "moment in time" assessment provides little usable information when making curricular decisions. Individual lives are not static events to be probed once and permanently plotted. They are fluid, ongoing experiences that involve a variety of factors. Only through continual assessment and reassessment, combined with the construction and use of the IEP, can we begin to address real-life issues and needs in the curricula that we design and implement.

VOCATIONAL CURRICULUM DESIGN

Although existing curricula offer comprehensive listings of skill domains, skill clusters, and specific skills needed for work, none of them are all inclusive, nor could they ever be. An effective vocational curriculum is one that teaches the individual the skills that she or he will need to function in his or her adult world. This adult world will be different for every individual. Because there is no way to be exhaustive in listing the ideal skills for inclusion in work curricula, we will not replicate the work done by many authors in compiling skill listings. However, it is important to list those domains and skill clusters identified in many curricular materials. These are woven within the curricular areas of the proposed model. This section includes a description of the model proposed and a discussion of the design and use of this model.

Successful movement from school to work requires that the individual receive a solid educational foundation that prepares him or her for various adult roles, careful longitudinal planning, and the provision of postschool supports and services that were identified in the planning process (Wehman, Kregel, & Barcus, 1985). Locating and linking with those postschool services are also critical aspects of the process. Much of the current conception of work preparation and related best practices appears to focus on the secondary and postsecondary years. In fact, Michaels (1994) equates transition with adolescence as he describes the life events of that time period. "Adolescence (and transition) is a time of . . . taking responsibility for one's self, separating from parental control and values, separating from the control of the school system, and developing an internal locus of control" (p. 12). However, understanding the basic premises of the entire preparation process provides a guide for evaluating decisions related to what, why, when, where, and how teachers assess, plan, and teach (Stodden & Leake, 1994) throughout the educational years.

Students must be provided instruction throughout their school careers on the options, skills, and outcomes that are selected by representatives from four perspectives: individual, family, community, and society. This emphasis on the importance of all aspects of an individual's life has been called the life-space perspective by Szymanski (1994). When combined with the life-span issues, which include career development, the result is a curricular model that not only teaches basic skills and processes with the idea of providing the individual with generalizable skills to use in making independent and meaningful life decisions, but also provides a multitude of experiences related to career and work options throughout the schooling process.

The curricular structure developed in this section builds on the model proposed by Udvari-Solner, Jorgensen, and Courchane (1992). Like the longitudinal vocational model (Udvari-Solner et al., 1992), it organizes skills to be taught from the primary grades on up. It differs in that it does not incorporate skills by traditional domains. The number and exact nature of instructional domains varies across the current literature (Jackson cited in Michaels, 1994). However, there are four generally accepted skill domains covering the academic, social, vocational, and independent living areas. This model moves away from these domains and proposes a different way of identifying and organizing critical skills. In addition, it is designed to be used with curricula already in place in the classroom.

The proposed structure is intended as a working model to make identification of and incorporation into the classroom curriculum of targeted skills more manageable and thus more successful. In this model, the skills that make up the areas or domains typically listed fall into three categories: (1) foundation or fundamental skills, (2) integrative skills, and (3) application skills or those skills that are needed by an individual for specific reasons having to do with the community in which he or she lives, the job he or she desires, or his or her abilities and limitations. These categories, depicted in Figure 7.1 are introduced in a semisequential manner beginning in preschool and elementary school and continuing through high school and into adult services.

FIGURE 7.1   Curricular Model

Elementary School	Middle School	High School	Employment
Foundational Skills ──→			X
Academic			
Reading			
Writing			
Math			
Personal Care			
Behavior			
Integrative Skills ──────────────────────────────────────→			X
Problem Solving			
Self-Efficacy			
Self-Advocacy			
Planning			
Personal Values			
Social Skills			
Application Skills ──────────────────────────→			X
Applying for a job			
Interviewing			
Job Tasks			
Job Maintenance			
Job Changes			

FOUNDATION OR FUNDAMENTAL SKILLS

This category or level of skill development includes those skills that have been identified as being the most basic skills essential for school and postschool functioning. These skills provide the foundation for more complex skills, as well as for a variety of occupations later in life, and span a continuum from the simplest to the most complex skills (Ford et al., 1989; Gajar, Goodman, & McAfee, 1993). They include skills in the following general areas: academics, personal care, communication, and behavior.

Academic Skills.   Academic skills identified as critical to adult functioning are those identified in the SCANS report (U.S. Department of Labor, 1991), current professional texts and curricular materials, and some follow-up research. They include reading, math, and writing. Each of the academic areas represents a continuum of performance demands that range from basic survival to meaningful use to highly technical use.

Reading encompasses understanding the meaning of pictures, figures, symbols, and words. Basic reading skills entail identification of sounds, performance skills, and being able to define word meanings. More advanced skills involve prediction, synthesis, and analysis. Examples of practical applications of reading skills include reading universal signs, single word signs, newspaper want ads, job listings, job applications, maps, phone books, and instructions.

Math skills identified as useful in work settings include the application of basic skills and operations to everyday tasks. Basic skills include working with whole numbers, adding, subtracting, money use, time telling, measurement and estimation.

More advanced skills include multiplication, division, decimals, fractions, percent, mixed operations, word problems, and mathematical reasoning. Practical skills include measuring liquids and solids, using the calculator, using money, balancing a checkbook, and using simple math operations in everyday tasks.

Writing skills are identified as important components in a variety of work-related tasks. At a minimal level, writing includes signing contracts, checks, tax forms or other legal agreements. Writing is also necessary for completing job applications and encompasses the generation of information that is included in written materials. Examples include resumes, letters of interest, and job-specific requirements (e.g., correspondence memos, billing). More sophisticated forms of writing are used for specific kinds of jobs and careers (e.g., journalism, editing, authoring).

Personal-Care Skills.   Personal skills include activities of daily living, dressing, grooming, hygiene, eating, mobility, and other activities needed to function in everyday life, as well as to prepare for work. These skills, while not directly related to the job, impact on the individual's success in the employment community (Gajar et al., 1993; Karge, Patton, & de la Garza, 1992; McCrae, 1991).

Communication Skills.   Communication skills include both listening and speaking (verbally and nonverbally). Communicating basic needs, following instructions, answering questions, asking for help, giving instructions, asking questions, offering assistance, asking for a raise, interviewing, giving criticism/feedback, and decoding nonverbal messages are skills specifically mentioned as critical communication skills on the job (Carnevale et al. cited in White, 1992; Karge et al., 1992; McCrae, 1991; U.S. Department of Labor, 1991).

All learners must have these fundamental skills. But the level of achievement in any one skill area is dependent on the characteristics of the student and the end goals as determined through thorough and ongoing assessment as a part of the IEP process.

Existing curricular models (e.g., Brolin, 1983; Gajar et al., 1993; Snell, 1987; West, 1989) attend to individual skills, such as fundamental skills, rather than the processes of learning and problem solving (i.e., generalization and maintenance). Michaels (1994) calls this the "basic skills approach" (p. 135) and expresses concern that too little attention is given to "higher level skill areas" (p. 135). He proposes an expanded basic skills approach that includes process skills of task approach and problem solving, self-efficacy skills (e.g., self-monitoring), and social skills as critical fundamental skills for all students (Michaels, 1994). In concert with Michael's approach, the second category of skills described in this model attends to the "what" (e.g., performance skills) but also emphasizes the acquisition of learning processes that will allow the student to acquire new skills, perform variations of old skills, and be flexible under new demands.

INTEGRATIVE SKILLS

While still considered important for postschool success, the skills at this level are more complex skills that will enable an individual to be more adaptable to changes in work and living settings. This area includes skills that must be taught within the context of other activities and instructional programs. The skills presented in this section are grouped only for the purpose of this discussion. As will become clear, many of these skills are interrelated. The skill groupings include problem-solving skills, self-efficacy skills, self-advocacy skills, planning skills, and personal values. It also includes social skills, the skills that relate to the ability to get along and communicate with others. Most of the skills at this level reflect various combinations of foundation skills and the covert cognitive skills that underlie functional skill usage. For example, problem solving requires the integration of communication and behavior performance skills with the internalized cognitive behaviors of decoding, deciding, and evaluation. The kinds of skills involved in each of the skill groupings at the integrative level are presented separately as follows.

Problem-Solving Skills. Problem-solving skills have recently been the center of discussions about the preparation of students for adult work roles. Specifically mentioned in the SCANS report (U.S. Department of Labor, 1991) and other employer research, problem-solving skills have taken on a new level of importance in recent transition literature. Problem solving includes identifying the problem, potential solutions, potentially needed resources, and potential outcomes; selecting one solution; and assessing that solution's success (Chadsey-Rusch, 1986). Mithaug, Martin, and Agran (1987) recommend steps in teaching students to enhance their adaptability through problem solving. These steps are (1) identify the problem, (2) define alternate solutions, (3) determine action, (4) take action, (5) evaluate the consequences, and (6) determine the need for adjustment.

Self-Efficacy. In addition to problem solving, students should be taught to take charge of their own behavior. These skills, similar to those found in problem solving, are part of the larger constellation of skills known as self-efficacy. Self-efficacy skills include self-knowledge, including interests and abilities; self-consequation, including reinforcement and correction; self-monitoring; self-control; and self-assertion (Martin, Marshall, & Maxson, 1991; Mithaug et al., 1987). These skills are required if the individual is to be a flexible, responsible, and independently functioning adult. As in problem solving, being able to identify and respond to natural cues and consequences is an important component of self-efficacy, and a critical part of independence building for adulthood (Berg, Wacker, & Flynn, 1990; Renzaglia & Hutchins, 1988). Responding to natural consequences requires the individual to (1) identify potential consequences, (2) identify and respond to natural reinforcers, and (3) use feedback to guide future behavior. Although the research literature indicates that skills such as problem solving and self-management are critical skills for all learners to acquire, these are rarely addressed in existing curricular offerings that are identified as school-to-work transition (Hanley-Maxwell & Collet-Klingenberg, 1995).

Self-Advocacy Skills. Self-advocacy skills are considered important skills from both employer and employee perspectives. Initiating contact, convincing others, and being self-assertive integrate the fundamental skills in the areas of communication and behavior with the skills of problem solving and decision making. Responding to the behavior of others is also an important part of self-advocacy. Avoidance of victimizing situations, letting one's needs and desires be known, and responding to/offering criticism are skills that would be included here.

Planning Skills.   Planning skills require the individual to accomplish many tasks including resource identification and acquisition, goal setting, personal organization, and task ordering. Planning is demonstrated in such tasks as IEP participation, stress management, and time management. Planning is critical to the development of long-term career goals and the identification of personal needs as they relate to work. Planning and problem solving are often combined in the decision-making process.

The IEP plays a pivotal role in long-range planning. However, if the IEP process does not progressively enhance the control that the individual students exert over their lives, then these students become victims of the process (Michaels, 1994). The IEP should be viewed as a tool that can be used to assist students in learning planning, self-advocacy, and responsibility skills. Students should not have IEPs completed for them "or to [them]" (Michaels, 1994, p. 14), they should be vitally involved in all aspects of the process. This is especially true in adolescence. "Adolescence is a critical period for the development of skills related to self-determination" (Wehmeyer, 1992, p. 308). During this period, individuals learn the skills necessary to develop realistic expectations. These skills include identifying physical and psychological needs, planning how to meet these needs, gathering necessary resources, and creating the actions required to meet those needs (Wehmeyer, 1992). The IEP process provides the vehicle for learning how to perform these self-determination skills.

Students and parents should be considered and treated as active and important members of the multidisciplinary team, not as passive participants there to okay a plan of action decided in advance by school staff. Home-school collaboration and active parent involvement are discussed and strategies are provided in a number of sources (e.g., Wehman, Moon, Everson, Wood, & Barcus, 1988). Additionally, utilizing the quality of life planning strategies (McGill Action Planning System, Vandercook, York, & Forest, 1989; Lifestyles Planning Process, O'Brien & Lyle, 1987; Personal Futures Planning, O'Brien, 1987; and Choosing Options and Accommodations for Children or COACH, Giangreco, Cloninger, & Iverson, 1993) will enhance the involvement and direction of the planning process by students and their families. These processes are designed to help parents and students "vision" for the future. This ensures that planning takes a lifelong perspective and students are provided with the vehicle to take charge of their own lives.

Recent research has raised clear questions about the ability of 17- and 18-year-old students to make career choices that will continue after exiting school (Shapiro & Lentz, 1991). The results of this research support the notion that involved planning on the part of students must take place throughout the school career, not just in the later high school stages of transition planning, in order for them to learn to make choices, follow through with choices, and revise their plans accordingly. Furthermore, these results support the career development literature that suggests no individual (disabled or not) is ready to make long-term career decisions at the age of 17 or 18. Any plans that students and their families make must be flexible enough to accommodate the real changes that will occur in the postschool environment. Once again, the skills of problem solving and decision making are highlighted. If an individual has the skills and the opportunities to make decisions from a very young age, what becomes important is involvement in the planning process—not what career choices are actually made upon leaving high school. With the acquisition and use of foundation and integrative skills, the individual will leave the school environment with the tools to make ongoing and flexible career and life plans.

Personal Values.   Personal values are repeatedly emphasized by employers as critical employment skills (Carnevale et al. cited in White, 1992; Karge et al., 1992; U.S. Department of Labor, 1991). Personal value skills refer to self-esteem, responsibility and dependability, quality of work, personal ethics, and response to peer pressure. Again, these skills overlap with skills in other areas, such as problem solving and self-efficacy. This area tends to be problematic for many educators, who ask, "Whose values do I teach?" While this is a complicated question, worthy of exploration, suffice it to say that what is important is to provide the opportunities and experiences for all students (regardless of race, ethnicity, socioeconomic status, or gender) to explore a range of personal values as they move through school. By doing this, we provide them with the background from which to form their own values.

Social Skills.   Extensive research (Chadsey-Rusch, 1986; Chadsey-Rusch & Gonzalez, 1988; Greenspan & Shoultz, 1981; Hanley-Maxwell, Rusch, Chadsey-Rusch, & Renzaglia, 1986) has shown that social skills or the lack of appropriate social skills can have a dramatic impact on the success of any individual in any adult role, especially in employment roles as demonstrated by the following facts: The most common reason for job termination is inappropriate social skills (Hanley-Maxwell et al., 1986); the most commonly reported problems in the work environment are related to interpersonal communication (Chadsey-Rusch & Gonzalez, 1988); and the most common interaction in the work environment is joking and teasing (Chadsey-Rusch & Gonzalez, 1988). Critical social skills identified in the SCANS report (U.S. Department of Labor, 1991) include cooperating, negotiating conflict, perspective taking, and team work. Minskoff and Demoss (1994) surveyed employers in relation to the identification of workplace social skill needs. The following skills were identified by more than 70% of the employer respondents: accepts supervision, follows directions, asks for information or assistance when needed, accepts constructive criticism, accepts help from coworkers, helps others when appropriate, does not bully or boss, speaks appropriately to supervisors, does not use profanity in workplace conversations, and listens to other person when involved in conversations.

APPLICATION SKILLS

The third level of the proposed curricular model is the most difficult group to ascertain. Application skills should be targeted based on an individual's interests, abilities, and needs, as well as the idiosyncrasies of the community in which he or she will work. This final set of skills currently receives the most attention at the secondary and postsecondary levels (Halpern, 1992). These skills are the academic and specific technical skills required for targeted jobs or further academic training, and include those skills needed to get and keep jobs.

In general, application skills are made up of fundamental and integrative skills. Whereas fundamental and integrative skills can be considered generic, application skills are specific to the individual and the community in which he or she lives. Application skills build on the first two levels of the model (i.e., fundamental and integrative skills) to support successful and meaningful outcomes. The first two levels of the model, fundamental and integrative skills, are the crux of the model. Application skills are the extension between those critical foundation skills and the use of those skills to succeed in employment settings. Without a solid foundation of the funda-mental and integrative skills, application instruction will ultimately fail.

Skills within and across the three levels of the model do not have to be acquired in sequential order. Many will be taught and learned simultaneously (e.g., social and communication skills, problem solving and community survival skills). But, when skills must be sacrificed because of time constraints or learner-related issues, sacri-ficed skills *must not* be those in the fundamental or integrative categories: the personal survival skills, community survival skills, social/interpersonal skills, and integrative cognitive skills. The reason for this is simple. Adult lives are recreated each day. Early goals and plans, those identified in school, are reworked, revised, and often discarded as self-understanding increases. The experiences of childhood, adolescence, and even young adulthood reveal more about what is not wanted in adult life than what is wanted. In fact, many individuals change jobs several times in their adult lives. Thus, if only job and career-specific skills are learned, young people are trapped into prede-termined targets and flexibility as adults is reduced.

CURRICULUM ACROSS THE SCHOOL AGES

Transition curriculum, including fundamental, integrative, and application skills lends itself to an organized and logical timeline for instruction. Fundamental skills can and should be infused into the regular (functional and/or academic) curriculum during the preschool and elementary years. Higher-order skills should be intro-duced during the early elementary years and refined during middle/junior-high and high school. Finally, goal-specific skills should be explored and identified dur-ing the later elementary grades, and continued into the middle/junior-high school years. These skills should then be targeted intensively during high school. As might be apparent when reviewing the three categories of skills, each category builds on the previous one(s). Specifically, minimal skills (e.g., task completion, working coop-eratively, sharing tasks and materials, asking for assistance, offering assistance) are combined and augmented considering generalization and maintenance issues to form integrative skills (e.g., time management, problem solving, conflict resolution). Combined fundamental and integrative skills then become the basis from which goal-specific skills (e.g., specific job skills, specific community skills, specific leisure skills) are taught. Thus, skills within each level are not taught and then abandoned (i.e., assumed a part of the learner's repertoire). They are retaught (often at greater or more complex levels) throughout the schooling process.

ELEMENTARY SCHOOL

The elementary school years are critical to acquiring foundational skills and begin-ning to acquire the integrative skills necessary for later flexibility. Krumboltz's the-ory (1979) highlights the importance of all life's activities. Based in social learning, this theory describes career development as an interaction between genetics, past learning experiences, current tasks, environment conditions and events. A variety of early learning experiences, role models, and acquisition and reinforcement of self-concept and work concepts will build a solid foundation for such critical career skills as self-observation, decision making, and entry behavior skills.

The elementary years fall within the first stage of Super's (1957, 1974) career development model, the growth stage. This theory reinforces the need for early and frequent opportunities to explore career alternatives as part of the early learning experiences. Career development results from the interaction of the individual with the various learning experiences as he or she synthesizes and compromises along the way. The result of this interactive and dynamic process is occupational self-concept. The growth stage ends with the development of (1) work attitudes and behaviors and (2) a progressive narrowing of career options. Critical activities during the elementary years include exploratory behavior that develops the concepts of self and careers, development of autonomy, development of time perspective, and development of self-esteem.

Translating career theory and desired exit skills into elementary curriculum is somewhat difficult. However, there are target skills, evolving knowledge, and specific activities, summarized in Figure 7.2 and discussed in this section, that are consistently identified as important. Example IEP goals and objectives for selected skills are provided in Figure 7.3.

While there is no current literature that recommends work experiences during the elementary years, Banks and Renzaglia (1993) report that there is a substantial number of authors who advocate for school-based jobs for students with disabilities. Additionally, home chores and neighborhood jobs provide important foundation experiences to learn work attitudes and related behaviors (Banks & Renzaglia, 1993; Hershenson, 1981; Szymanski, 1994). Additionally, elementary school is the time to start vocational awareness through exposure to a variety of career opportunities. Initial efforts should use fantasy (e.g., "What do you want to be when you grow

FIGURE 7.2   Elementary School

Target Activities	Target Skills	Evolving Knowledge
Career fantasy	Grooming/hygiene	Self-awareness
Home chores	Mobility	Self-appraisal
Neighborhood jobs	Interpersonal interaction	Self/familial/cultural
School jobs	Direction following	Values
Work role models	Task completion	Autonomy
Career exploration	Punctuality	Time perspective
	Attendance	Careers
	Communication	Self-esteem
	Basic math	Independence
	Basic reading	
	Basic writing	
	Behavior control	
	Initial Phase	
	Time Management	
	Organization of resources	
	Decision making	
	Reasoning	
	Self-efficacy	

FIGURE 7.3   Example Elementary School IEP Goals and Objectives

Goal: To improve grooming and hygiene skills.

Objectives:

    a. After using the rest room, the student will wash her hands with 100% accuracy for 4 out of 5 days.

    b. The student will arrive at school dressed in clothes appropriate for the weather with 100% accuracy for 4 out of 5 days.

    c. Given the task of setting the table for snack or mealtime, the student will initiate and complete washing her hands prior to the task 5 out of 5 times.

Goal: To improve time management and punctuality skills.

Objectives:

    a. When the morning bell rings, the student will be in his seat in the classroom, with the proper materials, and ready to begin instruction for 4 out of 5 days.

    b. Given in-class activities or assignments, the student will complete the work in the allotted time period 75% of the time for a 2-week period.

    c. When allowed to choose an activity for free period, the student will choose an activity that can be completed within the allotted time period (she may ask for information regarding the time required for a chosen activity) for 3 out of 4 activities for 2 consecutive weeks.

Goal: To improve on behavioral and interaction skills with peers.

    a. When faced with a conflict involving a peer, the student will talk to the peer about possible ways to resolve the situation, before getting a teacher to intervene for 2 out of 3 situations for a 3-week period.

    b. When feeling angry with a peer, the student will talk to the peer or a teacher about how she feels and will refrain from hitting the peer for 2 out of 3 situations for at least a 2-week period.

    c. The student will initiate an activity of her choice with a small group of peers (2 to 3) during recess time for 3 out of 5 days across 2 consecutive weeks.

Goal: To increase career awareness skills.

Objectives:

    a. The student will participate in at least two tours of jobs during the semester.

    b. The student will ask at least one question related to work of a guest speaker during career awareness week.

    c. The student will participate in an in-class activity related to career awareness week.

up?") to focus on the awareness of work as an adult outcome and the variety of occupations available.

Work-related skills learned at this time should cut across traditional and academic curricular domains. Skill development should include the fundamental skills of grooming and hygiene, mobility, interpersonal interaction, direction following, task completion, punctuality, attendance, communication, basic math, basic reading, basic writing, and behavioral control. Elementary curriculum should also include initial phases of development of the skills considered integrative. These skills include time management, organization of resources, independence, behavior, decision making, self-esteem, reasoning, awareness of self/familial/cultural values, and self-awareness/appraisal.

MIDDLE SCHOOL

Super (1957, 1974) sees the exploration stage starting during the middle school years. This is when the student progressively and naturally narrows the occupational options. During this stage, which continues into high school, students move from the career fantasies they have carried over from the growth stage to tentative career options to final career choices. They do this in a circular manner that includes exploration of breadth of occupations to depth in an occupational area, back to breadth and into depth until the student finds the "right" occupation. Students also continue to work on self-appraisal skills and acquisition of knowledge about work environments (Holland, 1985). Other skills that are targeted for continued refinement are those fundamental and integrative skills started during the elementary years. Special focus should be given to self-knowledge, values clarification, problem solving and decision making, social skills, and applied academics. Middle school is the time to start work on application behaviors as well. These include career awareness, sharpening work support behaviors (attendance, punctuality, work quality, time management, independence), development of self-efficacy skills, continued career exploration, and the initiation of that exploration for students with moderate to severe disabilities. Middle school is the time to focus on skill acquisition of generalizable core skills. Core skills are those skills needed for specific job types, regardless of exact location of the job (e.g., floor sweeping in janitorial jobs). Core skills are determined through survey and analysis of common job types available in local communities (e.g., filing, janitorial, fast food, retail). Additionally, they recommend continued development of work habits through ongoing school-based vocational experiences and when possible, movement into the community for work experience to begin job sampling.

Figure 7.4 summarizes the middle school curriculum in relation to target activities, target skills, and evolving knowledge. Figure 7.5 presents IEP examples of skills selected from the middle school years.

FIGURE 7.4   Middle School

Target Activities	Target Skills	Evolving Knowledge
School-based jobs	Social skills	Career awareness
Career exploration	Applied academics	Values clarification
Specific skill training in	Attendance	Self-appraisal
the community (for	Punctuality	Self-awareness
certain students)	Work quality	
	Time management	
	Self-efficacy	
	Problem solving	
	Decision making	
	Initial Phase	
	Career selection	
	Job searching	

FIGURE 7.5   Example Middle School IEP Goals and Objectives

Goal: To improve career awareness skills.

Objectives:

  a. Given access to and instruction on using the Career Portfolio Computer system in the school library, the student will complete a self-assessment on career interests, choose three careers to explore and complete a one-page report on each one.

  b. Given a school-based job (e.g., snack bar, canteen, office helper) that he helped to choose, the student will be punctual in arriving at work, will complete the tasks required with minimal assistance (i.e., by asking questions if needed, but completing tasks independently), and with 90% accuracy for at least 3 consecutive weeks.

  c. During career awareness week, the student will choose four vocations/careers to explore via attendance at talks, tours of businesses, and job shadowing. He will document this exploration by submitting a one-page written report on the vocations/careers at the beginning of the following week.

Goal: To improve problem-solving and decision-making skills.

Objectives:

  a. When confronted with the opportunity to make a decision regarding what to work on during academic resource period, the student will verbally list the options to the teacher (i.e., what assignments he needs to work on), when the assignments are due, which are the most difficult, and what he would like to work on. He will then choose what to work on and review this decision with the teacher. After discussing it with the teacher, he will have the option to revise the decision one time. He will do this for each resource period and, with the teacher, will rate his decisions based on completion of work in a timely fashion.

  b. When given a choice of activities during class time, the student will independently (i.e., without input from peers or teachers) choose an activity and stay with that activity for the required time for 4 out of 5 periods for 2 consecutive weeks.

  c. When faced with a conflict of interests for use of free time (at home and at school), the student will evaluate the situation by verbally listing his options with a peer or adult, talking about the pros and cons of each options, choosing an option, and following through with it. He will later evaluate the outcomes of his choices with a peer or adult and talk about whether or not he would make the same choice in the future. He will do this at least 2 times a week.

HIGH SCHOOL

Because the end goals of career interventions are career development, decision-making skills, career choice making, increased self-concept, appropriate work attitudes and increased competence in locating and securing employment (Rojewski, 1994), the high school work curriculum needs to focus on honing these skills. Wehmeyer (1992) also reminds us that adolescence is the time that individuals typically develop the self-appraisal skills needed to identify physical and psychological needs (Roe, 1956; Roe & Lunneborg cited in Rojewski, 1994), plan how to meet these needs (resource identification and planning), and gather resources to create the actions needed to meet those needs. Students should be assisted in the development of these skills. Furthermore, students should be assisted to make career selections that match their interests, needs, and abilities to targeted work environments (Dawis & Lofquist cited in Rojewski, 1994; Holland, 1985). Matching on these variables will result in higher job satisfaction (Holland, 1985). High school programs should ensure training in specific work skills if appropriate, based on the functioning level of the student.

Banks and Renzaglia (1993) make recommendations related to specific skill training. They recommend that students are given the opportunities to gather enough information about themselves and potential work environments to make career choices (Rojewski, 1994).

Keeping these issues in mind, Mithaug et al.'s (1987) focus on curricula designed to promote generalization and adaptation seems particularly appropriate. Skills emphasized in this type of curriculum include decision making, independence, self-evaluation, and adjustment based on feedback. When these skills are added to the specific vocational skills of seeking, securing, and maintaining employment through generalizing foundation skills and integrative skills, a comprehensive vocational curriculum begins to emerge. The reader is cautioned to remember the importance of academic skills in job success. While continuation of reading, math, and writing skill programs that are showing little success in skill acquisition is not recommended (Gajar et al., 1993), many students with special needs will need or want to continue to focus on the acquisition of these skills within a functional/applied context. Again, this decision is to be made with the student and his or her family in relation to postschool goals. Finally, *all* students should obtain work during their high school years, either in work experience programs and as part-time or summer jobs. While follow-up research has shown that early job choices rarely match up with later career choices (Shapiro & Lentz, 1991), the importance of early work experience to making career choices and ultimate success in obtaining and keeping employment is clear (Rojewski, 1994). These skills, activities and knowledge are summarized in Figure 7.6. Selected IEP examples are presented in Figure 7.7 with a full example of an IEP for Donna presented in Figure 7.8.

FIGURE 7.6   High School

Target Activities	Target Skills	Evolving Knowledge

Part-time or summer employment
Work experience
Locating and securing employment
	Self-appraisal
	  Identify needs
	    Psychological
	    Physical
	  Plan to meet needs
	    Identify resources
	    Plan resources
	  Gather resources
	Job seeking
	Job securing
	Job maintaining
	Career choice making
	  Interests
	  Needs
	  Abilities
	Specific job skills (when appropriate)
	Decision making
	Self-efficacy
	Applied academics
		Self-concept
		Specific work skills
		Work attitudes

FIGURE 7.7   Example High School IEP Goals and Objectives

Goal: To gain work-related knowledge via course work.
Objectives:
   a. The student will register for, attend, and pass (C or better) at least two vocational education classes per semester.
   b. The student will register for, attend, and pass (C or better) the course entitled, "Work Experience in the Classroom," while involved in the work-experience setting.

Goal: To gain direct work-related skills via work experience.
Objectives:
   a. Having worked with the teacher to identify at least two potential work experience sites, the student will choose a site, apply for the job, and interview for the job.
   b. Given a work experience opportunity, the student will attend work for the required hours per week.
   c. Given a work experience opportunity, the student will learn the skills or tasks required of the job with 95% accuracy.

Goal: To gain experience finding, applying and interviewing for jobs.
Objectives:
   a. Using such resources as the newspaper, employment services, and word-of-mouth, the student will identify at least three part-time jobs that are of interest to her. She will do this by the middle of the second week of the first semester.
   b. Upon identifying at least three part-time jobs of interest, the student will ask for, fill out, and submit applications for each. She will do this by the end of the second week of the first semester.
   c. Upon being notified by potential employers for an interview, the student will attend the interview at the scheduled time and complete the interview. She will also follow up the interview with a phone call, within 3 to 5 days.

Goal: To practice work-related time-management skills.
   a. Within the context of work-experience and/or part-time work, the student will be to work on time every day, for a 3-week period.
   b. Within the context of work experience and/or part-time work, the student will complete all of her assigned duties within the time allotted by the employer. She will do this with 75% accuracy for two consecutive weeks (criterion to be raised as student gains experience).
   c. Within the context of work-experience and/or part-time work, the student will sign-out and sign-in at the correct times for beginning and ending work, and for all breaks and lunches. She will do this with 90% accuracy for 2 consecutive weeks (criterion to be raised as student gains experience).

Goal: To continue to build on the academic skills necessary for entry into post-secondary education.
Objectives:
   a. The student will enroll in a freshman prealgebra course, complete all the course work (with the assistance/adaptations of the resource teacher), and pass the course (C or better).
   b. The student will enroll in an English composition course, complete all of the course work (with the assistance/adaptations of the resource teacher), and pass the course (C or better).

FIGURE 7.8 Sample IEP for Case Study

Meeting date: 5/21/96	Beginning date of IEP: 8/20/96	Ending date of IEP: 5/20/97

Student name: Donna Ray	Birth Date: 11/27/81	Sex: F

Parent/Guardian: John and Joan Ray	Address: 201 Way	Phone: 555-5555

District of residence: Anywhere	District of placement: Anywhere	Amount of Special Education (amount/percentage of time): 30%

Extent to which student will participate in regular education programs (describe any modifications required): 70%
- all except resource for math, reading, vocational education activities, and related services specified below.

Related Services (specify weekly amount of time for each service):

_____ assistive technology	_____ parent counseling/training	_____ recreation
_____ audiology	_____ physical therapy	_____ rehabilitation counseling
30 min counseling	1hr–2x psychological services	1hr–2x school health services (sex ed.,
_____ medical services	(assertion trng.)	_____ birth control counseling)
	_____ occupational therapy	_____ social work services

	1x mo transportation services to job shadow
	_____ other (specify) _____
	_____ other (specify) _____

Physical Education: ☒ Regular ☐ Specially Designed   Vocational Education: ☐ Regular ☒ Specially Designed

Participation in standardized testing?
eighth or tenth grade testing ☐ Yes ☐ No ☒ With modifications   Competency based testing: ☐ Yes ☒ No ☐ With modifications   Achievement testing: ☐ Yes ☒ No ☐ With modifications
resource provided oral testing

Justification for removal from regular education or regular education environment (include nature and severity of disability and any potential harmful effects on the child or on the quality of services): Moderate mental retardation. Student needs extra assistance with basic academics, as well as an increased emphasis on post-secondary vocational needs. Parents have requested assertion training, sex education and a consult with DVR.

Sp. Ed. Teacher:	LEA Rep:
Parents/Guardians:	Student:
Agency Rep: none	Other (specify):

Efforts to involve parents: phone call to set date/letter of invitation to meeting

(continued)

FIGURE 7.8 *(Continued)*

Student Name: Donna Ray   Date: 5/21/96

Annual Goal: To maintain and expand functional reading and writing skills as they relate to work.

Present levels of performance: Donna can complete simple forms with minimal assistance, filling in her name, address, phone number, social security number, birth date, etc. She often needs assistance in filling in essay type information (e.g., what are your goals, what do you like, where have you worked). She can read simple signs (e.g., men, women, bus, exit), but has trouble with non-routine reading of maps, instructions, directions, etc.

Short Term Objectives	Objective Criteria	EVALUATION Methods of Measurement	Schedule
Donna will complete a variety (at least five) of job applications independently	Completed applications with fewer than 3 errors.	Career Ed. teacher review of completed applications	fall semester
Donna will travel to businesses in the community, acquire, and complete a variety of job applications (at least three) independently	Completed applications turned in to employers	Employer feedback (follow-up phone call)	spring semester
Donna will read signs in the community in order to move about independently	Read and respond appropriately to all signs encountered in community	Teacher monitoring, parent monitoring, self monitoring	fall/spring semester
Donna will construct a grocery list, and shop from that list at the store	All items on list bought or accounted for with 100% accuracy for 4 out of 5 trips	Teacher/parent monitoring	fall/spring semester

Specific special education and related services needed to achieve this goal: Community instruction and travel time.

Action taken on this goal at IEP review (i.e., continue as is, continue with modifications, discontinue-met, discontinue-revised/replaced):

Student Name: Donna Ray | Date: 5/21/96

Annual Goal: To maintain and expand functional math skills.

Present levels of performance: Donna can tell time on an analogue (traditional) clock or watch. She can use money appropriately (e.g., make change, round-up to the nearest dollar to pay), although she sometimes takes a while to do so. She sometimes has difficulty estimating the cost of items and if she has enough money. She can compute basic math problems but has difficulty in applying the concepts to real-life situations.

Short Term Objectives	EVALUATION		
	Objective Criteria	Methods of Measurement	Schedule
Donna will use a calculator while shopping at the grocery store to add up her total and estimate how much she has spent.	She will do this with 100% accuracy for 4 out of 5 trips.	Self-recording of total from calculator compared to total on receipt. Teacher/parent monitoring.	fall/spring semester
Donna will count out to the nearest dollar the total requested by the cashier, hand it to the cashier, and wait for change.	She will do this with 100% accuracy for 4 out of 5 trips.	Self-report, teacher/parent monitoring	fall/spring semester
Donna will take a basic accounting class to learn how to use a checking/savings account.	Enrollment in class, passing grade (C or above)	Self-report to resource teacher; Reports from accounting teacher to resource teacher	Beginning, middle and end of spring semester
Donna will open a savings account at her parents' bank in her name. She will deposit her weekly allowance (from chores) in the account.	Account opened - passbook in Donna's possession.	Parent report to resource teacher	spring semester
Donna will be listed on her parents' checking account - and will use checks to pay for some purchases (e.g., large grocery trips, items for home, clothing)	Checks will be written with 100% accuracy.	Checks with Donna's name on them. Self and parent report to resource teacher.	Monthly reports
Using a calculator, task analysis and the reconciliation form provided by the bank, Donna will balance the family checkbook	2 out of 3 months with 100% accuracy	Completed reconciliation form to be reviewed by parents/or resource teacher	Monthly

Specific special education and related services needed to achieve this goal: Community instruction and travel time.

Action taken on this goal at IEP review (i.e., continue as is, continue with modifications, discontinue-met, discontinue-revised/replaced):

(continued)

175

FIGURE 7.8 (Continued)

Student Name: Donna Ray	Date: 5/21/96

Annual Goal: To increase awareness of career options for after high school.

Present levels of performance: Donna does not seem particularly concerned about the kind of work she will be involved in after she finishes high school. She has a variety of interests that need to be explored further.

		EVALUATION	
Short Term Objectives	Objective Criteria	Methods of Measurement	Schedule
Donna will take the Careers class (open to freshman, sophomores, and juniors)	Enrollment and passing grade (C or above)	Careers Class teacher report	Beginning, Middle, and End of fall semester
Donna will complete career related activities on the Career Options computer software package available in the school library.	Print-outs of self interest inventory, computer matches to careers, and brief reports on at least 3 careers	Self monitoring and report to resource teacher; print-outs to be reviewed with Careers Class teacher and resource teacher	Fall/Spring semesters
Donna will participate in Career Week activities within the high school. This will include attending at least 3 presentations, going on at least 1 tour, and participating in 1 job shadow.	Donna will complete reaction sheets on each of these experiences	Reaction sheets to be reviewed with Careers Class teacher and resource teacher	Spring semester

Specific special education and related services needed to achieve this goal: Resource time/teacher to assist with written documentation (e.g., reaction sheets)

Action taken on this goal at IEP review (i.e., continue as is, continue with modifications, discontinue-met, discontinue-revised/replaced):

Student Name: Donna Ray | Date: 5/21/96

Annual Goal: To increase/improve employment related skills.

Present levels of performance: Donna has no work history. In addition, she has had few responsibilities at home. While eager to please, she shows little initiation to find or complete tasks, and needs supervision to stay on task in the academic setting. However, the tasks that she does complete are usually done quite well.

Short Term Objectives	EVALUATION		
	Objective Criteria	Methods of Measurement	Schedule
Donna will initiate and complete two daily chores (making bed and doing dinner dishes) and three weekly chores at home (taking out garbage, cleaning upstairs bath, cleaning room).	Daily chores will be completed 4 out of 5 days; weekly chores, 3 out of 4 weeks.	Both Donna and her mom will check-off on a chart to be hung in the kitchen at home. Reports via Donna and her mom to resource teacher	Reports between home and school 3 times a semester, fall and spring semester.
Donna will work in the school library, reshelving returns, for three hours a week.	Attendance at school job.	Librarian and self-report	Fall semester
Donna will work in the student-run snack bar, re-stocking snack items, and managing the cash box for two hours a week.	Attendance at school job.	Teacher supervisor (varies) and self-report	Spring semester

Specific special education and related services needed to achieve this goal: none

Action taken on this goal at IEP review (i.e., continue as is, continue with modifications, discontinue-met, discontinue-revised/replaced):

(continued)

FIGURE 7.8 (Continued)

Student Name: Donna Ray	Date: 5/21/96

Annual Goal: To improve social interaction skills, esp. regarding assertiveness and sexual responsibility.

Present levels of performance: Donna appears to get along well with others (adults and peers), and reports that she enjoys being with her friends. However, her teachers and parents are concerned that Donna is too passive and is often taken advantage of - to the point of being sexually promiscuous.

Short Term Objectives	EVALUATION		
	Objective Criteria	Methods of Measurement	Schedule
Donna will take an after-school assertiveness training class with a small group of students and the school guidance counselor.	Attendance in course; Completion of course	Report by counselor, self-report to resource teacher	First six weeks of Fall semester
Donna will take an after-school sex education class with a small group of students and the school nurse/health educator.	Attendance in course; Completion of course	Report by nurse/health educator, self-report to resource teacher	Second six weeks of Fall semester

Specific special education and related services needed to achieve this goal: Involvement of related services staff(i.e., school counselor, school nurse/health educator). Waiver of enrollment fees due to family's economic status.

Action taken on this goal at IEP review (i.e., continue as is, continue with modifications, discontinue-met, discontinue-revised/replaced):

TRANSITION PLANNING SUMMARY PAGE

Yes	No	*Transition Services are Included in the IEP (indicate location in IEP)
X		*Transition related instruction pgs. 40, 41-42, 43, 44, & 45
X		*Community experiences pgs. 40, 41-42
X		*Employment objectives pgs. 40, 44
X		*Post-school adult living objectives pgs. 40, 41-42, 44, and 45
X		**Acquisition of daily living skills pgs. 40, 41-42, 44
	X	**Functional vocational evaluation to be conducted during fall of junior year

* if not included as annual goals and short term objectives in the IEP, write an annual statement of needed services or if not needed, write a statement regarding the basis upon which the services were excluded.
** if not included as goals and objectives in the IEP, these require an annual statement of needed services, if appropriate.

If the student did not attend the IEP meeting, what steps were taken to ensure that the child's interests and preferences were considered in the planning? NA

Participating Transition Service Agencies and Name of Representative	Date Agency Representative Invited, and Method of Invitation	Statement of Responsibilities /Linkages Related to Each of the Needed Transition Skill Areas
DVR - Scott Hall - DID NOT ATTEND MEETING	4/1/95 - phone call 4/15/95 - letter 5/15/95 - phone call	Has agreed to consult with the family at the school at the end of the school year regarding services available to Donna

If an invited agency representative did not attend the IEP meeting, what steps were taken to obtain the participation of the agency in the planning of transition services? see above

179

CONCLUSION

As seen in the Case Study IEP, work-related curriculum crosses traditional curricular domains (both academic and functional), "borrows" skills from each of these domains, and supplements those skills with work-targeted content. Work-related curriculum should lead the learner to acquire skills in decision making and career choice making, increase his or her self-concept, develop appropriate work attitudes, increase his or her competence in locating and securing employment, develop skills that support job maintenance (e.g., social skills, communication, problem solving), and develop skills that lead to lifelong learning. Early and varied learning experiences contribute to each of these areas, while career fantasy, informal and formal work experiences, and part-time jobs provide the vehicle for the development of career-specific skills and interests. The goal of work-related curriculum should not be to prepare a student for a particular occupation, but to prepare him or her to make relevant career decisions throughout life. Without thoughtful, ongoing assessment and planning, individualized work related curricula cannot be adequately developed. Thus, as intended from the outset, the IEP becomes the critical planning tool for effective education.

REFERENCES

Banks, R., & Renzaglia, A. (1993). Longitudinal vocational programs: A review of current recommended practices for individuals with moderate to severe disabilities. *Journal of Vocational Rehabilitation, 3*(2), 5–16.

Berg, W. K., Wacker, D. P., & Flynn, T. H. (1990). Teaching generalization and maintenance of work behavior. In F. R. Rusch (Ed.), *Supported employment: Models, methods, and issues* (pp. 145–160). Sycamore, IL: Sycamore.

Brolin, D. E. (1983). *Life Centered Career Education: A competency based approach* (Rev. ed.). Reston, VA: Council for Exceptional Children.

Brolin, D. E. (1991). *Life Centered Career Education: A competency based approach* (3rd ed.). Reston, VA: Council for Exceptional Children.

Browder, D. M., & King D. (1987). Comprehensive assessment for longitudinal curriculum development. In D. M. Browder (Ed.), *Assessment of individuals with severe handicaps* (pp. 25–53). Baltimore: Paul H. Brookes.

Brown-Glover, P. (1992). Applications for youth with mild mental retardation. In P. Wehman (Ed.), *Life beyond the classroom: Transition strategies for young people with disabilities* (pp. 237–260). Baltimore: Paul H. Brookes.

Chadsey-Rusch, J. (1986). Identifying and teaching valued social behaviors. In F. R. Rusch (Ed.), *Competitive employment: Issues and strategies* (pp. 273–287). Baltimore: Paul H. Brookes.

Chadsey-Rusch, J., & Gonzalez, P. (1988). Social ecology of the workplace: Employers' perceptions versus direct observation. *Research in Developmental Disabilities, 9*, 229–245.

Dewey, J. (1929). *The sources of a science of education.* New York: Horace Liveright.

Ford, A., Schnorr, R., Meyer, L., Davern, L., Black, J., & Dempsey, P. (1989). *The Syracuse community-referenced curriculum guide for students with moderate and severe disabilities.* Baltimore: Paul H. Brookes.

Gajar, A., Goodman, L., & McAfee, J. (1993). *Secondary schools and beyond: Transition of individuals with mild disabilities.* New York: Macmillan.

Giangreco, M., Cloninger, C., & Iverson, V. (1993). *Choosing Options and Accommodations for Children (COACH): A guide for planning inclusive education.* Baltimore: Paul H. Brookes.

Greenspan, S., & Shoultz, B. (1981). Why mentally retarded adults lose their jobs: Social competence as a factor in work adjustment. *Applied Research in Mental Retardation, 2,* 23–38.

Halpern, A. (1973). General unemployment and vocational opportunities for EMR individuals. *American Journal of Mental Deficiency, 80,* 81–89.

Halpern, A. (1974). Work-study programs for the mentally retarded: An overview. In P. Browning (Ed.), *Mental retardation: Rehabilitation and counseling* (pp. 120–137). Springfield, IL: Charles C. Thomas.

Halpern, A. (1992). Transition: Old wine in new bottles. *Exceptional Children, 58*(3), 202–211.

Halpern, A., Irvin, L., & Landman, J. (1979). *Test for everyday living.* Monterey, CA: CTB/McGraw-Hill.

Hanley-Maxwell, C. (1986). Curriculum development. In F. R. Rusch (Ed.), *Competitive employment: Issues and strategies* (pp. 187–197). Baltimore: Paul H. Brookes.

Hanley-Maxwell, C., & Bordieri, J. (1989, Fall). Purchasing supported employment: Evaluating the service. *Journal of Applied Rehabilitation Counseling, 20*(3), 4–11.

Hanley-Maxwell, C., & Collet-Klingenberg, L. (1995). *Design of effective curricular practices in transition from school to the community.* Eugene, OR: National Center to Improve the Tools of Educators (NCITE).

Hanley-Maxwell, C., Rusch, F. R., Chadsey-Rusch, J., & Renzaglia, A. (1986). Reported factors contributing to job terminations of individuals with severe disabilities. *Journal of the Association for Persons with Severe Handicaps, 11*(1), 45–52.

Hershenson, D. B. (1981). Work adjustment, disability, and the three r's of vocational rehabilitation: A conceptual model. *Rehabilitation Counseling Bulletin, 25,* 91–97.

Hershenson, D. B. (1984). Vocational counseling with learning disabled adults. *Journal of Rehabilitation, 50,* 40–44.

Holland, J. L. (1985). *Making vocational choices: A theory of vocational personalities and work environments* (2nd ed.). Englewood Cliffs, NJ: Prentice-Hall.

Individuals with Disabilities Education Act Amendments of 1990. 20 U.S.C. § 1400 (formerly the Education of the Handicapped Act Amendments of 1990, Pub. L. No. 101–476).

Karge, B. D., Patton, P. L., & de la Garza, B. (1992). Transition services for youth with mild disabilities: Do they exist, are they needed? *Career Development for Exceptional Individuals, 15,* 47–68.

Kellogg, A. (1995). Guidelines for conducting functional vocational evaluations. Madison: State of Wisconsin, Department of Public Instruction.

Krumboltz, J. D. (1979). A social learning theory of career decision making. In A. M. Mitchell, G. B. Jones, & J. D. Krumboltz (Eds.), *Social learning and career decision making.* Cranston, RI: Carroll.

Linkenhoker, D., & McCarron, L. (1980). *Street Survival Skills Questionnaire.* Dallas, TX: McCarron-Dial Systems.

Martin, J. E., Marshall, L. H., & Maxson, L. L. (1991). Transition policy: Infusing self-determination and self-advocacy into transition programs. *Career Development of Exceptional Individuals, 16*(1), 53–61.

McCrea, L. D. (1991). A comparison between the perceptions of special educators and employers: What factors are critical for job success? *Career Development for Exceptional Individuals, 14,* 121–130.

Michaels, C. A. (1994). *Transition strategies for persons with learning disabilities.* San Diego, CA: Singular.

Minskoff, E. H., & Demoss, S. (1994). Workplace social skills and individuals with learning disabilities. *Journal of Vocational Rehabilitation, 4,* 113–121.

Mithaug, D. E., Martin, J. E., & Agran, M. (1987). Adaptability instruction: The goal of transition programming. *Exceptional Children, 53,* 500–505.

O'Brien, J. (1987). A guide to lifestyle planning. In T. Bellamy & B. Wilcox (Eds.), *The activity catalogue: A programming guide for youth and adults with severe disability* (pp. 75–189). Baltimore: Paul H. Brookes.

O'Brien, J., & Lyle, C. (1987). *Framework for accomplishment.* Decatur, GA: Responsive Systems Associates.

Pancsofar, E. (1986). Assessing work behavior. In F. R. Rusch (Ed.), *Competitive employment: Issues and strategies* (pp. 93–102). Baltimore: Paul H. Brookes.

Parker, R. M., Szymanski, E. M., & Hanley-Maxwell, C. (1989). Ecological assessment in supported employment. *Journal of Applied Rehabilitation Counseling, 20*(3), 26–33.

Renzaglia, A., & Hutchins, M. (1988). A community-referenced approach to preparing persons with disabilities for employment. In P. Wehman & M. S. Moon (Eds.), *Vocational rehabilitation and supported employment* (pp. 91–110). Baltimore: Paul H. Brookes.

Roe, A. (1956). Early determinants of vocational choice. *Journal of Counseling Psychology, 4,* 212–217.

Rojewski, J. W. (1994). Applying theories of career behavior to special populations: Implications for secondary vocational transition programming. *Issues in Special Education and Rehabilitation, 9*(1), 7–26.

Sands, D. J., Woolsey, T., & Dunlap, W. R. (1985). *National Independent Living Skills Screening Instrument.* Tuscaloosa: University of Alabama.

Schnorr, R., Ford, A., Savern, L., Park-Lee, S., & Meyer, L. (1989). *The Syracuse curriculum revision manual: A group process for developing a community referenced curriculum guide.* Baltimore: Paul H. Brookes.

Shapiro, E. S., & Lentz, F. E. (1991). Vocational-technical programs: Follow-up of students with learning disabilities. *Exceptional Children, 58,* 47–59.

Snell, M. E. (1987). *Systematic instruction of persons with severe handicaps* (3rd ed.). New York: Macmillan.

Stodden, R. A., & Leake, D. W. (1994). Getting to the core of transition: A reassessment of old wine in new bottles. *Career Development for Exceptional Individuals, 17,* 65–76.

Super, D. E. (1957). *The psychology of careers.* New York: Harper & Row.

Super, D. E. (1974). Vocational maturity theory: Toward implementing a psychology of career education and guidance. In D. E. Super (Ed.), *Measuring vocational maturity for counseling and evaluation* (pp. 9–24). Washington, DC: American Personnel and Guidance Association.

Szymanski, E. (1994). Transition: Life-span and life-space considerations for empowerment. *Exceptional Children, 60*(5), 402–410.

Udvari-Solner, A., Jorgensen, J., & Courchane, G. (1992). Longitudinal vocational curriculum: The foundation for effective transition. In F. R. Rusch (Ed.), *Transition from school to adult life: Models, linkages and policy.* Sycamore, IL: Sycamore.

U.S. Department of Education. (1991). *America 2000: The President's education strategy.* Washington, DC: Author.

U.S. Department of Labor. The Secretary's Commision on Achieving Necessary Skills. (1991, June). *What work requires of schools: A SCANS report for America 2000.* Washington, DC: Author.

Vandercook, T., York, J., & Forest, M. (1989). The McGill Action Planning System (MAPS): A strategy for building a vision. *Journal of the Association for Persons with Severe Handicaps, 14,* 205–215.

Wehman, P. (1992). *Life beyond the classroom: Transition strategies for young people with disabilities.* Baltimore: Paul H. Brookes.

Wehman, P., Kregel, J., & Barcus, J. M. (1985). From school to work: A vocational transition model for handicapped students. *Exceptional Children, 52*(1), 25–37.

Wehman, P., Moon, S. M., Everson, J. M., Wood, W., & Barcus, J. M. (1988). *Transition from school to work: New challenges for youth with severe disabilities.* Baltimore: Paul H. Brookes.

Wehman, P., Wood, W., Everson, J. M., Goodwyn, R., & Conley, S. (1988). *Vocational education for multihandicapped youth with cerebral palsy.* Baltimore: Paul H. Brookes.

Wehmeyer, M. L. (1992). Self-determination and the education of students with mental retardation. *Education and Training in Mental Retardation, 27,* 303–314.

West, L. (Ed.). (1989). *Functional curriculum for transition: A resource guide.* Columbia: University of Missouri, College of Education, Missouri Linc.

Wheeler, J. (1995). *Conducting functional vocational assessments: A train the trainers workshop.* Prairie du Chien, WI.

White, W. J. (1992). The postschool adjustment of persons with learning disabilities: Current status and future projections. *Journal of Learning Disabilities, 25,* 448–456.

Will, M. C. (1986a). Educating children with learning problems: A shared responsibility. *Exceptional Children, 52*(5), 411–416.

Will, M. C. (1986b). *Educating children with learning problems: A shared responsibility. A report to the secretary.* Washington, DC: U.S. Department of Education.

8

Travel and Mobility Training

An Essential Component of Increasing Student Choice and Self-Determination

Michael West

Kathe Wittig

Vicki Dowdy

Case Study: Alex

Alex is a 16-year-old adolescent with mild mental retardation who also experiences moderate levels of depression. He is ambulatory, highly verbal, and reads on a second-grade level. Alex can do simple math such as counting and making change to $1.00. He lives with an older brother in a government-subsidized apartment in a rural town. Alex's parents live in a large, midwestern city. They do not wish for Alex to live with them there because he had previously become fascinated with gang-related activities, particularly drug running, when the family lived in another large city. He misses his parents a great deal and has been dejected and morose about his perceived rejection by them.

Alex is enrolled in a local high school and participates in supported employment training services. His Individualized Education Plan (IEP) and Individualized Transition Plan (ITP) place a strong emphasis on work-related activities. Alex is currently working in a small restaurant as a busboy and dishwasher, and hopes to continue there after graduation and perhaps take on additional duties. This job site is 4 miles from Alex's apartment and 10 miles from his school. There is an effective public transportation system in Alex's area, but he is currently dependent on others to provide transportation.

How can Alex's school personnel plan for him to be able to get to his job and to his apartment, both before and after he graduates?

DESCRIPTION OF CURRICULUM

Mobility and travel refers to movement both *within* and *between* environments. Assisting students to move about in the school, workplace, home, stores, or other public areas would be mobility within environments. "Between environments" refers to getting from one environment to another, such as from the home to school, work, or shopping centers.

Both aspects of mobility are essential components of educational planning and instruction. Increasing a student's mobility within environments increases the likelihood of achieving successful educational outcomes. Being able to maneuver about and locate specific areas within an environment increases the student's competencies and independence in that particular setting, and increases the likelihood that the student will be successful there (McGregor, 1995). For example, instructing a student in work-related skills will be more likely to result in successful employment if the student is also able to move about within the building, locate work areas, or access common areas such as rest rooms, cafeterias, break rooms, and conference areas.

Attention to student mobility between environments is an important educational goal for a second reason: Increasing mobility between environments has a positive effect on student self-determination. Student self-determination is a concept that has received much attention in educational research and policy in recent years, and is increasingly being promoted as both a means and an outcome in special education programs. Some background information may be helpful in understanding self-determination and the role that mobility plays in it.

WHAT IS SELF-DETERMINATION?

Most people value their ability to make decisions about the style of clothing they prefer, the individuals with whom they live, the decor of their home, where they work, the job they perform, and many other facets of life. These decisions are expressions of personal autonomy by which individuals define themselves. The ability to make choices that are meaningful is self-determination. The two key components of self-determination are *choice* and *control* (Deci & Ryan, 1985; Lovett, 1991; Price, 1990). Self-determination will be in evidence when individuals are free to exercise choice and to have those choices be the prevailing controlling factors in their lives, free from coercion or artificial constraints.

In recent years, choice and self-determination have been recognized as expressions of dignity and autonomy for people with disabilities, and have become a focus of educational and habilitative programs (Guess, Benson, & Siegel-Causey, 1985; Shevin & Klein, 1984; West & Parent, 1992). A number of strategies have been demonstrated for enabling choice for persons with even very severe and multiple disabilities (Reid & Parsons, 1990, 1991; Wacker, Wiggins, Fowler, & Berg, 1988). Choice and self-determination lead to improved service outcomes, in the case of VR services to more satisfying and successful employment, with decreased social and economic dependence.

Why Is Self-Determination a Critical Issue for Students with Disabilities?

Research over the past two decades indicates that individuals, disabled or not, tend to participate more and receive greater benefit from activities in which they can experience choice and control. Dattilo and Rusch (1985) found that students with disabilities engaged in a leisure activity more when given the choice of participation than when the choice was eliminated. Children with autism have been found to exhibit fewer antisocial or challenging behaviors when they are allowed choices from among activities (Dyer, Dunlap, & Winterling, 1990; Keogel, Dyer, & Bell, 1987), as have adults with cognitive disabilities (Ip, Szymanski, Johnston-Rodriguez, & Karls, 1994). Parsons, Reid, and Baumgartner (1990) studied clients of a sheltered workshop and found that attendance improved when participants were allowed to choose their own jobs, rather than being assigned to a particular job by the workshop staff.

As students approach transition, self-determination becomes even more critical (Ward, 1989). For most students, the end of high school brings decisions about college, careers, housing, social outlets, and other adult concerns—decisions in which the students are active participants. For many students with disabilities, however, the end of schooling means being placed on waiting lists for residential or vocational services, and lifelong dependence on family, friends, and service agencies. Teaching students with disabilities to be self-directing and self-determined will increase the likelihood of successful transition to a more independent life as an adult (Gerber, Ginsberg, & Reiff, 1992; West, Barcus, Brooke, & Rayfield, 1995).

The Individuals with Disabilities Education Act of 1990 (IDEA) requires that student's goals and preferences be considered in transitional planning. New strategies for promoting student self-determination in the transition process have been developed in recent years. Examples include the Life Centered Career Education model (Brolin, 1993), and student-directed transitional planning models (Wehmeyer & Kelchner, 1995).

How Does Mobility Increase Self-Determination?

In a study of self-determined adults with disabilities conducted by West and colleagues (1995), available means of transportation and independent mobility in the community were major factors in promoting self-determination. Having a means of accessing different environments increased the range of options that were available in the areas of work, socialization, recreation, and housing. Being mobile also enabled those individuals to exercise control, allowing them to decide where and how they lived, rather than relinquishing that control to service agencies, family members, or others.

These are important considerations in educational programs as well, particularly as the student approaches the transition to adult life. Students who are dependent on family or social service agencies for transportation will be functionally limited in the jobs and housing options that are available to them, as well as the friends with whom they can socialize and the types of social, community, and recreational outlets they can enjoy as adults. Increasing mobility and transportation skills and resources therefore increases the amount of choice and control that they experience.

INSTRUCTION, ADAPTATION, AND SUPPORT

It is important to understand that mobility instruction is only one option available to the teacher. Many students with disabilities can be taught to drive or bicycle, negotiate a large and complex building, use public transportation, cross streets safely, and achieve other mobility and transportation needs independently. If students can learn to accomplish these skills independently, then certainly they should be taught to do so. But what if a student is not able to move within or between environments independently because of cognitive or physical limitations? In these cases, the teacher must plan to provide for either *adaptations* or *support* to assist the students to meet their mobility and transportation needs (Sharpton & West, 1996).

Mobility and transportation adaptations involve a redesign of an existing option so that the student is able to use it. When this redesign involves the use of mechanical or electronic devices, it is often termed *assistive technology* (Carr, 1994). Adaptations can also be made to the ways in which tasks or skills are performed, maximizing the physical or cognitive skills that the student possesses, or in the cues to which the student must attend, such as substituting color or pictorial cues for written words. Often, an adaptation also requires some degree of training as well. Adaptations might include any of the following options:

1. Modifications to an automobile or van so that the student can learn to drive it.
2. Providing a student who has problems with balance with a three-wheel bicycle.
3. Use of a wheelchair, motorized cart, walker, or other mobility aid.
4. Environmental modifications for wheelchair or walker accessibility, such as widening aisles, installing ramps or electronic doors, and raising worktables.
5. Installing handrails along walkways to provide support for students with orthopedic or health impairments that impair balance or stamina.
6. Strategic placement of markers, such as signs or color-coded lines, to assist a student in locating target destinations.
7. Providing the student with a map of an area, or written or taped directions.
8. Developing templates for assisting students to identify correct change for bus fares and transfers.

To select a method of adaptation or assistive technology, and to evaluate its effectiveness in meeting the student's mobility needs, teachers should use the following questions, presented by Sharpton and West (1996) and The Arc (1994):

1. Will the adaptation be effective in meeting the student's needs?
2. Will the adaptation be convenient and easy to use?
3. Is the adaptation safe, durable, and reliable?
4. What are the repair and maintenance needs for an assistive device?
5. Can the adaptation be used in multiple environments?
6. Does an adaptation draw unnecessary attention to the student?
7. Is the student happy with the adaptation? Are there alternative methods that make them feel more comfortable?

If an appropriate adaptation is not available to meet an identified need, then the teacher must look for ways of supporting the student. Support refers to the identification and utilization of alternative means for enabling students to be mobile within or between environments (Sharpton & West, 1996). Support options typically involve the assistance of another person or organization. Some examples include:

1. Using a personal assistant, friend, or family member to assist the student in movement within work or community environments;

2. Identifying students without disabilities to serve as "buddies" or helpers to assist students with cognitive or orthopedic disabilities to reach target destinations, such as the library, cafeteria, and classrooms, or to assist with such chores as reaching library books on high shelves.

3. Locating other workers within an employment setting or, in the case of recreational outings, persons having similar interests, with whom the student can ride, and assisting the student in scheduling and reimbursement.

4. Assisting the student to make contacts with coworkers within employment sites to assist in reaching common areas, such as restrooms or cafeterias.

5. Arranging for transportation through paratransit services or human service agencies.

Locating mobility and transportation supports often requires the teacher to explore creative alternatives. When using support options for mobility and transportation needs, teachers should identify both main support options and backup options (Parent, Unger, Gibson, & Clements, 1994). If a student utilizes a ride-share to get to work, there will be days when the coworker is unable to drive to work due to illness, vacations, car problems, or time conflicts. Having the student worker totally dependent on the coworker would mean that both would be absent or late those days, and would reflect poorly on the student. The same principle applies for assisting students to be more mobile within the school setting.

GENERAL APPROACHES TO ASSESSMENT

FUNCTIONAL ASSESSMENT

Regardless of a student's age, the assessment of mobility and transportation needs should take a functional approach, first identifying the environments that students with disabilities want or need to reach, and those in which students are expected to function. Then, an assessment of the student's capacities and resources will help determine if the necessary skills can be taught, or if adaptations or support options are more appropriate (McGregor, 1995). It would be a waste of precious instructional time to teach a student to use public transportation if the student will not live in an area with bus service; likewise, mobility and transportation supports utilized in the school setting will not necessarily be feasible or available in community settings. These situations underscore the need for the instruction of functional mobility and transportation within *natural environments* and *ecological assessment* of mobility needs and resources (Bailey & Head, 1993; Everson, 1993).

NATURAL ENVIRONMENTS

Natural environments are those in which the student currently engages or is likely to engage in the future. For students in elementary grades, school-based activities are generally limited to the classroom and a few other settings, such as the library, cafeteria, and music classroom. Students in a classroom typically travel to these settings as a group (disregarding resource rooms, communication training, and other therapeutic settings for students with disabilities). Middle schools typically schedule classes so that students in the same homeroom take different courses or attend the same course at different times. For students with disabilities, this method of scheduling increases the complexity and difficulty of getting from one area of the school to another and identifying mobility needs and potential support persons. In secondary school, additional complexity arises with the inclusion of community-based training, such as work experience and job training programs, training in shopping and money-handling skills, and the like. Following exit from school, students will enter diverse work, social, and residential environments.

No two students will have identical needs and solutions during any of these stages. The most effective means of identifying a student's mobility and transportation needs is through an individualized assessment of the mobility requirements of the environments into which he or she functions or is expected to function (e.g., ecological assessment), and matching those requirements to training, adaptation, or support options that are available (Bailey & Head, 1993).

CURRICULUM DESIGN

This section presents three case studies of instructional objectives plans for students with disabilities, one each in elementary, middle, and secondary levels. These case studies illustrate the combination of training and support services that can be used to increase students' mobility, and the use of instruction and support in natural environments based on real needs.

Case Study—Elementary School: Amy

Amy is a second grader enrolled in a suburban elementary school in Virginia. Amy sustained a spinal cord injury during an accident when she was two years old. Amy's spinal column was injured at the fifth vertebrae, resulting in complete paralysis of her lower extremities. Amy uses a motorized wheelchair controlled by a touch control mechanism located on a small laptray. Amy's parents are very interested in her program and increasing her mobility and independence. They have requested that Amy's full-time instructional assistant be faded as much as possible. The IEP team was convened and developed the plan presented in Figure 8.1.

The instructional method used by Amy's teachers and aides was to develop task analyses for getting to each destination (see Chapter 2 and Figure 8.2) and, using a system of least prompts, give Amy verbal or gestural prompts to assist her in deciding which routes to take to her destinations. During initial training sessions, they pointed out directional signs and landmarks in the hallways that she could use. When Amy took a wrong turn, they corrected her with either verbal prompts ("Try it again, Amy") or by pointing in the correct direction. Using the task analysis, they were able to monitor her progress and determine the points at which she was having difficulty, and to determine

FIGURE 8.1   Mobility Training Portion of Individualized Education Plan for Amy

Current Skill Level: Amy independently navigates her electric wheelchair down one corridor of her school.

Travel/Mobility Goal: Amy will independently travel from her classroom to at least three school-based destinations.

Instructional Objectives:

1. Amy's teacher will develop a mobility plan with assistance from Amy's occupational and physical therapists by 10/2/95.
2. Amy will utilize her wheel chair independently to reach the cafeteria on five of five trials, by 11/1/95.
3. Amy will utilize her wheelchair independently to reach the library on five of five trials, by 12/6/95.
4. Amy will utilize her wheelchair independently to reach the gym on five of five trials, by 2/1/96.

when she had reached the instructional criterion for each objective. After Amy reaches these criteria, she will be informally monitored to ensure that she continues to reach each destination independently.

Case Study—Middle School: Logan

Logan is a 12-year-old boy with severe visual impairment. He has recently transferred to his local middle school after attending a segregated private school for persons with visual impairments. Logan is on the same grade level (seventh) as his peers in all subjects. Logan's parents are anxious for him to assimilate into the seeing world.

FIGURE 8.2   Sample Task Analysis for Amy

Objective: Amy will utilize her wheelchair independently to reach the cafeteria on five of five trials, by 11/1/95.

Instructional Method: Least prompts will be utilized for correction. Use gestural prompts for error correction (pointing in correct direction) or verbal prompt ("Try it again, Amy"). Record V for verbal prompt required; G for gestural; check for correct performance.

Date										
1. Exit classroom door.										
2. Make right turn.										
3. Proceed to second hallway intersection.										
4. Turn left.										
5. Proceed to third door on right (cafeteria sign).										
6. Turn right.										
7. If door is shut, push open w/wheelchair.										
8. Enter cafeteria.										

Logan's case manager is a resource room special education teacher whose case-load comprises students with learning disabilities. She has expressed some concerns that she lacks the knowledge and experience to "work with blind kids." A meeting was scheduled to develop Logan's IEP. Participants included Logan himself and his parents, the IEP case manager, the school occupational therapist, assistant principal, and guidance counselor, and Logan's counselor from the state department for visual impairments. The mobility plan that was developed for Logan is presented in Figure 8.3.

Because Logan's difficulties were related to the time required to get from one place to another and his fear, and not necessarily learning routes, his teachers and aides focused on training the walker buddies in how to ease his fears and provide encouragement. They also used a stopwatch to time him on each route during the instructional period, and tracked the amount of time he required on a daily basis. This charting enabled them to see when Logan had reached the 15-minute criterion they had established.

Case Study—Secondary School: Tim

Tim is an 18-year-old student with mild mental retardation and behavior disorders. He is ambulatory and very articulate. Tim has had various community-based work experiences including working at a local grocery store. With the support of his parents, Tim has obtained a part-time job bagging groceries at a grocery store in his neighborhood. Tim's parents and teachers are concerned about his safety during the frequent traveling in the parking lot that would be required. At Tim's IEP meeting, the mobility plan presented in Figure 8.4 was developed.

Because of the potential danger to Tim in this training, the IEP team felt that every effort should be taken to ensure error-free learning. This is why the instructional objectives require 100% performance criteria on five consecutive days (see a sample task analysis in Figure 8.5). This level of mastery should ensure that Tim has ingrained safe mobility into his work routine before supervision is reduced. The team also felt that a teacher or aide should be with Tim until complete mastery is attained.

The instruction methods include task analyses of the correct behaviors for initial skill instruction, a daily charting form for recording the number of attempts for one of

---

FIGURE 8.3   Mobility Support and Training Portion of Individualized Education Plan for Logan

Current Skill Level: Logan is able to locate classrooms within his homeroom wing only. He is somewhat fearful of crowds between classes, but has indicated a strong interest in utilizing some of his new friends as "walker buddies."

Travel/Mobility Goal: Given a time frame of not more than 15 minutes, Logan will independently ambulate from one end of the school to the other (from the gym to his homeroom) by June 1996.

Instructional Objectives:

1. The school will allow early release time from long-distance classes for Logan and two identified "walker buddies" from each class during mobility training (October–December). The state agency counselor will provide supervision and program development.
2. Logan will ambulate from the gym to the B-wing with a buddy within arm's reach, in 15 minutes or less, by 12/20/95.
3. Logan will ambulate from the gym to his English class with early release time only, in 15 minutes or less, by 2/15/96.
4. Logan will ambulate from the gym to his homeroom, in 15 minutes or less, by 6/1/96.

FIGURE 8.4   Mobility Training Portion of Individualized Education Plan for Tim

Current Skill Level: Tim can ambulate from one place to another, but does not appear to do so safely. He has been observed walking across a road without looking, and must be reminded to look for oncoming cars.

Travel/Mobility Goal: Tim will exhibit safe travel at all times during the two-hour training session as a grocery bagger.

Instructional Objectives:

1. Tim will look both ways before crossing the street adjacent to the grocery store and correctly judge when safe to cross, five consecutive work sessions, 100% of attempts, under teacher supervision.
2. Tim will exhibit safe travel in the grocery store parking lot while pushing carts to and from the store, five consecutive work sessions, 100% of attempts, under teacher supervision.

FIGURE 8.5   Sample Task Analysis for Tim

Objective: Tim will exhibit safe travel in the grocery store parking lot while pushing carts to and from the store, five consecutive work sessions, 100% of attempts, under teacher supervision.

Instructional Method: Record performance for *each* opportunity; use additional sheets if necessary. Record check mark for performed correctly; X for correction by verbal warning or physical interruption.

Task Analysis: Returning Carts to Store	1	2	3	4	5	6	7	8	9	10
1. Exit store to front drive.										
2. Look both ways prior to crossing.										
3. Cross when clear.										
4. Walk along car row to cart return area.										
5. Push together carts (up to 20).										
6. Connect carts with strap and clip harness.										
7. Check for oncoming cars.										
8. Maneuver carts to center of aisle.										
9. Push toward store.										
10. If car approaches, move to one side.										
11. Stop at front drive, check for traffic.										
12. Cross when clear.										
13. Push carts into store to cart rows.										
14. Undo harness.										

the objectives (which should be varied daily) and the times Tim performs correctly, and immediate cessation of incorrect behavior through either a verbal warning or a physical prompt (putting an arm in front of him to block him from moving forward). After Tim reaches the instructional criteria, the teacher will fade her presence, first by observing him from a conspicuous position, and then by surreptitious monitoring, and finally by random observations.

SAMPLE INDIVIDUALIZED TRANSITION PLAN

We began this chapter with a case study for Alex, who had a personal and educational goal for full-time employment in the restaurant industry. Now we will see

---

FIGURE 8.6   Individualized Transition Plan for Alex

I. Postsecondary Education

Current Skill Level: Alex is currently enrolled in a vocational special needs program at his school. He is not earning Carnegie units toward a regular diploma; rather, Alex will earn a Vocational Certificate in Supported Employment.

Postsecondary Education Goal: Alex will explore available options in his area.

Objective: Alex will explore postsecondary options with his teacher to include:
   a. Job Corps.
   b. Project Work and Education at Franklin Pierce College.
   c. Adult education programs offered through the school system.

II. Postsecondary Employment Goal

Current Skill Level: Alex is part of a small enclave of students with vocational special needs who work in a shopping mall. Alex works in a small restaurant as a busboy and dishwasher. Another student from his class shares these duties. A job coach monitors progress for 15 minutes during each of the three hours they are working at the site. Wages are paid by the restaurant.

Postsecondary Employment Goal: Full-time supported employment in an individual job placement in the restaurant industry.

Objective: Alex will work independently for up to two hours a day by June 1996.
   a. Alex will load and unload the dishwasher independently by December 1995.
   b. Alex will bus tables independently by February 1996.
   c. Alex will clean and sanitize his workstation independently by May 1996.

III. Postsecondary Adult Living

Current Skill Level: Alex is dependent on others for transportation.

Postsecondary Adult Living Goal: Alex will increase his independent mobility skills.

Objective: Alex's special education teacher will develop a daily bus training program by October 19, 1995, to include:
   a. Procurement of bus schedule.
   b. 1:1 training for the initial three weeks, with Alex and teacher riding bus together, fading to teacher following in car.
   c. Independent bus travel for supervised trip within four weeks.
   d. Independent bus travel including one transfer at Main Street depot within eight weeks.
   e. Independent bus travel from school to work within 12 weeks.

---

how Alex's Individualized Transition Plan team addressed that goal and the mobility and transportation needs that coexist with that goal.

Figure 8.6 provides an overview of the Individualized Transition Plan that was developed for him. This Individualized Transition Plan shows the integration of postschool environments and transportation needs and resources. Because bus service was available in Alex's area, and because he was capable of learning to access it, that was the option selected for getting him to his place of employment.

CONCLUSION

This chapter has examined mobility and transportation skills within the context of increasing student success and self-determination, and ultimately the quality of the student's school experiences and adult life. Instruction in mobility and transportation can be most effectively conducted in natural environments, guided by ecological assessment of each student's individualized abilities and mobility needs. Instruction in mobility and transportation is but one option; adaptation and support can be used when a student is unlikely to be able to attain independence through instruction alone.

REFERENCES

Bailey, B. R., & Head, D. N. (1993). Providing O&M services to children and youth with severe multiple disabilities. *RE:view, 25*, 57–66

Brolin, D. (1993). *Life Centered Career Education: A competency-based approach.* Reston, VA: Council for Exceptional Children.

Carr, T. (Ed.). (1994). Assistive technology: Enhancement for daily living. *HKNC-TAC News, 7*(2).

Dattilo, J., & Rusch, F. R. (1985). Effects of choice on leisure participation for persons with severe handicaps. *Journal of the Association for Persons with Severe Handicaps, 10*, 194–199.

Deci, E. L., & Ryan, R. M. (1985). *Intrinsic motivation and self-determination in human behavior.* New York: Plenum Press.

Dyer, K., Dunlap, G., & Winterling, V. (1990). Effects of choice making on the serious problem behaviors of students with severe handicaps. *Journal of Applied Behavior Analysis, 23*, 515–524.

Everson, J. M. (1993). *Youth with disabilities: Strategies for interagency transition programs.* Boston: Andover Medical.

Gerber, P. J., Ginsberg, R., & Reiff, H. B. (1992). Identifying alterable patterns in employment success for highly successful adults with learning disabilities. *Journal of Learning Disabilities, 25*, 475–487.

Guess, D., Benson, H. A., & Siegel-Causey, E. (1985). Concepts and issues related to choice-making and autonomy among persons with severe disabilities. *Journal of the Association for Persons with Severe Handicaps, 10*, 79–86.

Individuals with Disabilities Education Act of 1990, 20 U.S.C. § 33, 1400–1485.

Ip, S. M. V., Szymanski, E. M., Johnston-Rodriguez, S., & Karls, S. F. (1994). Effects of staff implementation of a choice program on challenging behaviors in persons with developmental disabilities. *Rehabilitation Counseling Bulletin, 37*, 347–357.

Koegel, R. L., Dyer, K., & Bell, L. K. (1987). The influence of child-preferred activities on autistic children's social behavior. *Journal of Applied Behavior Analysis, 20*, 243–252.

Lovett, H. (1991). Empowerment and choices. In L. H. Meyer, C. A. Peck, & L. Brown (Eds.), *Critical issues in the lives of people with severe disabilities* (pp. 625–626). Baltimore: Paul H. Brookes.

McGregor, M. L. (1995, April 5–9). *Orientation and mobility for students with multiple severe disabilities.* Paper presented at the 73rd Annual International Convention of the Council for Exceptional Children, Indianapolis, IN.

Parent, W., Unger, D., Gibson, K., & Clements, C. (1994). The role of the job coach: Orchestrating community and workplace supports. *American Rehabilitation, 20*(3), 2–11.

Parsons, M. B., Reid, D. H., & Baumgartner, M. (1990). Effects of choice versus assigned jobs on the work performance of persons with severe handicaps. *Journal of Applied Behavior Analysis, 23,* 253–260.

Price, E. B. (1990). Independence and the individual with disabilities. *Journal of Rehabilitation, 56,* 15–18.

Reid, D. H., & Parsons, M. B. (1990). Assessing food preferences among persons with profound mental retardation: Providing opportunities to make choices. *Journal of Applied Behavior Analysis, 23,* 183–195.

Reid, D. H., & Parsons, M. B. (1991). Making choice a routine part of mealtimes for persons with profound mental retardation. *Behavioral Residential Treatment, 6,* 249–261.

Sharpton, W., & West, M. (1996). Severe and profound mental retardation. In P. J. McLaughlin & P. Wehman (Eds.), *Mental retardation and developmental disabilities* (2nd ed., pp. 131–145). Austin, TX: Pro-Ed.

Shevin, M., & Klein, N. (1984). The importance of choice-making skills for students with severe disabilities. *Journal of the Association for Persons with Severe Handicaps, 9,* 159–166.

The Arc. (1994). *How to evaluate and select assistive technology.* Arlington, TX: Author.

Wacker, D. P., Wiggins, B., Fowler, M., & Berg, W. (1988). Training students with profound or multiple handicaps to make requests via microswitches. *Journal of Applied Behavior Analysis, 21,* 331–343.

Ward, M. J. (1989). The many facets of self-determination. *National Information Center for Children and Youth with Handicaps: Transition Summary, 5,* 2–3.

Wehmeyer, M., & Kelchner, K. (1995). *Whose future is it anyway? A student-directed transition planning process.* Arlington, TX: The Arc.

West, M., Barcus, J. M., Brooke, V., & Rayfield, R. G. (1995). An exploratory analysis of self-determination of persons with disabilities. *Journal of Vocational Rehabilitation, 5,* 357–364.

West, M., & Parent, W. S. (1992). Consumer choice and empowerment in supported employment services: Issues and strategies. *Journal of the Association for Persons with Severe Handicaps, 17,* 47–52.

9

Community Living

STACY K. DYMOND

Erika is 13 years old and attends the eighth grade at the middle school. Her classes consist of home economics, technology education, science, social studies, art, adaptive physical education, and computer science (some are scheduled daily for the school year, others for only a quarter). She also receives instruction in a variety of other environments throughout the school building and local community. In the school, she is sampling office, cafeteria, laundry, and maintenance jobs, and in the community she is learning to utilize stores, restaurants, and public recreation facilities.

Erika is identified as having severe mental retardation and mild cerebral palsy. A variety of staff with expertise in special education, physical therapy, occupational therapy, and speech therapy provide supports that ensure her participation and integration into the school and community. These individuals, along with a paraprofessional staffperson, work closely with the eighth grade teachers to embed Erika's Individualized Education Program (IEP) objectives into the curriculum and make appropriate adaptations when necessary. As a team, they provide direct instruction and therapy to Erika in her eighth-grade classes, school-based jobs, and community activities.

During the past couple of years, Erika's IEP team has begun to shift the focus of instruction from classroom-based activities to school and community-based options. Erika's parents would like their daughter to maintain her current level of integration in the school; however, they recognize that increasing attention must be placed on teaching skills that will enhance her transition to adulthood. In addition to developing social relationships with peers, their priorities for Erika's instruction include building independent self-care, domestic, and community skills; expanding vocational exploration and training in the school building; and increasing Erika's ability to communicate her wants and needs. Due to the severity of Erika's disability, a transition plan has been established as part of the IEP to ensure appropriate planning for her transition from school to adulthood.

TABLE 9.1 Erika's Community-Based Instruction Program

Erika's Objectives	Activities	Environments	Instructor	Frequency	Peer Involvement
When provided with a coupon picture (or other picture) of an item in a store, Erika will pick up the item that matches the picture and release it in her cart/basket within 20 seconds. (Erika will be positioned two to three feet in front of the item before she is asked to locate it.)	Purchase items for cooking class.	Ukrops Grocery Store, Kmart	Home Economics Teacher	Mondays (first two quarters)	A small group of home economics students accompany Erika and the teacher to work on comparison shopping and/or learn about nutrients and calories contained in the food purchased.
Given the checkout line of a store or restaurant and money to cover the cost of the purchase, Erika will hand the cashier the money, wait for change, and deposit the change in her purse, with no more than one gestural cue. (The instructor will provide Erika with the appropriate amount of money prior to reaching the checkout line.)	Purchase and deliver groceries and drugstore items to a homebound senior citizen.	Ukrops Grocery Store, CVS Drug Store	Paraprofessional	Wednesdays (all four quarters)	Student(s) participating in the school volunteer program accompany Erika (during their study hall) to purchase groceries for other homebound seniors living in the same apartment building.
In a fast-food restaurant, Erika will hand the cashier pictures of the items she wishes to order, 100% of the time.	Purchase food for making lunch.	Ukrops Grocery Store	Speech Therapist	Fridays (all four quarters)	None.
	Eat lunch at a fast-food restaurant.	Burger King, Wendy's, or Ukrops Cafeteria	Paraprofessional	Tuesdays (all four quarters)	Peers from Erika's homeroom sign up (with parental permission) to go out to lunch with Erika during their normal lunch period.
	Order a drink at a fast-food restaurant.	Burger King, Wendy's, or Ukrops Cafeteria	P.E. Teacher, Paraprofessional, or Speech Therapist	Once a week (all four quarters, on the way back from a recreation or shopping trip)	Members of adaptive P.E. class purchase a soda with Erika on the way home from a community outing.

This year, Erika's community skills training will focus on locating items in a store, purchasing items, and ordering food at a fast-food restaurant. Stores and restaurants have been targeted based on Erika's preferences and the frequency that her family uses these businesses. Whenever possible, situations have been arranged that allow Erika to participate in community activities with her peers. Table 9.1 lists each of Erika's community objectives, the environments and frequency in which they will be addressed, and strategies for involving nondisabled peers in each activity.

Since Erika has a difficult time generalizing the things she learns in one setting to other similar environments, the IEP team has decided to address each of Erika's community skills objectives in the community environments where the skills are normally performed. When possible, these objectives will also be taught during functional school routines (e.g., in the school cafeteria Erika will use pictures to choose which lunch she wants and pay for her lunch as stated in her community objectives). The team has also identified strategies for incorporating many of Erika's other IEP objectives into her community skills training (see Table 9.2). A copy of her complete IEP is included at the end of this chapter.

TABLE 9.2   Objectives Embedded into Community Skills Training (for Erika)

Domain	Objective	Community Skills Activity
Domestic	Making a sandwich.	Using supplies purchased in the community to make lunch 2–3 times a week at school.
Domestic	Wiping face with a napkin.	During lunch in the school cafeteria; during lunch or when stopping for a soda at a restaurant.
Functional Academics	Using a picture schedule.	Pictures of community activities will be placed in the schedule.
Communication	Making picture choices.	Choosing school cafeteria lunches; choosing type of soda/meal to purchase at a restaurant.
Communication	Requesting a break.	Signing break, as needed, during all community activities.
Communication	Requesting the bathroom.	Pointing to picture of bathroom, as needed, during all community activities.
Social	Greeting others.	Greeting the cashier at a restaurant/grocery store; greeting another shopper in the store; greeting the bus driver.
Social	Saying "thank-you."	After receiving change from a cashier; when someone holds a door open.
Motor	Bilateral hand usage.	Pushing a grocery cart; carrying a bag of groceries; carrying a lunch tray in the cafeteria or restaurant; zipping coat.
Motor	Alternating legs when climbing stairs.	Exiting/entering the school building, stores, and restaurants; getting on/off the bus.

Through community-based instruction, Erika is learning skills that will increase her participation and inclusion in the community. As in many schools today, her IEP team is struggling to determine the appropriate amount of time that she should spend in general education classes with her peers versus in the community. Whereas the majority of her day was spent in activities with her same-age peers during elementary school, instructional time in community environments has become increasingly important as she prepares for adulthood. Balancing the need for school inclusion with that of community inclusion will be an issue that Erika's IEP team will continue to address as she approaches graduation.

In the 1990s, research on school inclusion has expanded to demonstrate the effectiveness of educating students with disabilities in general education classrooms (Evans, Salisbury, Palombaro, Berryman, & Hollowood, 1992; Ferguson, Meyer, Jeanchild, Juniper, & Aingo, 1992; Hunt, Farron-Davis, Beckstead, Curtis, & Goetz, 1994; Hunt, Staub, Allwell, & Goetz, 1994; Kennedy & Itkonen, 1994). As a result, many school divisions have shifted the location of instructional programming from self-contained classrooms to integrated environments. In some cases, this shift has created a gap in services, depending on the way a school has interpreted the meaning of inclusion. For example, some schools have eliminated or significantly reduced their community-based instruction program (for all students) in favor of developing an inclusive school program. Others have interpreted inclusion to mean placement in age-appropriate general education classes even when an activity cannot be appropriately adapted to meet the needs of the student (e.g., adaptations involve simulated work and/or developmental activities that are not age-appropriate or functional for the student). This is not the intent of inclusion.

Inclusion refers to the membership of all individuals (both with and without disabilities) in their schools and communities (Ferguson, 1995). To say that it can only take place when students are located in a general education classroom with their peers is misleading. Inclusion can easily occur in both school and community environments. School personnel and parents can choose both of these types of service; a choice of one does not exclude the other. Many proponents of school inclusion agree that a student's placement in integrated classes must be balanced with their need for instruction in the community (Beck, Broers, Hogue, Shipstead, & Knowlton, 1994; Browder & Snell, 1993; Ferguson & Jeanchild, 1992). Equally important, community-based instruction can and should include students without disabilities, when it can assist all students to meet their educational goals (Table 9.1 illustrates how Erika's community objectives were structured to promote peer involvement).

The purpose of community training is to teach students the competencies they need to function in their community both now (given their present age) and in the future. The emphasis of this training is on teaching functional skills that have longitudinal application throughout the individual's life. Although community experiences have been a mandated component of transition plans since the Individuals with Disabilities Education Act of 1990, many schools began developing community-based instruction programs in the early 1980s. These programs were designed to serve not only transition-aged youth, but all students with disabilities. Community-based instruction was viewed as a method for helping students with disabilities to increase their independence in the community and improve their chances for successful postschool employment and other adult outcomes (Wehman, Kregel, & Barcus, 1985).

Since the development of these initial programs, research has repeatedly demonstrated that systematic instruction in the community leads to skill acquisition

FIGURE 9.1   Benefits of Community-Based Instruction

1. Teaches skills that allow the student to more fully participate in activities outside the school setting with peers and family members.
2. Exposes students to a variety of experiences, thus broadening the choices available to them and increasing their ability to impact their environment.
3. Provides opportunities for students to learn social skills with members of the greater community (not just family, school staff, and other students).
4. Enhances quality of life by increasing community inclusion, independence, and participation.
5. Prepares a student for adulthood by teaching skills that will have longitudinal usage.
6. Raises the family's expectations for their child.
7. Increases the community's expectations for individuals with disabilities.
8. Helps school staff and other IEP members to determine student preferences and plan for postschool opportunities that reflect those preferences.

(Browder & Snell, 1993). Most students with severe disabilities are unable to generalize skills learned under simulated conditions (ones that use artificial materials and settings that approximate the real thing) to the actual environments and situations where they are normally performed. For example, a teacher in a classroom that houses a mock grocery store may find that students learn to grocery shop appropriately in the classroom but fail to use the skill correctly when taken to an actual grocery store. Community-based instruction overcomes this problem by teaching skills in the location where they are expected to be performed. Other benefits of community-based instruction are listed in Figure 9.1.

The desired outcome of education is to teach all students to become productive, independent, and contributing members of society (Everson, 1988). Many skills can and should be taught within the school setting; however, others are better learned in the community. Although community skills instruction is traditionally emphasized at the high school level, elementary and middle school personnel should consider its appropriateness for the students they serve. If we have learned one thing in the field of education, it is that there is no one best way of educating all students. To say that all students should receive inclusive education or all students should receive community-based instruction is inappropriate. For some students, a given educational program may not be suitable at a particular age or during a particular year; for others it may be in conflict with the student's or a parent's preferences. This chapter is designed to assist teams of school personnel, families, and community members to determine when and where community skills instruction is appropriate by describing the components of a community skills curriculum, providing strategies for student assessment and the selection of objectives, and outlining a series of steps that teams can use to develop their own longitudinal community skills program.

DESCRIPTION OF CURRICULUM

Up to this point, the terms "community skills instruction" and "community-based instruction" have been used interchangeably. Community skills instruction refers to the types of skills that are taught whereas community-based instruction signifies the location of the training. Ford et al. (1989) define the major goal areas of community skills instruction to include travel, community safety, grocery shopping, general shopping, eating out, and using services. These skills are usually taught in the community (community-based instruction); however, they can often be embedded into functional school-based routines (community-referenced instruction). Unlike simulations that seek to approximate the materials and conditions of the community environment, community-referenced instruction "references" the community by addressing skills that have joint applicability within both the school and community environments. Some examples of how community-based instruction, community-referenced instruction, and simulated instruction differ are provided in Figure 9.2.

A well-developed community skills curriculum provides students with opportunities for both community-based and community-referenced instruction. While this chapter will focus primarily on community-based instruction, one should not forget the importance of teaching skills in the school setting that reference the same skills being taught in the community. The more opportunities that students have to use a new skill and apply it across multiple settings, the greater the probability of skill acquisition. The following identifies and explains some of the core components of the curriculum.

FIGURE 9.2   Differences Among Community-Based Instruction (CBI), Community-Referenced Instruction (CRI), and Community Simulations (CS)

Skill: Dressing

CBI   Putting on a coat to go into the community; taking off a coat when you arrive at the community location (if appropriate); trying on clothes in a department store; changing clothes at the YMCA to participate in swimming or aerobic dance.

CRI   Changing clothes for gym; putting on/taking off a coat during school arrival/departure; changing shirts after lunch (if the current one becomes soiled); putting on a painting smock in art class.

CS   Five trials of putting on and taking off a shirt in the classroom during a dressing program; tying shoelaces on a dressing board; buttoning clothes on a doll.

Skill: Purchasing

CBI   Purchasing items at the drug store; paying for a game of bowling; purchasing a soda at a restaurant; buying stamps at the post office.

CRI   Purchasing lunch in the cafeteria; buying a drink from the soda machine; purchasing a ticket to a school basketball game; buying school buttons/ribbons to wear on color day.

CS   Counting money in the classroom (e.g., "Show me $6.25"); pretending to shop and pay for items in a classroom grocery store; sorting coins (nickels, dimes, and quarters).

Skill: Communicating/Understanding Pictures

CBI   Locating items in the store from a picture grocery list; ordering in a restaurant using a picture menu; presenting a picture to a store clerk to determine the location of a bathroom.

CRI   Reviewing the school lunch choices and selecting pictures of the items desired; choosing a leisure activity from a series of picture choices; using a picture schedule throughout the school day.

CS   Matching pictures of various foods with their plastic replicas; identifying a picture by pointing to it when the teacher verbally requests "Show me the _____."

INSTRUCTION THAT REFLECTS LOCAL COMMUNITY OPPORTUNITIES

Community instruction emphasizes skills and activities that are valued by the students, their parents, and the community. Since communities differ, schools must develop a curriculum based on the opportunities available in their particular locality. For example, using public transportation might be an appropriate instructional objective for many students living in urban environments; however, it has limited applicability in rural areas where the primary method of transportation may be a family member or friend's car.

Instruction must not only reflect the opportunities available in the community, it should also take place in each student's community of residence. Students with disabilities are increasingly being served in their home school (the school they would attend if they did not have a disability). Community-based instruction for these students naturally occurs in their local community. In rural areas where two or three centrally located schools serve all students in the county or urban areas where all students (regardless of disability) attend regional high schools, many schools find it necessary to transport students to their neighborhoods so that instruction can occur in the businesses the family normally frequents.

FUNCTIONAL SKILLS

Functional skills are ones that have immediate applicability in a student's life (Brown et al., 1979). In a community skills curriculum, they result in increased participation and involvement in valued community activities. Functional skills also include those activities that teach students to participate in future environments. By focusing on skills that will be needed in the near future, teachers can encourage a smooth and successful transition between current and subsequent environments (e.g., elementary to middle school, school to work, etc.).

Within a functional community skills curriculum, skills are taught in the natural environment(s) where they are normally performed. This allows the student to use the actual materials involved with the activity and to learn skills within the context of the normal sights, sounds, smells, lighting, and distractions associated with the environment where the activity occurs. For example, rather than teaching students to use a play phone in a cardboard box that is painted to look like a telephone booth (simulated instruction), telephone skills would be taught at an actual pay phone in the community (community-based instruction).

AGE-APPROPRIATENESS

Choosing skills that reflect an individual's community and teaching them in the environment(s) where they are normally performed will do little to ensure functionality if the activities in which the skills are taught are not age-appropriate. An activity is age-appropriate if a person of the same age without a disability would find the activity acceptable. Within a community skills curriculum, instruction and participation in the community increase with age and parallel the opportunities available to students without disabilities. Children in elementary school may accompany their parents to the grocery store and participate by choosing a favorite cereal or snack item. In contrast, a high school student may be responsible for traveling to the store independently and picking up several grocery items needed for that night's dinner. Examples of age-appropriate community skills training are examined later in this chapter.

INDEPENDENCE VERSUS PARTICIPATION

The ideal goal of functional programming is for students to acquire independent life skills. Many students, however, will always require some level of assistance and may not reach full independence in the activities in which they participate. Although surveys have indicated that teachers do not feel adequately prepared to provide integrated school and community instruction to students with profound, multiple disabilities (Izen & Brown, 1991) or severe challenging behaviors (Horner, Diemer, & Brazeau, 1992), effective strategies do exist for including these individuals in integrated environments.

One method that has frequently been used is partial participation (Baumgart et al., 1982). With this strategy, a student participates in (and receives instruction on) a portion of a task and an adult or peer assists the student to perform all other skills. For example, when using the post office, a student with a significant motor impairment may need assistance with placing a stamp on the correct location of an envelope. Once this assistance is provided, the student would participate by dropping the envelope in the mail slot. Although the student may never reach full independence in this activity, partial participation enables him to exert control over his environment and participate to the maximum extent possible.

OMISSION OF THE READINESS THEORY

The readiness theory states that students must learn certain prerequisite skills before they will be "ready" to go into the community (Wilcox, 1987). School personnel subscribing to this theory often use it to justify why students with severe disabilities and/or challenging behaviors should not receive community-based instruction. They believe that if students exhibit challenging behaviors in the classroom, they will also exhibit these challenging behaviors in the community. As a result, they list community-based instruction as a future objective and spend the present school year trying to teach the student appropriate behaviors.

One of the major problems with the readiness theory is that some students may spend their entire lives "getting ready" without ever arriving at the place they are trying to reach. By preventing students from accessing integrated settings, teachers may in fact be promoting the challenging behaviors they are trying to change. Teaching age-appropriate, functional skills in normalized community environments contributes to positive behaviors. It provides natural opportunities for students to learn appropriate behaviors in the settings where they are needed. It also enhances the student's quality of life by promoting independence, providing opportunities to develop relationships, and increasing the variety of activities and number of choices available to the student.

A COLLABORATIVE MODEL

Community skills programs are designed and implemented using a team approach. Parents and students are key participants in determining which goals and objectives should be targeted for instruction. Other members of the team may include general and special educators, paraprofessionals, and therapists. Although a community skills curriculum may be used to provide direction regarding the types of skills that are appropriate for each age level, it is up to the team to decide which of these skills best meet the instructional needs and preferences of each individual. The team also shares responsibility for providing instruction on the skills, both in the school and the community.

SYSTEMATIC INSTRUCTION

Most community skills for students with disabilities are taught in the community rather than the school. Unlike field trips, which occur sporadically, community-based instruction involves regular, repeated training on specific IEP objectives. Systematic instructional procedures (task analyses, specific teaching strategies, natural cues and corrections, reinforcement, and data collection) are used to teach each skill. Although a variety of techniques have been used successfully to train students in the community, instructors should consider approaches that increase students' inclusion rather than call attention to their differences. In a sample of sheltered workshop staff, job coach staff, fast-food restaurant staff, and business students, Wolfe (1994) found that physical prompts were viewed as less appropriate by the fast-food staff and business staff than by the sheltered workshop staff and job coaches. In addition, most respondents found antecedent and data collection strategies to be more socially acceptable than consequential strategies. These results reinforce the importance of choosing teaching strategies that are both effective with students and do not inadvertently stigmatize them.

GROUPING STUDENTS

Community-based instruction can be provided either one-on-one or in small groups. It has been suggested that no more than four students accompany an adult in the community at one time (Hamre-Nietupski, Nietupski, Bates, & Maurer, 1982). This ensures that each student's needs will be adequately met and that the students will blend in with the community environment. Large groups of students with disabilities do not reflect the natural proportions of people with disabilities in the community and call attention to themselves as being different. If more than four students must go into the community at one time (e.g., because of transportation availability) the group should be split up to receive instruction in different businesses.

Whenever possible, students should be heterogeneously grouped. This might mean that a student with a disability participates in community-based instruction with his or her nondisabled peers or that he or she is grouped with other students who have varying levels of disabilities. A number of schools have developed strategies for providing community-based instruction to students both with and without disabilities (see Beck et al., 1994, for an example). For students without disabilities, community-based instruction can be a method for applying what has been learned in the classroom (e.g., triple digit addition) to the real world (e.g., figuring the cost of groceries to make sure that one does not overspend a budget). Since these students may not need to participate in community skills instruction as frequently as their peers with disabilities, a teacher may decide to rotate small groups of students through the experience. For example, Joe (a student with a disability) may need to receive community-based instruction three times a week. Each day Joe goes into the community, the teacher schedules a group of three peers without disabilities to participate in the training. These groups rotate each day so that all students receive community-based instruction at least once a month. While Joe and his peers may complete the activity (e.g., grocery shopping) together, Joe may be working on learning to locate items in the store while his peers address a math class objective (e.g., using a calculator, comparing unit prices of items, or figuring the cost of the grocery bill).

FREQUENCY OF INSTRUCTION

The amount of time devoted to teaching community skills depends primarily on the preferences of the family and the goals they have for their child. Other factors that the IEP team may wish to consider include the student's age and severity of disability. In general, as a student grows older, the need for community skills instruction increases. For students who have severe disabilities and do not easily generalize what they learn in one setting to another setting, community skills instruction (whether it be community-based, community-referenced, or a combination of these) may be a priority throughout the student's entire school career.

GENERAL APPROACHES TO ASSESSMENT

To maximize the benefits of community skills instruction, goals and objectives should be chosen for each student based on their interests, preferences, and needs. Traditional models of assessment and service delivery for individuals with disabilities have focused on a systems-centered approach (Bradley, 1994). With this approach, assessment has emphasized a consumer's (student's) deficits, and services have been chosen based on the programs offered by the organization (the school). Recognizing that this model prevents consumers from obtaining access to opportunities not offered by "the system," many organizations are beginning to create supports based on the preferences of the individual. Known as person-centered planning, this approach seeks to understand an individual's hopes, needs, and dreams for the future. Control for developing appropriate student objectives shifts from the professional (teacher) to a team that includes the person with a disability, family members, friends, and professionals who can assist the student to achieve his or her goals. Services and supports are created for the person based on his or her vision for the future, rather than just the programs currently offered by the school.

In Erika's team, members used a variety of assessment tools to learn about her skills and preferences in the community, her parent's priorities for instruction, and the dreams she and her family had for the future. The team's knowledge about the businesses and agencies in the community were then combined with this information to identify instructional priorities. This section suggests four steps for completing a comprehensive person-centered assessment that focuses on a person's skills and talents rather than his or her deficits. The steps include (1) inventory the community, (2) determine student and parent preferences, (3) gather information about student skills, and (4) prioritize student goals and objectives. An example of how these steps were used by Erika's team to plan for her community skills training is provided in Figure 9.3.

STEP 1. INVENTORY THE COMMUNITY

Community skills instruction should reflect the activities and opportunities available in the student's community. For many students, families, and school personnel, the assessment process begins by determining all the possibilities that exist in the community. Sitting around a table and discussing options does little good unless all team members are familiar with the activities that occur in the student's community. Ecological inventories have frequently been used to obtain this information prior to beginning a student's individualized planning process.

An ecological inventory involves canvassing the community and identifying all the environments (agencies, organizations, or businesses) where instruction can take place (Brown et al., 1979). One of the best ways to complete an ecological inventory is by walking or driving around the community. Since most people only access a portion of their community, it is often difficult to recall all the options that exist when one is sitting at school or at home. A teacher conducting his first ecological inventory once commented that he thought his community was so rural that it had little to offer the students. When he took his inventory (originally completed at school) into the community and compared it with the businesses and agencies he saw, he was amazed at the wealth of opportunities that were available for his students.

After the environments in the community have been identified, the next step in an ecological inventory is to determine the subenvironments. The subenvironments are the different physical areas of a business. For example, within a grocery store, some of the subenvironments might include the cart area, the canned goods aisle, the meat section, the dairy case, the bakery, the deli, the salad bar, and the checkout lines. These subenvironments can further be broken down into the activities that occur in each area and the skills required to participate in these activities. An example of a partial ecological inventory that Erika's team developed for Wendy's is shown in Figure 9.4.

Many schools find it helpful to organize the results of their ecological inventory into a districtwide file that can be accessed by school personnel. Periodically, the file can be updated to include new businesses and remove ones that have left the area. Other helpful information to include with the inventory results are the location of the business, its distance from the school building(s), its proximity to other businesses where instruction could occur, and environmental aspects that may affect students (e.g., noise, temperature, visual distractions, walking distance involved, long lines at the checkout counter, etc.). This type of filing system can be particularly helpful to new school personnel, staff who live in a different community from that of the school, and families who are trying to evaluate different instructional possibilities for their child.

A second part of assessing the community involves taking the information obtained from the ecological inventory and defining the types of activities and skills that are most often performed at each age level (elementary, middle, and high school). This can be done by observing what students without disabilities do independently, with family, and with friends in the community at various ages. Another effective strategy is to interview parents and students to obtain their perspectives.

FIGURE 9.3   Assessment Strategies Used by Erika's Team

Step 1. Inventory the Community

Erika lives within 5 miles of the middle school and her parents frequently use the businesses within that locality. Since the school division had previously completed an ecological inventory of the area, team members began the assessment process by reviewing the inventory results so that they could be prepared to share the existing possibilities with Erika's parents. Their inventory indicated that a variety of restaurants, stores, and other businesses (roller-skating rink, bowling alley) were located in the community and that transportation would require use of the school bus or car since public transportation was not available.

Step 2. Determine Student and Parent Preferences

Erika's family decided to participate in a Making Action Plans (MAPs) planning process to help them determine some long-range plans for her future. They invited several of Erika's friends, teachers, and therapists to attend. Two of the dreams Erika's family have for her future are that she participate in meaningful activities (maybe a job?) in the community and that she have friends and family who are actively involved in her life. Although Erika was not able to articulate these goals, she smiled and nodded when asked what she thought about them. As a result of the MAP, a number of steps were identified that the group could take to help Erika achieve these goals. At school it was determined that Erika should learn skills that would increase her ability to participate in the community. Since Erika has limited methods for expressing herself, the team assessed her preferences by developing a list of activities and activity qualities that they knew she liked. Preferred activities involved being with other people, eating, preparing food, keeping/retrieving things from her bookbag, and walking. The team decided that possible environments of interest to Erika would be the grocery store and a fast-food restaurant because both environments encourage social interactions, each centers around food, and opportunities for walking would be available. In addition, Erika could learn to retrieve money from a purse instead of a bookbag to purchase items in each environment.

Step 3. Gather Information About Student Skills

Erika's parents involve her in most activities; however, she has never actively participated in the community environments they frequent. As a result, the team decided to take Erika into a grocery store and a fast-food restaurant to observe her reactions and any attempts she made to participate. Erika responded favorably to both environments. She was able to push the grocery cart with some assistance in steering and she carried a light grocery bag when one was put in her hand.

Step 4. Prioritize Student Goals and Objectives

After Erika sampled both community environments, her IEP team reconvened to review the assessment results and identify specific community skills objectives. Erika's parents thought that instruction in both environments would help her to participate in the community both now and after she exits school. They also thought the experiences would expose her to different jobs that she might be able to sample in the future. Since Erika demonstrated limited skills in each environment, the team targeted three objectives that would allow her to partially participate in five different activities (see Table 9.1). These objectives were also chosen because they can be applied in the school environment and will have long-term potential usage in many other community environments.

Parents can identify the variety of activities and skills that their child performs at a certain age, whereas students will be able to define the activities that are most valued by their peer group.

There are several commercially available curriculums that can be used to augment an ecological inventory. For example, *The Activities Catalog* (Wilcox & Bellamy,

FIGURE 9.4 Partial Ecological Inventory for a Fast-Food Restaurant

Domain: Community
Environment: Wendy's

Subenvironment	Food Counter
Activity	Ordering food
Skills	Waiting in line; looking at the menu; greeting the cashier; making a choice; placing an order; waiting for the food
Activity	Paying for food
Skills	Obtaining money; handing money to the cashier; receiving change; putting change in wallet; saying thank-you
Subenvironment	Condiments Section
Activity	Obtaining condiments
Skills	Obtaining a straw, ketchup/mustard/relish, napkins, and silverware
Subenvironment	Seating Area
Activity	Obtaining a table
Skills	Carrying tray; locating a table; sitting down; removing coat
Activity	Eating lunch
Skills	Unwrapping food; unwrapping silverware; putting straw in drink; putting mustard/ketchup/relish on burger; using a napkin; eating
Activity	Socializing with others
Skills	Greeting friends; asking for help or helping others; commenting on food; talking with friends about shared interests

1987) and *The Syracuse Community-Referenced Curriculum Guide* (Ford et al., 1989) both suggest possible community activities and the ages at which they are appropriate. Each provides a listing of activities and possible skills to teach in the community, and offers strategies for assessment, individualized planning, and management of a community skills program. When used in combination with an ecological inventory, these curriculums can help schools to examine numerous possibilities for instructional programming.

STEP 2. DETERMINE STUDENT AND PARENT PREFERENCES

In addition to reflecting the opportunities available in one's locality, community skills instruction should also be based on student and parent preferences for instruction. This information can be gathered through questionnaires, interviews, observations, community sampling, and personal futures planning. Multiple methods are often needed to obtain an accurate understanding of each party's interests and preferences.

Questionnaires are one of the most frequently used strategies for assessment. For parents, they often include a series of questions about the child's current level of participation and skills in the community, areas where they experience difficulty, community activities that the child seems to enjoy, and the parent's priorities for skill instruction. Student questionnaires generally seek to identify the student's personal interests and previous experiences in the community. The benefit of questionnaires is that they allow people to think about their responses privately before responding. However, they sometimes neglect to obtain complete or accurate information. For this reason, they are often most beneficial when used in combination with an interview.

Interviews can occur by phone or face-to-face. In some cases, they are used to review the results of a questionnaire and clarify parent/student responses. In other cases, interviews may involve the use of pictures of community activities or a copy of the school's ecological inventory file. Using pictures and lists allows parents and students to look at a variety of options without having to recall specific examples in their minds. This option can be especially helpful when obtaining information from parents who have a disability or are unable to read.

Observations are a particularly effective assessment strategy for students who have severe disabilities and may not be able to respond to questionnaires or picture choices. The process involves observing the student in a variety of activities at home and school. Based on these observations, a list of activities and activity qualities that the individual likes and dislikes is developed. The list is then compared with opportunities in the community that reflect the qualities the person most enjoys. For example, if a student enjoys participating in activities that involve music (an activity quality), community instruction might occur in environments that naturally involve music (e.g., music store, roller-skating rink, department stores). Skills can then be selected for instruction based on the activities that occur in that preferred environment.

Community sampling, an extension of the observation process, involves taking students into the community to observe their reactions to various environments. This method is helpful when the student's team is trying to decide among a number of alternative environments or when logistical arrangements (e.g., length of the activity, amount of walking involved, etc.) may affect the student's perception of an activity. By visiting the environment with the student, additional information can be gathered before a decision is made about the appropriateness of that environment for instruction.

Personal futures planning is a method for assisting someone with a disability to plan for their future and take steps toward achieving their goals (Mount, 1994). It supports a long-term planning approach and can be used with people of all ages. While there are many ways of conducting personal futures planning, one of the tools most frequently used with school-age students is the Making Action Plans System, also known as MAPS (see Furney, 1993; Pearpoint, Forest, & Snow, 1992, for more information on conducting MAPS). Unlike the other models of assessment profiled in this section, the MAPS process provides a comprehensive view of an individual's life and assists team members to structure community instruction within the context of how it will help the individual to reach overall life goals.

STEP 3. GATHER INFORMATION ABOUT STUDENT SKILLS

When completed, Step 2 should result in a list of community environments and activities that reflect the student's and parent's preferences. In Step 3, these activities are explored in greater detail and information is gathered about the student's skills and abilities in each activity. Much of this information can be obtained by interviewing people who know the student well and have observed him or her in the environments of interest. In some cases, this information may be sufficient for the team to move to the prioritization process in Step 4. In others, where a student may not have had previous opportunities for participation (e.g., the student accompanies a parent to the post office but does not actively engage in any activities), further assessment of the student's skills may be warranted.

Informal assessments of student skills are most accurate when they occur in the environment where the skill is normally performed. One method for conducting an informal assessment is to develop a task analysis for each of the activities in question, observe the student performing the skills (without teacher instruction), and record which steps the student implements correctly, incorrectly, or does not attempt. By allowing the student to sample the activity, the team may find that the student already has many of the needed skills and that instructional time would be better spent in another area. The team might also determine that a number of skills could be targeted for instruction and that efforts will need to focus on identifying which skill(s) should receive primary focus during the upcoming year. Step 3 should result in a list of specific skills and activities from which the team will select goals and objectives for the student.

STEP 4. PRIORITIZE STUDENT GOALS AND OBJECTIVES

Organizing the assessment results to determine priority areas for instruction is one of the most difficult, yet most essential steps for identifying student objectives. It is a time for teams to evaluate each of the proposed areas for instruction and determine which ones have the greatest potential value for the student. A number of factors have been suggested for consideration when prioritizing objectives (Falvey, 1989). Figure 9.5 encompasses these and other components that teams may wish to consider as they weigh the value of each potential community skill. For a more detailed student assessment and planning strategy, the reader is encouraged to refer to the *COACH* (Choosing Options and Accommodations for Children), developed by Giangreco, Cloninger, and Iverson (1993).

FIGURE 9.5   Questions to Consider When Prioritizing Community Skills Objectives

1. Does the skill reflect the student's strengths and interests?
2. Has the student's family identified the skill as a priority?
3. Is the skill chronologically age-appropriate? Do students without disabilities of the same age participate in this activity?
4. Will learning this skill increase the student's level of participation in the community with family and friends during nonschool hours?
5. Can the skill be taught and applied in a variety of community environments?
6. Is it possible to embed the skill into natural school-based routines (community-referenced instruction)?
7. Is the skill reasonable?
8. Will acquiring this skill help the student to function more independently in future environments?

CURRICULUM DESIGN

A key factor to the development of a successful community skills program is the inclusion of a diverse group of people in its planning. Although a special education teacher or community skills coordinator is usually responsible for maintaining the day-to-day organization of the program once it is in place, he or she should not be the only person to develop the curriculum. During the design phase, school personnel (special and general education teachers, therapists, paraprofessionals, administrators), parents, and community members need to work together as a team to generate a vision for the program, address concerns, and develop procedures and guidelines for curriculum implementation. This ensures that multiple perspectives are gathered and that commitment for the program is obtained from the different groups who will be directly or indirectly impacted.

There are a variety of approaches that schools can use to develop their community skills program. *The Syracuse Curriculum Revision Manual* (Schnorr, Ford, Davern, Park-Lee, & Meyer, 1989) provides some excellent strategies for school personnel to consider. Ideally, the curriculum should be longitudinal in nature (K–12) and address the needs of all children, regardless of disability level. In some instances, it may be desirable to develop and pilot the program with one group of students before expanding its implementation across the school division. This method was chosen in Greensville County, a rural community where students with disabilities obtained all their instruction in the school building (most, in self-contained classrooms). Since the community was not accustomed to seeing students with disabilities receive instruction in the community, the school division decided to initiate the program with interested students with moderate and severe disabilities at the high school. This class was chosen because of the teacher's interest and involvement in developing the community skills program and because of the students' age (high school level) and need for instruction in community skills. Appendix 9.B illustrates the length of time it took Greensville County to develop its program, the number of people and programs consulted, and the value placed on keeping everyone in the community informed of the project's progress.

OVERCOMING OBSTACLES TO COMMUNITY SKILLS TRAINING

During the initial stages of curriculum development, a number of questions arise about the feasibility of providing instruction in the community. Issues related to liability, transportation, staffing, and program expense are often viewed as obstacles that could prevent the school system from adopting a community skills program. Several strategies identified for addressing each of these issues are now widely accepted and practiced in the field. In addition to considering the ideas offered in this chapter, teams would be wise to consult with professionals from other school divisions in their region who are implementing successful programs to determine the strategies they use.

Liability. Since students participate in community training as part of their IEP, the school system is responsible for students while they are in the community in the same way that they are responsible for them when they are on school grounds. Many schools initially fear that the risks involved with providing students instruction in the community may increase their susceptibility to claims of liability and, in particular, negligence. Liability refers to *who* is responsible if a student is injured in the community or if property is damaged. In many instances, an individual is deemed liable on the basis of negligence (not providing appropriate supervision or care). To protect staff from liability and claims of negligence, schools should consider the following steps before implementing community instruction:

1. Present the program to the school board and obtain their approval.
2. Contact the school's insurance carrier and review the current policy to make sure that it covers all students and staff engaged in community-based instruction. In some cases, a clause may need to be added if staff will be providing instruction outside normal school hours.
3. Develop a manual that identifies professional conduct during training and includes procedures for handling emergencies.
4. Make sure that all staff are trained in CPR and basic first aid.
5. Obtain written parental permission for training in the community.
6. Verify that each student is covered by a parent's or guardian's health insurance or a school insurance policy.
7. Include all community-based training objectives on the student's IEP.

Transportation.   Depending on the nature of a community and the location of its schools, transportation can be a logistical nightmare. In one school division, both the elementary and high school are located at a rural crossroads centrally located for three towns. Within a five-mile radius, the schools have access to two convenience stores, a small "mom and pop" grocery store, and a church. Although instruction occurs in these environments, the staff and students also regularly travel a minimum of 20 miles one way to provide instruction in the three towns where most of the students live. A school car that was donated to the driver education program (by a car dealership) is used to transport students.

A number of options exist for transporting students to and from the community. These include:

- *Walking.* Walking helps students to work on mobility goals and also provides opportunities for students to learn street-crossing skills. In many urban areas, it may also be the most convenient method for accessing the community.

- *School Buses.* Teachers, paraprofessionals, and other school staff who have a bus driver's license may be able to use the school bus during the day to transport students. In addition, scheduling community outings to coincide with the current school bus schedule (e.g., dropping students in the community on the way to school, picking up students from the community on the way home, riding with other students traveling to work-study programs, etc.) can maximize school resources.

- *School Cars/Vans and Driver Education Vehicles.* More economical than a school bus, these vehicles can often be stationed at the school and designated specifically for students receiving community training.

- *Private Vehicles.* Use of staff and volunteers' cars provides maximum flexibility when scheduling community instruction; however, care should be taken to make sure that the school's insurance will cover this transportation option.
- *Public Transportation.* In urban areas, public buses, subways, taxis, and specialized transportation (e.g., buses for people with disabilities) all provide excellent methods for accessing the community throughout the day.
- *Transportation Provided by Other Agencies.* In some instances, schools can access transportation provided by adult service agencies (e.g., The Arc, Community Services Board) when additional seats are available on their vans.

Staffing.   Community-based instruction should occur with small groups of students (no more than three or four per instructor). Most schools rarely have the luxury of such high staffing ratios; however, creative ways do exist for maximizing existing resources. In addition to the special education teacher, the following arrangements can be made for other staff to provide community-based instruction:

- Therapists who normally schedule their time during student's classes can arrange to provide therapy goals as part of a student's community instruction.
- Peer tutors, adult volunteers, and college students can assist school staff with instruction.
- Job descriptions for paraprofessionals can be changed to include the provision of community instruction. (Although paraprofessionals work under the general supervision of a teacher, there is no reason they cannot independently provide instruction in the community once they have received appropriate training.)
- Team teaching among special education teachers or between special and general education teachers promotes a shared responsibility for all students. Small group instruction (in the school or community) is possible while other students receive large group instruction.
- General education teachers can provide instruction in the community to a small group of students (both with and without disabilities) to address individual needs.

Program Expenses.   Although the most cost-effective method for providing community training is to access environments and activities that do not require money (e.g., public library, window shopping, music store "listening library," community center, street crossing, mall walking), many student's objectives cannot be completed without some level of funds. Families have frequently been requested to contribute money for their son or daughter's instruction in the community. Not all families, however, are financially able to offer assistance. Lack of money should not prohibit any student from receiving community instruction. Instead, the following alternatives should be considered:

- Convert a portion of the classroom supply budget for community skills training. Obtain permission for staff to procure cash advances so that students can use real money to make purchases.

- Have students use their lunch money to purchase lunch supplies at the grocery store. Provide instruction on meal preparation during the week.
- Conduct fund raisers (e.g., bake/sell cookies during lunch hour, sell coffee and muffins to teachers throughout the school day, obtain orders for cakes/cookies from school staff, grow plants for the holidays, hold car washes). Students' other IEP objectives can be embedded into these activities.
- Have families send in money and a list of purchases they need. Obtain similar lists from school staff or elderly people in the community who need assistance.

DEVELOPING GUIDELINES AND PROCEDURES FOR IMPLEMENTING COMMUNITY-BASED INSTRUCTION

Providing students with quality instruction in the community requires extensive up-front planning. It is important that school personnel develop procedures and guidelines for implementing community-based instruction prior to training students in the actual community. Many school systems find it helpful to compose a manual or handbook documenting the decisions that have been made. This method has several benefits. First, it reinforces the school division's commitment to providing students with instruction in the community. Second, it provides staff with specific procedures for implementing the program. Third, it helps maintain consistency in the delivery of services throughout the school division.

Although a community-based instruction manual may have many components, the following areas should be emphasized:

- *School Philosophy or Mission Statement.* This might include the importance of preparing students to enter the adult world, the benefits of teaching in real settings where students need to perform the skills they learn, and the school system's commitment to teaching students to live as independently as possible.
- *Liability.* The school's liability for students who are receiving instruction in the community should be explained as well as strategies the school division has taken to prevent claims of negligence. Decisions made regarding school insurance coverage of staff and students during instruction in the community should be explicitly stated.
- *Handling Emergencies.* Specific procedures for handling emergencies in the community should be identified. Requirements for students to carry personal identification cards and staff to carry important phone numbers might also be included.
- *Transportation.* This section should identify which types of transportation are acceptable for training (e.g., school bus, public transit, personal vehicle, walking) and who is responsible for making the travel arrangements.
- *Training Expenses.* Identify how community skills training will be funded. For example, families might be requested to fund all activities where the child performs a service for the family while the school covers the cost of all other expenses. Describe how funds will be accessed and by whom.

- *Staff Responsibilities.* Clearly define which school personnel will be responsible for setting up training sites, analyzing the tasks, training students, supervising paraprofessionals, and teaching those students at school who are not receiving community instruction at that time. Guidelines might be provided on how to write IEP goals for community environments.

- *Release Forms.* Parental permission forms should be obtained for transportation to and participation at each new training site. Although community-based instruction goals will be included in the IEP, parents should be informed and agree to the specific skills to be taught, activity location, and training dates and times.

DESIGNING THE CURRICULUM FOR DIFFERENT AGE LEVELS

Although students of all ages access the community, the types of activities in which they engage are often dependent on their age. For example, a 6-year-old child may accompany his parents to the food court of a mall and choose the type of food he wants to eat (e.g., hamburger); a 12-year-old may decide the specific eatery in the food court she wishes to use and order a meal with money provided by the parent; and an 18-year-old will choose the time of day he goes to the mall to eat, the amount of money he will spend, and the friends or family members with whom he will eat. As a person grows older, the number of choices and responsibilities increase.

The design of a community skills curriculum should reflect the natural range of choices and responsibilities that are available to most children as they mature. Although some students with disabilities may require adaptations or assistance to participate in an activity, the types of activities they access should be determined by their preferences and chronological age rather than their ability to independently perform the skills involved with the activity. Naturally, a variety of other considerations will influence the type of community skills instruction any one student receives. The purpose of a curriculum, however, is to provide information about the kinds of skills needed to participate in the community and the ages at which those skills are normally acquired.

In addition to the identification of age-appropriate skills, a community skills curriculum must also consider the extent to which students should receive instruction in the school and/or community. While this decision should be based on the individual needs of the student and preferences of the family, Sailor et al. (1989) suggest several guidelines for teams to consider. They advocate that during the elementary school years most instruction occur in the school building (general or special education classrooms). The focus during these years should be on increasing students' proximity and contact with their nondisabled peers. Beginning in the late elementary years and throughout middle school, instruction in community environments takes on greater importance. Students still receive instruction in integrated school environments; however, the percentage of time they spend in the community increases. In high school, community instruction intensifies as students prepare for adulthood and other postschool living objectives. The following sections illustrate how this model can be used to determine the types of community skills instruction students receive during elementary, middle, and high school.

Elementary School. Community skills instruction is provided primarily in the school building during the elementary years. Skills are selected that reference those needed to participate in the community at that age. For example, learning to carry a tray in the cafeteria can be applied in fast-food restaurants or other cafeterias in the community. Instruction also prepares students to function in future environments. Students who are taught to board and exit a school bus during arrival and departure from school will use these same skills when traveling to a business in the community when they are older. Although providing instruction in the school setting does not guarantee that the student will be able to apply the skill in the community, it does provide natural opportunities for students to learn functional skills with their nondisabled peers.

Occasionally, there may be situations that require instruction in the community. A student's behavior may be so difficult that it precludes the family from accessing the community with their child; the severity of a student's disability may prevent him or her from generalizing the skills learned at school to similar community settings; or the parent may simply prefer that instruction occur in the community environments that the family frequents. The type of training provided (community-referenced or community-based) should reflect the individual needs of the student. When possible, this instruction should include a student's same-age peers (see previous section, "Grouping Students" for strategies on how to involve nondisabled peers in community activities). Some examples of the types of objectives that might be targeted for a student at this age level can be found in Table 9.3.

Middle School. Instruction at the middle school level begins to focus on teaching skills in the community environments that a student's family accesses. Although

TABLE 9.3   Elementary School (Selected IEP Objectives)

Objective	Environment	Activities/Skills
Find destination.	School building	Get meds at the clinic; go to lunch in the cafeteria; return books to the library; take attendance to the office; locate classroom when arriving from the bus.
Use the school bus.	School bus	Get on/off the school bus; find a seat; identify correct bus; put on a seatbelt.
Walk with an adult, peer buddy, or group of students.	School building	Move to the next activity in the classroom; go with the class to lunch, P.E., or another activity; run an errand with a peer; stay with the group during fire drills.
	Convenience store Fast-food restaurant	Walk with an adult from the car/bus to a store or restaurant; stay with an adult while browsing in a store.
Purchase items.	School cafeteria	Hand lunch ticket/money to cashier; buy ice cream.
	Convenience stores	Purchase gum, candy, drink, or other snack.
Use a cafeteria/fast-food restaurant.	School cafeteria Fast-food restaurant	Obtain utensils, condiments, napkin, straw; carry tray; dump trash.

community-referenced instruction remains an important component of a student's in-school experiences, many age-appropriate skills become increasingly difficult to reference in the school setting. For instance, teaching a student to locate personal care items in a drug store can only be taught in the community drug store. To approximate these skills in the school setting would entail the creation of artificial simulations that have limited meaning for most students. Certainly many skills can still be referenced in the school; however, the goal at this stage is to provide students with opportunities to perform skills in the actual environments where they will be used.

During middle school, the amount of time devoted to community skills instruction gradually increases. By being exposed to a number of community environments and receiving instruction in critical areas, students can begin to acquire the skills they will need in adulthood. These opportunities can also help students to identify preferred community activities and potential options for future employment. For some individuals, community skills objectives may be included in the transition component of the IEP at this time. As with elementary school, opportunities for participating in community skills training with the student's peers should be identified whenever possible. Sample IEP objectives for students at the middle school level are provided in Table 9.4.

TABLE 9.4   Middle School (Selected IEP Objectives)

Objective	Environment	Activities/Skills
Use a change machine.	Arcade store, laundromat, post office	Obtain change for playing arcade games, using washers and dryers, and purchasing stamps from vending machine.
Cross the street.	Parking lots Single lane roads Double lane highways	Navigate a parking lot from one's car/bus to the business; cross a single lane road; cross a double-lane highway; use pedestrian "walk" signs.
Use a vending machine.	School cafeteria Grocery store YMCA or community center Post office Laundromat	Purchase a drink; obtain a snack; buy stamps; purchase laundry soap.
Use a pay phone.	Community pay phone	Call school to inform staff of location and anticipated return time; call a business to determine hours of operation.
	School pay phone	Call parent to obtain an item left home, to obtain a ride after school, or to inform of sickness; call a business to determine hours of operation.
Rent a video or Nintendo®.	Video rental store	Select a video or game; present the cashier with desired item; show video card; pay rental fee; walk through turnstile.

TABLE 9.5   High School (Selected IEP Objectives)

Objective	Environment(s)	Activities/Skills
Clothes shopping.	Department stores, discount stores, the mall	Window shop; browse through clothes; select and try on clothes; return unwanted clothes to rack; purchase clothes.
Use public transportation.	Public bus	Select the correct bus; pay bus fare; locate a seat; exit the bus.
Eating out.	Sit-down restaurant	Locate a table; order from the menu; play the jukebox; signal the waiter/waitress for assistance; pay for the meal.
Grocery shop.	School building	Plan a meal; develop a shopping list; clip coupons.
	Grocery store	Push the grocery cart; select items from grocery list; transfer items to checkout counter; pay for items.
Get a haircut.	Beauty salon Barber shop	Schedule an appointment; secure transportation; communicate needed services; pay for services; leave a tip.

High School.   Community training during the high school years builds on skills learned at the elementary and middle school levels. Instruction in community environments continues to take on increased importance as the length of time devoted to community skills, and community functioning in general, expands. Once a student graduates with their peers at age 18, special education services may focus exclusively on instruction in community environments (across all instructional domain areas) in order to prepare students to transition from school at age 21.

During high school, all students begin to make curriculum choices based on the goals they have for their life as adults. Some students focus on advanced academics that will prepare them for college while others pursue training in a vocational trade. Due to the diversity of student goals at this level, inclusion in community activities with one's peers may be more likely to occur after school or on weekends. In one rural school system, community skills instruction includes Junior ROTC training because a large proportion of the student body participates in this activity. Although some of the training occurs during school hours, students also participate in raising the flag at football games, presenting the colors at school board meetings, and marching in local parades. Other ideas for community skills training at the high school level are provided in Table 9.5.

CONCLUSION

Training in community skills is essential for students of all ages and all abilities. Whether it takes place in the school, the community, or some combination of both settings, depends on the needs and preferences of the student and their family. This chapter has defined the major components of a community skills curriculum and suggested guidelines that school personnel can use to develop their own program. While many of these ideas have worked in other school divisions, each program has looked significantly different depending on the opportunities available in that particular community. The success of any community skills program lies in the degree to which it teaches students the skills they need to access their community and participate in valued activities with friends and family.

APPENDIX 9.A

ERIKA'S IEP GOALS AND OBJECTIVES

DOMESTIC

GOAL   To increase independence in dressing, food preparation, eating, and cleaning activities.

1. Given a shirt and an activity that necessitates changing clothes, Erika will independently put on the shirt within three minutes.
   (Examples: changing for gym class; changing from bathing suit to regular clothes at the YMCA; changing shirt after lunch [if it becomes soiled during eating]; changing into home economics uniform [a shirt to protect students' clothes during cooking].)
2. Given bread, cold cuts, a knife, and mayonnaise or mustard, Erika will make a sandwich for lunch (2–3 days a week), with 90% accuracy.
   (Erika will bring her sandwich to the lunchroom (in a lunch bag) and eat with her peers as usual on the days this objective is addressed.)
3. Given a paper napkin during lunch or snacks, Erika will wipe her mouth without prompts, 90% of the time.
   (Environments where this objective will be addressed include the school cafeteria, the classroom, Wendy's, Ukrops Cafeteria, and Burger King.)

RECREATION/LEISURE

GOAL   To expand Erika's leisure skills in integrated school and community environments.

1. Given free time, Erika will participate in board games with her peers, twice a week.
2. Given pictures of leisure activities in the community, Erika will point to one picture and participate in that activity for at least 15 minutes, once a week.
   (Leisure choices will include bowling, swimming, aerobics/dance, arcade games, exercise machines, browsing in stores, movie rentals, movie theaters, the public library.)
3. Given breaks between activities, Erika will select an age-appropriate free-time activity and engage in the activity independently for five minutes, 90% of the time.

COMMUNITY

GOAL   To develop skills in the community that will promote increased independence and inclusion.

1. When provided with a coupon picture (or other picture) of an item in a store, Erika will pick up the item that matches the picture and release it in her cart/basket, within 20 seconds.
   (Stores used will include Ukrops Grocery Store, Kmart, and CVS pharmacy. Erika will be positioned two to three feet in front of the item before she is asked to locate it.)

2. Given the checkout line of a store or restaurant and money to cover the cost of the purchase, Erika will hand the cashier the money, wait for change, and deposit the change in her purse, with no more than one gestural cue.
   (The instructor will provide Erika with the appropriate amount of money prior to reaching the checkout line.)

3. In a fast-food restaurant, Erika will hand the cashier pictures of the items she wishes to order, 100% of the time.

VOCATIONAL

GOAL   To sample four different jobs within the school building during the year. (Erika will sample only one job each semester. Each objective will be targeted for 30 minutes, 3–5 times per week.)

1. Given the school cafeteria dishwasher, Erika will stack dirty plates, cups, and silverware in the dishrack with 90% accuracy.
   (Erika will partially participate in all aspects of running the dishwasher; however, instruction in this environment will focus only on this objective.)

2. Given a maintenance cart and a job duties checksheet, Erika will clean the teacher's lounge, with 100% accuracy.
   Cleaning the teacher's lounge will consist of emptying the trash, wiping down the vending machines, and washing the worktable.

3. Given clean towels and aprons in the home economics room, Erika will fold each item with 90% accuracy.
   (Erika will partially participate in washing dirty towels/aprons and drying them. This objective will be targeted once Erika takes the items out of the dryer.)

4. Given the daily announcements, Erika will insert one announcement into each teacher's mailbox, 100% of the time.
   (Erika and another office assistant who does not have a disability will work together to complete this task.)

FUNCTIONAL ACADEMICS

GOAL   To improve math, time management, and money skills within the context of functional routines.

1. Given a functional task or activity that requires one-to-one correspondence, Erika will pick up and distribute one item to each person/place, with 100% accuracy.
   (Examples: inserting one copy of the daily announcements in each teacher's mailbox; passing out one set of pastel chalks to each student in art class; dealing one card to each player during a free-time board game; inserting one new handout or other material into students' social studies or science folders; passing out jerseys during gym class.)

2. Given a picture schedule in a notebook, Erika will open her notebook, pick up the first picture, velcro it to the outside of her notebook, and walk to the location of that activity with a peer, with no more than one gestural prompt.

(One picture will be velcroed on each page of Erika's notebook and pictures will be sequenced according to the order in which they occur. Once Erika has arrived at the next activity, the picture on the cover of her notebook will be placed in a "discard" pocket in the back of the notebook.)

3. Given coins and a "change card," Erika will match the correct coins to the card to purchase a drink or snack from a vending machine with 90% accuracy.

(A change card will be developed that shows pictures of each snack in the school vending machines and the corresponding coins necessary to purchase each item.)

COMMUNICATION

GOAL   To increase Erika's ability to influence and control the events in her environment.

1. Given a choice of three pictures, Erika will point to one picture and obtain the item or activity chosen, 90% of the time.

(Examples: choosing a leisure activity; choosing a peer with whom to work; indicating which job to perform first; making choices among cafeteria lunch options; determining a soda choice for break time.)

2. Given a difficult task and the need to take a break, Erika will sign "break" to request a break in instruction, 80% of the time.

3. Given the need to use the bathroom, Erika will initiate pointing to the picture of a toilet, 100% of the time.

SOCIAL

GOAL   To develop socially appropriate methods for interacting with others.

1. When initiating a greeting with a friend or stranger (not a relative), Erika will wave, shake hands, say "hello," and/or give "fives," 100% of the time.

2. After receiving assistance with a task or activity, Erika will look at the individual who provided the assistance and say "thank-you," 90% of the time.

(Examples: receiving change from a school cafeteria or store cashier; receiving assistance from a peer or teacher; receiving medication from the nurse.)

MOTOR

GOAL   To maximize Erika's strength and use of both sides of her body to perform daily routines.

1. Given an activity that requires bilateral hand usage, Erika will use both hands to complete the task, 100% of the time.

(Examples: rolling a maintenance or grocery cart; catching/holding/rolling a ball during gym class; carrying a tray in the cafeteria or a restaurant; zipping pants or coat; opening a can of soda; folding towels; putting on a shirt.)

2. When going up or down stairs, Erika will alternate right and left legs for at least six consecutive steps.

(Examples: entering and exiting the school building; walking to the cafeteria; walking from the cafeteria to the nurse's office.)

APPENDIX 9.B

Process for Developing a Community-Based Instruction Program
Greensville County Schools*

September–October 1993. Greensville County's high school teacher for students with moderate and severe disabilities met with the special education director and school principal to gain support for developing a community-based instruction program (CBI) for students in his class. These individuals requested long-term assistance on this project from the Severe Disabilities Technical Assistance Center (SD TAC) at Virginia Commonwealth University.

November 1993. An initial meeting was held with members of the school division and the SD TAC to clarify the goals and objectives of the program and to develop an action plan. The SD TAC agreed to provide the school with technical assistance on a monthly basis through December of 1994. Information about the addition of community-based instruction and vocational training to the curriculum was announced through the school newsletter.

December 1993. The teacher began reviewing other school division's CBI manuals to determine possible guidelines and procedures that would need to be implemented. A letter was sent to parents to explain about the changes in the curriculum and to invite their participation in the process. An article was also published in the local newspaper outlining the proposed curriculum changes.

January 1994. The special education director coordinated a review of the school's insurance policy to ensure that staff and students would be covered during CBI. Transportation possibilities were explored.

February 1994. The teacher and SD TAC representative presented an inservice to the high school faculty on the importance of transition planning. A videotape was shown illustrating students with severe disabilities receiving instruction in the community as part of their transition from school to work and an explanation was given of how this could happen in Greensville County. The teacher presented a similar inservice to the Special Education Steering Committee, the Lions Club, and the Rotary Club. An Advisory Council was formed (members included school personnel, parents, business leaders, and community service personnel) to participate in the design and review of the CBI guidelines. The teacher and special education director also observed students from a similar school setting in the community and talked with that county's community training coordinator about issues specific to developing a program in a rural environment.

March 1994. An inservice on ecological assessments and curriculum development was provided by the SD TAC representative to elementary and high school staff who serve students with severe disabilities. The Advisory Council held its first meeting, discussed the program's progress, and decided to submit a grant proposal to the statewide transition system (Project UNITE) in order to obtain funding for (1) a job coach, and (2) an extended summer contract for the teacher.

---

* From "Hard Work and Accomplishments . . . A Time for Celebration," by Stacy Dymond and Trish Angle, 1995, *Four Runner*, 10(5), p. 5. Copyright 1995 by the Severe Disabilities Technical Assistance Center at Virginia Commonwealth University. Reprinted with permission.

April 1994. An ecological inventory of the community was conducted to determine potential training sites. Procedures and guidelines for implementing CBI were developed. A grant was submitted to Project UNITE.

May–June 1994. The CBI program was piloted with two students at nonvocational community training sites. Greensville County received full funding from Project UNITE. The teacher leading the development of the school's community skills program was voted "Teacher of the Year" by his high school faculty.

July–August 1994. The teacher visited several adult service agencies to learn about their programs (many already had staff who had participated on the Advisory Council). Time was also spent meeting with parents and students to determine their preferences for instruction, developing appropriate objectives, and revising IEPs. A project brochure was developed for the community-based vocational program and initial vocational and nonvocational training sites were identified. A job coach was hired, and she and the teacher attended a two-day training seminar on supported employment. The SD TAC representative provided inservices on the labor laws and community-based instructional training strategies for all school staff who serve students with disabilities.

September 1994. An updated article on the CBI program was published in the local newspaper. A schedule of student training times was solidified. By the end of the month, seven of the eight students were receiving community skills training twice a week (one student's parents opted not to have their son participate). The community-based vocational training program was piloted with three of these students.

REFERENCES

Baumgart, D., Brown, L., Pumpian, I., Nisbet, J., Ford, A., Sweet, M., Messina, R., & Schroeder, J. (1982). Principle of partial participation and individualized adaptations in educational programs for severely handicapped students. *Journal of the Association for the Severely Handicapped, 7,* 17–27.

Beck, J., Broers, J., Hogue, E., Shipstead, J., & Knowlton, E. (1994). Strategies for functional community-based instruction and inclusion for children with mental retardation. *Teaching Exceptional Children, 26*(2), 44–48.

Bradley, V. J. (1994). Evolution of a new service paradigm. In V. J. Bradley, J. W. Ashbaugh, & B. C. Blaney (Eds.), *Creating individual supports for people with developmental disabilities: A mandate for change at many levels* (pp. 11–32). Baltimore: Paul H. Brookes.

Browder, D. M., & Snell, M. E. (1993). Daily living and community skills. In M. E. Snell (Ed.), *Instruction of students with severe disabilities* (4th ed., pp. 480–525). New York: Merrill.

Brown, L., Branston, M. B., Hamre-Nietupski, S., Pumpian, I., Certo, N., & Gruenewald, L. (1979). A strategy for developing chronological age appropriate and functional curricular content for severely handicapped adolescents and young adults. *Journal of Special Education, 13*(1), 81–90.

Clark, G. M. (1994). Is a functional curriculum approach compatible with an inclusive education model? *Teaching Exceptional Children, 26*(2), 36–39.

Evans, I. M., Salisbury, C. L., Palombaro, M. M., Berryman, J., & Hollowood, T. M. (1992). Peer interactions and social acceptance of elementary-age children with severe disabilities in an inclusive school. *Journal of the Association for Persons with Severe Handicaps, 17,* 205–212.

Everson, J. M. (1988). An analysis of federal and state policy on transition from school to adult life for youth with disabilities. In P. Wehman & M. S. Moon (Eds.), *Vocational rehabilitation and supported employment* (pp. 67–78). Baltimore: Paul H. Brookes.

Falvey, M. A. (1989). *Community-based curriculum: Instructional strategies for students with severe handicaps* (2nd ed.). Baltimore: Paul H. Brookes.

Ferguson, D. L. (1995). The real challenge of inclusion: Confessions of a "rabid inclusionist." *Phi Delta Kappan, 77,* 281–287.

Ferguson, D. L., & Jeanchild, L. (1992). It's not a matter of method: Thinking about how to implement curricular decisions. In S. Stainback & W. Stainback (Eds.), *Curriculum considerations in inclusive classrooms: Facilitating learning for all students* (pp. 159–174). Baltimore: Paul H. Brookes.

Ferguson, D. L., Meyer, G., Jeanchild, L., Juniper, L., & Zingo, J. (1992). Figuring out what to do with the grownups: How teachers make inclusion "work" for students with disabilities. *Journal of the Association for Persons with Severe Handicaps, 17,* 218–226.

Ford, A., Schnorr, R., Meyer, L., Davern, L., Black, J., & Dempsey, P. (Eds.). (1989). *The Syracuse community-referenced curriculum guide for students with moderate and severe disabilities.* Baltimore: Paul H. Brookes.

Furney, K. S. (1993). *Making dreams happen: How to facilitate the MAPS process.* Burlington, VT: University of Vermont, Center for Transition Policy and Development.

Giangreco, M. F., Cloninger, C. J., & Iverson, V. S. (1993). *Choosing options and accommodations for children: A guide to planning inclusive education.* Baltimore: Paul H. Brookes.

Hamre-Nietupski, S., Nietupski, J., Bates, P., & Maurer, S. (1982). Implementing a community-based educational model for moderately/severely handicapped students: Common problems and suggestions. *Journal of the Association for the Severely Handicapped, 7*(4), 38–43.

Horner, R. H., Diemer, S. M., & Brazeau, K. C. (1992). Educational support for students with severe problem behaviors in Oregon: A descriptive analysis from the 1987–1988 school year. *Journal of the Association for Persons with Severe Handicaps, 17,* 154–169.

Hunt, P., Farron-Davis, F., Beckstead, S., Curtis, D., & Goetz, L. (1994). Evaluating the effects of placement of students with severe disabilities in general education versus special classes. *Journal of the Association for Persons with Severe Handicaps, 19,* 200–214.

Hunt, P., Staub, D., Allwell, M., & Goetz, L. (1994). Achievement by all students within the context of cooperative learning groups. *Journal of the Association for Persons with Severe Handicaps, 19,* 290–301.

Individuals with Disabilities Education Act of 1990, Pub. L. No. 101-476, 20 U.S.C. § 33, 1400–1485, 104 Stat. 1103–1151.

Izen, C. L., & Brown, F. (1991). Education and treatment needs of students with profound, multiple handicapping and medically fragile conditions: A survey of teachers' perceptions. *Journal of the Association for Persons with Severe Handicaps, 16,* 94–103.

Kennedy, C. H., & Itkonen, T. (1994). Some effects of regular class participation on the social contacts and social networks of high school students with severe disabilities. *Journal of the Association for Persons with Severe Handicaps, 19,* 1–10.

Mount, B. (1994). Benefits and limitations of personal futures planning. In V. J. Bradley, J. W. Ashbaugh, & B. C. Blaney (Eds.), *Creating individual supports for people with developmental disabilities: A mandate for change at many levels* (pp. 97–108). Baltimore: Paul H. Brookes.

Nietupski, J., Hamre-Nietupski, S., Houselog, M., Donder, D. J., & Anderson, R. J. (1988). Proactive administrative strategies for implementing community-based programs for students with moderate/severe handicaps. *Education and Training in Mental Retardation, 23,* 138–146.

Pearpoint, J., Forest, M., & Snow, J. (1992). *The inclusion papers: Strategies to make inclusion work.* Toronto, Canada: Inclusion Press.

Sailor, W., Anderson, J., Halvorsen, A. T., Doering, K., Filler, J., & Goetz, L. (1989). *The comprehensive local school: Regular education for all students with disabilities.* Baltimore: Paul H. Brookes.

Sailor, W., Goetz, L., Anderson, J., Hunt, P., & Gee, K. (1988). Research on community intensive instruction as a model for building functional, generalized skills. In R. H. Horner, G. Dunlap,

& R. L. Koegel (Eds.), *Generalization and maintenance: Lifestyle changes in applied settings* (pp. 67–98). Baltimore: Paul H. Brookes.

Schnorr, R., Ford, A., Davern, L., Park-Lee, S., & Meyer, L. (1989). *The Syracuse curriculum revision manual: A group process for developing a community-referenced curriculum guide.* Baltimore: Paul H. Brookes.

Wehman, P., Kregel, J., & Barcus, J. M. (1985). From school to work: A vocational transition model for handicapped students. *Exceptional Children, 51*(1), 25–37.

Wilcox, B. (1987). Why a new curriculum? In B. Wilcox & G. T. Bellamy (Eds.), *A comprehensive guide to The Activities Catalog: An alternative curriculum for youth and adults with severe disabilities* (pp. 1–10). Baltimore: Paul H. Brookes.

Wilcox, B., & Bellamy, G. T. (1987). *The Activities Catalog: An alternative curriculum for youth and adults with severe disabilities.* Baltimore: Paul H. Brookes.

Wolfe, P. S. (1994). Judgment of the social validity of instructional strategies used in community-based instructional sites. *Journal of the Association for Persons with Severe Handicaps, 19,* 43–51.

10

Living at Home

Daniel E. Steere

Teri L. Burcroff

A person's home is a unique environment. It is a place of privacy where the individual can relax at the end of a workday, spend time with family, or simply be alone. It is therefore a place that in some ways has fewer demands than places of employment or other community environments. Being successful at home, however, requires that people be able to complete a number of complex activities:

- Planning a balanced nutritional menu of meals, and then cooking and preparing the food.
- Cleaning their home or apartment.
- Cleaning their clothes.
- Bathing and maintaining appropriate hygiene.
- Using electrical appliances safely.
- Using the telephone.
- Engaging in leisure activities within the home.
- Getting along with family members or roommates, who also live in the home or apartment.
- Knowing what to do in an emergency.
- Caring for themselves when ill.

The authors wish to thank Kim Troxell, Rebekah Seltzer, Margaret Howard, and Kathleen Steere for their willing feedback, which helped to improve our manuscript. Requests for correspondence should be sent to Daniel E. Steere, Department of Special Education and Rehabilitation, East Stroudsburg University, 200 Prospect Street, East Stroudsburg, PA 18301.

- Interacting with neighbors.
- Managing finances to maintain the home.

This brief list illustrates the complexity and importance of skill development related to living at home. An underlying concern with all of these areas is the need for people to plan and manage their time effectively to complete all these activities. Consequently, the development of effective self-management skills (Agran, Fodor-Davis, Moore, & Deer, 1989; Hughes & Agran, 1993) is a common thread throughout all the activities described in this chapter. In addition, because most people have more than one home during their lifetime, the skills that are described here must be generalized skills. For example, a person who can operate more than one type of vacuum cleaner, stove, or telephone will be in a better position to be successful in a new house or apartment. For this reason, multiple examples of activities should be systematically provided throughout the years of instruction to enhance generalization (Horner, Sprague, & Wilcox, 1982; Steere, Pancsofar, Powell, & Butterworth, 1989).

In this chapter, our orientation is that instruction related to living at home should be based on the presumption that all students, including those with severe disabilities, can master many of the skills required for success in this area. Certainly, many students will continue to require support for some areas of home living well into adulthood (Racino & Walker, 1993). However, our instruction during the educational years should prepare students for maximum independence in these skill areas. This chapter addresses major skill areas that need to be mastered for success at home. Some activities that are completed in part at home (e.g., financial management, leisure activities, and health and fitness) are addressed elsewhere in this book, and readers should refer to those chapters for additional ideas.

In the remainder of this chapter, we describe eight key activities areas that are needed for success in the home and that should be included in the curriculum. We then describe four considerations for assessment of home living activities. Specific considerations in curriculum development at the elementary, middle, and secondary level are then provided along with sample objectives. Finally, we provide a brief discussion of some additional considerations for teaching home living skills. First, however, the following case study is provided as a point of reference for our discussion of the development of home living activities. We will return to this case study later in the chapter to discuss the development of appropriate IEP objectives related to home living.

Case Study: Mark

Mark is 13 years old and lives with his family. He has autism and requires extensive support. Mark has many skills, including the ability to dress himself, to brush his teeth, and to wash himself if the shower is prepared for him. In addition, Mark can operate the toaster to make himself toast, and he can prepare himself a bowl of cold cereal with milk. He is able to operate the TV set and likes to watch television. He can also operate the stereo system to play CDs, tapes, and record albums, which is one of his favorite leisure activities, along with watching television. Mark has a pet cat and can feed it without assistance. Mark is verbal and can greet visitors to his family's home, although his rapid speech, awkward syntax, and limited vocabulary make it difficult to understand him. Mark's parents are very aware of the need for him to develop greater independence and have developed a system of chores that need to be completed every day. Mark is responsible for setting the dinner table, feeding his cat, making his bed, and brushing his teeth. He is also responsible for vacuuming the living room floor and sweeping the kitchen on the weekends. He accompanies his family when they go grocery shopping and helps pick out items from a list. He also assists them at the laundromat, where he loads laundry into the washing machines and inserts the coins. He has a job chart on which he checks off completed activities. Mark's parents provide him with an allowance that is paid when he completes a designated series of chores. Mark uses his earnings to purchase additional tapes and CDs for his collection.

Despite his many abilities and his parents' active efforts to teach and support him, Mark lacks skills in many areas. For example, he cannot cook a meal other than toast or cereal. He can clean the dishes but requires verbal and gestural prompting to do so. Mark is not able to plan a balanced diet for shopping and, if left by himself, would rely on potato chips and other preferred snack food. He can speak on the telephone but would not know what to do in an emergency that required him to call the fire or police departments or a neighbor. Although Mark can shower and dress himself, he requires prompting to initiate these activities. In fact, he is often resistant to changing his clothing, particularly during changes of the seasons from cold to warm weather. Mark has not been taught to regulate the heat or air conditioning in his home and does not know when or how to do so. Finally, Mark requires considerable prompting from his family to stop one activity and begin another. For example, unless prompted by his parents to begin his chores or get dressed, he would remain in his pajamas and watch television for hours. Mark will need continued instruction in a number of areas to become more independent in his family's home and to enhance the likelihood of success in future homes away from his family.

DESCRIPTION OF GENERIC CURRICULUM CONTENT

As illustrated, numerous activities need to be completed at home. In this section, we describe eight general activity areas that are needed for success in most homes. The areas addressed in this section are:

1. Planning and preparing meals within a balanced diet.
2. Self-care, bathing, and hygiene.
3. Cleaning and care of the home.
4. Cleaning and care of clothing.
5. Telephone use.
6. Leisure-time activities.
7. Correct safety procedures to react to emergencies within the home.
8. Time management and scheduling of the activities to be completed at home.

Under each of the eight areas, key activities that should be considered for inclusion in the curriculum are highlighted. Table 10.1 lists the eight areas and the key activities discussed in the following sections.

PLANNING AND PREPARING MEALS

A major activity that is completed at home is planning, preparing, and then eating meals. A key consideration for this set of activities is that the meals prepared are

TABLE 10.1   Generic Curriculum Areas and Activities for Living at Home

Curriculum Area	Key Activities
1. Planning and preparing meals.	Planning a menu. Preparing meals. Using cooking equipment. Storing food safely.
2. Self-care, bathing, and hygiene.	Showering or bathing. Hair care. Caring for nails. Dental care. Toileting. Washing hands and face.
3. Cleaning and care of the home.	Vacuuming. Dusting/wiping surfaces. Neatening and organizing.
4. Cleaning and care of clothing.	Washing and drying clothes. Changing clothes as needed. Folding and storing clothes.
5. Telephone use.	Calling for appointments or services. Calling friends and acquaintances. Calling in emergencies. Answering calls from others.
6. Leisure activities in the home.	Watching television. Listening to music. Hobbies. Entertaining visitors.
7. Safety procedures.	Calling 911 in an emergency. Evacuating during a fire. Responding to smoke detectors. Using a fire extinguisher. Calling an ambulance or doctor if one becomes very sick. Safely answering the door.
8. Time management and scheduling of completion of activities.	Adhering to a daily schedule. Following a calendar. Using alarm clocks.

nutritious and balanced. There is a danger that, without active instruction, people with disabilities may eat only foods that are high in calories and low in nutritional value. Therefore, it is essential that students learn that meals must have variety and must include foods from the major food groups. This can be taught creatively by designing menu planning forms that contain categories to be filled in, as shown in Figure 10.1. Such menu planners can then be used as shopping lists to enhance the likelihood that healthy foods will be purchased.

A second consideration is the ability to prepare both simple meals, such as making a sandwich, as well as meals that require cooking, such as a dinner with

FIGURE 10.1   Sample Menu Planner for a Nutritious Diet

Menu Planner
Menu for *Monday*

	What I Need to Buy (Put These on the Shopping List!)
Breakfast	
Toast and butter	Bread
Cereal and milk	Milk
Banana	
Orange juice	Orange juice
Coffee	
Lunch	
Bologna sandwich	
Apple	Apples
Chips	
Soda	
Dinner	
Frozen fish fillets	
Frozen French fries	
Canned corn with butter	Canned corn
Milk	
Coffee	
Ice cream	Ice cream

meat, vegetables, and rice or potatoes. Such skills should be systematically taught over the years, so that the ability to prepare increasingly complex meals is developed as the student becomes older. Some students who learn to read will be able to follow recipes from food packages or from cookbooks. Others will require adaptations such as picture recipes or recipes recorded onto audiotapes. An underlying skill to meal preparation is the ability to follow a set of directions and to sequence steps within a more complex set of activities. The ability to develop simple task analyses of cooking activities in written or pictorial form is therefore an important instructional strategy.

A third consideration for this curriculum area is the ability to use cooking equipment correctly and safely. This includes the ability to use simple utensils, such as a cutting knife, as well as the ability to operate appliances such as a stove, oven, microwave oven, coffeemaker, or toaster. As discussed earlier, using a range of examples of appliances systematically can enhance the likelihood of generalization of skills to new appliances that may be encountered. In addition, because the preparation of different foods requires the ability to time the length of cooking, the ability to use a watch or a simple kitchen timer is an important component skill to be incorporated.

Finally, the appropriate storage of food is an essential skill. Because food that is left out or stored improperly can present a danger, students should be taught how to correctly freeze or refrigerate perishable foods. A simple chart as shown in Figure 10.2 can help students who have difficulty in this area.

**FIGURE 10.2   Sample Reminder Sheet for Where
to Store Food Correctly**

Where to Put the Food

Put These in the Freezer
 Frozen waffles
 Frozen orange juice concentrate
 Meat (unless you will use it today)
 Ice cream
 Vegetables (frozen)
 French Fries

Put These in the Refrigerator
 Apple juice in jars and boxes
 Butter
 Milk
 Lettuce, tomato
 Cheese
 Soda
 Jelly

Put These in the Cabinet
 Granola bars
 Rice
 Potatoes
 Vegetables in cans
 Cookies

SELF-CARE, BATHING, AND HYGIENE

This is a key part of the home living curriculum that can have an impact on many other areas, including success in employment and in general community environments. Students must learn to master a number of key skills in this area, including the ability to shower or bathe on a regular basis. Hair care and care of nails are also essential.

Dental care is an important consideration for self-care. Students must learn to brush and floss their teeth regularly. In addition, some students may need to learn to use mouthwashes or fluoride supplements.

Appropriate hygiene skills include self-care during toileting and washing hands and face when necessary. In addition, the use of deodorants is an important consideration as students enter adolescence.

CLEANING AND CARE OF THE HOME

A home that is not cared for can become unsanitary. In addition, visitors are less likely to return to a home that is dirty or smells. It is essential that students learn to care for their home correctly and then do so on a frequent and regular basis.

Cleaning and care of the home entails the activities of vacuuming, dusting, and wiping surfaces. Of particular concern in any home are the kitchen and bathroom areas. In completing these activities, students will need to learn how to use equipment such as vacuum cleaners, carpet sweepers, brooms, and mops, as well as chemical cleaners. This, in turn, requires the ability to use spray bottles and other dispensers. An additional cleaning activity is the use of an automatic dishwasher (if available) or hand washing of dirty dishes.

In addition to cleaning, an important skill is the ability to neaten and organize one's living environment. Although personal choice of the degree of neatness is a consideration, the ability to make one's bed, put away dishes and dirty clothing, or clear off chairs and tables is important, particularly when other people live in the home or are visiting. Thus, where to put things and when to put them away are important skills to master.

CLEANING AND CARE OF CLOTHING

Students need to learn to change their clothing on a regular and frequent basis. For example, Mark's tendency to want to keep winter clothing on in warm weather results in hygiene problems which, in turn, makes people want to stay away from him. For students who lack judgment in this area, a simple rule of changing all clothing after a daily shower can be an effective strategy.

In addition to knowing when to put on new clothing, students must learn to wash soiled clothing. If a washing machine is available within a home, then students can learn to use it on a regular basis. For others, the use of coin-operated machines at a laundromat will be necessary. In either case, separating clothes into light and dark washes, measuring detergent and fabric softener, and selecting correct wash cycles are important skills. Finally, students need to learn to fold or hang clothes correctly and put them away.

TELEPHONE USE

There are multiple uses of a telephone at home. First, telephones are used for personal management activities such as calling for a doctor's appointment or calling for a repairperson to fix something in the home. Second, calls are made to family and friends. Third, answering phone calls from others is an important skill. Finally, telephones are essential during an emergency.

Component skills of using a telephone include dialing and speaking clearly into the speaker. In addition, in some homes the use of an answering machine may be necessary.

LEISURE ACTIVITIES IN THE HOME

A variety of leisure and recreational activities may be completed at home. Watching television, listening to music, or reading or looking at books and magazines are common activities. In addition, hobbies such as coin collecting, building models, and crafts are appropriate leisure activities. As with other areas of home living, many of these leisure activities involve the use of electronic equipment such as stereo equipment, televisions, or videocassette recorders (VCRs). In addition, the use of remote controls is a component skill for many of these activities.

A second major category of leisure activities involves those completed with visitors to the home. Inviting a friend over for dinner or lunch is an activity that many people value. Although this incorporates much of what has been discussed earlier, additional skills include appropriate greeting, interactions, and providing additional food or beverages to visitors. Scheduling and time management, as discussed later in this chapter, are also important to the success of hosting leisure activities within the home.

SAFETY PROCEDURES IN THE HOME

Although emergencies rarely arise, people must be prepared to handle them quickly. Generally, emergencies in the home can involve fire, illness, or unwanted visitors.

To respond to a fire emergency, a student must be able to dial 911 and report the emergency. For students with little verbal language, adaptations such as a direct emergency line to the fire or police department are appropriate alternatives. In addition, it may be necessary to use a home fire extinguisher. Finally, knowing how and where to evacuate the home is important.

An additional safety issue concerns sudden or extreme illness. Knowing how to contact a hospital or ambulance is an essential skill, especially for people who live on their own. Again, being able to contact emergency personnel is essential.

Finally, in some areas it is important to know whom to let into your home. Knowing how to answer the door when a stranger calls is important, particularly for someone with a disability, who may be more vulnerable. Basic information relating to interaction with strangers can be incorporated into this aspect of the curriculum.

TIME MANAGEMENT AND SCHEDULES FOR COMPLETING ACTIVITIES IN THE HOME

Although self-management skills are addressed elsewhere in this book, it is important to reiterate that all the preceding activities rely on the ability to manage time and schedule activities effectively. For example, it is insufficient to know how to cook a healthy dinner if the person does not remember to make it. In addition, being able to clean clothes is not enough if the person does not make time to do so. Consequently, for success in the home, it is important to teach careful scheduling of chores, menus, and other self-management or leisure activities. For many people, a calendar hung near the telephone is the best way to plan. Others may require formal menus for planning that can be hung on the refrigerator. Additional alternatives include a date book and a hand-held tape recorder to enter important activities to remember. Most important, teaching regular schedules throughout each day and week will help students establish routines, such as always getting up at 6:00 A.M. with an alarm clock; always eating dinner, at 6:30 P.M.; or always doing the laundry on Saturday mornings.

CONSIDERATIONS FOR ASSESSMENT OF HOME LIVING ACTIVITIES

Assessment of home living activities should provide the instructor with useful information to assist in instructional decision making. In particular, instructors need to know what activities to teach, what steps need to be worked on, what materials should be incorporated into instruction, and when and where to teach. To determine the answers to these key questions, four approaches to assessment—

ecological inventory, task-analytic assessment, assessment of choices of the student and family, and social validation—are discussed in this section. These are not mutually exclusive approaches to assessment, and all four should be incorporated into an assessment plan.

ECOLOGICAL INVENTORY

As discussed in Chapter 1, ecological inventories are an essential element in longitudinal curriculum design (Brown, Branston-McClean, et al., 1979). Within the context of teaching skills necessary for living at home, instructors must conduct careful inventories of each student's current home environment as well as potential future environments. For younger students, more emphasis may be placed on teaching skills needed within their current family home. For older students, however, potential new homes, such as apartments within likely neighborhoods, should be considered.

The use of an ecological inventory approach is particularly important in identifying activities that may be unique to particular environments. For example, removal of trash from containers within the home will vary from one situation to another. This is particularly true in light of specific recycling requirements in different areas. Although this is just one activity that is important in maintaining a clean and healthy home environment, the variations in how the activity is completed illustrate the need for instructors to conduct careful ecological inventories of current and likely future environments.

When the likely future environment for a student is not known, the instructor and the student's family members can conduct inventories of apartments or homes that are representative of possible options. For example, they could conduct inventories of three apartments that are within the likely geographic area and price or rental range that the student would be likely to afford. By analyzing more than one such apartment or home, possible variations in activities could be identified and then incorporated into instruction using a general case programming strategy (Horner, Sprague, & Wilcox, 1982). To illustrate this, activities that are important in most homes and that may well vary from home to home are listed in Figure 10.3. Instructors who are aware of such potential generalization challenges will incorporate a variety of examples into their teaching, for example, teaching a student with severe disabilities to use different types of faucets or cabinet latches.

TASK-ANALYTIC ASSESSMENT

Once important activities are identified from ecological inventories, specific assessment of students' abilities to complete important activities should be conducted. The task-analytic assessment approach is recommended, in which the natural cue for the performance of each step in a task analysis is provided (Pancsofar, 1986). In using this approach, the instructor first develops a task analysis of a particular activity identified through ecological inventory. Next, the natural cue that sets the occasion for each step in the task analysis is identified. For example, Table 10.2 shows a task analysis of operating a home dishwasher. The natural cues that are identified for each step in this task are also shown in Table 10.2. These natural cues describe how the materials and environment look just before the completion of the next step. These cues become the "clue" for the learner to perform the next step (Pancsofar, 1993). The

FIGURE 10.3   Common Home Activities That May Be Performed in Multiple Ways

Opening cabinet latches.
Turning on water faucets.
Operating microwave ovens.
Using stoves and ranges.
Operating TV sets.
Operating VCRS.
Operating home phones.
Operating tape, CD, or record players.
Operating lock mechanisms and different doorknobs and latches.
Turning on/off light switches.
Using alarm clocks.
Opening different refrigerators and freezers.
Disposing of the garbage.
Putting on and fastening different articles of clothing.
Obtaining mail from a mailbox.

instructor then assesses learners' ability to complete the activity by noting their responses to the salient natural cues. If a learner performs a step correctly, then this is recorded in the assessment data. If, however, the learner does not perform a particular step correctly, then the instructor can stop the learner and arrange the natural cues for the next step in the activity. This strategy allows the instructor to pinpoint steps that need to be taught, thereby increasing the efficiency of instruction. In addition, the instructor can also assess the type of assistance that is required for a learner to perform a step correctly.

ASSESSMENT OF CHOICES OF THE INDIVIDUAL AND FAMILY

A third aspect of assessment is the analysis of choices of both students and their family members. Because so many activities that are performed in the home are

TABLE 10.2   Task Analysis of Operating a Dishwasher

Natural Cue for the Step	Step in the Task Analysis
Dishwasher door closed.	Open the dishwasher door.
Door opened; soap receptacle in opened position.	Pour in liquid soap to fill the soap receptacle.
Receptacle filled with soap.	Close the soap receptacle.
Receptacle closed.	Close the dishwasher door.
Door closed.	Set temperature cycle.
Cycle button depressed.	Turn knob to "on" position to start the wash cycle.

based on choices (e.g., the choice of foods to eat, music to listen to, television programs to watch, and what to wear), it is essential that the choices and preferences of students be known. These choices and preferences will need to be balanced with those of family members who are the primary advocates for students. For example, a student's preferences in foods should be balanced with the family's interests in a healthy diet for their son or daughter.

Because this is such an important aspect of assessment, we suggest that an on-going profile of choices be maintained and updated on an ongoing basis. This should include not only a listing of preferences that have been expressed, but also those that have been acted on (Pancsofar, 1993). Figure 10.4 shows an example section of a profile of choices for a student for activities related to home living. A number of materials are available that provide structured inventories of choices, including those by Allen (1989) and by Butterworth et al. (1993).

FIGURE 10.4   Sample Section of Choice Profile

Things to Eat and Drink
Ice cream for dessert!
Chicken casserole and chicken pot pie
Mexican dinners (frozen)
Apples
Grilled cheese sandwiches
Tuna sandwiches
Apple juice

Things to Watch on TV
Music videos
Half-hour sitcom reruns *(MASH, Taxi)*

Favorite Music
Michael Jackson
Madonna

Favorite Things to Do in His Free Time
Look at *TV Guide*
Watch TV
Call friends or family members on the telephone

Preferred Times to Go to Bed and Get Up
Weekdays: up at 7:00 A.M.; in bed by 10:00 P.M.
Weekends: up at 8:30 A.M.; in bed by 11:30 P.M.

Preferred Times to Do In-Home Chores
Cleaning house on Saturday mornings
Making bed and cleaning dishes, daily
Laundry on Sunday mornings

Preferred Times to Do Shopping
Saturday afternoons

Favorite People to Invite Over to Visit
Rob and Liz (neighbors)
Teresa (sister)

The direct teaching of choice-making skills has been identified as important for people with disabilities (Guess, Benson, & Siegel-Causey, 1985; Schloss, Alper, & Jayne, 1993). This implies that students not only are taught to make choices, but also that they have opportunities to exercise choices (Bambara, Koger, Katzer, & Davenport, 1995) and then reflect on their experiences in choice making (Pancsofar, 1993). Assessment in this area should be as systematic as the other approaches described in this chapter.

SOCIAL VALIDATION

Social validity refers to the degree to which behavior change is socially meaningful as assessed by the reactions of others or by comparison with the performance of others (Wolf, 1978). Increasingly, the need for a social validation component to assessment is recommended. This is particularly important for the development of home living skills.

The importance of this aspect of assessment is perhaps best illustrated by the following situation. An individual with severe disabilities was living in an apartment by himself with support for specific activities through a supported living program. His support professionals reported to the family that he was doing well and that they were satisfied with his performance of home activities. A friend of the family, however, stopped by at the individual's apartment one afternoon to visit. During the visit, the friend noted that the bathroom was dirty and smelled; she also noted that there was little healthy food in the refrigerator: What the supported living staff felt was acceptable was not acceptable to this close friend. This situation illustrates the importance of a social validity component to assessment. Questions such as those listed in Figure 10.5 should be incorporated into assessment of skill development on an ongoing basis. A negative response to any of these questions would indicate the need for additional instruction or support.

FIGURE 10.5   Social Validation Questions

1. Is the student able to plan a healthy diet?
2. Can the student prepare meals in a safe manner?
3. Can the student safely store and handle food?
4. Is the student able to keep the home clean, sanitary, and odor-free?
5. Is the student able to operate equipment in the home safely?
6. Can the student occupy his or her free time?
7. Does the student know how to respond in an emergency or when the smoke detector sounds?
8. Does the student know how to call for help using 911?
9. Does the student have any friends to spend free time with?
10. Does the student have acceptable personal cleanliness and hygiene?
11. Can the student dress him- or herself?
12. Can the student care for his or her own toileting needs?
13. Can the student manage his or her own time effectively?
14. For any of the preceding questions to which the answer is "no," what type of instruction or support needs to be provided?

CURRICULUM DESIGN

A general overview of the recommended components of a curriculum for home living activities is provided in the preceding section. Readers should note that there are several available curriculum materials that contain excellent ideas related to home living skills development. Table 10.3 lists five sample curriculum models that contain objectives related to living at home. We recommend that instructors consult all available material, including those shown in Table 10.3, as they develop IEP objectives for specific learners.

In this section, we describe important general considerations for addressing the curriculum areas at the elementary, middle, and secondary levels. Keep in mind that all curricular decisions should be based on the unique profiles of students with the active input of their families. The assessment strategies described earlier are key approaches to targeting objectives that are tailored to each student.

One of the major challenges to teaching skills needed for success within the home is when and where to teach these skills. Teachers rarely have regular access to the student's current home as a teaching environment, and families cannot be expected to assume the additional challenge of becoming full-time instructors within their own homes. Consequently, teachers must use creativity at all levels in teaching home living activities within the context of naturally occurring opportunities throughout the day. Table 10.4 illustrates some of the naturally occurring opportunities that could be used for teaching skills related to home living at the elementary, middle, and secondary levels.

An additional consideration across the span of the educational years is the gradual and subtle shift from focusing only on teaching students, to also putting necessary supports and adaptations into place (Steere, Pancsofar, Wood, & Hecimovic, 1990). Teachers should attempt to teach important skills throughout students' educational years, and beyond. However, some students with more severe disabilities may never fully master some activities, and they may require adaptations and supports to be successful. By clarifying the needed supports and adaptations and then putting these into place prior to the end of educational services, teachers can contribute to the likelihood of students' success in adulthood.

The remainder of this section addresses considerations at the elementary, middle, and high school levels. Sample objectives are included in Table 10.5 to illustrate how these considerations are included in curriculum design. Readers may wish to refer back to Table 10.4 as they read this information.

ELEMENTARY LEVEL

The elementary school years, from approximately ages 5 through 11, form the foundation for future learning throughout a student's educational career. Curriculum planning, therefore, is a multifaceted set of activities that enables the teacher to prepare a student for later learning experiences. Many factors are taken into account when beginning to plan appropriate goals and objectives for a child at a given point in time. In most cases, the teacher is responsible for selecting curriculum materials that can be utilized with relative ease to meet students' instructional needs. The purpose of this section is not to describe available curriculum materials and models, as that has been done elsewhere (Snell, 1993; Spooner & Test, 1994), but to provide a conceptual framework to use in selecting goals and objectives.

TABLE 10.3   Sample of Currently Available Curriculum Materials

	COACH Choosing Options and Accommodations for Children (Giangreco, Cloninger, & Iverson, 1993)	Syracuse Community Referenced Curriculum Guide (Ford, et al., 1989)	The Community Based Curriculum (Falvey, 1989)	Community Living Skills (Dever, 1988)	The Activities Catalog (Wilcox & Bellamy, 1987)
Domains/Areas Covered	Communication *Socialization *Personal management *Leisure and recreation Applied academics *Home School Community Vocational	*Self-Management and home living Vocational *Recreation and leisure General community functioning Functional academics Embedded social, communication, and motor skills	Community *Domestic Recreation Employment Motor Communication Functional academics	*Personal maintenance and development *Homemaking and community life Vocational and leisure Travel	*Leisure *Personal management Work

* An asterisk indicates curricular areas directly related to goals and objectives for living at home.

TABLE 10.4   Naturally Occurring Opportunities to Teach Home-Related Skills in School

Skill Areas	Elementary School Years	Middle School Years	Secondary School Years
Planning and Preparing Meals	Making lunch request in cafeteria. Setup and cleanup for snack and lunch.	Making lunch requests to cafeteria. Community outings for fast food. Health class unit on nutrition.	Preparing meal for lunch (lunchbox). Working with kitchen staff. Reading newspaper food sections for recipes.
Self-Care, Bathing and Hygiene	Taking off jacket or coat in morning on arrival. Putting on coat in afternoon for dismissal. Dressing aspects of toileting.	Cleaning teeth after meals. Responding to medical emergencies. Washing hands after restroom. Using tissues for nose blowing.	Using rest rooms at community work sites. Using rest rooms in community restaurants.
Cleaning and Care of the Home	Cleaning up after each activity. Washing chalkboards. Washing desktops. Watering plants. Care of classroom pets.	Cleaning up after meals in cafeteria. Organizing materials for cleaning up. Changing lightbulbs, towels, and other disposable items.	Assist in cleaning the chemistry lab. Cleaning up work area at community work site.
Care and Cleaning of Clothing	Wearing paint smocks during art.	Sewing on buttons. Sorting of objects by color. Folding clothes after dressing for gym.	Caring for uniforms and other work clothing. Using laundromats.
Telephone Use	Calling friends for homework assignments. Calling home from school. Calling the office from the classroom. Dialing 911.	Receptionist activities in school office. Using telephone book to order supplies for a project.	Using telephones as part of job duties at community work sites.
Leisure Activities in the Home	Cooperative classroom games. Reading time (SSR). Computer games.	Reading activities. Use of VCR. Use of CD player.	Engaging in conversations in school cafeteria.
Safety Procedures in the Home	Responding to fire drills. Helping with first aid in class. Pairing up with another student to walk to the nurse.	Fire drills. Using extension cords. Checking for placement of objects near heat sources.	Learning safety procedures in roles at community work sites.
Time Management and Scheduling	Taking responsibility for homework folder. Calendar activities. Self-responsibility for homework. Stating schedule for day.	Following transportation schedules. Following class schedules. Writing important calendar dates. Reading television program schedules.	Maintaining a personal calendar. Assuming responsibility for following a work schedule.

TABLE 10.5   Sample IEP Objectives at the Elementary, Middle, and High School Levels

Elementary Level	Given two slices of bread, jelly, and peanut butter, the student will correctly make a peanut butter and jelly sandwich, without assistance, for three consecutive opportunities.
	At recess time, the student will put on her coat without assistance, on three consecutive occasions.
Middle School Level	In the school cafeteria, the student will successfully retrieve the utensils needed for lunch, proceed through the lunch line to obtain food, and then clean up after lunch, without assistance, on three consecutive days.
	During the preparation for gym class, the student will change into her gym clothes without assistance, on five consecutive opportunities.
High School Level	Given a weekly menu planner, the student will develop a written menu for each meal of the week. In addition, the student will make a check next to those items for which he needs to shop. The completeness and accuracy of the menu planner will be assessed by his parents. Criterion will be met when three consecutive menu planners are completed to the parents' satisfaction.
	Prior to going to a community-based work site, the student will independently dress for work, on five consecutive workdays.

Factors to consider within the context of this conceptual framework include the student's present and future living circumstances, the needs of the family, the use of naturally occurring opportunities for instruction, the age-appropriateness of skills, and the introduction of choice making and its consequences. Each of these considerations is important for curricular decision making.

Brown, Branston, et al. (1979) refer to the necessity of identifying a student's current and future environments to ensure that the goals and objectives selected for a student are functional and relevant to that student's life. For a child living at home, the current environment is obvious. The range of potential future living environments may not be so clear. Will the child be living with his or her family after high school or in some form of supported or independent living arrangement in the community? During the elementary school years, this question may not be easily answered, but it should be considered within the context of providing multiple opportunities to practice a skill in a range of naturally occurring situations, conditions, and settings (Brown & Snell, 1993).

The needs and desires of the family, especially within their own home, are of critical significance, as siblings and parents spend more time with the student than any other people (Giangreco, Cloninger, & Iverson, 1993). Family needs, desires, and aspirations must be identified and prioritized in a respectful, nonjudgmental, and supportive manner (Forest & Pearpoint, 1992). Expectations of parents as teachers should be tempered with the reality that most parents work outside the home and have barely enough time to prepare meals, do the laundry, and keep up with the cleaning. It is realistic, however, to teach parents specific instructional strategies to help them make the most of naturally occurring opportunities for teaching within their homes.

Selection of individualized educational goals and objectives must also be guided by the concept of chronological age-appropriateness (Brown, Branston, et al., 1979). Application of this concept involves assessing the skills, activities, and level of independent performance of chronological age peers. In examining the skills of age peers, the teacher can then identify the critical elements of the task and decide which, if not all, of the components are appropriate for inclusion in the child's curriculum. For example, what would one expect of a 5-year-old child without a disability, an 8-year-old, or a 10-year-old child, in the area of meal planning and preparation? For the 5-year-old, assistance and supervision in spreading peanut butter onto one slice of bread and jelly onto another would be a reasonable expectation. As students grow older, they would be expected to complete the task with increasing independence.

Another important aspect of this conceptual framework is the introduction of choice and the consequences of making choices (Houghton, Bronicki, & Guess, 1987). During the elementary school years, opportunities to teach children about making choices are provided with guidance and supervision from adults. In the home environment, choice is incorporated into many activities, such as choosing what to eat for breakfast or selecting a television program. A child without a disability makes many choices throughout the day, and a child with disabilities should be afforded these same opportunities.

Naturally occurring opportunities, conditions, and settings for teaching should be used to their full advantage. This is of most significance when we consider that more and more children with disabilities are included in regular education classes for a major portion of their school day. In addition, the typical elementary curriculum is being taught, which highlights the need to make every teachable moment count.

MIDDLE SCHOOL LEVEL

During later elementary years and the beginning of middle school, the focus begins to shift toward the future needs of students once they are more independent of their families. Planning for the future begins to take shape at this point. Preparation for transition from school to adulthood begins for many children at 14 years of age or younger. Planning during the middle school years, therefore, entails a broader examination of the future potential home environments for students. The independent performance of many tasks becomes more a focus than in previous years, and more complex activity sequences are introduced. An increasing emphasis is placed on the inclusion of community-based activities and the preparation for life as an adult (Clark, Field, Patton, Brolin, & Sitlington, 1994; Halpern, 1994). All components of the conceptual framework discussed for the elementary school level continue to be considered in curriculum planning at the middle school level. In fact, many of the activities taught in the elementary school years will continue, but with a focus on increasing complexity and independence. For example, the complexity of meal preparation increases from making a simple sandwich to making an entire lunch or learning how to make a simple dinner. In addition, adaptations and supportive environments that allow student participation are designed for students who are not expected to be completely independent.

The partnership between families and teachers must be maintained during the middle school years, as this is the time when many families first begin to think about their children's life after the end of educational services. Teachers can assume the role of supporter and consultant to families during the transition planning process. Likewise, families are essential partners with teachers for the identification of important teaching activities that can happen during naturally occurring opportunities within the school.

SECONDARY SCHOOL LEVEL

At the secondary school level, finding time for direct instruction in home living activities becomes a major challenge. At this level, particularly as students approach the end of educational services, they should be spending a major portion of their day in natural community environments, particularly work sites (Wehman, 1992). Teachers, therefore, need to be extremely creative in finding opportunities to teach home living skills within different contexts. For example, as shown in Table 10.5, dressing and grooming skills can be taught within the context of preparing to go to work or gym class. Similarly, lunch planning and preparation can occur as students prepare their own lunch to take to a work site. Finally, students can assume greater responsibility for following a schedule to meet all of their obligations throughout the school day.

A second consideration is that students should have experiences completing more complex activity sequences. For example, students may be expected to plan and prepare their own lunch, or they may clean an entire area at a work site, if appropriate. It is particularly important that these activities are completed with less direct instruction from teachers, and that students extend their abilities to follow pictorial or written checklists.

Well-designed classroom activities can augment, but not replace, community-based instruction. For example, menu planning and other similar activities could well be taught within a classroom, particularly during home economics or English classes, if the student is included in these subjects. In addition, the use of videotapes allows teachers to expose students to different home environments that may otherwise not be available for teaching. For example, a teacher could videotape different ways of making a telephone call, or could use videotapes to demonstrate the use of different types of ranges for cooking. With creativity, teachers can use this type of classroom instruction to expand the range of examples to which students are exposed. Experience and instruction in natural community environments, including students' homes should be included on a frequent and regular basis and will allow teachers to assess the effectiveness of classroom-based instruction.

At the secondary level, students and their families should be actively involved in transition planning. They should therefore be considering carefully the home environments in which students will live after the end of educational services. For some students, this will remain their family homes. Others may wish to rent or even to purchase their own homes. These decisions will have impact on the instruction that is provided for students, and professionals and families must work together to focus on skills that will be needed for future success.

Finally, the continued development of home leisure activities should not be neglected at the secondary level. Students with specific areas of interest can develop a number of leisure activities around their interests. For example, a student who enjoyed stock car racing subscribed to racing magazines and looked at the pictures. In addition, he watched races on TV. He developed scrapbooks of stock car pictures and trading cards, and assembled models of famous cars. By building a number of leisure activities around an existing area of interest, as in this example, instructors increase the likelihood that students will engage in some type of leisure activities, and may even expand those activities. In addition, building on areas of interest within the home can lead to community-based leisure activities, such as going to the library, joining a club, or attending a sporting event such as a real race.

MARK'S INDIVIDUALIZED EDUCATION PLAN

In this section, we provide a sample section of an Individualized Education Plan (IEP) related to activities needed for success in living at home. This sample IEP was developed for Mark, who was profiled at the beginning of this chapter. Mark's IEP for home living activities is shown in Figure 10.6.

FIGURE 10.6   Mark's IEP, Home Living Skills

Goal 1.0	Mark will develop his ability to complete all washing, grooming, and hygiene activities according to a written schedule.
Objective 1.1	When provided with a written daily schedule with specific times written on it for washing his hands for lunch and changing his clothes to get ready to go to his work site, Mark will initiate these activities without additional prompts for seven consecutive days, within no more than three minutes of the time listed on the daily schedule.
Goal 2.0	Mark will learn to prepare shopping lists and then prepare simple dinners.
Objective 2.1	When given a preprinted menu template with food categories listed on it, Mark will prepare written menus for two dinners for himself. Each dinner must contain a meat, vegetable, and potato or rice, dessert, and a beverage.
Objective 2.2	When provided with a microwave-preparation TV dinner, Mark will correctly read the directions, set the microwave, and cook his meal, for three different meals, over three consecutive opportunities.
Goal 3.0	Mark will learn to respond to home emergencies.
Objective 3.1	Upon hearing the sound of a home smoke alarm without prior notice, Mark will correctly follow the steps of (1) notifying his parents (or teacher in school) that he hears the alarm, and then (2) going outside to the front lawn of his home or school. All steps must be correctly followed within 15 seconds of hearing the alarm, over five consecutive opportunities at different times of the day. This objective will be taught within the school and generalization will be assessed within his home.
Objective 3.2	Given a home-style telephone, Mark will demonstrate how to call 911 and state his name, address, and the nature of the emergency (fire, somebody's sick). This objective will be accomplished using a simulated situation in which Mark can speak to an instructor via the in-school telephone. He will have met this objective when three new school personnel who do not know him well are able to understand his requests for assistance.
Goal 4.0	Mark will learn to regulate the temperature in his home.
Objective 4.1	Given photographs of a variety of home thermostats, Mark will correctly state the current temperature on each thermostat, over three consecutive occasions.
Objective 4.2	When provided with a home thermostat within a home or apartment setting, Mark will correctly and accurately set the thermostat as requested by the instructor. He will demonstrate mastery by setting temperatures from 65 to 70 degrees, over three consecutive sessions.

Mark's IEP is based on his learning of more complex activities, such as planning and preparing a meal, and following a schedule of when to complete daily activities. In addition, current skills that he completes with assistance are continued with a focus on increasing his independence. Mark will also begin to learn about regulating the temperature in his home, and he will learn about how to respond to a home emergency. These objectives will extend his competence with home living activities. At age 13, Mark has the opportunity to continue to master the necessary skills so that, by the time he leaves school, he is able to perform most activities within the home with far less support.

ADDITIONAL CONSIDERATIONS

Before leaving the topic of curriculum development in the area of home living activities, several additional considerations for effective instruction in this area should be noted. First, the selection of environments for teaching is an important consideration. Although some skills related to home living can be taught within a school setting, instruction within natural settings is also essential. Although this is a major challenge for many educators, a variety of strategies can be used to address it. Some programs have model or simulated apartments that can be used for instruction. An additional strategy is to ensure that materials and equipment that are found in many homes are used for instruction in school. For example, learning to use a microwave oven that is placed in a central location within the school is possible and can help students learn this important skill. Conducting instruction within a real apartment or home setting can be implemented on a regular basis to assess skill development and generalization of skills learned in school. The key point is that instruction must not rely entirely on simulations of home living environments, but instead must incorporate real materials and settings. Effective simulations, however, can increase the students' exposure to home living activities, particularly if slides or videotapes are used to show the range of environments to which students are expected to generalize.

A second consideration for instruction is that it occur within logical and appropriate contexts. For example, meals should be prepared at mealtimes, and dressing skills should be taught when students are going to gym or are changing to go to a community job. This will require instructors to be organized in their scheduling so that activities can be taught in appropriate situations.

A third consideration is the need for close collaboration with families. Family members provide ongoing support within the home and can provide valuable information about skill development in the activities described in this chapter. This does not imply that educators should view home skills development as the sole province of families, rather that they are essential partners in the curriculum design and instructional processes. The importance of this partnership is highlighted by Szymanski's (1995) description of the importance of home chores in establishing a work ethic and work habits, which are important not only in later employment settings but also in completing necessary activities at home.

A fourth consideration is the need to identify skill areas in which additional support may be required over time. Although active and systematic instruction in home living skills should continue throughout a student's education, not all students will master all activities necessary for success in living at home. However, as described by Racino and Walker (1993), people with disabilities can live successfully in their own homes if support is provided, and many people aspire to owning their own homes with support from others (O'Brien, 1991). Educators can play a key role in helping to identify the minimal level of support that is necessary for success.

The need for the development of strong self-management skills must be reiterated. People can be successful in their homes if they are able to manage their time and remember to complete necessary activities. Teaching self-management skills will have major impact on the area of successful home living. Finally, getting along with others within a home setting is an important aspect of success. Even people who choose to live with others do not get along with them at all times.

CONCLUSION

In this chapter, we have described curriculum development related to activities that are necessary for successful living in one's home. Although the home is a place for relaxation and private time, numerous activities must be performed well in order to be successful. Many of these skills have direct impact not only on success in other environments, such as work, but on more general health and safety. In this chapter, we have focused on eight key activity areas. Each of these areas requires careful, systematic, and longitudinal instruction for mastery. In addition, we have described four key approaches to the assessment of home living skills. Finally, we have provided considerations for the development of home living curriculum development during the elementary, middle, and secondary school levels.

As a final consideration in this chapter, we suggest that Szymanski's (1994) recommendation that longitudinal and early experiences have positive impact on transition outcomes is most relevant to the topic of living at home. Skill development that is carefully and systematically structured is more likely to result in generalized and durable skills. Close, collaborative partnerships between educators and family members is essential to this effort and can have substantial positive impact on the abilities of people with disabilities to live successfully in their future homes.

REFERENCES

Agran, M., Fodor-Davis, J., Moore, S., & Deer, M. (1989). The application of a self-management program on instruction following skills. *Journal of the Association for Persons with Severe Handicaps, 14,* 147–154.

Allen, W. (1989). *Read my lips: It's my choice . . . .* St. Paul, MN: Governor's Planning Council on Developmental Disabilities.

Bambara, L., Koger, F., Katzer, T., & Davenport, T. (1995). Embedding choice in the context of daily living routines: An experimental case study. *Journal of the Association for Persons with Severe Handicaps, 20,* 185–195.

Brown, F., & Snell, M. (1993). Meaningful assessment. In M. E. Snell, (Ed.), *Instruction of students with severe disabilities* (pp. 61–98). New York: Merrill.

Brown, L., Branston, M. B., Hamre-Nietupski, S., Pumpian, I., Certo, N., & Gruenewald, L. (1979). A strategy for developing chronological-age-appropriate and functional curricular content for severely handicapped adolescents and young adults. *Journal of Special Education, 13,* 81–90.

Brown, L., Branston-McClean, M., Baumgart, D., Vincent, L., Falvey, M., & Schroeder, J. (1979). Using the characteristics of current and subsequent least restrictive environments in the development of curricular content for severely handicapped students. *AAESPH Review, 4,* 407–434.

Butterworth, J., Hagner, D., Heikkinen, B., Farris, S., DeMello, S., & McDonough, K. (1993). *Whole life planning: A guide for organizers and facilitators.* Boston: Institute for Community Inclusion.

Clark, G., Field, S., Patton, J., Brolin, D., & Sitlington, P. (1994). Life skills instruction: A necessary component for all students with disabilities. A position statement of the Division of Career Development and Transition. *Career Development for Exceptional Individuals, 17,* 125–134.

Dever, R. (1988). Community living skills: A taxonomy. In M. J. Begab (Ed.), *Monograph of the American Association on Mental Retardation, 10.* Washington, DC: American Association on Mental Retardation.

Falvey, M. (1989). *Community-based curriculum: Instructional strategies for students with severe handicaps.* Baltimore: Paul H. Brookes.

Ford, A., Schnorr, R., Meyer, L., Davern, L., Black, J., & Dempsey, P. (1989). *The Syracuse community-referenced curriculum guide for students with moderate and severe disabilities.* Baltimore: Paul H. Brookes.

Forest, M., & Pearpoint, J. (1992, October). Putting all kids on the MAP. *Educational Leadership, 49,* 26–31.

Giangreco, M., Cloninger, C., & Iverson, V. (1993). *COACH: Choosing options and accommodations for children.* Baltimore: Paul H. Brookes.

Guess, D., Benson, H., & Siegel-Causey, E. (1985). Concepts and issues related to choice-making and autonomy among persons with severe disabilities. *Journal of the Association for Persons with Severe Handicaps, 10,* 79–86.

Halpern, A. (1994). The transition of youth with disabilities to adult life: A position statement of the Division of Career Development and Transition. *Career Development for Exceptional Individuals, 17,* 115–124.

Horner, R. H., Sprague, J., & Wilcox, B. (1982). General case programming for community activities. In B. Wilcox & G. T. Bellamy (Eds.), *Design of high school programs for severely handicapped students* (pp. 61–98). Baltimore: Paul H. Brookes.

Houghton, J., Bronicki, G., & Guess, D. (1987). Opportunities to express preferences and make choices among students with severe disabilities in classroom settings. *Journal of the Association for Persons with Severe Handicaps, 12,* 18–27.

Hughes, C., & Agran, M. (1993). Teaching persons with severe disabilities to use self-instruction in community settings: An analysis of applications. *Journal of the Association for Persons with Severe Handicaps, 18,* 261–274.

O'Brien, J. (1991). *Down stairs that are never your own: Supporting people with developmental disabilities in their own homes.* Decatur, GA: Responsive Systems Associates.

Pancsofar, E. (1986). Assessing work behavior. In F. R. Rusch (Ed.), *Supported employment issues and strategies* (pp. 93–102). Baltimore: Paul H. Brookes.

Pancsofar, E. (1993). *Community connections.* Manchester, CT: Communitas.

Racino, J., & Walker, P. (1993). "Whose life is it anyway?": Life planning, choices, and decision making. In J. Racino, P. Walker, S. O'Connor, & S. Taylor (Eds.), *Housing, support, and community: Choices and strategies for adults with disabilities* (pp. 57–80). Baltimore: Paul H. Brookes.

Schloss, P., Alper, S., & Jayne, D. (1993). Self-determination for persons with disabilities: Choice, risk, and dignity. *Exceptional Children, 60,* 215–225.

Snell, M. (1993). *Instruction of students with severe disabilities* (4th ed.). New York: Merrill.

Spooner, F., & Test, D. (1994). Domestic and community living skills. In E. C. Cipani & F. Spooner (Eds.), *Curricular and instructional approaches for persons with severe disabilities* (pp. 149–183). Boston: Allyn & Bacon.

Steere, D., Pancsofar, E., Powell, T., & Butterworth, J. (1989). Enhancing instruction through general case programming. *Teaching Exceptional Children, 22,* 22–24.

Steere, D., Pancsofar, E., Wood, R., & Hecimovic, A. (1990). Principles of shared responsibility. *Career Development for Exceptional Individuals, 13,* 143–153.

Szymanski, E. (1994). Transition: Life span and life space considerations for empowerment. *Exceptional Children, 60,* 402–410.

Szymanski, E. (1995, September). *Transition from school to adulthood.* Presentation at State-wide Conference on Transition from School to Work, Montana State University-Billings.

Wehman, P. (1992). *Beyond the classroom: Transition strategies for young people with disabilities.* Baltimore: Paul H. Brookes.

Wilcox, B., & Bellamy, G. T. (Eds.). (1987). *A comprehensive guide to The Activities Catalog: An alternative curriculum for youth and adults with severe disabilities.* Baltimore: Paul H. Brookes.

Wolf, M. (1978). Social validity: The case for subjective information or how applied behavior analysis is finding its heart. *Journal of Applied Behavior Analysis, 11,* 203–214.

11

*Teaching Personal
Care and Hygiene Skills*

FRED SPOONER

WENDY M. WOOD

Cleanliness, good health, and being able to handle one's personal needs such as toileting, eating, menstrual care, and dressing are highly valued in our culture. In many ways, these basic skills are viewed as essential as evidenced by the emphasis placed on personal care and hygiene skills by parents of infants and toddlers, (toileting, independent eating); children aged 5 to 12 (independent bathing, dressing, toothbrushing); adolescents (independent personal hygiene including menstrual care, use of deodorant); to adulthood (meal preparation, clothing care and maintenance, medications management, nutrition, etc.). As children grow, they are expected to become more independent with these basic tasks. The degree to which children with disabilities can acquire these skills will impact their lives in many ways.

The greater one's independence with basic tasks of daily living, the less one will have to depend on others for support. With greater independence, comes more choices, more freedom to participate in community settings and activities, and more decision-making control over when, where, and with whom one lives, works, recreates, and otherwise participates in society. Unlike public education services, some adult service organizations are not operating under entitlement mandates (i.e, they are without a public mandate, or law, requiring that all individuals identified with a disability be served regardless of severity or financial means). Therefore, some adult service programs *may* set limits on who will be served. These adult service programs *may* establish eligibility criteria that restrict participation of certain individuals (e.g., individuals who are not toilet trained, individuals who cannot eat independently).

In other settings, individuals who do not follow a routine of regular showering/bathing and do not use deodorant, may be rejected by peers in social situations or coworkers in employment settings because they smell bad or are perceived to be dirty. Individuals who can eat independently, toilet, shower and dress themselves, shop for groceries, plan and prepare meals, and work in a real job for real pay (i.e., not sheltered employment) will likely be able to live in community settings with less supervision and support. A general rule might be that the more a person can do without the involvement of another person in a supervision or assistance role, the more an individual can enact his or her choices.

WHAT SKILLS COMPRISE PERSONAL CARE AND HYGIENE?

Working Americans typically start their day with a quick breakfast, a shower, and a routine composed of various steps to get ready (dressed, primped, etc.) to leave for the day. Each of these activities includes a subset of activities that must be completed. For example, a quick breakfast might also include taking prescribed medications and/or vitamins; after showering, an individual will typically need to brush and floss his or her teeth, use mouthwash, get dressed in clean clothes, and style his or her hair. In addition, at some point during the aforementioned routine, many women may want to apply makeup and most men will need to shave. Other daily activities might include meal planning, food storage and disposal, selection of clothing for the day's activities, and laundry and clothing maintenance.

During the day, most people eat a midday meal, use the bathroom, and wash their hands several times throughout the day. In the evening after returning from work, individuals typically undress from their work clothes and put on more comfortable clothes, prepare and/or eat an evening meal, engage in some household chores (see Chapter 10), enjoy some leisure/recreation activities, ending the evening by undressing from evening leisure clothes into bedclothes, brushing and flossing teeth, and washing face and hands before bed. In addition, one may want to see that appropriate clothing is clean and available for the next day. Of course, there are always variations of sequence (i.e., some people prefer to shower or bathe in the evenings before bed, some individuals' work clothes are just as comfortable for evening leisure clothes, some people do not require hair styling on a daily basis, many individuals work on schedules other than 8 to 5).

Although the above daylong scenario has not been tested on a representative sample of adult Americans, the personal care and hygiene (PCH) tasks listed approximate what would be included in a daily routine for many adult Americans. Based on this assumption, this chapter addresses the preceding topics in addition to those PCH tasks that are *not* typically addressed on a daily basis such as cutting and styling hair, cutting fingernails and toenails, painting fingernails, cleaning ears, and for women—menstrual care, shaving legs and underarms. Instructional strategies and content span across the school years for students aged 5 through 21 with varying levels of disability (mild to severe). Strategies include provisions for training students to perform skills to full independence as well as to various levels of partial participation (Baumgart et al., 1982; Ferguson & Baumgart, 1991; Snell, 1993).

These tasks have been listed in an approximate order of when during the day and in what relation to each other they may occur to establish the context of what

TABLE 11.1   Brainstorm of Daily PCH Activities and Lists from Previous Literature

Brainstorm Based on Competent Peers in Future Environments	Ford et al. 1989	Snell, 1993	Spooner & Test, 1994	Falvey, 1995
Toileting	Toileting	Toileting	Toileting	Toileting
Menstrual care	Eating	Eating	Dressing	Dressing
Showering	Food preparation	Dressing	Eating	Eating
Washing hair	Clean up after	Undressing	Grooming	Toothbrushing
Styling hair	meal	Selecting clothing	Brushing teeth	
Using deodorant	Food storage	Evaluating one's	Washing hands	
Shaving	Serving food	appearance	Washing face	
Face	Showing/	Showering/bathing	Clothing care	
Legs	bathing	Using deodorant	Clothing	
Underarms		Washing face	selection	
Nail care		Hands		
Washing hands		Brushing teeth		
Washing face		Clipping/filing		
Toothbrushing		nails		
Flossing		Painting finger-		
Using mouthwash		nails		
Dressing		Shaving face or legs		
Undressing		Menstrual hygiene		
Clothing				
Maintenance				
Clothing selection				
Eating				
Drinking				
Meal preparation				
Food				
Handling/storage				
Washing dishes				
Taking				
medications				
Responding to				
illness				

might be a typical person's daily schedule. When planning a program for an individual, variations should be accommodated for any given individual's particular situation and/or preference. Table 11.1 compares the tasks delineated in the preceding brainstorm of a daily routine of PCH activities with skills that have been delineated in previous literature.

WHO ARE INDIVIDUALS WHO WILL NEED ASSISTANCE WITH PERSONAL CARE AND HYGIENE?

Almost by definition, most people with special needs will require some assistance in the area of personal hygiene whether it would be a few of the finer, more advanced, points of hygiene like flossing teeth and using mouthwash on a regular basis or picking a clothing selection that is seasonally appropriate to some of the more basic skills like independent toileting or showering. On the other hand, it is likely that those people with the most severe deficits will be the ones who will require the most systematic instruction over an extended period.

INDIVIDUALS WITH SEVERE DISABILITIES.

Although there are several different definitions that have been posited in the professional literature, there appear to be two perspectives on the strategies that one uses to formulate a definition. The first perspective is based on a deficit model (e.g., ABT Associates, 1974; Justin, 1976). That is, people with severe disabilities have traditionally been explained by their paucity of skills (e.g., severe intellectual deficits, self-injurious behavior, stereotypic behavior, not toilet trained). In some cases, the litany of problems was so long that an automatic mind-set was formed that people who functioned at this level, with this many deficiencies could not learn.

A second perspective, and a more recent one, is based on the supports needed to participate in a meaningful lifestyle (e.g., McDonnell, Hardman, McDonnell, & Keifer-O'Donnell, 1995). Sailor and Haring (1977) were probably among the first authors to identify the supports necessary to promote successful to community participation based on primary service need. They indicated that if the student's need was of an academic nature, then referral to a program for students with severe disabilities would be inappropriate. If, on the other hand, the student's needs were assessed to be basic, then placement in a program for students with severe disabilities would be suitable. The second perspective is the direction that clearly identifies people with severe disabilities in a positive light, and also continues to suggest that in most cases, these people will require extensive support, to participate in integrated community settings with a lifestyle that is commensurate with their chronological age-appropriate peers.

People with severe disabilities are individuals who, in most cases, will require training at the most basic level in the area of personal hygiene, and in some cases will need additional environmental modification due to the multiple nature of their disability. At the other end of the continuum might be people who have been mislabeled. Individuals who will rapidly move through a systematic training program dress themselves, toilet themselves, bathe themselves, care for their own basic hygiene and graduate to more advanced training in clothing selection, evaluation of their appearance, and clothing maintenance.

THE CURRICULUM: BASED ON COMPETENT PEERS IN FUTURE ENVIRONMENTS

In this chapter, the PCH curriculum is based on what is typical for *working adults* in American culture. By focusing on working adults, we are designing these curricular components around competent peers in future (i.e., subsequent) environments (Spooner & Test, 1994). As such, content is focused on developing PCH skills in the context of a typical daily routine for an individual who participates in paid and integrated employment.

Content is not presented in "cookbook" fashion. Rather, a process of identifying and analyzing current and future environments of a particular individual (ecological analysis) is discussed, which is to be implemented in conjunction with a process of gathering information on the particular skills of the individual, followed by an assessment of the learner's skills level in relation to the skills determined necessary to function in the current and future environments (Ysseldyke, Christenson, & Kovaleski, 1994). Then a process is discussed that describes how members of a transdisciplinary team can use this information to formulate an individualized educational program (IEP) that will build the necessary repertoire of PCH skills to achieve maximum independence in current and future environments where competent peers live and work. In addition, this chapter examines teaching individuals with special needs to attain partial independence or partial participation in conjunction with arranged public or natural supports. For students who need partial independence or partial participation with supports, the IEP process described includes emphasis on working with family members of young children and adult community service agencies for students who are nearing transition age to determine to what degree these students can achieve independence with their PCH skills and to what degree they will need to be supported.

Table 11.2 delineates approximate levels of support available in our communities for both current and future environments. Incorporating accommodations, modifications, and assistive technology is also discussed.

Because of the commitment to individualized planning and instruction, two longitudinal case examples are used. Both case examples start with each student at age 5 and continue through their exiting secondary school. The cases are used to illustrate how teams of concerned educators should work together with parents to focus on current needs and future environments and goals for students with special needs. For the purpose of these case examples, the process of planning for the development of PCH skills in the student's Individualized Education Plan (IEP) is framed by discussions of what skills are important (1) to increase independence in current environments (and in effect, will serve to reduce the burden on their primary caregivers), (2) to increase

TABLE 11.2   Levels of Independence and Support Needs and Community Support Options

Total Independence	Independent on Some Tasks, Needing Partial Support on Others	Partial Participation with Support Needed on All Tasks	Full Care Needed
Can live independently in private home or apartment.	Can live in community with natural supports from family and/or friends, case management support, long-term follow-along support through a supported living and/or employment program, or personal care assistant part-time support.	Can live in community with natural supports from family and/or friends, long-term follow-along support through a supported living program, or personal care assistant part-time support.	Can live in community with ongoing support from family and/or friends, in a supervised apartment program with full-time staff, group home placement, with full-time PCA services, in-home nursing care.

independence in future environments, and (3) to enhance their integration by their current and future age peers. Case 1, Carol, is a young girl with severe intellectual disability and physical disability caused by cerebral palsy. Case 2, Michael, is a student with mild to moderate intellectual disability and a difficult home life.

Case 1. Carol

Carol is a 5-year-old girl scheduled to attend a regular elementary school in the fall. At the request of her parents, she will be served in a regular kindergarten classroom with collaborative support from a special education teacher. Carol has multiple disabilities including severe intellectual (IQ 30) and physical disability. She uses a manual wheelchair for mobility and has good use of her right hand and arm, limited use of her left. She can stand for brief periods if supported by another person. Carol has not yet demonstrated an ability to pull herself up with a handrail, but the physical therapist indicated that she should be capable of this with practice. She has some functional receptive language and uses some one-word utterances. Carol enjoys being around people, which is evident by her smiles when her sister or her sister's friends include her in their activities. Carol's older sister, Sarah, lets Carol come in her room when she has friends over because many of her friends appreciate Carol's friendliness. Sarah and her friends help Carol eat, take her for walks around the neighborhood, and help her change clothes.

Carol is not yet toilet trained even though her doctor says that she is physically capable (i.e., she has bladder and bowel control) of accomplishing this objective. Her mother explained to the two new teachers that Carol has not been able to access the bathroom at home because the room and the doorway are too small. Sometimes, she and Carol's father ask Carol if she needs to go, and they lift and carry her into the bathroom even when they are uncertain about her indication. Sometimes she goes and sometimes she does not. "Most of the time, we keep a diaper on her, because we never know when she is going to need to go," Carol's mother explained.

Recently, however, Carol and her family moved into a new house. Her mother said that the large bathroom was a big selling point of the house. Carol's father is putting in a wide door that opens into the hallway instead of into the bathroom to allow Carol to get through the doorway and pull the door closed behind her for privacy: something she never had in their previous house. Now, she needs to know how and when to respond to her bodily sensations indicating when she needs to go to the bathroom and how to transfer from her wheelchair to the toilet without assistance.

In addition to not being toilet trained, Carol eats most foods with her fingers. She has not been able to hold a spoon and transfer food from the plate or bowl to her mouth without spilling all or most of the food. She has not learned to use a fork because of poor hand grip. Carol also needs help to brush her teeth, brush her hair, get dressed, and her mother provides total assistance with bathing. Other areas of need involve language and communication, functional reading, and socialization and participation with age peers without disabilities.

Case 2. Michael

Michael is a 5 year-old boy with moderate intellectual disability (IQ 50) caused by Down's syndrome. Although small in stature, Michael is physically capable, and strong. With regard to expressive language, he is very vocal about what he wants or needs although his vocabulary is very limited. His preschool teacher says that she suspects he may be somewhat selective regarding his receptive language in that he seems to have trouble understanding her directions, particularly when she instructs him to change from an activity he likes. He likes to look at pictures of cars in magazines.

As for Michael's PCH skills, he can eat independently with a spoon, although his mother says that she wishes he didn't spill so much food. He can dress himself but needs help zipping and snapping his jeans and he cannot tie his shoes. He is toilet trained but his mother reports that he still wets his bed two to three times per week. Michael participates in brushing his teeth but is very slow. His mother puts toothpaste on his toothbrush every morning and helps him brush his teeth. The preschool teacher added that he does not have any pattern established for brushing his teeth; he seems to move the brush around inside his mouth randomly. Michael does not know how to wash his face without assistance and has to be told to wash his hands after each visit to the bathroom.

An attractive boy, with freckles and brown hair, he lives alone with his mother. Michael's father is not present in his life. His mother works full-time for the local newspaper as a clerical support person, and has a second job as a waitress Saturday and Sunday mornings. She says that the extra money is critical since she gets no support from Michael's father for his care. She works from 7:00 A.M. until 3:30 P.M., Monday through Friday at the newspaper office and Saturday and Sunday from 6:30 A.M. to 2:30 P.M. at her waitress job. Her mother, Michael's grandmother, takes care of him until she comes home from work. According to his mother, his grandmother has a difficult time "controlling" Michael and so to help "keep him busy" she lets him watch videos or play with his matchbox toy cars until his mother gets home from work. She places very few demands on Michael. She does have him put his toy cars away after he finishes playing with them and sometimes lets him help her set the dinner table.

CASE EXAMPLE 1. PLANNING A PROGRAM FOR CAROL'S ELEMENTARY SCHOOL YEARS

At the end of Carol's preschool program for students with disabilities, a meeting was scheduled to facilitate Carol's transition to the elementary school program. Carol's preschool teacher and occupational therapist met with the K–5 special education, and regular education kindergarten teachers, the special education coordinator, Carol, her mother and father, her two sisters, a neighbor who is a friend of the family, physical therapist (PT), occupational therapist (OT), and other members of the school transdisciplinary team near the end of the year before Carol was to enter kindergarten. The team looked at Carol's current strengths and needs and worked together as a group to decide what educational goals would comprise Carol's IEP for her year in kindergarten. Being in the regular classroom, the regular education teacher would be the person who had primary contact with Carol for instruction. In addition to deciding what goals would be included, the team needed to design an optimum service delivery and support system to enable Carol to participate as fully as possible in the regular classroom with her age peers and to achieve the goals that were most essential to her current and future needs in the classroom and other environments.

The special education teacher facilitated the meeting and encouraged Carol's family to talk about what goals and objectives they felt would be important for Carol. The teacher also asked Carol, her parents, and her older sister to talk about what types of things she liked to do in her free time and what things might be important to her. The special education (SE) teacher also initiated planning with the regular education (RE) teacher and the special services support staff to design the optimum service and support system for Carol in the regular classroom. The SE teacher asked for members of the IEP team to discuss and prioritize Carol's needs with regard to (1) current environments, (2) near future environments (for the next two to four years), and (3) skills and or behaviors that would enhance Carol's acceptance by her current and future age peers (Fredericks & Brodsky, 1994).

Understandably, some basic needs in PCH were discussed by all because improving these skills would enhance Carol's ability to participate in the classroom activities. All agreed that independent toileting was a high priority with independent eating, hand washing, and toothbrushing also on the list. Since this was kindergarten, the RE teacher said that she could very easily include a unit on "Care of Your Teeth" for her class that would be good for all the students. At the conclusion of the unit, toothbrushing practice could be moved home with continued practice and monitoring being provided by Carol's parents and older sister. The occupational therapist (OT) was asked to provide some input in relation to how best to position Carol for tooth brushing and how to set up the task so that Carol could best reach and manipulate the materials, (e.g., toothbrush, toothpaste, glass, water faucet, towel). In addition, she said that teaching her students to wash their hands after leaving the bathroom and before lunch were regular activities for her kindergarten students. Correct positioning for Carol to brush her teeth will also be appropriate for washing hands and face.

For Carol to toilet independently, she will initially need more intensive involvement of the SE teacher and the OT as teaching her this skill will involve (1) having her indicate her need to go to the bathroom, (2) learning the optimal positions for her to wheel her chair up to the toilet, (3) learning to hold on to the handrail and pulling herself up, and so forth. Training her in this skill will need to be approached in a well-planned sequence with cooperative teaming between the SE teacher and the OT before her performance of the skill can be transferred to the classroom teacher to support. Additionally, the OT will make a visit to Carol's home to assess the bathroom in her new home and give Carol's father guidance on how best to install the handrail in the bathroom and Carol's mother on how best to assist Carol in practicing her transfer from her chair to the toilet seat and back again. As Carol meets separate objectives during the in-school training, the SE teacher and/or the OT will make contact with Carol's parents to assist in generalizing her independent toileting skills to her home environment. Starting to work on this difficult skill while Carol is young takes advantage of her small body weight for lifting and transferring herself, and encourages development of the necessary muscle groups early in life.

Table 11.3 lists the goals and objectives that were delineated for Carol for her year in kindergarten and the service design to achieve those goals and objectives.

ARRANGING PEER TUTORING FOR CAROL

Because Carol is receiving her education in a regular classroom, the team has to devise effective and efficient ways to unobtrusively provide instruction to Carol in the skills she needs within the regular classroom routine. It is decided that after some initial training by the RE teacher, that some of Carol's classmates, functioning as peer tutors, can work with her on learning how to wash her hands at the natural times of the day—before lunch, in the bathroom, after art class, and before the afternoon snack. The peer tutors will be selected by observing which students in the class

TABLE 11.3 Carol's Goals and Objectives for Kindergarten

Instructional Goals	Objectives	Person Responsible	Projected Completion
1. The student will toilet herself independently.	1.1 During class, lunchroom, and recess activities, Carol will indicate her need to go to the bathroom by saying "Bathroom, please" to the teacher or classroom assistant for 95% of the opportunities for 7 consecutive days.	RE teacher & SE teacher	11/1/96
	1.2 When wearing pants with an elastic band, Carol will slide her outer- and underpants down around her knees while holding onto the side bar handrail without assistance for 7 consecutive days.	PT & OT	1/1/97
	1.3 Given a toilet with a side bar handrail, Carol will transfer to the toilet seat without assistance for 7 consecutive days.	PT & OT	3/1/97
	1.4 After urinating or defecating, Carol will dry/wipe herself without assistance for 7 consecutive days.	PT & classroom assistant OT & SE teacher	3/1/97 4/1/97
2. The student will eat independently.	2.1 Given an adaptive spoon, a bowl of food appropriate for eating with a spoon (oatmeal, Brunswick stew, cereal, baked beans, jello), Carol will eat using a spoon with less than 5% spillage for 5 consecutive days.	OT & classroom assistant	11/15/96
	2.2 Given bite-sized pieces of food on a plate, Carol will eat 10 out of 10 pieces with a fork, on 5 consecutive days.	Classroom assistant and peer tutors	12/15/96
	2.3 Given a plate of food, Carol will eat using a spoon or a fork with less than 5% spillage for 5 consecutive days.	SE teacher w/transfer home to parent	4/1/97
3. The student will wash her hands and face independently.	3.1 At appropriate times during the day, Carol will wash her hands with 100% accuracy within a 3-minute time period, for 5 consecutive days.	RE teacher & peer tutors	11/1/96
	3.2 After brushing her teeth, Carol will wash her face using a washcloth and warm water within a 3-minute period, for 5 consecutive days.	SE teacher w/transfer to parent at home	2/1/97
	3.3 After brushing her teeth, Carol will wash her face using a washcloth, warm water, and a nontear soap, within a 3-minute period, for 5 consecutive days.	Parent at home	4/1/97
4. The student will brush her teeth independently.	4.1 Given a toothbrush with an adapted handle, and toothpaste in an adapted dispenser, Carol will put toothpaste on her toothbrush with 95% accuracy for 5 consecutive days.	OT	11/1/96
	4.2 After lunch, Carol will brush her teeth with 85% accuracy for 5 consecutive days.	SE teacher	2/1/97
	4.3 After breakfast and before bed, Carol will brush her teeth with 95% accuracy for 5 consecutive days.	Parent with SE teacher in consulting role Home visit initially	4/1/97

Personnel codes: OT = occupational therapist; PT = physical therapist; RE = regular education; SE = special education.

showed an interest in helping with Carol; students who asks the teacher if they can push Carol's wheelchair, help her eat her lunch, or otherwise assist her during the schoolday. As it is a natural occurrence for all kindergartners to wash their hands, Carol will be put in a group with the peer tutors for hand washing. The RE teacher will work with Carol on learning to wash her hands within this group. The RE teacher plans to let their natural curiosity about Carol and their interest in helping her lead them through observing the teacher or classroom assistant working with her and then volunteering to help her themselves. Gradually, after allowing for observation by peer students, the RE teacher will let the peer tutors begin to play a role in Carol's teaching. The SE teacher developed a simple task analysis in the form of a peer tutor guide sheet. The peer tutor task analysis is available in Table 11.4.

During Carol's kindergarten year, her IEP team met to plan what goals and objectives should be addressed for her next several years in school in an attempt to design her IEP to maximize her independence in current and future environments and to enhance her participation with her age peers. The list in Table 11.5 represents the skills to be taught and the approximate schedule for these to be included across Carol's elementary school years.

CASE EXAMPLE 2. PLANNING FOR MICHAEL'S ELEMENTARY SCHOOL YEARS

Prior to his enrollment in kindergarten, Michael attended a preschool program for three days each week. The month before he transitioned out of preschool, Michael, his preschool teachers, the special education coordinator, and his mother, met to discuss what goals and objectives would be important for Michael to have on his IEP for the coming year as well as what goals might be appropriate for the next several years. Because the team was looking at what skills Michael was going to need in future environments, it was apparent that all could not be accomplished in any one year.

The team worked with Michael's mother to identify some of her needs for Michael. Because she was a single parent to a child with a disability and was working two jobs, she did not have much assistance in caring for Michael and even less free time for herself or quality time with Michael. She said that getting Michael ready for school in the morning was a real challenge. Because of her early morning work schedule, she wished that Michael could do more to get himself ready for school in the morning. It was decided by the team that the SE teacher would analyze the activities required for Michael to get ready to leave for school in the morning, and begin instructional planning and implementation efforts designed to increase Michael's independence in a morning "get ready for school" routine. Table 11.6 represents a tentative plan developed to address PCH skills during Michael's elementary school years. This plan was developed based on the analysis of Michael's home life, his mother's schedule, and other factors.

MAKING PERSONAL CARE AND HYGIENE SKILLS DEVELOPMENT MEANINGFUL

For the most part, PCH skills are implemented from the home setting (e.g., bathing, brushing teeth, dressing, hair care). Although skills training can be carried out in the school setting, provisions must be made for generalizing the learned skills to

TABLE 11.4   Peer Tutor Task Analysis

Peer tutor instructions: Scoring: J if she does a step by herself
H if you *help* her do a given step

Tutoring Sessions

Task Steps									
Please say to Carol:									
1. Carol, let's wash our hands. (Count to 5, then)									
2. Pull up under the sink.									
3. Get in position (wheelchair under sink).									
4. Turn on the cold water (rotate handle ¼).									
5. Turn on the hot water (rotate handle ¼).									
6. Wet both hands.									
7. Rub hands on soap.									
8. Rub hands together.									
9. Rinse hands in water.									
10. Turn off cold water.									
11. Turn off hot water.									
12. Dry hands with paper towel.									
13. Put paper towel in trash.									
No. of steps correct									
Percentage of task correct									

TABLE 11.5   Carol's Elementary School Goals in Personal Care and Hygiene

Goals for K–2nd Grade	Goals for 3rd–4th Grade	Goals for 5th Grade
Goals for Kindergarten IST on: *Waking to alarm.* *Transferring from bed to wheelchair.* *Independent toileting.* *Washing hands and face.* *Eating using a spoon and fork.* *Brushing teeth independently.* *Goals for 1st Grade* IST on: Improving proficiency with toileting. Improving proficiency with eating skills. Improving proficiency brushing teeth. GTH of independent toileting skills, independent eating, hand and face washing across three target environments. (home, fast-food restaurant, grandmother's house). *IST on combing hair.* *IST on putting on and taking off coat.* *Goals for 2nd Grade* Build Morning Routine 1. GTH waking to alarm. 2. GTH independent toileting. 3. GTH eating breakfast independently. 4. Go to bathroom for brushing teeth, washing face and hands, combing hair (mother will assist and/or supervise for remainder of morning routine—dressing, etc.). 5. *Leaving for bus stop.*	*Goals for 3rd Grade* *Extend and Maintain Morning Routine* 1. GTH waking to alarm. 2. IST on transferring from bed to chair—PP. 3. Independent toileting. 4. Eating breakfast independently. 5. Go to bathroom for brushing teeth, *washing face,* washing hands. 6. IST on putting on a pullover shirt, at home—*dressing with PP.* 7. GTH combing hair. 8. *Putting bathroom materials away.* 9. GTH putting on coat to leave for school. 10. *Leaving for bus stop.* *Goals for 4th Grade* 1, 3, 4, 5, 7 maintain skills. 2. GTH transferring from bed to chair. 6. Dressing: *In-school training on putting on jeans; GTH pullover shirt to home; remainder dressing—PP.* 8. *IST putting on a hair band.* 9. *Leaving for bus stop.*	*Goals for 5th Grade* *Maintain Morning Routine and Improve Proficiency* Maintain 1, 2, 3, 4, 5, 7. 6. GTH putting on shirt and pants, remainder dressing—PP. 8. GTH putting on a hair band. 9. Leave for bus stop. *Build Evening Routine* 1. *IST on selecting outfit for next day.* 2. *CWP on training bathing skills.* 3. *CWP dressing for bed.* 4. Brushing teeth.

Codes: PP = partial participation; IST = in-school training; GTH = generalize to home; CWP = consultation with parent; *italicized print* = new skills.

TABLE 11.6   Michael's Elementary School Goals in Personal Care and Hygiene

Goals for K–2nd Grade	Goals for 3rd–4th Grade	Goals for 5th Grade
Goals for Kindergarten	*Goals for 3rd Grade*	*Goals for 5th Grade*
IST on:	*Extend and Maintain Morning*	*Maintain Morning Routine and*
Waking to alarm.	*Routine*	*Improve Proficiency*
Independent toileting.	1. Wake to alarm.	1. Wake to alarm.
Washing hands and face.	2. Go to bathroom.	2. Go to bathroom.
Eating using a fork.	3. *Fixing breakfast (PP:*	3. Go to kitchen:
Brushing teeth in reasonable time	*Get glass from cabinet.*	Get glass from cabinet.
frame.	*Get orange juice from*	Get orange juice from
Buttoning and zipping.	*refrigerator.*	refrigerator.
	Pour juice in glass.	Pour juice in glass.
Goals for 1st Grade	*Carry to seat at table.*	Carry to seat at table.
CWP on training bathing skills.	*Eat cereal prepared by*	Eat cereal prepared by
CWP on training washing hair,	*mother.*	mother.
IST on combing wet hair and	*Wipe mouth with napkin.*	Wipe mouth with napkin.
hanging up towel.	4. Go to bathroom for	Carry dishes to sink after
CWP on training independent	brushing teeth, *washing*	finished.
nighttime toileting.*	*face,* washing hands.	4. Go to bathroom for:
IST on dressing independently.	5. *Getting dressed.*	brushing teeth, washing
	6. *Picking up packed lunch for*	face and hands, combing
Goals for 2nd Grade	*school.*	hair, and putting
Build a Morning Routine	7. *Leaving for bus stop.*	materials away.
1. CWP waking to alarm.		5. Getting dressed.
2. Independent toileting.	*Goals for 4th Grade*	6. Picking up packed lunch
3. GTH eating breakfast	Maintaining 1, 2, 3 above and	for school.
using a fork. *IST on putting*	adding into 4):	7. Leaving for bus stop.
dishes in sink.	*Combing hair.*	*Build Evening Routine*
4. GTH go to bathroom for	*Putting materials away—*	1. Select outfit for next day.
brushing teeth, washing	*toothbrush; cap on toothpaste*	2. Packing a lunch.
hands.	*tube; washcloth on hook;*	3. Taking bath.
(Mother will assist with tasks for	*comb in drawer; soap in soap*	4. Dressing for bed.
remainder of morning routine)	*dish.*	5. Brushing teeth.
5. *Getting dressed.*	5. *Getting dressed.*	6. Going to the bathroom.
6. *Picking up packed lunch for*	6. *Picking up packed lunch for*	7. Getting into bed.
school.	*school.*	
7. *Leaving for bus stop.*	7. *Leaving for bus stop.*	

Codes: PP = partial participation; IST = in-school training; GTH = generalize to home; CWP = consultation with parent; *italicized print* = new skills.

* See references Azrin, Sneed, & Foxx (1973); Baller (1975).

their more natural settings. In Carol's and Michael's cases, the school staff would work on skills development in the school setting and then work with Carol's parents and Michael's mother to generalize those skills to the home setting in a routine that would fit their particular schedule and activities. In almost all cases, the in-school training followed by generalization to the home setting would require a good consultative effort between the school staff and Michael's mother. Tables 11.5 and 11.6

include tentative plans for developing a morning routine for Carol (Table 11.5) and Michael (Table 11.6) including provisions for *in-school training* (IST), followed by a process to generalize the skills to the home setting (*generalize to home* = GTH), and cases where *consultation with the parent* (CWP) might be needed for training and generalization to be successful.

Arranging a stream of skills into a consistent sequence avoids ending up with the student knowing how to do several different activities, but unsure about which to do first and which second, and so on. By arranging the different morning "get ready for school" activities into a consistent routine, there is a higher likelihood that ending one activity will cue the student as to what activity he or she should do next. If training is successful, the child will be more capable of completing the various activities independently (he or she will not need to prompted in between each activity as to what activity to do next) and more likely to maintain the skills as a pattern is developed in which completion of each activity in the stream cues the next activity in the stream (Alberto & Troutman, 1995). In this regard, students or individuals with disabilities may be able to maintain their level of independence with an entire routine more successfully than they might be able to with separate and disconnected skills.

PLANNING FOR MIDDLE SCHOOL YEARS

In middle school, Carol and Michael have a new set of PCH needs. With adolescence comes puberty and a host of changes in their interests and their bodies. If we were to examine a group of competent adolescent peers, we would find students dealing with changes in their bodies such as breast development and the onset of menstruation for girls, chest hair on boys, underarm and pubic hair on both, skin problems, more active sweat glands, a developing interest in sex, and the emotional upheaval which accompanies all of this change and uncertainty. Social relationships with peers become the dominant focus of their universe. PCH skills become critical to an individual being successful in developing secure social relationships with age peers. The biological changes and needs for students with disabilities are no different than those for students without disabilities.

Physical attractiveness becomes very important (near life or death) for adolescents. Therefore, exercise and nutrition become important. For students with physical impairments, weight gain may become an issue because their ability to burn calories may be hindered by their impaired mobility. Weight gain can further hinder mobility for individuals with physical disabilities thereby impeding their ability to be independent at various PCH tasks. Students with physical disabilities need to develop patterns early in life (during elementary school) that include practicing good nutrition and regular exercise to avoid complicating their physical limitations by weight gain. Table 11.7 delineates what PCH skills might be included for Carol as she moves through her middle school years. All skills should be taught within the context of expanding and maintaining the morning and evening routines.

Planning for Michael's middle school years will involve adding a few activities into his morning and evening routines. With recent information emerging on the prevention of gum disease (National Institutes of Health [NIH], 1995) using mouthwash would be a valuable activity to add to the morning bathroom routine immediately following tooth brushing. Using deodorant fits logically in the morning

TABLE 11.7   PCH Skills to Be Addressed During Carol's Middle School Years

Skill Areas	Subskills and/or Related Skills	Training (T), Maintenance (M), and Generalization (G) Concerns
Menstrual Care	1. Feeling dampness in pants or recognizing menstrual soiling. 2. Pulling pants down and up. 3. Transferring to and from toilet. 4. Wiping. 5. Using sanitary napkin.	1. (T) Selection of a menstrual care product best suited for Carol. 2. (T&M) Gross motor range of motion for reaching. 3. (T&M) Fine motor skills for manipulating sanitary napkins and/or tampons. 4. (G) Consistency of menstrual care product used. 5. (G) Physical placement of materials in home setting. 6. (G) Access to materials in community settings.
Use of Deodorant	1. Removing a lid from deodorant container (a certain container type, e.g., round screw-off top, or oval pull-off, may facilitate Carol's independence with this task).	1. (T) Selection of product for Carol. 2. (T&M) Fine motor skills for manipulating deodorant container. 3. (T&M) Gross motor range of motion for reaching and holding applicator under both arms. 4. (G) Physical placement of materials in home setting.
Nutrition and Weight Control	1. Selecting nutritious low-calorie foods. 2. Independent eating. 3. Physical exercise.	1. (T&M) Best if patterns are started and maintained early. 2. (T) Will require developing a controlled repertoire of food choices. 3. (T&M) Will depend on close collaboration with parents from beginning throughout program.
Developing and Maintaining a Personal Look	1. Selecting clothes (fit, style, season, laundering instructions, cost, maintenance). 2. Independent dressing. 3. Using accessories if desired. 4. Applying makeup if desired.	1. (T&M) Will depend on close collaboration with parents. 2. (T&M) Fine motor skills for manipulating deodorant container. 3. (T&M) Gross motor range of motion for reaching. 4. (G) School staff will need to inform parents how Carol can make clothing selections. 5. If by middle school, Carol is unable to make clothing selections, work with parents on selecting clothes and accessories that are compatible with Carol's competent age peers.
Shaving Legs and Underarms		1. (T&M) Fine motor skills for manipulating electric shaver. 2. (T&M) Gross motor range of motion for reaching all areas of both legs and underarms.

bathroom sequence right after washing face and hands (see Table 11.6, under Goals for the 5th grade, number 4). After completing the task, Michael would return the deodorant top to the deodorant container and then put this and his other morning bathroom materials (toothbrush, toothpaste, comb, etc.) away. When training these skills and routines in the classroom, it is important to plan ahead for generalization to the home setting by having materials that are the same as or similar to what students will be using at home. In addition, generalization will be more efficient if the storage and retrieval of materials can approximate the same process in the home. For example, since it is unlikely that the school bathroom setting can be remodeled to approximate the home bathroom settings for all of the students, it may facilitate transferring the storage and retrieval steps home if students are taught to return all their materials to a shoe box or plastic storage box to then be put in one specific place.

ACCOMMODATING PERSONAL STYLE AND CULTURAL DIVERSITY IN PCH TRAINING

When given an opportunity, people like to have choices about how they look. To a large degree, style decisions for persons with disabilities have often been made according to the convenience and style preference of the caregiver, not the individual who would be wearing the style. Personal style should not be overlooked for the preference or convenience of the caregiver but rather should be accommodated as much as possible. Clothing selections, how clothes fit, color preferences, hair styles, use of accessories and/or jewelry, use of makeup (for girls), are all matters of personal style that should be accommodated as much as possible for people with disabilities. Having a certain look may enhance an individual's acceptance and inclusion with their valued age peers.

Usually, kids begin to make style choices during their middle school years. Many of their selections are inevitably influenced by styles put forth by the media as well as trends that develop among their peers. The "hip-hop" look, which originated with African American gang members and rap artists, is an example of a fashion trend that was not endorsed by the fashion industry, but which, nevertheless, caught on like wildfire among school-age youth across the country. This look is or was (depending on whether or not the trend lasts through the publication of this book) characterized by sagging jeans, males often wearing one earring, various hat styles turned backward, and big tennis shoes with oversize pants stacked on top of the shoes. The "punk" look was another trend that grew out of alternative art and music subcultures of the late 1970s and early 1980s. Parents with teenagers wearing dog collars and pink-tipped Mohawks found themselves avoiding extended family get-togethers until this fad ran its course. The "punk" look has evolved into the "grunge" look which might be identified by black Chuck Taylor tennis shoes, jeans torn across the knees and just below the buttocks, and oversize t-shirts and sweaters. The "grunge" look evolved from West Coast bands, skateboarders and beach bums. Most of these trends and fads are disseminated to a large extent by the "kid"-dominated cable network, MTV. Parents of adolescents and preadolescents with disabilities can monitor style trends by watching MTV and competent age peers in the schools. Thankfully, not all the styles modeled on MTV are followed and most that are, are done so temporarily. Wise parents know better than to incite rebellion when they can just wait until the trend changes to something a little less shocking.

Adolescent youth in middle school who choose a look to model or to imitate are perhaps in the initial stages of forming an identity, asserting some independence from parent domination of their earlier years. Attention to styles is also very important to kids "fitting in" with their age peers. For this reason, attending to personal style preferences of youth with disabilities is just as important, perhaps even more so, as it is for youth without disabilities. Issues such as affordability and the ability of the individual to maintain the look independently are fair considerations just as they would be for anyone.

In addition to personal choice, many individuals have preferences that are related to their cultural or ethnic backgrounds. Thankfully, America offers a rich diversity of different races, cultures, and ethnic backgrounds. Native Americans, African Americans, Asian Americans, European Americans and others can all trace roots back to a wide variety of culturally rich tribes and clans. Today, we are enjoying a rejuvenation of interest in cultural heritage and dress that should be considered and even encouraged when supporting a child's desire to develop a personal look.

FACILITATING AGE-APPROPRIATE DRESS

If students are not interested in making personal choices or if their choices are grossly out of sync with their competent age-appropriate peers, the teacher may need to offer the parents some guidance in assisting their teenage sons and daughters to make appropriate clothing selections. Many special education professionals have had teenage students with disabilities come to school dressed in clothing or equipped with accessories that are more appropriate for students in their early elementary school years (e.g., Barney lunch boxes, Barbie doll sweatshirts, Mickey Mouse notebooks, immature hairstyles and/or clothing). Some parents (and some professionals) tend to treat their sons and daughters as if they are much younger than they are. As we move toward inclusive education systems, it is critical that we help students with disabilities and their parents recognize the importance of chronologically age-appropriate dress. Teachers often struggle with the awkwardness of how to tell parents that they are dressing their teenager in baby clothes. A possible way to address this is to prepare one-page flyers to go home to parents monthly or every other month that address various issues pertaining to growing up. Figure 11.1 offers an example of a flyer that teachers might use to communicate one of these potentially awkward issues to parents. Other topics that may be addressed with a send-home flyer include students' use of deodorant and "Down with Baby Talk." Sending home a flyer gets the message across while avoiding an uncomfortable confrontation with parents who might react defensively if approached directly.

PLANNING FOR ADULTHOOD: TRANSITION FROM SCHOOL TO ADULT LIFE

PCH skills that would be desirable to address in high school for Carol (or other female students at this age) might include wearing light makeup, learning to dress in clothes appropriate for work, revising morning and evening routines to accommodate work schedules, preparing simple meals (e.g., frozen waffles, instant oatmeal, cereal

FIGURE 11.1   Sample Flyer to Keep Parents Informed About Their Children's Growing Up

Hey ~~Mommy~~ and ~~Daddy~~
(Ooops!! no more baby talk.)
Hey Mom and Dad

Your son or daughter is growing up.
Help him or her to blend in to the scene
here at middle school.
As a middle school student, your son or daughter
needs to wear clothes that teenagers wear.

No more Barney!

No more Care Bears!

No more Mickey Mouse!
(unless teenager approved)

If you need help knowing what kinds of clothes
teenagers are wearing, . . .
watch their classmates, watch MTV,
ask a teenager in your neighborhood.

with milk, lunchmeat sandwich, various microwave entrees, frozen vegetables, warming up leftovers) and storage of different food types, after-meal cleanup, etc. However, some time will be needed to maintain and generalize the skills learned during elementary and middle school years.

Looking into our crystal ball for Carol (and other students with the most severe disabilities), support systems will likely be needed to support her on a daily basis for some of the tasks for which she may only achieve a level of partial participation (e.g., medications management, first aid, grocery shopping, banking, housecleaning, shopping for clothes, laundering clothes). In addition, she will inevitably undergo changes during her life that may cause disruptions to her daily living routines. These disruptions might be caused by changes in her environment (e.g., moving to a new setting with different conditions), changes in her schedule (e.g., a supported employment opportunity which presents her with a different time to leave and return to her home or apartment); emotional upheaval (e.g., death of a parent(s)), changes in support personnel involving a caregiver (e.g., parent or relative, group home, or personal care provider). For each of these changes in her life, Carol will need her support systems (family, friends, and/or public community service system) to assist her in adjusting to the change or disruption. The supports and services will be designed based on a personal futures plan (Mount, 1987; Vandercook & York, 1990) which will be initiated before Carol graduates in conjunction with her Individualized Transition Plan (ITP) and will continue for as long as needed to support Carol's personal goals as an adult in the community.

In our crystal ball for Michael, we see that given his abilities and anticipated improvements in community support services, that by the time Michael graduates, there will be a community support service system to help him set up house in a shared apartment for which he will choose his roommate. Supported living personnel will work with the supported employment staff, his friends, and family to help Michael adjust his morning and evening routines to fit his new independent life and job in the community. Between his family, friends, and the community support services, there will be ongoing support to ensure that Michael meets all his responsibilities and achieves his needs and desires. As for Michael's preparation for adulthood, his ITP team, again using a personal futures planning approach, should examine some or all of the following skills to be addressed during Michael's final years in school. To live as independently as possible, Michael will need to learn to shave, dress for work, shop for clothes, apply basic first aid (how to care for minor cuts, abrasions, fever, etc.), manage any medications that may be prescribed, do his laundry, prepare simple meals, clean up after meals, and master the basics of food storage. In addition, he will need to expand, maintain, and generalize his daily and weekly routines to new settings, new conditions, and changing schedules. If he develops a healthy social life, he may meet and fall in love with someone, which will necessitate his learning and practicing safe and responsible sex.

By addressing PCH skills early in an individual's life, educators and parents enhance the likelihood that individuals will be able to live independently as adults in the community. Designing and training students to carry out PCH tasks within a logical daily routine (thereby chaining one task with another early in life), provides for a block of daily living skills that can be *efficiently* transferred from the family home setting to another setting when the time comes. The more independent individuals are with their PCH skills, the less restrictive their adult living and community participation arrangements can be. Adults who have clean hair, smell clean, and have clean breath will be more likely to be able to gain and maintain paid employment in integrated community employment settings. Individuals who can toilet themselves with little or no assistance and can eat independently will not have to depend on others to assist them with these essential daily activities. For these reasons, educational programs serving very young children have a real responsibility to address these issues so that behavioral and physical patterns can be established early in life. Looking at PCH skills development as a long-term process, starting at the earliest point in public education and continuing to build and link PCH skills over time, helps to ensure maximum independence for adulthood.

In this section, we have identified the scope and sequence of PCH skills; the individuals who will most likely need significant systematic and longitudinal intervention; the curriculum, which is based on PCH skills needed in subsequent environments and competent peers; provided longitudinal examples with Carol and Michael, taking them through key chronological milestones (e.g., the middle school years), and have addressed the issue of diversity and making personal choices about appearance and clothing selections. The next section is devoted to the implementation of instructional strategies for training PCH skills to persons with special needs.

INSTRUCTIONAL STRATEGIES

The underlying approach to teaching new skills is called applied behavior analysis. Applications of using behavior analysis to teach basic domestic skills like tooth brushing or more advanced skills like clothing selection to people with special needs are prevalent in the literature (e.g., tooth brushing, Horner & Keilitz, 1975; Snell, Lewis, & Houghton, 1989; Wolber, Carne, Collins-Montgomery, & Nelson, 1987; toileting, Azrin & Foxx, 1971; dressing, Day & Horner, 1986; Diorio & Konarski, 1984; washing clothes, Cuvo, Jacobi, Sipko, 1981; mending clothes, Cronin & Cuvo, 1979; selecting clothes, Nutter & Reid, 1978). Implementation of the behavioral approach for teaching persons with severe disabilities is also prevalent in recent texts devoted to developing instructional strategies for this population (Cipani & Spooner, 1994; Ryndak & Alper, 1996; Snell, 1993). Additionally, there are numerous documented success stories in teaching persons with special needs personal care and hygiene (menstrual care, Epps, Prescott, & Horner, 1990; Richman, Ponticas, Page, & Epps, 1986; Richman, Reiss, Bauman, & Bailey, 1984; use of roll-on-deodorant, Elium & McCarver, 1980; grooming, Brown, Evans, Weed, & Owen, 1987; Doleys, Stacy, & Knowles, 1981; Thinesen & Bryan, 1981).

Over the years as instructional applications for persons with special needs have matured, we have found collectively that there is more to teaching skills than acquisition alone. If a skill is to be valuable to an individual, the skill not only has to be acquired, but the learner must also be fluent in using the skill, be able to generalize the newly acquired skill to other environments, be likely to perform the skill for other people (other than the original trainer) and be able to maintain the skill across time (e.g., Billingsley, Liberty, & White, 1994; Haring, Liberty, & White, 1980). For example, an individual acquires the skill of making an appropriate clothing selection (i.e., picking out a color-coordinated outfit to wear to work the next day). The individual mastered the accuracy criterion that was set (i.e., five trials consecutive without error or assistance), and demonstrated that she was appropriately dressed on the job, day after day, with clothing selections that were socially validated by chronologically aged peers without disabilities. Yet, the data indicated that it took the individual one hour each evening to make the selection. Most people do not spend an hour deciding what they will wear to work the next day. Some folks may not even make the decision of "what to wear" until they begin to get dressed for the day's activities. Many people know what is clean, what combinations work together, and where various articles of clothing are stored. Decisions for each clothing item are made; based on the coordinated outfit, these items are put together; the total outfit is chosen; and the person gets dressed. Total time to make the decisions of "what to wear" and laying-out the items, should take maybe 15 minutes or less.

CONSIDERATIONS PRIOR TO STARTING INSTRUCTION

If instruction is to be successful, various considerations need to be weighed before actual training begins. For example, keeping the goals of the overall instructional process at the forefront of planning is important. Assessing what the individual needs to know now to be successful in the current environment, in addition to what skills will be needed in future environments will also provide useful information. Making some assessment of the discrepancy between the individual's current level of performance and what the final performance of the skill will look like when the individual has mastered it, will give still more information. Preparing appropriate task analyses that articulate the sequence of steps the student must perform accurately to accomplish the skill is also a necessary part of the pretraining process. How the skill will be taught is another essential decision (Billingsley et al., 1994).

Goals of the Instructional Process.   The overall goal of any instructional application is to produce an individual who cannot only perform the skill accurately, but who can also execute the skill fluently, maintain the skill across time, and generalize the skill to new situations. Skills that are not transferable to other environments, skills that are performed too slowly, and skills that are forgotten in a short period will not be useful to the learner. The continued emphasis on additional phases of learning fluency, maintenance, generalization, and skill development requires planners and trainers to seek more than mere acquisition of the skill. The goal of the instructional process should also keep in mind three additional considerations: encouraging personal choice, teaching skills that have immediate use, and teaching skills that are chronologically age-appropriate (Test & Spooner, 1996).

Making Initial Assessments of the Learner's Skill Level.   An assessment of the learner's current functioning level compared with the performance of where the learner would be when that particular skill is considered to be learned, is necessary to determine what skills, and what part of what skills, need to be taught. Analyzing skills that the learner will need in the immediate environment as well as those skills that he or she will need in subsequent environments involves what Brown and colleagues (1979) and Falvey (1995) call an *ecological inventory.* An ecological inventory assists the instructor in determining what skills are most functional for the individual. It is also necessary that the assessment process not stop at the initial assessment level, but rather should continue as an ongoing process in determining how both curriculum and methods should be modified to keep pace with changing student performance (Billingsley et al., 1994; Browder, 1991; Falvey, 1995).

Analyzing the Number of Steps for Instructional Tasks.   In most cases, many personal hygiene tasks (e.g., tooth brushing, dressing, toileting) will comprise a series of steps. The process of delineating the sequence and order in which steps will be performed is called *task analysis.* Table 11.8 is an example of a task analysis to teach tooth brushing.

Although there is no magic number of steps that a task analysis should contain, the literature provides some guidelines. Crist, Walls, and Haught (1984) indicate that task analyses with smaller increments of learning and more steps in the analysis produced fewer errors by students with severe disabilities. Sailor and Guess (1983)

TABLE 11.8   Brushing Teeth Task Analysis*

1. *Check for materials* (toothbrush, toothpaste, drinking cup).
2. *Pick up toothpaste* (with nondominant hand).
3. *Unscrew toothpaste cap* (with dominant hand).
4. *Lay cap on countertop.*
5. *Turn on cold water* (light flow).
6. *Pick up toothbrush* (use dominant hand, bristle end protruding from palm through thumb and forefinger).
7. *Wet* bristles of *toothbrush.*
8. *Put toothpaste on toothbrush* (small amount on top of bristles).
9. *Lay toothpaste tube on countertop.*
10. *Bring toothbrush* with paste up *to mouth.*
11. *Begin brushing teeth* (left back: top—outside then inside, then bottom—outside then inside; front: top—outside then inside, bottom—outside then inside; then right back: top—outside then inside, then bottom—outside then inside.)
12. *Spit out toothpaste into sink.*
13. *Rinse toothbrush* under water stream.
14. *Put toothbrush away.*
15. *Fill drinking cup with cold water.*
16. *Rinse mouth with water.*
17. *Spit water* from cup *into sink.*
18. *Rinse cup with water.*
19. *Put cup away.*
20. *Put toothpaste cap on tube.*
21. *Put toothpaste tube away.*

* For Carol or other individuals with physical limitations, the trainer might want to add onto the front of this task her steps for approaching and positioning next to or up under the sink. She may need the handle of her toothbrush adapted to facilitate her grasping and moving it through the motions of brushing her teeth. It may also be helpful to have a stand-up pump toothpaste dispenser for Carol rather than the squeeze tube. In some cases, it may be helpful to stabilize the toothpaste tube or pump by devising some kind of jig to hold it in place while squeezing or pumping to extract the toothpaste. In any of the preceding alterations, the task analysis would need to be written to accommodate the specific details for the particular learner.

as well as Neel and Billingsley (1989) suggest that task analyses with long chains of behavior (in excess of 20 or so steps) should be avoided. In the final analysis, the number of steps that are delineated to be learned is based on a relationship between the level of the learner and the complexity of the task. Test and Spooner (1996) suggest that there are three steps in developing task analyses; (1) determining critical steps in the instructional process, (2) considering partial participation and other adaptations, and (3) field-testing the task analysis.

As the task at hand is being considered and the steps to completion are being developed, a number of steps are usually critical to effective performance of the task. These steps are called *critical steps* (Wright & Schuster, 1994). For example, when training a person to brush his or her teeth, actually brushing the teeth is an important component of the tooth-brushing task, but equally important, or critical, to the process of brushing teeth is the use of toothpaste or tooth powder. Only a portion of the task is effectively accomplished if toothpaste is not applied to the toothbrush. Therefore, applying toothpaste to the toothbrush and brushing would be viewed as critical steps in the tooth-brushing process.

Once the task analysis is developed, it is necessary to *field-test the task analysis.* Again, due to the private nature of many personal hygiene tasks, testing the steps to see if the finished product is achieved is different than with many community-based tasks. However, to accomplish a field test, you can give the task analysis to another staff member, to a roommate, or to a spouse, and ask them to follow the steps just as they are delineated in the task analysis. See if that individual can perform the steps as they have been delineated. Do the steps make sense? Are the steps sequenced in a logical order? The process of having another individual perform the steps as they are detailed in the task analysis is discussed in the literature as the "stranger test" (Test & Spooner, 1996). Of course, it still may be necessary to make adjustments to the task analysis to accommodate the particular style or abilities of the learner.

Deciding How the Skill Will Be Taught.   Many, if not all personal hygiene skills, are skills that have multiple steps. In the case of grooming hair, even for an individual who functions at a mild level of disability, grooming instruments need to be chosen (comb and/or brush, hair clips, spray or mousse), and the instrument needs to be oriented (e.g., with a comb, the fine teeth are at one end and the widely spaced teeth are at the other end). The individual will place the comb either to the right or the left of the head (depending on the part), point comb teeth or brush bristles into hair, or perhaps place the comb at the front and move toward the back of the head, and continue the hair-combing process until satisfied with the results. The steps of this grooming process become the task analysis as discussed in the preceding section (analyzing the number of steps for instructional tasks). After the steps have been determined, then the way in which the steps of the task analysis will be taught needs to be decided based on the particular hair style of the individual.

The decision of which way to teach the task usually means the application of a chaining procedure. Chaining is a way to teach tasks that have several steps. Technically, a chain is a specified series of steps, each associated with a unique stimulus condition. Each behavior, except for the first and the last steps, reinforces the previous step. A very practical way to explain a relatively complicated behavioral phenomenon is to use the example of a person following a set of directions to get dressed, specifically to put on a pair of jeans. The steps of the task analysis can vary depending on the abilities of the learner for which the steps have been delineated. For example, some people with adequate foot and leg dexterity may be able to stand and remain standing while putting on a pair of jeans. Other people may start out sitting and then stand, while others may prefer to remain seated through the whole process.

The directions to put on the jeans have been written in a series of steps, a portion of which will be used to illustrate how a chain works. The directions read: (1) Find the zipper; (2) lay pants against legs with zipper facing out; (3) move hands to waistband of pants; (4) put left hand on waistband above left pocket; (5) put right hand on waistband above right pocket; (6) with both hands grasp waistband tightly with a pincer-type grasp; (7) lower pants toward floor while at same time lifting left leg, . . . The second step in the sequence, "lay pants against legs with zipper facing out" gives the learner a form of a "landmark" as to where to place the jeans. The learner picks up the jeans, finds the zipper, and places the jeans with zipper facing out on his or her legs. When the learner has the jeans on legs, he or she begins to look for the next step in the sequence. The placement of the jeans on the legs indicates the completion of one step and signals the beginning of the next step in the sequence. The remainder of the steps also work in the same way with the completion of the previous step indicating what the next step in the sequence should be. The diagram in Figure 11.2 illustrates the relationship between the cue, the response, and the reinforcer. As you can see from the diagram, placing pants on legs, zipper out functions both as a reinforcer for "finding the zipper" and as a cue for the next response, "placing hands." As such, steps in a task analysis serve the "dual function" as both a reinforcer for the previous step in the chain and a cue for the next step in the chain. This dual function holds the sequence of steps together in a task analysis.

Considerations About the Instructional Context

Where will instruction take place? Who will teach the skill? Will the skill be taught in multiple environments? When will instruction occur? These queries are all examinations into components of the instructional context. Judgments about where the skill is taught (if the skill is ultimately to be performed in an environment other than the original teaching environment), are likely to affect the degree to which the skill is maintained and, perhaps, generalized to other settings. Information about the instructional setting, the instructional ratio, and scheduling of instruction are important factors to weigh when deciding about instruction, and its physical, temporal, and human dimensions (Billingsley et al., 1994).

Where Will Instruction Take Place?   Personal care and hygiene skills, to a certain extent, are somewhat different than skills from other curriculum domains (e.g., vocational job skills). Most job skills will likely be performed in the work situation. On the other hand, personal care and hygiene are usually performed in multiple environments. For example, an individual may only take a shower at home but may go to the restroom at home, at work, or at a friend's house. Major grooming tasks like washing, drying, and combing hair may be done at home; yet the student may need to check appearance at other times during the day and, if necessary, freshen up and

FIGURE 11.2   Chaining Illustration

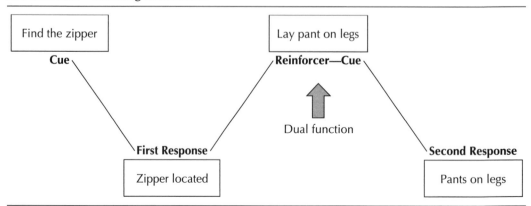

fix hair. Some people may get dressed two or three times a day (e.g., changing from workclothes into exercise clothes, and then into pajamas), but there are additional times during the day when portions of the dressing task need to be executed (e.g., after one has used the rest room). The nature of multiple environment contexts needs to be estimated when training personal care and hygiene skills. The trainer or teacher needs to examine the primary environment where this skill will take place (at home, at school), as well as other places where the skill is likely to be used. The multiple environment context of using personal hygiene and grooming skills suggests that *generalization is a key feature* in successfully transferring skills (e.g., hand washing) from home to school to a friend's house to a public rest room.

Generalization may be described as an expansion of the individual's performance beyond the initial conditions under which the skill was taught (Alberto & Troutman, 1995; Stokes & Baer, 1977). Learner performance may be expanded in one of three ways or in multiple combinations: (1) *across stimuli* (called stimulus generalization by researchers), (2) *across time* (called maintenance), and (3) *across responses* (called response generalization). When performance is extended across stimuli, the individual may perform the skill with new or different cues, materials, or trainers, or in new environments. In the case of *stimulus generalization,* applying soap in the shower, or applying soap when washing hands is an example where "lathering up" will take place in separate parts of the bathroom (e.g., the shower for washing the total body, and a public rest-room sink for washing hands). The ability to *maintain* personal hygiene skills across time is also important. Once an individual learns to brush teeth, the teacher hopes that brushing teeth will take place two times a day, perhaps more, across several environments (e.g., at home, at grandparent's for an overnight visit), and that brushing teeth will occur, 7 day's a week, 365 day's a year. Skills that are practiced the most are usually the skills that will transcend the passage of time (Horner, Williams, & Knobble, 1985). When the response is different from the original trained response, it is called *response generalization.* From a personal hygiene perspective, some of the same steps that are used in putting on and buttoning a shirt are similar to putting on and buttoning a coat, yet the response outcomes are different. Buttoning and putting arms in sleeves are similar maneuvers that should transfer from putting on a shirt to putting on a coat. Personal care and hygiene skills are no different than any other skill area; these skills will not automatically transfer to a new environment or to new people. If PCH skills are to generalize, specific training strategies must be implemented to increase the likelihood of the skill being transferred across environments, across time, and across people.

When Will Instruction Take Place? Decisions about when instruction will take place impact on the scheduling and frequency of training. Personal care and hygiene skills should be taught in relation to other temporal events which suggest that the hygiene skill needs to be performed as a consequence of the preceding event. For example, the student should wash hands after using the toilet in the rest room and at other times when hand washing would naturally occur. Natural opportunities for instruction are also discussed and described as naturally distributed training trials. These natural opportunities provide the contextual sequence for the skill and will be the discriminative stimuli and consequences that will be present in the environment after instruction is concluded. As such, scheduling instruction at natural times when the skill would likely take place can improve acquisition and generalization

(Bambara, Warren, & Komisar, 1988; Mulligan, Guess, Holvoet, & Brown, 1980; Neel & Billingsley, 1989).

Based on the temporal relationship between some natural occurring events throughout the day and personal hygiene, personal hygiene skills should be taught in a temporal sequence to those events. Instruction for skills like dressing, hand washing, combing hair, and toileting should not be scheduled at arbitrary times during the day (e.g., dressing training at 10:00 A.M. for Melba, Fred, and Jason); instead, these skill sequences should receive instruction during the times of the day when these events would naturally occur (Billingsley et al., 1994; Gaylord-Ross & Holvoet, 1985). Gaylord-Ross and Holvoet have suggested that the training of skills in their naturally occurring sequences is addressing the "When and Why" of instruction. Most people do not put on a coat just after taking off the coat. Yet, in many cases, we have given people with severe disabilities multiple trials of dressing (e.g., putting on a coat) in a discrete trial format training sequence.

USING SYSTEMATIC INSTRUCTIONAL STRATEGIES TO TEACH PERSONAL CARE AND HYGIENE SKILLS

In the case examples discussed in this chapter, various PCH skills are suggested for instruction according to Carol and Michael's unique needs. We have discussed breaking down each PCH task into a sequence of discrete steps called a *task analysis* and teaching the skill using this sequence in a consistent and systematic fashion. We have also suggested that the daily PCH skills be built into a consistent routine for the morning and the evening to maximize the degree to which each student will ultimately be able to perform a sequence of PCH activities independently. Much like a supported employment specialist would analyze a specific job organizing the various daily job duties into a logical sequence, and then task analyze each duty (Moon, Inge, Wehman, Brooke, & Barcus, 1990), the teacher can work with parents to help structure a series of PCH activities into a logical routine that can facilitate a student's ability to function within and across tasks more independently. Various instructional strategies that have been demonstrated effective with students with mild and severe disabilities have been discussed in general terms. In this section, we will take a slice out of the morning routines of both Carol (Table 11.5) and Michael (Table 11.6) and illustrate how, when, and where some of these instructional strategies might be utilized.

THE ALARM CLOCK SETS THE MORNING IN MOTION

In order to make the best of *natural conditions* for training some tasks in the school setting, it helps to plan ahead—in some cases, way ahead. For example, most working Americans wake up every morning to an alarm clock, which sets into motion a stream of activities designed to get them ready for the day's activities, either a workday or a weekend leisure activity. The alarm clock is one of many steps to independence that youth begin to use during middle or high school. The alarm clock takes over the role of the parent for waking the child up at the necessary time of day. Because kindergarten is usually the last year that schoolchildren take naps during school hours, it offers a naturally occurring time for the teacher to have children learn to wake to an alarm clock. Thus in Tables 11.5 and 11.6, "waking to alarm" is listed as a goal for both Carol and Michael. It will be the starting point for a morning routine for both of these students and is initially linked to going to the bathroom as the logical first activity of the morning.

Students with severe cognitive and/or physical disabilities will need intensive and extensive instruction. In Carol's case, before she can respond to the alarm clock by going to the bathroom independently, she will need intensive intervention from the OT and/or PT to help her develop a strategy and the skill to transfer from the bed, cot, or floor pad to her chair, so that she can then be encouraged to wheel herself from her bedroom (or the nap area) to the bathroom where she is learning to transfer from her chair to the toilet.

Carol's independent toileting must be treated as a complex task with a full task analysis. She will need *physical guidance* while learning to get up from her prone position and move her body from her bed to her chair. The teacher should identify *positive reinforcers* that Carol can receive for correctly completing parts of this task.

As stated earlier, Carol will need assistance from the OT and/or PT to help her devise the best method for her to transfer from her bed to her wheelchair. *One possible* strategy for Carol to independently transfer from her bed to her wheelchair is as follows:

1. She rolls herself onto her side so that she is facing the outside of the bed. (If necessary, side bars can be added to her bed to give her places to grasp to roll herself on her side.)
2. Once on her side, she rolls her legs and hips out of bed first, so that she slides out of bed on her stomach with her feet landing on the floor.
3. Steadying herself with both hands on the side of the bed, she will then need to lower her body backward into the chair.
4. Placing both of her arms on top of the armrests of the wheelchair, she pushes herself up to a straight position in the chair.
5. Put the foot pedals down on the chair.
6. Unlock the brakes on the chair.
7. Back away from the bed.
8. Turn the chair in the direction of the door.
9. Wheel to the bathroom.

The preceding sequence written as a task analysis is shown in Table 11.9.

CONCLUSION

Personal care and hygiene skills are just one component of a total longitudinal independent living curriculum for persons with special needs. Of the skill training areas listed in this longitudinal sequence (e.g., recreation and leisure skills, health fitness and safety, financial planning and money management), personal care and hygiene would likely be the skill area that is most often taken for granted. Not only is being

TABLE 11.9   A Task Analysis for Transferring from the Bed to Wheelchair

1. Roll onto your side.																		
2. Roll your legs out of bed.																		
3. Hold onto the side of the bed.																		
4. Come back into the chair.																		
5. Pull yourself up straight.																		
6. Put your foot pedals down.																		
7. Unlock the brakes.																		
8. Back away from the bed.																		
9. Turn the chair toward the door.																		
10. Wheel to the bathroom.																		
No. of steps correct																		
Percentage of task correct																		

Note. Each strategy for transferring must be individualized to the particular individual.

able to take care of one's personal needs taken for granted in our culture, it is also a highly valued basic component of self-sufficiency and personal independence. With personal independence comes the ability to make choices and more opportunities to participate in community living.

Many Americans naturally assume that practically everyone will be able to take a shower, get dressed, and eat something for breakfast. On the other hand, as we have indicated, many people with special needs—especially those with severe intellectual disabilities—will need systematic and longitudinal training in PCH skills. The ability to manage one's personal needs (e.g., grooming) is one of the skill hierarchies which, usually, sets apart those who function on an independent level from those who do not.

The personal care and hygiene skill area (e.g., toilet training, dressing) was one of the first skill areas where researchers concentrated their early training efforts. The literature that has accumulated over the past 20 years in the field of developmental disabilities emphasizes that people at all levels of disability and retardation can learn to perform many of these skills independently. In the past 20 years an effective, efficient, and validated technology for training numerous skills to persons of all walks of life and levels of functioning has emerged. We encourage trainers, developmental care technicians, and teachers to use this technology to not only train skill sequences, but to also validate the progress of their learners. The behavior approach is one of the few approaches that allows for switching training tactics midstream when the learner is not acquiring the skill at the level which was anticipated. We have attempted to show a longitudinal sequence of these skills and the application of instructional strategies through Carol and Michael's case examples.

REFERENCES

Abt Associates. (1974). *Assessment of selected resources for severely handicapped children and youth* (Vol. 1). Cambridge, MA: Abt Associates.

Alberto, P. A., & Troutman, A. C. (1995). *Applied behavior analysis for teachers* (4th ed.). Columbus, OH: Charles E. Merrill.

Azrin, N. H., & Foxx, R. M. (1971). A rapid method of toilet training the institutionalized retarded. *Journal of Applied Behavior Analysis, 4,* 89–99.

Azrin, N. H., Sneed, T. J., & Foxx, R. M. (1973). Dry bed: A method of eliminating bedwetting (enuresis) of the retarded. *Behaviour Research and Therapy,11,* 427–434.

Baller, W. R. (1975). *Bed wetting: Origins and treatment.* New York: Pergamon Press.

Bambara, L. M., Warren, S. F., & Komisar, S. (1988). The individualized curriculum sequencing model: Effects on skill acquisition and generalization. *Journal of The Association for Persons with Severe Handicaps, 13,* 8–19.

Baumgart, D., Brown, L., Pumpian, I., Nisbet, J., Ford, A., Sweet, M., Messina, R., & Schroeder, J. (1982). Principle of partial participation and individualized adaptation in educational programs for severely handicapped students. *Journal of The Association for Persons with Severe Handicaps, 7*(2), 17–27.

Billingsley, F. F., Liberty, K., & White, O. (1994). Instructional technology. In E. Cipani & F. Spooner (Eds.), *Curricular and instructional approaches for persons with severe disabilities.* Needham, MA: Allyn & Bacon.

Browder, D. M. (Ed.). (1991). *Assessment of individuals with severe disabilities: An applied behavioral approach to life skills assessment* (2nd ed.). Baltimore: Paul H. Brookes.

Brown, F., Evans, I., Weed, K., & Owen, V. (1987). Delineating functional competencies: A competent model. *Journal of The Association for Persons with Severe Handicaps, 12,* 117–124.

Brown, L., Branston, M. B., Hamre-Nietupski, S., Pumpian, I., Certo, N., & Gruenwald, L. (1979). A strategy for developing chronological-age-appropriate and functional curricular content for severely handicapped adolescents and young adults. *Journal of Special Education, 13*(1), 81–90.

Cipani, E. C., & Spooner, F. (1994). *Curricular and instructional approaches for persons with severe disabilities.* Needham Heights, MA: Allyn & Bacon.

Crist, K., Walls, R. T., & Haught, P. A. (1984). Degrees of specificity in task analysis. *American Journal of Mental Deficiency, 89,* 67–74.

Cronin, K. A., & Cuvo, A. J. (1979). Teaching mending skills to mentally retarded adolescents. *Journal of Applied Behavior Analysis, 12,* 401–406.

Cuvo, A. J., Jacobi, L., & Sipko, R. (1981). Teaching laundry skills to mentally retarded students. *Education and Training of the Mentally Retarded, 16,* 54–64.

Day, H. M., & Horner, R. H. (1986). Response variation and the generalization of a dressing skill: Comparison of single instance and general case instruction. *Applied Research in Mental Retardation, 7*(2), 189–202.

Diorio, M. S., & Konarski, E. A. (1984). Evaluation of a method for teaching dressing skills to profoundly mentally retarded persons. *American Journal of Mental Deficiency, 89,* 307–309.

Doleys, D. M., Stacy, D., & Knowles, S. (1981). Modification of grooming behavior in adult retarded: Token reinforcement in a community-based program. *Behavior Modification, 5,* 119–128.

Elium, M. D., & McCarver, R. B. (1980). *Group vs. Individual training on a self-help skill with the profoundly retarded* (EC 150 366). Tuscaloosa, AL: Partlow State School and Hospital. (ERIC Document Reproduction Service No. ED 223 060)

Epps, S., Prescott, A. L., & Horner, R. H. (1990). Social acceptability of menstrual-care methods for young women with developmental disabilities. *Education and Training in Mental Retardation, 25,* 33–44.

Falvey, M. A. (1995). *Inclusive and heterogeneous schooling: Assessment, curriculum, & instruction.* Baltimore: Paul H. Brookes.

Ferguson, D. L., & Baumgart, D. (1991). Partial participation revisited. *Journal of The Association for Persons with Severe Handicaps, 16,* 218–227.

Ford, A., Davern, L., Meyer, L., Schnorr, R., Black, J., & Dempsey, P. (Eds.). (1989). *The Syracuse community-referenced curriculum guide for students with moderate and severe disabilities.* Baltimore: Paul H. Brookes.

Fredericks, H. D., & Brodsdy, M. (1994). Functional assessment. In E. Cipani & F. Spooner (Eds.), *Curricular and instructional approaches for persons with severe disabilities* (pp. 31–49). Needham, MA: Allyn & Bacon.

Gaylord-Ross, R., & Holvoet, J. (1985). *Strategies for educating students with severe handicaps.* Boston: Little, Brown.

Haring, N. G., Liberty, K. A., & White, O. R. (1980). Rules for data-based strategy decision in instructional programs: Current research and instructional implications. In W. Sailor, B. Wilcox, & L. Brown (Eds.), *Methods of instruction for severely handicapped students* (pp. 159–192). Baltimore: Paul H. Brookes.

Horner, R. D., & Keilitz, I. (1975). Training retarded adolescents to brush their teeth. *Journal of Applied Behavior Analysis, 8,* 301–309.

Horner, R. H., Williams, J. A., & Knobble, C. A. (1985). The effect of "opportunity to perform" on the maintenance of skills learned by high school students with severe handicaps. *Journal of the Association for Persons with Severe Handicaps, 10,* 172–175.

Justin, J. E. (1976). Who are the severely handicapped?: A problem in definition. *AAESPH Review, 1*(5), 1–12.

McDonnell, J. J., Hardman, M. L., McDonnell, A. P., Kiefer-O'Donnell, R. (1995). *An introduction to persons with severe disabilities: Educational and social issues.* Boston: Allyn & Bacon.

Moon, M. S., Inge, K., Wehman, P., Brooke, V., & Barcus, J. M. (1990). *Helping persons with severe mental retardation get and keep employment.* Baltimore: Paul H. Brookes.

Mount, B. (1987). *Personal futures planning: Finding directions for change* [Doctoral dissertation, University of Georgia]. Ann Arbor, MI: UMI Dissertation Information Service.

Mulligan, M., Guess, D., Holvoet, J., & Brown, F. (1980). The individualized curriculum sequencing model (1): Implications from research on massed, distributed, or spaced trial training. *Journal of The Association for the Severely Handicapped, 5,* 325–336.

National Institutes of Health (NIH). (1995, December). *What you need to know about periodontal (gum) diseases* [On-line NIH Publications No. 94–1142]. Available Internet: Hostname: http://tsw.ingress.Com Directory: tsw/talf/ftc File: gum-dis.html.

Neel, R. S., & Billingsley, F. F. (1989). *Impact: A functional curriculum handbook for students with moderate to severe disabilities.* Baltimore: Paul H. Brookes.

Nutter, D., & Reid, D. H. (1978). Teaching retarded women a clothing selection skill using community norms. *Journal of Applied Behavior Analysis, 11,* 475–487.

Reid, D. H., & Favell, J. E. (1984). Group instruction with persons who have severe disabilities: A critical review. *Journal of The Association of Persons with Severe Handicaps, 9,* 167–177.

Richman, G. S., Ponticas, Y., Page, T. J., & Epps, S. (1986). Simulation procedures for teaching independent menstrual care to mentally retarded persons. *Applied Research in Mental Retardation, 7,* 21–35.

Richman, G. S., Reiss, M. L., Bauman, K. E., & Bailey, J. S. (1984). Teaching menstrual care to mentally retarded women: Acquisition, generalization, and maintenance. *Journal of Applied Behavior Analysis, 17,* 441–451.

Ryndak, D. L., & Alper, S. (1996). *Curriculum content for students with moderate and severe disabilities in inclusive settings.* Boston: Allyn & Bacon.

Sailor, W., & Guess, D. (1983). *Severely handicapped students: An instructional design.* Boston: Houghton Mifflin.

Sailor, W., & Haring, N. G. (1977). Some current directions in education of the severely/ profoundly handicapped. *AAESPH Review, 2*(2), 3–24.

Snell, M. E. (1991). Foreword: Sad voices from the twentieth century. In L. H. Meyer, C. A. Peck, & L. Brown (Eds.), *Critical issues in the lives of people with severe disabilities* (pp. xv–xix). Baltimore: Paul H. Brookes.

Snell, M. E. (1993). *Instruction of students with severe disabilities* (4th ed.). New York: Merrill/Macmillian.

Snell, M. E., Lewis, A. P., Houghton, A. (1989). Acquisition and maintenance of toothbrushing skills by students with cerebral palsy and mental retardation. *Journal of The Association for Persons with Severe Handicaps, 14,* 216–226.

Spooner, F., & Test, D. W. (1994). Domestic and community living skills. In E. C. Cipani & F. Spooner (Eds.), *Curricular and instructional approaches for persons with severe disabilities* (pp. 149–183). Needham Heights, MA: Allyn & Bacon.

Stokes, T. F., & Baer, D. (1977). An implicit technology of generalization. *Journal of Applied Behavior Analysis, 10,* 349–367.

Test, D. W., & Spooner, F. (1996). *Innovations: Community-based training as an instructional support.* Washington, DC: American Association on Mental Retardation.

Thinesen, P. J., & Bryan, A. J. (1981). The use of sequential pictorial cues in the initiation and maintenance of grooming behaviors in mentally retarded adults. *Mental Retardation, 19,* 247–250.

Vandercook, T., & York, J. (1990). A team approach to program development and support. In W. Stainback & S. Stainback (Eds.), *Support networks for inclusive education: Interdependent integrated education* (pp. 95–120). Baltimore: Paul H. Brookes.

Wolber, G., Carne, W., Collins-Montgomery, P., & Nelson, A. (1987). Tangible reinforcement plus social reinforcement versus social reinforcement alone in acquisition of toothbrushing skills. *Mental Retardation, 25,* 275–279.

Wright, C. W., & Schuster, J. (1994). Accepting specific versus functional student responses when training chained tasks. *Education and Training in Mental Retardation and Developmental Disabilities, 29,* 43–56.

Ysseldyke, J. E., Christenson, S., & Kovaleski, J. F. (1994). Identifying students' instructional needs in the context of classroom and home environments. *Teaching Exceptional Children, 26*(3), 37–41.

12

Health and Safety

MARTIN AGRAN

Malinda is 16 years old and attends 11th grade at West Bench High School. Except for one period committed to intensive academic instruction in the resource room (reading and math instruction), Malinda is in regular classes.

Malinda was two months premature. She functions in the moderate to severe range of cognitive impairments and has been diagnosed with several autisticlike behaviors (e.g., self-stimulation, echolalia). Also, she is given medication to control seizures that occur once or twice a week. She can accomplish most basic living skills independently and adapts easily to routines. She does not know how to use various appliances at home but has expressed an interest in learning how to operate them; in particular, she has expressed an interest in learning to use the microwave and coffeemaker. She is generally friendly and social and is concerned about dressing nicely for school. She enjoys going shopping with friends for clothing. Although she has been invited to a number of dances and parties and has enjoyed these experiences, she appears to have little interest at this time in dating or interacting with boys during social situations. Once a week, she and a number of other students with disabilities clean the social/recreational center of a local church. Also, she works one hour a day at a store at school that sells snacks, supplies, and souvenirs.

Her parents have strongly expressed an interest in having her work in a part-time job in the community, and Malinda has indicated that she would like to live in an apartment with roommates and work in a grocery store one day. Additionally, her parents have indicated to Malinda's homeroom teacher that it is critical that Malinda be taught a variety of safety skills. These include crime prevention, fire safety, first aid, and relevant work safety skills. *Times have changed,* they noted, *all kids have to learn skills these days they didn't have to know before.*

No matter whether we believe that the world is becoming increasingly more dangerous and risky, all students may experience situations in which they either do not know how to identify risks that may be present (e.g., handling a "hot" wire) or not know how best to respond to them when they are present (e.g., reacting to a stranger). In the preceding case example, Malinda will be instructed to participate in varied settings where any of a number of present and future risks may be present. To ensure her well-being and good health, Malinda needs to learn how to use public transportation; to acquire a variety of home, community, and fire safety skills; and to learn numerous work safety skills and crime prevention skills. The consequences of not teaching her these skills are far too serious to ignore.

NEED FOR SAFETY SKILLS INSTRUCTION

Teaching students safety skills has been largely ignored as a curricular domain (Agran, Marchand-Martella, & Martella, 1994; Gast, Wellons, & Collins, 1994; Juracek, 1994); when these skills have been taught, fragmented and unsystematic procedures have often been used. There are several reasons for this oversight. First, many teachers and parents may assume that students already possess basic health and safety skills and that time could be better spent teaching students other deficient skills. Second, teachers and parents may have low expectations of their students or children and think it is unrealistic to teach them skills routinely performed by adult service providers. Safety skills may involve complex discriminations that students have difficulty making (e.g., appropriately identifying dangerous situations, assessing the seriousness of an injury). Instruction should be provided in essentially risk-free settings; if not, students are being exposed to unnecessary risk. Third, although injuries may be serious, the likelihood of sustaining one is small. Since the selection of instructional targets is largely based on the frequency of occurrence of target skills (i.e., functional skills that occur more frequently are prioritized), why teach a behavior such as a safety skill that occurs at low frequency? Even if there is a possibility that an accident may occur, a teacher or other service provider is usually present to intervene if needed. Last, many persons continue to equate safety or good health with having a positive attitude. Awareness of risks comes with such attitudes. Since safety is associated to a large extent by what one doesn't do (have an accident, sustain an injury), there's not really much to teach. Periodic counseling should be sufficient. In summary, many teachers may believe that students should not be intentionally exposed to risks and that learning is difficult enough for students with special needs, without adding the challenge of teaching them to deal with risks.

Although virtually any community can be dangerous for individuals unable to identify and respond appropriately to risk stimuli and accidents remain the leading cause of death for nondisabled children (Haller, 1970; Peterson, 1984), it is becoming increasingly clear that students with disabilities often do not know how to perform (Pelland & Falvey, 1986), and that teachers are not aware of the dangers that students may face (Lazar, 1980). This situation is compounded because there is sufficient evidence to suggest that persons with disabilities are at a particular risk for accidents and emergency situations due to such characteristics as "poor judgment; lack of awareness of danger; impulsiveness and restlessness; inability or difficulties in communicating; low pain threshold; abnormal muscle functioning causing difficulties in chewing, swallowing, standing, walking; and impaired vision and/or hearing" (Bryan, Warden, Berg, & Hauck, 1978, p. 8). Also, such health problems as seizures, vulnerability to infection (Blackman, 1984; Bryan et al., 1978), and other chronic health-related conditions (Lorr & Rotatori, 1985) may increase their risk for emergencies and accidents. With our increased efforts to prepare students for fuller participation in community settings, there is no question that there is a higher likelihood that an accident may occur. Injury rates may be as high for persons with disabilities as for nondisabled persons because of their physical and adaptive limitations (Matson, 1980).

While accident or victimization data for persons with disabilities are limited, the available reported data are indeed sobering. For example, Stimpson and Best (1991) reported that 73% of women with disabilities have been victims of violence. Chotiner and Lehr (1976) indicated that 70% of abused children had disabilities, and Muccigrosso (1991) stated that at least 90% of children with developmental disabilities have been sexually exploited. Jaskulski and Mason (1992) noted that in a sample of 108 rehabilitation facilities, approximately 30% of the consumers were HIV-positive. Last, Agran and Madison (1995) stated that, in a sample of 11,000 individuals served by 800 vocational rehabilitation facilities, over 4,000 injuries for these individuals were reported. These data underscore the need for safety skills instruction.

Agran et al. (1994) indicated that safety behavior is not a state of mind or an attitude, but a repertoire of discrete skills that allow individuals to discriminate risk situations and respond appropriately. As noted previously, students are often denied access to settings where risks may be present. Denying students the opportunity to respond to potentially risky situations endangers their dignity and prevents them from experiencing the risk-taking of ordinary life (Wolfensberger, 1972). Perske (1972) stressed the importance of risk-taking for persons with disabilities and indicated that "there can be such a thing as human dignity in risk. And there can be a dehumanizing indignity in safety" (p. 200). Students must be allowed to experience the consequences of their decisions and to realize that there will not always be someone to offer guidance when they need help (Vogelsberg & Rusch, 1979). Failure to teach students safety skills may lead parents and school boards to restrict students' access to community environments. Worse still, it may result in a student's total inability to avert a serious accident or assault.

The purpose of this chapter is to describe a health and safety curriculum for students with disabilities. Additionally, procedures to assess and teach health and safety skill performance are suggested and selected IEP objectives for elementary, middle, and secondary schools are presented. As Sobsey (1994) indicated, although steps can be taken to reduce individual risk, no amount of preventive behavior can eliminate risk entirely. It is not the purpose of this chapter to teach individuals skills that will totally keep them out of harm's way. But the health and safety skills addressed in this chapter comprise a repertoire of skills that will allow students to respond appropriately to many risks and dangers they will be exposed to at work, in their homes, and in the streets in their communities.

OVERVIEW OF CURRICULUM

Agran et al. (1994) noted:

> Given the exigencies of these times and rapidly evolving sociological, cultural, and medical changes in our society, the curricular domains we have formerly taught

remain important, but, ultimately, inadequate. There is no question that an individual unprepared to take responsibility for his or her health and safety represents an individual ill-equipped for contemporary living. (p. xii)

As indicated in this text, independent and functional living skills encompass a broad range of skills including, but not limited to, work, community, home living, academic, recreational and leisure, mobility, financial management, personal care, social, and a number of self-advocacy and self-determination skills. Appropriate and consistent performance of these skills allows individuals with disabilities to have normalized and valued life experiences, but, as indicated previously, expanding the range of environments for students will no doubt expose them to numerous risks. Many potential dangers are present in most home, work, and community settings for unknowledgeable persons or persons who do not behave safely. Failure to teach safety skills leaves individuals vulnerable to injury, limits their competence, and further promotes their dependence on caregivers or service providers.

Although the type of health and safety skills instruction depends on the individual's instructional needs and circumstances (the settings in which he or she participates, the medical needs of the individual), critical skill areas include the following: *home and community living, work, fire and crime prevention, HIV/AIDS prevention, substance use,* and *self-medication and health care.* In each of these skills areas, students need to be taught to recognize potentially dangerous conditions or stimuli and to execute actions that will correct or modify, on either a short- or long-term basis, these situations; the latter, in fact, may involve teaching the student how to respond to an actual emergency. This knowledge will lessen their vulnerability to the many dangers of contemporary life.

The following section presents justification for each of the preceding critical skill areas. Additionally, important instructional targets are identified and recommended assessment and teaching procedures are presented.

HOME AND COMMUNITY LIVING

Identifying Skills.   Accidents occur at home and in the community frequently. Foege (1988) reported, "Injury is the principal public health problem in America today. . . . It will touch one of every three Americans this year" (p. 1). One person in 11 has incurred an injury at home requiring medical attention or resulting in one half day or more of restricted activity (National Safety Council, 1988), and one percent of the population suffers serious burn injuries each year (Tarnowski, Rasnake, & Drabman, 1987). Risks abound in every setting and the child unaware of these dangers may be in grave danger. It is essential that students be taught to identify these risks and be able to complete a task that has an element of fear in a safe manner (Gast et al., 1994).

Figure 12.1 presents selected safety skills areas identified by a sample of parents (Collins, Wolery, & Gast, 1992). The respondents identified a diverse repertoire of skills across several key areas: safe tool/appliance use, pedestrian and mobility skills, interacting with animals, recognizing poisons, and knowledge of electrical problems, to name a few. Although this is an extensive list, it does not include a number of problems in other environments the child may frequent. For example, risks may be present in the living room, bedroom, garage, or hallway of a home.

FIGURE 12.1   Safety Skills Areas
Identified by Parents

Home safety
  Kitchen
  Bathroom
  General home areas
Community safety
  Yards/playgrounds
  Responding to strange animals
  Bicycle use
  Community mobility
Fire safety
First aid
Responding to strangers
Sex education

Further, the different stores, recreation facilities, restaurants, or public offices/services in the community may present common and unique risk factors. Risks abound across all aspects of our lives.

Ideally, students should acquire all the safety skills they may need, but available resources and circumstances warrant that skill selection will need to be prioritized. Gast et al. (1994) suggest the following procedure be followed when prioritizing skills. First, teachers need to identify the environments at home and in the community that the student participates in. This information can be obtained from parents, siblings, the student's friends, the student, and informal observations the teacher may make. Once obtained, the types of accidents that may occur in each of these environments can be identified. Thus, professionals can determine the environments in which the likelihood of an accident occurring are the highest. Prioritization is based on the student's frequency of participation in environments where risks are present.

Second, priority must be given to teaching skills that will prevent *immediate danger* (e.g., using a power tool/appliance, crossing the street). This is not to suggest that risks that may have more of a delayed effect (e.g., HIV/AIDS, recognizing hypothermia) are not important to teach, but only that more immediate dangers should be addressed first. Once immediate risks are addressed, responses to other potential threats and risks need to be incorporated into instruction. Last, priority needs to be given to the particular concerns of parents, the students, and significant others. Failure to do so will discourage collaborative planning and problem solving.

Teaching Safety Skills.   It is recommended that teaching be conducted in the natural setting, the actual environment where the skill is typically performed. Instruction in such environments will minimize transfer of learning difficulties the student may have and will expose him or her to the other stimuli in the setting that may influence responding (e.g., specific physical characteristics of setting, number of persons present). However, instruction in community settings may be neither safe nor practical (Gast et al., 1994). Because students should not be subjected to unnecessary risks, the use of simulations is recommended. Unlike naturally occurring events or the limited number of instructional trials that may be provided in community settings, simulations allow for frequent, repeated trials. They permit students to acquire and practice a variety of safety skills that would otherwise expose them to great danger or harm. Simulations provide both the teacher and student with information on skill mastery. Needless to say, target skills should frequently (at least once a week) be assessed in natural, community settings.

In addition to teaching in the natural environment, Gast et al. (1994) recommend that safety skills be taught in the context of a natural routine (e.g., safe use of appliances during meal preparation), not at an arbitrary time, convenient for the teacher. This allows the student to learn what to do if an accident occurs during the execution of a task (e.g., preparing a meal) when it would typically occur. Also, to minimize risk, instructional materials may need to be modified (e.g., knife blades dulled, removing tips from matches). These adaptations allow for instruction that would otherwise be too difficult to conduct. In all, systematic instructional procedures can be used to teach students a variety of home living and community skills that will promote their well-being and independence.

WORK SAFETY

Virtually every work environment can potentially be dangerous and students are not being adequately trained to respond appropriately to these risks (Agran & Martella, 1994). Mueller, Wilgosh, and Dennis (1989) indicated that employers rated safe work behavior and safety awareness as most important for the job survival of all employees. However, Heath (1983) pointed out, "Not only are workers entering the workforce with a minimum of job safety and health knowledge and skills, many of them receive little or no instruction on job risks upon entering the work force" (p. 22). Without assurance that students with disabilities can work safely, both employers and employment specialists may restrict placements and work opportunities. Martella and Marchand-Martella (1995) indicated that employers would be hesitant to employ individuals if they knew they either had no safety awareness or had a history of on-the-job injuries. Failure to provide students with appropriate work safety instruction not only limits their employability, but also may put them in a potentially dangerous situation.

Accident Causes. Work injuries are caused by either behavioral or environmental factors. Behavioral causes refer to the inappropriate actions of employees or their lack of an appropriate response to an injury-causing situation. Environmental causes include the physical characteristics of the job site that may cause an injury (e.g., exposed electrical wiring, spilled food on floor).

Agran and Madison (1995) identified selected causes of work accidents (see Figure 12.2). They are classified as either behavioral or environmental. Behavioral causes were reported to occur at a significantly higher level of frequency than environmental causes. The most frequently reported cause was general carelessness, followed by improper positioning, failure to adhere to safety procedures, and not wearing protective equipment. The most frequently reported environmental causes were objects on floor, congestion, and wet floors. What is compelling about these data is that, since most accidents were caused by inappropriate responses, most of these accidents were preventable. Teaching individuals to not engage in the behaviors listed in Figure 12.2,

FIGURE 12.2   Causes of Work Accidents

Environmental Hazards
  Slippery floors
  Objects on floor
  Flammables near heat source
  Exposed electrical wires
  Sharp objects
  Broken/defective equipment

Behavioral Causes
  Fighting
  Lifting heavy objects inappropriately
  Not wearing protective equipment
  Running/horseplay
  Inappropriate tool use
  Not following safety procedures

as well as to discriminate hazardous environmental stimuli, suggests a potentially useful curriculum.

Identifying Skills.   Work safety skills include both generic and job-specific skills. The generic skills include the skills described earlier (see Figure 12.2). For example, knowing how to lift a heavy box, attending to what you are doing, and not engaging in horseplay while working are necessary for all jobs. In addition, many jobs may present specific risks. To identify these risks, several procedures are recommended. First, job trainers should ask employers, supervisors, and coworkers about potential risks in the work setting and how best to respond to them. Second, a job safety analysis is recommended (see Table 12.1). The safety analysis includes the response sequence for the work task. For this task, all potential safety hazards are indicated, with the related environmental cues. Next, for each of these hazards, an appropriate safe response is suggested.

With this information, employees can be taught to respond appropriately to the work hazards at their jobs. Further, it allows safety instruction to be nested into ongoing work training and performance. This allows the student to have a better idea of the contexts in which an accident may happen, not as an event that occurs independent of the work routine.

Last, attention needs to be directed to the student's individual instructional needs. For example, a student with a sensory impairment or a physical challenge may need to be provided special instruction on how to respond to potential risks (e.g., operating machinery, using tools, maneuvering through the work setting). Such instruction is critical to the student's physical well-being and performance.

Martella and Agran (1994) suggest that the assessment of an individual's work safety skills should be an integral part of any work performance evaluation. Without having information on students' command of safety skills, we may be sending them ill-prepared into many work settings.

TABLE 12.1   Job Safety Analysis

Task Steps	Environmental Cue	Potential Safety Hazard	Safe Procedure

Teaching Work Safety.   As indicated previously, teaching work safety needs to be directed to changing behaviors, not attitudes. Work safety involves teaching students a set of specific and observable safe work skills. These skills are identified through the procedures discussed earlier.

Instruction in work safety involves two major components: identifying safety hazards and determining how to respond to them. It is best taught using a systematic behavior-analytic approach, in which the work behaviors of students are systematically modified (see Chapter 2). This allows teachers to shape behaviors over time and to motivate students by rewarding safe work behavior. In particular, a problem-solving strategy is suggested as an effective way to teach safety skills (Martella & Agran, 1994). First, students are taught to identify the common environmental hazards and behavioral causes of accidents; students can be taught a variety of them or only those specific to those environments they participate in. Second, students are taught to determine how an accident can be prevented. Specifically, students are taught to ask themselves:

- How would an accident happen?
- When would an accident be prevented?
- Who would you talk to?
- What would you do or say?

or the following set of questions:

- What is dangerous?
- Why is it unsafe?
- What can I do to make it safe?

Initially, students are taught to state that a problem exists and come up with a solution. Following, they are instructed to direct themselves to perform the planned response.

Instruction can be implemented using either one-on-one or group instructional formats. In one-on-one instruction, the student is asked to respond to the question after a risk stimulus is presented (either verbally or actually); in a group format, participants take turns suggesting solutions to problematical situations. Following, students are instructed how to respond appropriately to risk stimuli, then are observed responding to staged assessments (e.g., teacher spills a glass of water intentionally on the floor) or to naturally occurring risks in their work settings when they occur (e.g., a customer's spilled beverage on the floor of a fast-food restaurant). Also, teachers may want to teach their students to politely inform coworkers when risks are evident. Thus, teachers may want to ask coworkers to serve as confederates (i.e., intentionally engage in unsafe work behavior), and the students' response to these situations can be observed.

Students need to have skills so they can evaluate the safety of their work settings and the safety of their own work behavior (Martella & Agran, 1994). Without these skills, both their own safety and future job success are greatly in peril.

FIRE SAFETY

Home fires result in tragic deaths for many people each year and millions of dollars in property loss. To compound the problem, learning what to do during an emergency is a demanding task, and various case studies have demonstrated that many persons without disabilities have difficulty responding appropriately (Juracek, 1994). Although teaching students with disabilities fire safety skills is a challenging activity, there is sufficient evidence to suggest that students with disabilities (mild to severe) can learn a variety of fire safety skills (see Bannerman, Sheldon, & Sherman, 1991; Haney & Jones, 1982; Katz & Singh, 1986). It goes without saying that the survival of individuals with disabilities during a fire may depend on their ability to perform these skills.

Identifying Skills. Based on available data on home fires, individuals need to know how to respond appropriately to nighttime emergencies (most fire emergencies occur in the night), how to respond to cooking fires (a large percentage of fires occur in the kitchen), and how to use smoking materials appropriately (appropriate lighting and disposal of cigarettes and ashes) (Juracek, 1994). Figure 12.3 lists several critical fire safety skills. A difficulty in assessing and teaching fire safety skills

FIGURE 12.3   Selected Fire Safety Skills

Exit from home at the sound of an alarm.

Respond appropriately to smoke, hot door.

Extinguishing contained fires.

Preventive skills (e.g., safe lighting, disposal of ashes).

Selection and instruction in using assistive fire safety devices (e.g., appliance timer, sensitive smoke alarms, auditory monitoring devices).

is that fires, fortunately, occur infrequently. The infrequency of these events prevents students from practicing fire safety skills on a consistent basis and assessing and teaching related skills must rely extensively on simulations. Teachers must create situations to assess skill mastery.

Assessment of fire safety skills needs to be conducted across two dimensions. First, professionals need to conduct an analysis of the fire safety features of the resident's home and the projected fire emergencies that may occur in that residence (see Juracek, 1994, for detailed information). Second, the cognitive and physical capabilities of the individual need to be assessed. This will determine the ability of the individual to discriminate the type and seriousness of a fire and his or her ability to safely evacuate from one.

Teaching Fire Safety Skills.   All fire safety skills require that students follow a specified sequence. In teaching these sequences, Juracek (1994) recommends that teaching strategies include direct instruction, rationales, repeated practice, modeling, feedback, and self-evaluation (Did I follow each step of the sequence?). If possible, training should take place in the setting where the student is most likely to encounter a fire (e.g., home), and training probes should be scheduled at various times (especially in the nighttime). To accomplish this, the teacher will have to plan with the parents. Also, to promote maintenance, occasional probes will need to be conducted periodically (at least once a month).

Last, a critical skills area that should be addressed is preventive safety skills (see Figure 12.3). It must strongly be emphasized to students that everything must be done to ensure that a fire doesn't start in the first place. Appliances should be used appropriately, flammable objects should be stored safely, cigarettes should be extinguished properly, lit candles should be carefully monitored, and space heaters should only be used following manufacturers' recommendations. All these skills must become an integral part of the student's repertoire.

CRIME PREVENTION

Although precise figures on the number of persons with disabilities who have been victimized are not available, people with disabilities appear to be particularly vulnerable (especially persons with cognitive and/or physical impairments; Sobsey, 1994). Additionally, there is evidence to suggest that individuals with disabilities are particularly susceptible to child abuse and sexual assaults (Chotiner & Lehr, 1976; Stimpson & Best, 1991; West, Richardson, LeConte, Crimi, & Stuart, 1992). The reasons for this are several. Individuals with disabilities may be perceived by criminals as "easy prey." Also, they may be involved in dysfunctional familial and social relationships and may be isolated from more supportive and protective communities. Further, they may be unable to recognize a potentially dangerous situation or to extricate themselves from a criminal attack. Regardless of the reason, individuals with disabilities are more likely to be victimized than nondisabled individuals (Sobsey, 1994), and crime prevention needs to be recognized as a critical safety skills area.

There is widespread agreement that individuals with disabilities can reduce the likelihood of being victimized by acquiring skills in the following areas: assertiveness training, sex education, personal rights and safety, social and communication skills, property management, and responding to crimes (Sobsey, 1994). A brief discussion of each follows.

Assertiveness.   Individuals need to learn to be assertive, to express their preferences, and to protect their rights (e.g., control of one's own money, freedom from unwanted interventions or medications, freedom from coercion and abuse). Sobsey (1994) suggested that educators have spent excessive time teaching students to be compliant rather than to be assertive; by doing so, individuals become more vulnerable to crime. Teaching students to be more assertive may reduce considerably the likelihood of being a crime victim.

Sex Education.   The incidence of sexual abuse or sexual assaults may be greatly reduced by the individual's knowledge of sexuality and sexual relationships. Ignorance about sexuality appears to be a major factor in increasing an individual's risk for abuse (Muccigrosso, 1991). A comprehensive and accurate sex education curriculum is essential. Among the skill areas individuals should know are birth control, sexually transmitted diseases, hetero- and homosexual behavior, responsibility for sexual behavior, preventing abuse, hygiene, and choice making pertaining to sexual behavior (Sobsey, 1994).

Personal Safety.   Although the issue of teaching self-defense skills to persons with disabilities is somewhat controversial (opponents believe it will further jeopardize individuals), there is a growing opinion that these skills should be taught to persons with disabilities (Pava, Bateman, Appleton, & Glasscock, 1991). Such instruction will enable individuals to determine if, when, and how to fight back if attacked. Also, as Sobsey (1994) suggested, it may increase the individual's self-esteem and overcome feelings associated with learned helplessness. Generally, such training involves teaching individuals strategies to break free or temporarily disable an offender (Bodnar & Hodge, 1989). The use of these strategies will vary across individuals, based on their instructional needs.

Social and Communication Skills.   People who are isolated because of social or communication deficits are more often victims of crime. Conversely, individuals who have active friendships and community relationships are less likely to be victimized (Sobsey, 1994). Attention should be directed to teaching students to establish friendships, to date, and to develop leisure and recreational skills that provide opportunities for social interactions. Likewise, teaching practical communication skills related to crime prevention warrant more attention.

Property Management.   People with disabilities are typically not provided instruction in protecting personal possessions or money. Students need to be informed that they have the right to possess and secure money and personal property. Such skills as home security (how to safely secure doors and windows), securing valuables, discouraging others from taking their possessions, using checks and credit cards, and hiding money are routinely performed by parents or caregivers, with scant attention directed to teaching them to students. It is crucial to teach students these skills.

Responding to Crimes. Individuals need to learn how to report a crime and to whom it should be reported. They need to be taught how to communicate this information to the police and who in their community they can trust. In particular, they need to learn how to provide testimony and how to respond to questions from court officials.

Teaching Crime Prevention Skills. Crime prevention skills can be taught using the same instructional procedures used for any other functional response class (see Chapter 2). As with the other safety skills, instructional content should be based on the student's instructional needs. Also, most, if not all, of this instruction needs to involve simulation training with individual and small group instruction, discussion, role plays, modeling, repeated practice, and the use of pictures and audiovisual instructional materials. Students should also be provided opportunities to practice skills in natural community environments. For example, to assess how well a student responds to strangers, a teacher may want to recruit a confederate to approach a student in a selected site in the community. Additionally, Gast et al. (1994) suggest that, although it is inappropriate to have students experience aversive consequences, they should be exposed to consequences that may occur if they do not behave safely. Newspaper articles or television programs can be used for this purpose.

HIV/AIDS PREVENTION

Health Concern. People with disabilities are at great risk of acquiring HIV/AIDS because of inadequate sex education and HIV prevention training, ignorance about safe sex practices, engagement in high-risk sexual behavior, and vulnerability to sexual abuse (Mason & Jaskulski, 1994), individuals with disabilities may be at great risk of becoming infected with HIV. In a study involving member agencies of the National Association of Rehabilitation Facilities (NARF), 23% to 30% of the respondents reported that they were serving consumers who were HIV-positive (Jaskulski & Mason, 1992). In an additional study (NARF, 1989), over 75% of the members indicated that little or no prevention training was provided to consumers. The number of individuals who are infected with HIV is growing, and the seriousness of this health problem for persons with disabilities cannot be underestimated.

Effective Education Programs. The need to include HIV prevention training in a sex education program is critical if we are to ensure the safety of people with disabilities. Indeed, Mason and Jaskulski (1994) suggest that teaching objectives relating to HIV prevention need to be included in students' individualized education programs. Despite teachers' possible discomfort with this subject matter, students need to be provided frank and comprehensive information on sexuality and infectious diseases and the need for hygienic measures. Prior to instruction, teachers need to assess students' knowledge in these areas. Mason and Jaskulski suggest that students' knowledge of body parts, sexual activities, use of condoms, appropriate places to engage in sexual activity, and what to say and do when the individual is or is not interested in engaging in sexual activity should be examined. As with other safety skills, critical instructional targets can be determined based on these assessment findings and the students' instructional needs. In particular, efforts need to be made to determine if a student is engaging in high-risk behavior (e.g., multiple partners, needle use), so that appropriate targets can be identified.

Although AIDS prevention involves many skills (see Mason & Jaskulski, 1994, for more detailed information), at the minimum, students need to know that AIDS is a very serious disease that can result in death, that it is transmitted via sexual relationships or sharing intravenous needles, and that it can be prevented through safe sex practices, abstinence, and not sharing needles or syringes.

Individual or group instruction is recommended, and repeated practice of target skills should be provided as appropriate. For example, students can practice unrolling condoms several times during an instructional session (Mason & Jaskulski, 1994). Role plays are strongly encouraged and, if possible, target skills should be practiced in natural environments.

Substance Use

Although prevalence figures regarding alcohol and drug use vary across disability groups, there is growing evidence that students with disabilities may be consuming substances at levels comparable to or even higher than the general population (Morgan, 1994). Such prevalence levels are unacceptable. Additionally, several risk factors have been identified to predict substance use among youth with disabilities. These include failure at school, hyperactivity and socially aggressive behavior, emotional difficulties, and family management problems. These may produce stressors for students that result in increased use of alcohol and drugs (Prendergast, Austin, & deMiranda, 1990). As Morgan (1994) noted, substance use among youth with disabilities represents a largely undocumented yet serious problem. This situation is compounded because few prevention programs are designed for students with disabilities.

Effective Prevention Approaches. When teaching substance use prevention skills, the following practices are recommended (Morgan, 1994). First, it is best to *teach students specific skills* (e.g., problem solving, stress management) rather than attempt to change their attitudes, self-concepts, or self-esteem; changes in the latter may not produce changes in the former. Second, teachers should address both the *short- and long-term consequences of substance use.* Also, ways to respond to pressure (from peers as well as oneself) should be taught. Third, professionals should *conduct instructional programs on a continuous, long-term basis.* A one-time discussion will produce little or no benefits. Fourth, *parent involvement must be actively encouraged.* Parents need to be persuaded to have a strong interest in this curricular area and to serve as appropriate models. Additionally, several skills can be taught that may help prevent or ameliorate a substance use problem. Among these are listening skills, behavior management procedures, and learning how to identify their child's drug use. Fifth, *the use of peers is recommended.* Youth with disabilities may be greatly influenced by positive peer interactions. Last, teachers must *ensure that instructional activities are appropriate* for their students. Concepts need to be concretely presented, sufficient practice and reviews should be built into lessons, and instructional materials should be at appropriate reading levels for the students.

Prevention Skills. Prevention curricula include a diverse set of skills. Such instruction should start as early as possible (e.g., kindergarten) and continue through secondary school. (*Note.* According to the U.S. Department of Education, the fourth to ninth grades are the best times to provide instruction.) Major skills areas include stress reduction, assertiveness training, problem solving, decision making, and communication.

The curriculum should teach students that substance use represents an illegal and harmful activity. Also, in addition to learning about the harmful effects of drugs, students need to learn strategies to resist peer pressure. Recommended teaching procedures include role play, behavioral rehearsal, peer tutoring, cooperative learning experiences, and verbal instruction. Morgan (1994) suggests that students be actively engaged in instructional activities (e.g., role playing) rather than passive seatwork (e.g., responding to worksheets). Also, a motivation system should be used in which students receive points or other reinforcers for acquiring and performing desired target behaviors and completing homework assignments. Last, the information that teachers present needs to be accurate, candid, and complete. Prevention programs must present students with sufficient information and experiences so that they can conclude unequivocally that the risks of substance use far outweigh its benefits. This is indeed a serious challenge to educators, but one that certainly needs to be addressed.

SELF-MEDICATION AND HEALTH CARE

An increasing number of students with special health care needs are being served in public schools. These students may require highly specialized treatments that trained medical and school staff need to provide (e.g., tracheostomy care, gastrostomy care). Additionally, taking medication is a routine part of the day for many persons with disabilities (Harchik, 1994). In both cases, out of fear that a serious error may be committed, individuals with disabilities may have little or no involvement in their own health care or medication regimens. As Lehr and Macurdy (1994) suggested, health care procedures are typically *done to* students, rather than *with* or *taught to* students. This is unfortunate since it limits the autonomy and competence of students, and there are a number of skills students can perform to promote their participation, partially or fully, in their own health care. There is increasing evidence that individuals with disabilities can execute several procedures that have been routinely performed by caregivers.

Self-Medication.   Individuals with disabilities need to be taught to assume as much responsibility as possible for their medication regimens. Prior to the implementation of such a program, students need to demonstrate that they will consistently take the medication (i.e., not be resistant to its use), that they have the necessary administrative behaviors (e.g., consume pills with water), and that they have sufficient emotional stability.

Harchik (1994) suggests that a self-medication curriculum comprises three components: recognizing and understanding one's medication, learning self-medication skills, and learning to respond to problems that may occur. First, although there appears to be no strong evidence that the student's knowledge of the medication will aid in the self-medication procedure, such knowledge may be helpful since it will allow students to learn what they need to take medication. Self-medication skills involve being able to locate the medicine, remove it from its container, consume or apply it correctly, and monitor one's own quality of performance. Last, students need to respond appropriately to problems that may occur in the medication regimen (e.g., taking too little or too much medication, and what to do if medication is lost).

Teaching Self-Medication Skills.   Instruction may involve individual or group formats. Teaching should coincide with the times of the day the individual normally receives medication (Harchik, 1994), with additional sessions as needed. In these sessions, simulated medicines should be used (e.g., candies). Additionally, teachers may find it necessary to use adaptations (e.g., color-coded medication containers, picture schedules). Last, self-medication programs must be monitored to ensure that the individual is appropriately following the regimen. Harchik indicated that individuals can learn to monitor their own self-medication behavior or this information can be obtained through interviews or direct observation from teachers or service providers.

Health Care.   Students with special health care needs can be taught to have a critical role in the administration of their own health care. Lehr and Macurdy (1994) suggest that students can be taught to assist in varying degrees in tube feeding, tracheostomy suctioning, and catheterization, among a number of procedures. At the minimum, they should be instructed in performing appropriate toileting, hand washing, and oral and nasal hygiene. Ideally, students with health care needs should be taught to assume full responsibility for their own health care. However, the decision to teach self-administration of health care procedures needs to be carefully made by the student's IEP team, with the approval of the child's physician. As with the other skills discussed in this chapter, objectives should be determined on the basis of the child's medical, cognitive, and physical needs and abilities.

CURRICULUM DESIGN

Table 12.2 presents selected IEP objectives across different health and safety skills areas. They are organized across elementary, middle, and secondary school levels. With coordinated efforts by educators and parents, students can learn and practice these skills across school, home, and community settings.

TABLE 12.2   Selected Individualized Education Plan Objectives

	Grade Level		
Skills Area	Learner in Elementary School	Learner in Middle School	Learner in Secondary School
Home and Community[1]	Will not climb into a refrigerator or freezer	Will use knives safely	Will discriminate spoiled meat and other food
	Will not touch a hot stove/oven	Will use shower/bathtub safely	Will use hair dryer appropriately
	Will recognize marked poisons	Will use tools/appliances safely	Will change lightbulb appropriately

(continued)

TABLE 12.2 *(Continued)*

Skills Area	Learner in Elementary School	Learner in Middle School	Learner in Secondary School
		Grade Level	
	Will pick up toys on stairs	Will lock and unlock doors in his/her house	Will safely use gym equipment
	Will not play with matches	When outdoors, will know what to do in a thunderstorm	Will know how to respond to aggressive animals
	Will stay away from power sources outdoors	Will know how to enter/exit a public bus	Will treat burns appropriately
	Will use bicycle safety	Will select lighted streets in the evening	Will recognize hypothermia or frostbite signs
	Will walk on sidewalks	Will know how to treat minor injuries	Will call the humane society about stray animals
	Will not feed strange animals	Will clean up broken items appropriately	Will identify overloaded wall outlets
	Will use utensils properly		Will aid a drowning swimmer
Work Safety[2]	Will not play while engaged in a task	Will move safely on slippery floors	Will identify exposed wires
	Will not throw objects while engaged in a task	Will move safely around objects on the floor	Will use power tools appropriately
	Will attend to relevant stimuli for specified period	Will not place flammable objects near fire	Will lift heavy objects safely
	Will follow safety rules at school	Will use tools appropriately	Will wear appropriate clothing at work
	Will exit school building when alarm is heard	Will place and store work materials appropriately	Will follow company safety policies while working
	Will show care with sharp objects	Will not fight while working	Will keep work area clean
	Will clean up desk	Will identify safety symbols	Will ask for instruction on how to use equipment
	Will report an emergency to a teacher or other school representative	Will understand the function of protective devices	Will operate equipment at appropriate speed
	Will identify tools and their intended functions		Will use protective equipment

TABLE 12.2 *(Continued)*

Skills Area	Grade Level		
	Learner in Elementary School	Learner in Middle School	Learner in Secondary School
			Will identify dangerous conditions at work
Fire Safety[3]	Will respond to fire/smoke alarms	Will identify flammables	Will use matches/lighters safely
	Will call fire department	Will use a fire extinguisher appropriately	Will respond appropriately to person on fire
	Will leaving burning building	Will extinguish an electrical fire	Will respond appropriately to nighttime fires
	Will identify emergency exits	Will extinguish a grease fire	Will dispose of ashes safely
	Will feel door for heat	Will use a stove properly	Will know how to check whether a home fire alarm is operating correctly
	Will go to window to call for help if door is hot	Will keep flammables away from a fire or stove	
		Will extinguish a fire in a wastebasket	
Crime Prevention[4]	Will not talk to strangers	Will identify dangerous areas	Will learn about his/her rights as a citizen
	Will say no to physical approaches	Will exercise caution in public rest rooms	Will demonstrate knowledge of responsible sexual behavior
	Will attract attention when attacked	Will identify body parts	Will demonstrate how to provide police with a statement after an attack
	Will demonstrate proper care of body	Will demonstrate knowledge of maturation	Will identify who in the neighborhood can be trusted
	Will demonstrate how to build friendships	Will learn how to lock and unlock the doors in his/her house	Will know how to behave appropriately when questioned in court
	Will learn when to dial 911	Will demonstrate how to secure and protect private property	

(continued)

TABLE 12.2   (*Continued*)

Skills Area	Learner in Elementary School	Learner in Middle School	Learner in Secondary School
		Grade Level	
HIV/AIDS[5]	Will describe how diseases are transmitted	Will identify AIDS as a sexually transmitted disease	Will demonstrate knowledge of safe sex
	Will identify what HIV infection is	Will identify the risks of drug and alcohol use	Will identify resources in the local community for AIDS prevention
	Will describe different emotions/feelings	Will describe how blood can be contaminated	Will describe how HIV and AIDS impact relationships, families, and society
	Will describe functions of body parts	Will describe the function of a condom and its limitations	Will describe the function of testing for HIV infection
	Will identify various situations to avoid (e.g., playing with needles, talking to strangers)	Will describe the dangers of sharing needles and syringes	Will describe his/her responsibility to sexual partner
Substance Use[6]	Will indicate that alcohol and drugs are harmful	Will discuss the specific risks of drug use	Will describe how drug use is related to various disabilities
	Will state that most individuals do not use drugs	Will describe how drugs are sold	Will describe how drug use can be fatal
	Will state various drugs individuals use	Will describe the seriousness of the drug problem	Will describe how drug use can affect the fetus
		Will describe the legal and criminal consequences of drug use	Will describe the negative effects of drug use and driving and other physical tasks
		Will describe how drugs and AIDS are related	Will describe how drug use can negatively affect his/her education and professional development
			Will describe treatment and intervention resources
Self-Medication and Health Care[7]	Will identify function of medication prescribed	Will identify side effects of medication	Will seek appropriate attention or assistance in the event of an injury or illness

TABLE 12.2 *(Continued)*

Skills Area	Grade Level		
	Learner in Elementary School	**Learner in Middle School**	**Learner in Secondary School**
	Will identify medication prescribed	Will monitor his/her self-medication	Will consume appropriate medications as needed (e.g., aspirins, antacids)
	Will swallow pills	Will identify times for administration of medication	Will respond appropriately if too little or too much medication is taken
	Will follow proper toileting procedures	Will measure feeding liquid into feeding bag or syringe	Will clean feeding equipment
	Will wash hands properly	Will feed self independently using feeding equipment	Will wash and assemble catheterization materials
	Will demonstrate proper nasal and oral hygiene practices	Will describe steps necessary to suction	
	Will state reason for alternative eating method, suctioning, or catheterization	Will self-catheterize	
	Will turn on suctioning machine		
	Will identify need to be catheterized		

[1] Adapted from Gast, Wellons, & Collins (1994).
[2] Adapted from Agran & Madison (1995).
[3] Adapted from Bannerman, Sheldon, & Sherman (1991); Juracek (1994).
[4] Adapted from Sobsey (1994).
[5] Adapted from Mason & Jaskulski (1994).
[6] Adapted from Morgan (1994).
[7] Adapted from Harchik (1994); Lehr & Macurdy (1994).

IEP GOALS FOR CASE STUDY

Table 12.3 lists selected IEP goals established for Malinda. The goals are in the following skills areas: home and community safety, work safety, and crime prevention and personal safety. These skills will strongly promote Malinda's independence and safety at work and in the community.

TABLE 12.3 Goals for Malinda's Individualized Education Plan

ANNUAL GOAL: Malinda will increase her home and community safety skills.

Objectives/Activities	Person Responsible	Evaluation Criteria	Learning Environment S = School C = Community H = Home W = Work	Date Initiated	Date Completed	Quarterly Program		
With assistance from mother, Malinda will operate microwave	Mother, home economics teacher	100% correct performance	S, H					
With assistance from mother, Malinda will use coffeemaker	Mother, home economics teacher	100% correct performance	S, H					
Malinda will exit safely during simulated fire emergencies	Malinda, father	100% correct performance, parent evaluation	H					
Malinda will treat cuts and abrasions, sprains, and burns	Special education teacher, parents	90% correct performance	S, H					

When presented with different emergency situations (e.g., fire, severe injury), Malinda will call 911	Special education teacher, parents	100% correct performance	S, H			
Malinda will recognize marked poisons	Special education teacher, parents	100% correct performance	S, H			
Malinda will identify spoiled food	Home economics teacher, parents	100% correct	S, H			
Malinda will respond appropriately to cooking fires	Home economics teacher, special education teacher, parents	100% correct performance	S, H			

(continued)

TABLE 12.3 *(Continued)*

ANNUAL GOAL: Malinda will demonstrate critical work safety skills.

Objectives/Activities	Person Responsible	Evaluation Criteria	Learning Environment S = School C = Community H = Home W = Work	Date Initiated	Date Completed	Quarterly Program			
While working at a grocery store, Malinda will lift boxes appropriately	Special education teacher, employer	80% correct performance, employer's rating	S, W						
While working at a grocery store, Malinda will walk safely around objects on the floor or slippery floors	Special education teacher, employer	80% correct performance, employer's rating	S, W						
While assigned to clean areas of a grocery store, Malinda will safely use cleaning agents and materials	Special education teacher, employer	80% correct performance, employer's rating	S, W						

ANNUAL Goal: Malinda will demonstrate crime prevention and personal safety skills.

Malinda will initiate social interactions with peers at school and in the community	Special education teacher, parents	Self-report data, parents' satisfaction	S, C					
Malinda will lock and unlock the doors in her home	Parents	Parents' satisfaction	H					
Malinda will state what HIV/AIDS virus is and how it is transmitted	Special education teacher	100% correct performance	S					
Malinda will respond appropriately to strangers	Special education teacher, parents	100% correct performance, self-report data, parents' satisfaction	C					
Malinda will say no to physical approaches	Special education teacher, parents	100% correct performance, parents' satisfaction	S, C, H					

(continued)

TABLE 12.3 (Continued)

Objectives/Activities	Person Responsible	Evaluation Criteria	Learning Environment S = School C = Community H = Home W = Work	Date Initiated	Date Completed	Quarterly Program
Malinda will initiate social interactions with peers at school and in the community	Special education teacher, parents	Self-report data, parents' satisfaction	S, C			
Malinda will lock and unlock the doors in her home	Parents	Parents' satisfaction	H			
Malinda will state what HIV/AIDS virus is and how it is transmitted	Special education teacher	100% correct performance	S			
Malinda will respond appropriately to strangers	Special education teacher, parents	100% correct performance, self-report data, parents' satisfaction				
Malinda will say no to physical approaches	Special education teacher, parents	100% correct performance, parents' satisfaction	S, C, H			

REFERENCES

Agran, M., & Madison, D. (1995). Prevalence of injuries among supported employees. *Journal of Vocational Rehabilitation, 5,* 5–13.

Agran, M., Marchand-Martella, N. E., & Martella, R. C. (Eds.). (1994). *Promoting health and safety: Skills for independent living.* Baltimore: Paul H. Brookes.

Agran, M., & Martella, R. C. (1994). Safety skills on the job. In M. Agran, N. E. Marchand-Martella, & R. C. Martella (Eds.), *Promoting health and safety: Skills for independent living* (pp. 121–134). Baltimore: Paul H. Brookes.

Bannerman, D. J., Sheldon, J. B., & Sherman, J. A. (1991). Teaching adults with severe and profound retardation to exit their homes upon hearing the fire alarm. *Journal of Applied Behavior Analysis, 24,* 571–578.

Blackman, J. (1984). *Medical aspects of developmental disabilities in children: Birth to three.* Rockville, MD: Aspen.

Bodnar, M., & Hodge, M. (1989). *Personal security.* Wellington, New Zealand: GP Books.

Bryan, E., Warden, M. G., Berg, B., & Hauck, G. R. (1978). Medical consideration for multiple handicapped children in the public schools. *Journal of School Health, 48,* 84–89.

Chotiner, N., & Lehr, W. (1976). *Child abuse and developmental disabilities: A report from the New England regional conference.* Boston: New England Developmental Disabilities Communication Center.

Collins, B. C., Wolery, M., & Gast, D. L. (1992). A national survey of safety concerns for students with special needs. *Journal of Developmental and Physical Disabilities, 4,* 263–276.

Foege, W. H. (1988, November). *Newsletter of the Family Health Services Division, Utah Department of Health.* (Available from Stephen McDonald, 288 North 1460 West, Salt Lake City, UT 84116–0650)

Gast, D. L., Wellons, J., & Collins, B. (1994). Home and community safety skills. In M. Agran, N. E. Marchand-Martella, & R. C. Martella (Eds.), *Promoting health and safety: Skills for independent living* (pp. 11–32). Baltimore: Paul H. Brookes.

Haller, J. A. (1970). Problems in children's trauma. *Journal of Trauma, 10,* 269–271.

Haney, J. I., & Jones, R. T. (1982). Programming maintenance as a major component of a community-centered preventative effort: Escape from the fire. *Behavior Therapy, 13,* 47–62.

Harchik, A. E. (1994). Self-medication skills. In M. Agran, N. E. Marchand-Martella, & R. C. Martella (Eds.), *Promoting health and safety: Skills for independent living* (pp. 55–69). Baltimore: Paul H. Brookes.

Heath, E. D. (1983). Youth and safety for the world of work. *Vocational Evaluation, 58,* 23–24.

Jaskulski, T., & Mason, C. (1992). AIDS policies and education: What are vocational and residential rehabilitation providers doing? *American Rehabilitation, 19*(3), 12–19.

Juracek, D. B. (1994). Fire safety skills. In M. Agran, N. E. Marchand-Martella, & R. C. Martella (Eds.), *Promoting health and safety: Skills for independent living* (pp. 103–119). Baltimore: Paul H. Brookes.

Katz, R. C., & Singh, N. N. (1986). Comprehensive fire-safety training for adult mentally retarded persons. *Journal of Mental Deficiency Research, 30,* 59–69.

Lazar, A. L. (1980). Exceptional persons, careers, and health hazards. *Journal for Special Educators, 17,* 2–3.

Lehr, D. H., & Macurdy, S. (1994). Meeting special health care needs of students. In M. Agran, N. E. Marchand-Martella, & R. C. Martella (Eds.), *Promoting health and safety: Skills for independent living* (pp. 71–84). Baltimore: Paul H. Brookes.

Lorr, C., & Rotatori, A. F. (1985). Who are the severely and profoundly handicapped? In A. F. Rotatori, J. O. Schween, & R. A. Fox (Eds.), *Assessing severely and profoundly handicapped individuals* (pp. 38–48). Springfield, IL: Charles C. Thomas.

Martella, R. C., & Agran, M. (1994). Safety skills on the job. In M. Agran, N. E. Marchand-Martella, & R. C. Martella (Eds.), *Promoting health and safety: Skills for independent living* (pp. 121–134). Baltimore: Paul H. Brookes.

Martella, R. C., & Marchand-Martella, N. E. (1995). Safety skills in vocational rehabilitation: A qualitative analysis. *Journal of Vocational Rehabilitation, 5,* 25–31.

Mason, C. Y., & Jaskulski, T. (1994). HIV/AIDS prevention and education. In M. Agran, N. E. Marchand-Martella, & R. C. Martella (Eds.), *Promoting health and safety: Skills for independent living* (pp. 161–191). Baltimore: Paul H. Brookes.

Matson, J. L. (1980). Preventing home accidents: A training program for the retarded. *Behavior Modification, 4,* 397–410.

Morgan, D. P. (1994). Preventing substance use. In M. Agran, N. E. Marchand-Martella, & R. C. Martella (Eds.), *Promoting health and safety: Skills for independent living* (pp. 135–159). Baltimore: Paul H. Brookes.

Muccigrosso, L. (1991). Sexual abuse prevention strategies and programs for persons with developmental disabilities. *Journal of Sexuality and Disability, 9*(3), 261–272.

Mueller, H. H., Wilgosh, L., & Dennis, S. (1989). Employment survival skills for entry-level occupations. *Canadian Journal of Rehabilitation, 2,* 203–221.

National Association of Rehabilitation Facilities. (1989). *1989 NARF Education Needs Analysis Survey.* Washington, DC: Author.

National Safety Council. (1988). *Accident facts.* Chicago: Author.

Pava, W. S., Bateman, P., Appleton, M. K., & Glasscock, J. (1991, December). Self-defense training for visually impaired women. *Journal of Visual Impairment and Blindness,* 397–401.

Pelland, M., & Falvey, M. A. (1986). Domestic skills. In M. A. Falvey (Ed.), *Community-based curriculum: Instructional strategies for students with severe handicaps* (pp. 31–60). Baltimore: Paul H. Brookes.

Perske, R. (1972). The dignity of risk and the mentally retarded. *Mental Retardation, 10*(1), 24–26.

Peterson, L. (1984). Teaching home safety and survival skills to latch-key children: A comparison of two manuals and methods. *Journal of Applied Behavior Analysis, 17,* 279–293.

Prendergast, M., Austin, G., & deMiranda, J. (1990). *Substance use among youth with disabilities* (Prevention Research Update No. 7). Portland, OR: Northwest Regional Educational Laboratory.

Sobsey, D. (1994). Crime prevention and personal safety. In M. Agran, N. E. Marchand-Martella, & R. C. Martella (Eds.), *Promoting health and safety: Skills for independent living* (pp. 193–213). Baltimore: Paul H. Brookes.

Stimpson, L., & Best, M. C. (1991). *Courage above all: Sexual assault against people with disabilities.* Toronto, Ontario, Canada: DisAbled Women's Network.

Tarnowski, K. J., Rasnake, L. K., & Drabman, R. S. (1987). Behavioral assessment and treatment of pediatric burn injuries: A review. *Behavior Therapy, 18,* 417–441.

Vogelsberg, R. T., & Rusch, F. R. (1979). Training severely handicapped students to cross partially controlled intersections. *AAESPH Review, 4,* 264–273.

West, M. A., Richardson, M., LeConte, J., Crimi, C., & Stuart, S. (1992). Identification of developmental disabilities and health problems among individuals under child protective services. *Mental Retardation, 30,* 221–225.

Wolfensberger, W. (1972). *The principle of normalization in human services.* Toronto, Ontario, Canada: National Institute on Mental Retardation.

Index

About the Authors

Paul Wehman, PhD, is Professor at the Department of Physical Medicine and Rehabilitation, Medical College of Virginia, Virginia Commonwealth University and holds a joint appointment in the Department of Special Education. Dr. Wehman has taught many courses in special education, published in various special education journals, and has been involved in teacher training. Internationally recognized for his service and scholarly contributions in the fields of special education, psychology, and vocational rehabilitation, Dr. Wehman is the recipient of the 1990 Joseph P. Kennedy, Jr., Foundation Award in Mental Retardation, a 1992 Leadership Award from the Association for Persons in Supported Employment, and the Distinguished Service Award from the President's Committee on Employment for Persons with Disabilities in October 1992. He has received numerous awards, in both special education and rehabilitation. He is the author or editor of over 100 books, research monographs, journal articles, and chapters in the areas of traumatic brain injury, mental retardation, supported employment, and special education. He also is Editor of the *Journal of Vocational Rehabilitation*, an international journal published by Elsevier. Specific research interests include transition from school to work, supported employment, developmental disabilities, and brain injury.

Dr. Martin Agran, PhD, is a Professor in the Department of Special Education and Rehabilitation at Utah State University. He chairs the Moderate/Severe Disabilities Personnel Preparation Program. Dr. Agran has served as a principal investigator for several federally funded personnel preparation projects to prepare teachers of students with severe disabilities, served as a consultant for several research projects, published extensively in a number of professional journals and texts on self-management, health and safety, and other issues relating to the education of students with severe disabilities, authored or coauthored six books, presented at numerous national conferences, and served on the editorial boards of several professional journals. He served as a Fulbright Scholar in the Czech Republic. In addition to teaching at Charles University in Prague, he served as a consultant to the Ministry of Education and various parent groups on inclusion and the education of students with severe and multiple disabilities.

Kathryn Cleland Banks, EdS, began her special education career teaching mildly intellectually disabled students in 1975 for the Savannah/Chatham County Public School System. In 1981, she began working as a job-placement counselor and found that only those students with appropriate social skills and a high level of family support were successful on the job. This translated into a low percentage of students who were able to maintain even entry-level employment for an extended period. Kathryn is currently an active member of the Savannah/Chatham County Interagency Transition Council. Council members are organized into work teams and are responsible for field-testing methods and procedures designed to blur the barriers for disabled students and their families as students exit school programs and enter the world of work or postsecondary education as adults. She has presented at four Annual Conventions of the Council for Exceptional Children on the subjects of transition, parental involvement, and the interagency transition team process.

Teri L. Burcroff, PhD, is an assistant professor in the Department of Special Education and Rehabilitation at East Stroudsburg University of Pennsylvania. She received her doctorate in Special Education at the State University of New York-Buffalo. Prior to that time, she was a public school special education teacher. Dr. Burcroff has consulted extensively to public schools regarding the development of inclusive educational practices. Her professional interests include the provision of quality services to individuals with severe disabilities, development of inclusive practices, and positive behavioral support.

Shirley K. Chandler, PhD, is the Director of Florida's State Systems Change Project, *The Florida Blueprint for School to Community Transition,* and is a faculty member in the Center for Policy Studies in Education and teaches a transition course for the Special Education Department at Florida State University. Prior to her current position, she was an Instructor and Research Associate in the Department of Rehabilitation Counseling, The University of Texas Southwestern Medical Center at Dallas, where she directed a national study on partnership building within the rehabilitation process, as well as a study to identify and provide vocational services to individuals with traumatic brain injuries. She has also worked as an instructor and Training Associate for the Rehabilitation Research and Training Center on Supported Employment, at Virginia Commonwealth University. Dr. Chandler has taught numerous courses in Special Education, Rehabilitation Counseling, and Psychology. She was a Special Education teacher in the public schools in New York State, and is a certified rehabilitation counselor. Dr. Chandler is the author of an assessment instrument on vocational decision making, several book chapters, numerous journal articles, and training materials. Her research interests include policy development, program evaluation, transition issues, and vocational decision making. Dr. Chandler holds Master's degrees in Rehabilitation Counseling, and Special Education from Syracuse University, and a PhD from Virginia Commonwealth University.

Lana Collet-Klingenberg, PhD, is a doctoral candidate in Special Education at the University of Wisconsin-Madison. Her background includes teaching students with moderate and severe disabilities, conducting research in the areas of social skills and communication, and providing training and support to educators implementing transition services. Currently, while completing her degree work, Lana teaches an undergraduate level course on applied behavior analysis, and assists with data collection and technical support for a state transition systems change grant.

Victoria Dowdy, MEd, received both her Bachelor's and Master's degrees from Virginia Commonwealth University and holds endorsements in Mental Retardation, Severe and Profound Handicaps, and Vocational Special Needs. She began her teaching career in the Williamsburg-James City County School system working with adolescents and adults at Eastern State Hospital. Since 1990, Vicki has taught in Henrico County and is currently teaching secondary-school level students at Virginia Randolph Special Education Center.

Stacy K. Dymond, MEd, is a Program Specialist at the Virginia Commonwealth University Training and Technical Assistance Center, where she provides consultation and training to school personnel who serve students with disabilities. She has also coordinated several grant-funded projects including a technical assistance center for school personnel servicing children with severe disabilities and a community-based instruction and supported employment program for transition-aged youth. Currently, she is pursuing a PhD in Education and Human Services. Her areas of interest include community-based instruction and vocational training, positive behavioral supports, and curriculum development for students with severe disabilities.

Cheryl Hanley-Maxwell, PhD, is a professor and chairperson of the Department of Rehabilitation Psychology and Special Education at the University of Wisconsin-Madison. She has extensive experience in preparing a variety of professionals to work with students as they move from school to their adult lives and in providing technical assistance in the development of innovative transition programs. She is interested in how student experiences of the school years prepare young adults for their adult roles. She is especially interested in enhancing student and family participation in all aspects of transition.

Wendy A. Harriott, MS, is currently a PhD candidate and graduate assistant in the Special Education program at The Pennsylvania State University. She has a MS from Marywood College, Pennsylvania, and a BS from Bloomsburg University, Pennsylvania, in special education. She has been employed as a special education teacher and an educational consultant working with a variety of disabilities such as learning disabilities, mental retardation, and emotional disturbance. Her research interests include adaptations for regular education classrooms, administration, and teacher training.

John Kregel, EdD, is a Professor of Special Education at Virginia Commonwealth University, who also serves as the Associate Director and Research Director of the Rehabilitation Research and Training Center on Supported Employment. Currently, he is directing the Supported Employment Outreach Project which replicates a natural supports approach to supported employment in rural communities throughout the Southeast, as well as the VCU Career Connections Project, which is attempting to apply supported employment strategies to meet the job placement needs of college students with disabilities. He has published numerous articles and chapters on supported employment, focusing specifically on program evaluation and attitudes of employers. He was awarded the NARF Research Award by the American Rehabilitation Association for his significant research contributions in the field of rehabilitation.

James E. Martin, PhD, is a Professor of Special Education and Director of the Self-Determination Project at the University of Colorado. He received his MA from Eastern Illinois University in 1975 and worked as a teacher/counselor for several years in a private program in Illinois before going to graduate school. He earned his PhD from the University of Illinois in 1983, where he began his career-long interest in self-management, self-determination, and transition. He currently has over 75 publications including books, book chapters, and numerous journal articles. He has given presentations in Europe, Canada, and throughout the United States. Because Jim's mother had a severe disability, he grew up in a home that provided him with unique insights into the life of people with disabilities. Jim's dream is to develop and implement methods that will improve the quality of life for people with disabilities. His present work is the closest that he has come to reaching this goal. He is now working on infusing self-determination concepts and interventions into transition and supported employment programs. Jim is proud that all of his applied work is done in collaboration with practicing educators or employment specialists.

Sara C. Pankaskie, PhD, is an Assistant Professor in the Department of Exceptional and Physical Education at the University of Central Florida, where she teaches courses in special education methods, transition, parent and professional collaboration, and behavior and classroom management. Prior to her current position, she was a Program Specialist with the Florida Department of Education, Bureau of Student Services and Exceptional Education, where she provided leadership in the areas of mental retardation and transition. While at Florida DOE, Dr. Pankaskie developed the postschool follow-up model and a new competency-based Special Diploma for exceptional education students. She has also worked as the director of an Association for Retarded Citizens (ARC) where she implemented programs that integrated adults with mental retardation into the work and social environments of their community. Dr. Pankaskie has presented at state, regional, and national conferences in the areas of transition, dropout prevention, postschool follow-up, and self-advocacy for individuals with disabilities. Her research focus is on secondary special education, especially the effect of Florida's new competency-based diploma on the postschool outcomes of students with disabilities and use of simulation training in virtual community-based settings. Dr. Pankaskie holds a Master's degree and a PhD in Special Education from Florida State University.

Paul Sale, EdD, is an Associate Professor and Chair of the Special Education Program at the University of Colorado at Colorado. Dr. Sale teaches courses in methods of instruction for children with severe needs, career education and transition, and research methods. His current research interests include student and teacher outcomes associated with the inclusive schools movement and assistive technology applications for learners with significant challenges.

Fred Spooner, PhD, is an associate professor in the Department of Counseling, Special Education, and Child Development, College of Education, University of North Carolina at Charlotte. He coordinates the graduate-level personnel preparation program in severe disabilities. For the past eight years, he has served as the coeditor of the Council for Exceptional Children's practitioner-oriented journal, *TEACHING Exceptional Children*. His research interests have focused on instructional applications for persons with severe disabilities, classic articles in special education, and practitioner-oriented writing. At present, he is directing a five-year federally funded personnel preparation project in the area of severe disabilities that will collaborate with other institutions of higher education in the state of North Carolina and delivers its content over a satellite network via a distance learning model.

Daniel E. Steere, PhD, is an assistant professor in the Department of Special Education and Rehabilitation at East Stroudsburg University of Pennsylvania. Prior to his current position, he taught courses in rehabilitation counseling at Montana State University-Billings. In addition, he has worked as a special education teacher, directed a community residence for adults with severe disabilities, and served as a consultant to public schools and to rehabilitation agencies. His particular areas of interest are transition to adulthood for students with disabilities and supported employment.

Michael West, PhD, holds an MEd, in Special Education and Habilitative Services from the University of New Orleans in Louisiana. He received a Doctorate in Education from Virginia Commonwealth University in Richmond. His direct service experiences have included special education, residential programs, vocational services, and general community functioning. He currently is a Research Associate with the Rehabilitation Research and Training Center on Supported Employment at Virginia Commonwealth University. He has authored or coauthored numerous journal articles and book chapters on supported employment, special education, and other disability-related issues.

Katherine Mullaney Wittig, MEd, received her BA in Art/Elementary Education at the University of Rhode Island. She went on to receive her Master's degree in Severe/Profound Handicaps at Rhode Island College. Mrs. Wittig has worked in the fields of rehabilitation, supported employment, and special education for the past 20 years as a teacher and/or administrator. Mrs. Wittig coauthored a grant to develop Project Transition, in Bangor, Maine, which she directed until 1992. She is currently the Work/Transition Coordinator at Virginia Randolph Education Complex in Henrico County, Virginia. Kathe is married to Dr. Bill Wittig and resides in Ashland, Virginia, with their two sons, Matt and Timothy.

Pamela S. Wolfe, PhD, is an Assistant Professor at the Pennsylvania State University. She has over 11 years' experience in teaching and research in areas of severe disabilities and transition. Dr. Wolfe has published and presented at national conferences on topics such as instructional techniques, transition planning, sexuality, and implementation of the Americans with Disabilities Act (ADA). She is currently director of a grant to train graduate students in rural transition planning. Dr. Wolfe has a strong interest in fostering self-advocacy for persons with disabilities in integrated community settings.

Wendy M. Wood, PhD, is an Assistant Professor in the Department of Counseling, Special Education, and Child Development, College of Education at the University of North Carolina, Charlotte. She teaches special education coursework concentrating in supported employment, transition from school to work, and behavior management. Before coming to UNCC, Dr. Wood was executive director and cofounder of the Association for Persons in Supported Employment (APSE), and served as project coordinator for several national demonstration projects and director of Employment Services at the Rehabilitation Research and Training Center at Virginia Commonwealth University (VCU-RRTC) in Richmond, Virginia.